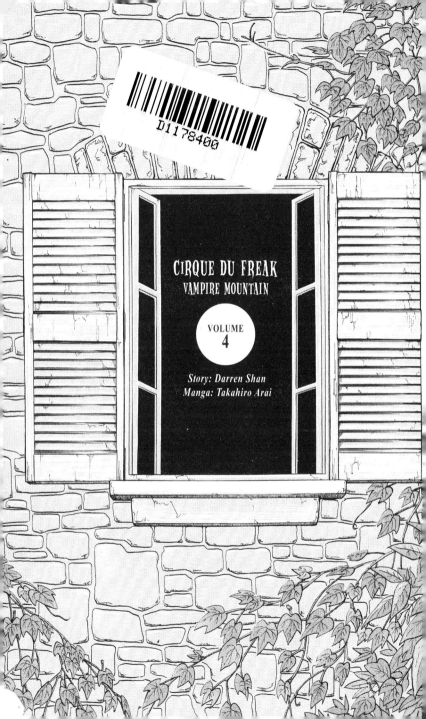

CIRQUE DU FREAK
VAMPIRE MOUNTAIN

VOLUME 4

Story: Darren Shan
Manga: Takahiro Arai

A SUMMARY OF TUNNELS OF BLOOD:

DARREN AND EVRA SET OUT WITH MR. CREPSLEY, LEAVING THE SAFETY OF THE CIRQUE DU FREAK FOR MR. CREPSLEY'S HOMETOWN. DARREN ENJOYS HIS TIME THERE, ESPECIALLY WITH HIS NEW ROMANTIC INTEREST, DEBBIE, BUT EVERYTHING CHANGES WHEN A STRING OF GRISLY MURDERS EMERGES. THE SLAUGHTER COMES FROM THE CLAWS OF THE VICIOUS VAMPANEZE, MURLOUGH! WITH MR. CREPSLEY'S HELP, DARREN JUST BARELY SUCCEEDS IN STOPPING MURLOUGH, AND THE THREE HEAD BACK TO THE CIRQUE. TIME PASSES ONCE AGAIN...

CIRQUE DU FREAK 4
CONTENTS

CHAPTER 25: DESTINY LENDS A HAND

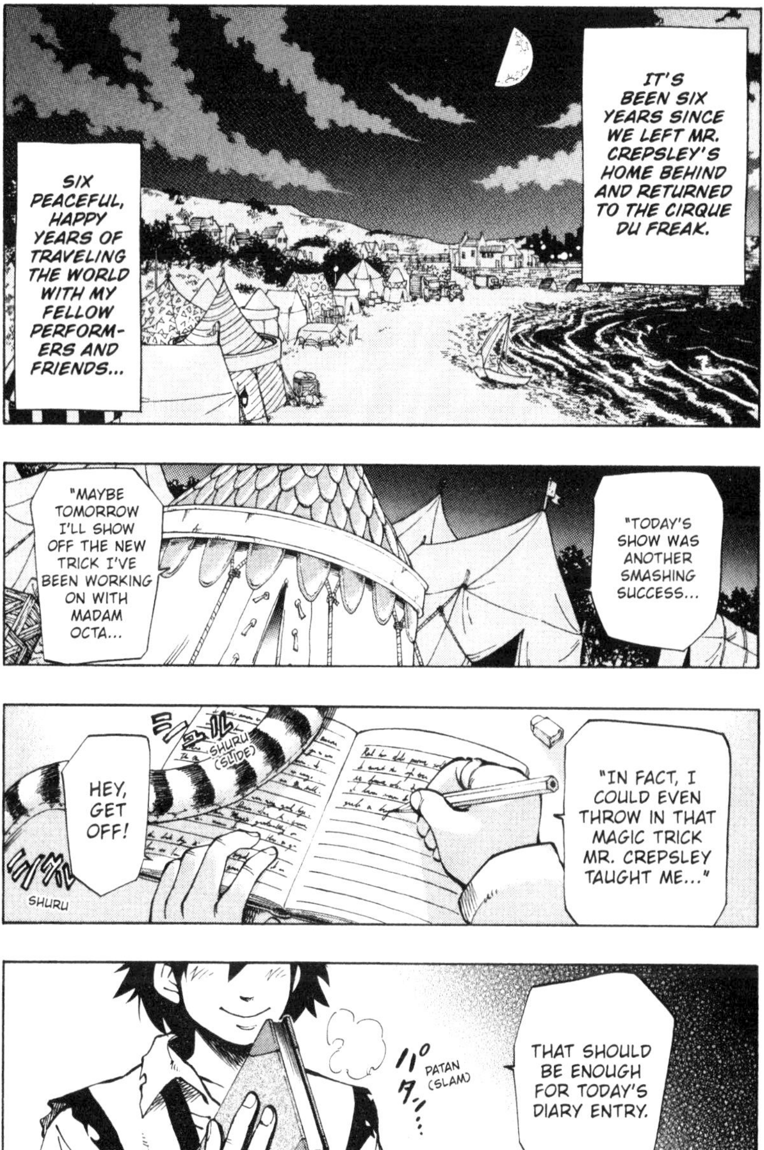
IT'S BEEN SIX YEARS SINCE WE LEFT MR. CREPSLEY'S HOME BEHIND AND RETURNED TO THE CIRQUE DU FREAK.
SIX PEACEFUL, HAPPY YEARS OF TRAVELING THE WORLD WITH MY FELLOW PERFORMERS AND FRIENDS...
"TODAY'S SHOW WAS ANOTHER SMASHING SUCCESS...
"MAYBE TOMORROW I'LL SHOW OFF THE NEW TRICK I'VE BEEN WORKING ON WITH MADAM OCTA...
"IN FACT, I COULD EVEN THROW IN THAT MAGIC TRICK MR. CREPSLEY TAUGHT ME..."
SHURU (SLIDE)
HEY, GET OFF!
SHURU
THAT SHOULD BE ENOUGH FOR TODAY'S DIARY ENTRY.
PATAN (SLAM)

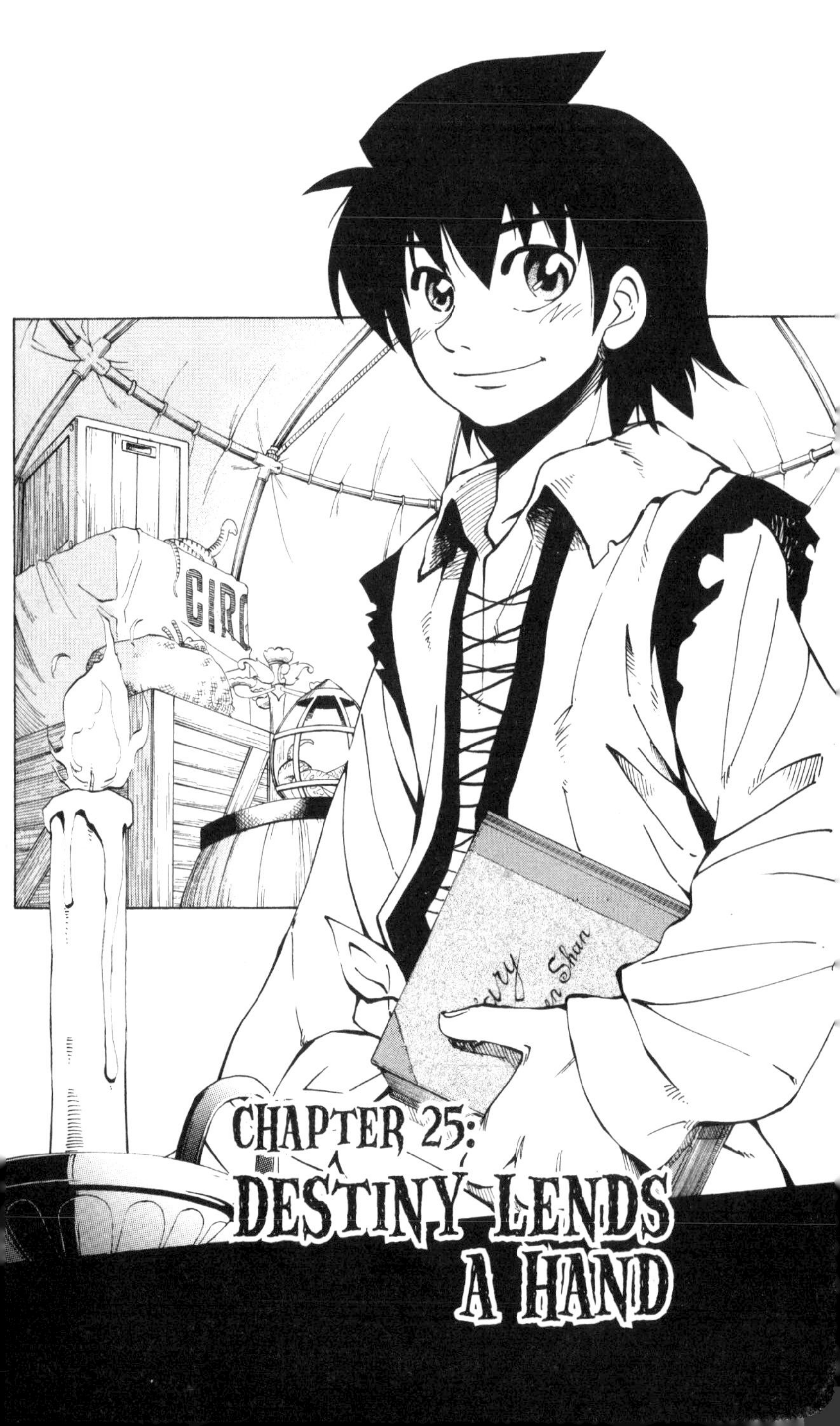
CHAPTER 25:
DESTINY LENDS A HAND

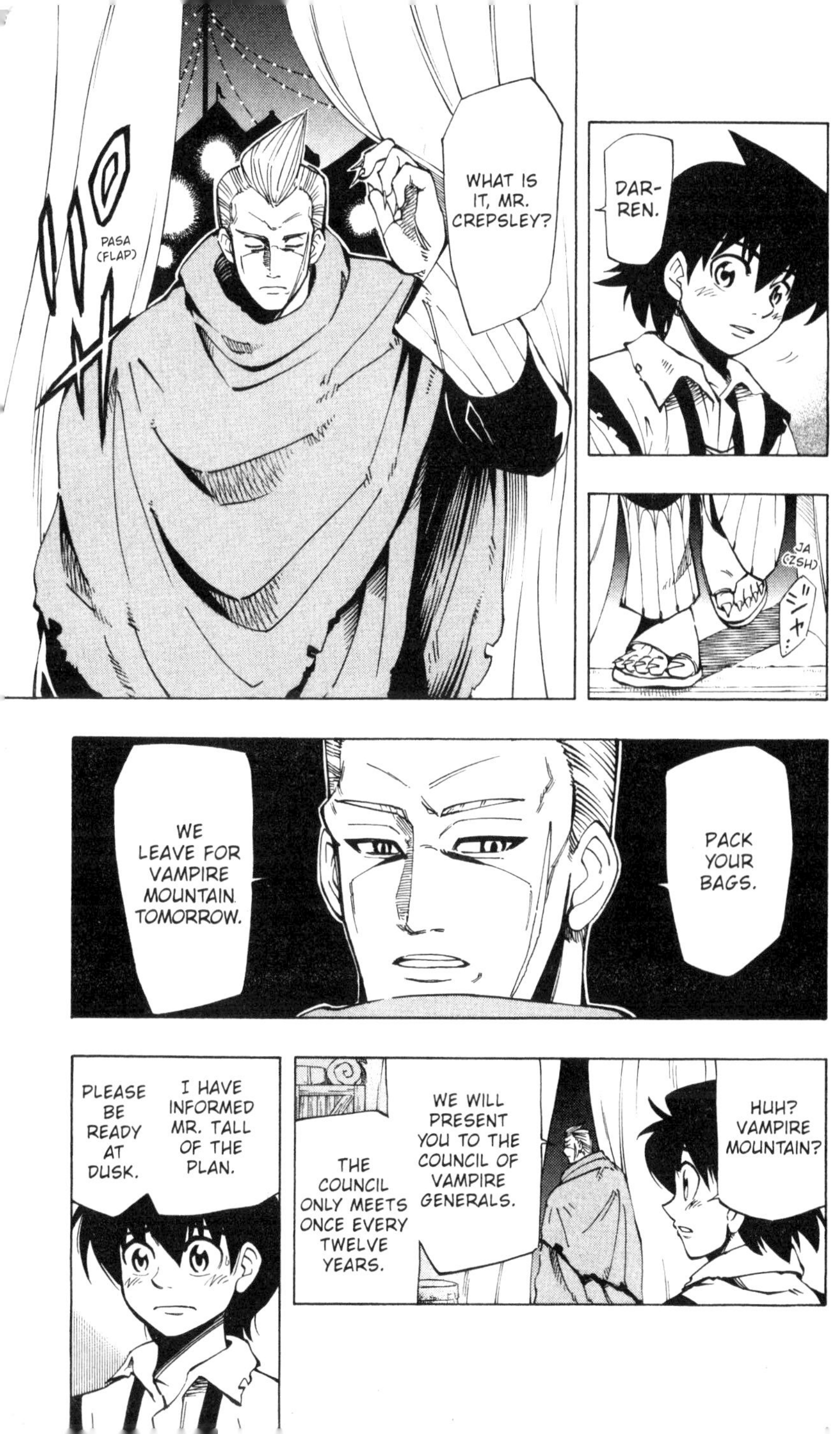
DAR-REN.
JA (ZSH)
WHAT IS IT, MR. CREPSLEY?
PASA (FLAP)
PACK YOUR BAGS.
WE LEAVE FOR VAMPIRE MOUNTAIN. TOMORROW.
HUH? VAMPIRE MOUNTAIN?
WE WILL PRESENT YOU TO THE COUNCIL OF VAMPIRE GENERALS.
THE COUNCIL ONLY MEETS ONCE EVERY TWELVE YEARS.
I HAVE INFORMED MR. TALL OF THE PLAN.
PLEASE BE READY AT DUSK.

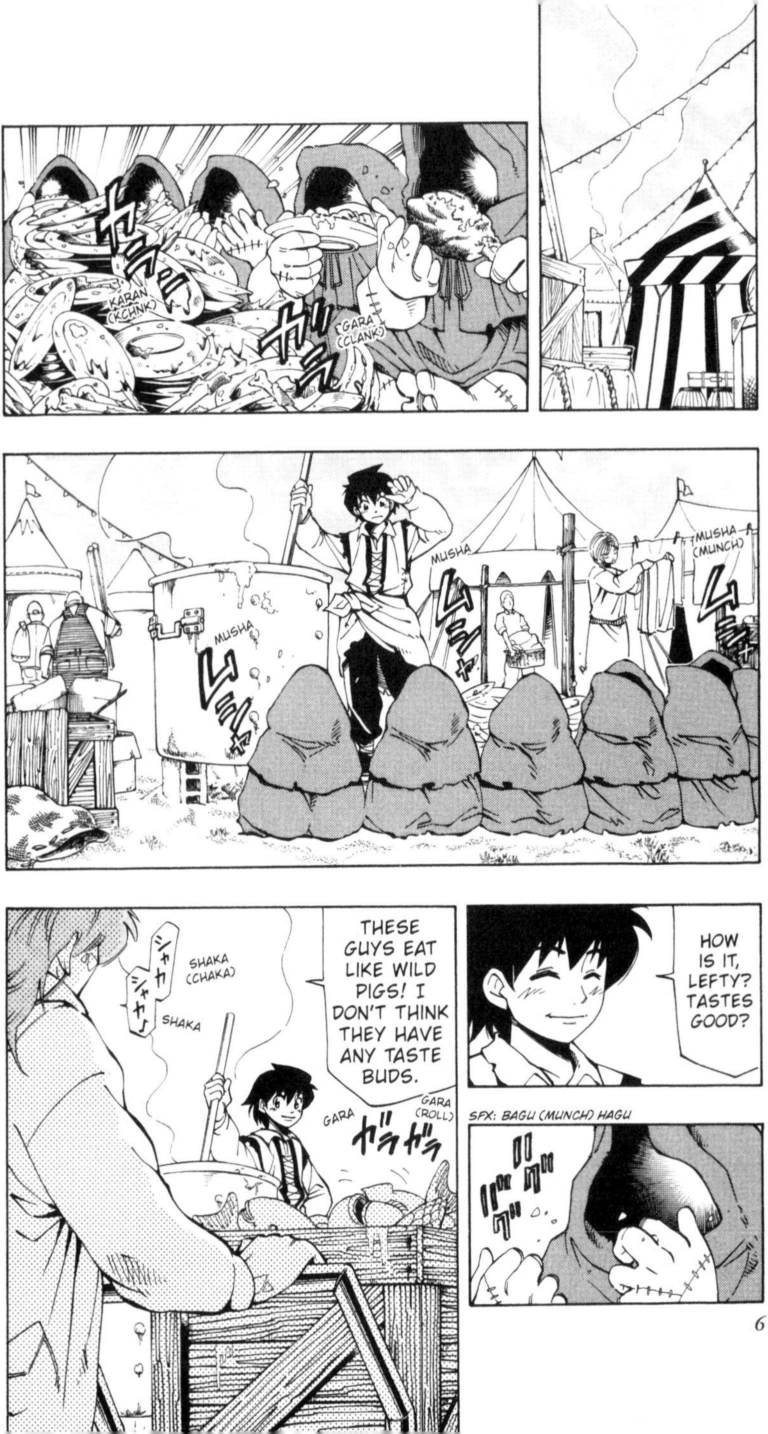
GARA (CLANK)
KARAN (KCHNK)
MUSHA (MUNCH)
MUSHA
MUSHA
HOW IS IT, LEFTY? TASTES GOOD?
SFX: BAGU (MUNCH) HAGU
THESE GUYS EAT LIKE WILD PIGS! I DON'T THINK THEY HAVE ANY TASTE BUDS.
SHAKA (CHAKA)
SHAKA
GARA (ROLL)
GARA

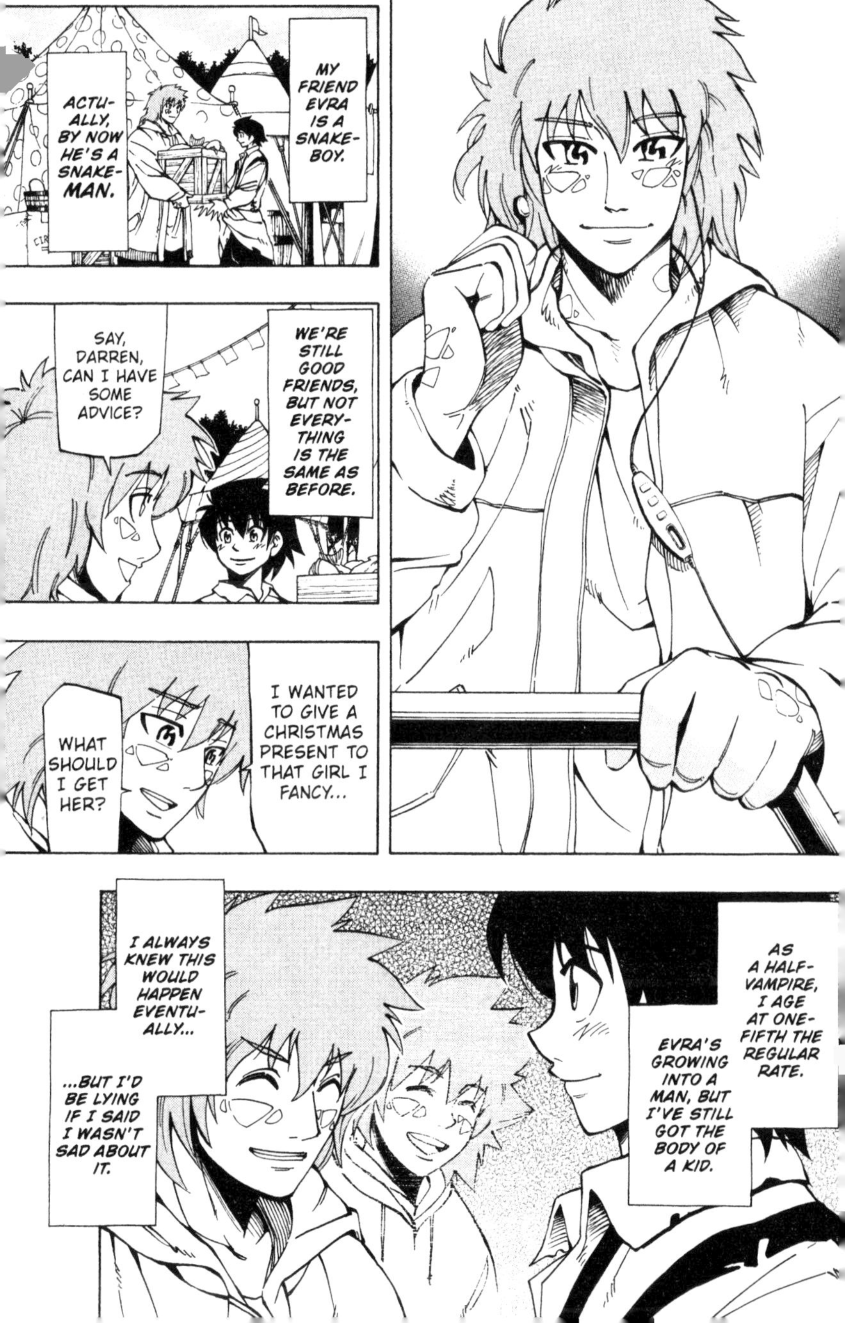
MY FRIEND EVRA IS A SNAKE-BOY.
ACTUALLY, BY NOW HE'S A SNAKE-MAN.
WE'RE STILL GOOD FRIENDS, BUT NOT EVERYTHING IS THE SAME AS BEFORE.
SAY, DARREN, CAN I HAVE SOME ADVICE?
I WANTED TO GIVE A CHRISTMAS PRESENT TO THAT GIRL I FANCY...
WHAT SHOULD I GET HER?
AS A HALF-VAMPIRE, I AGE AT ONE-FIFTH THE REGULAR RATE.
EVRA'S GROWING INTO A MAN, BUT I'VE STILL GOT THE BODY OF A KID.
I ALWAYS KNEW THIS WOULD HAPPEN EVENTUALLY...
...BUT I'D BE LYING IF I SAID I WASN'T SAD ABOUT IT.

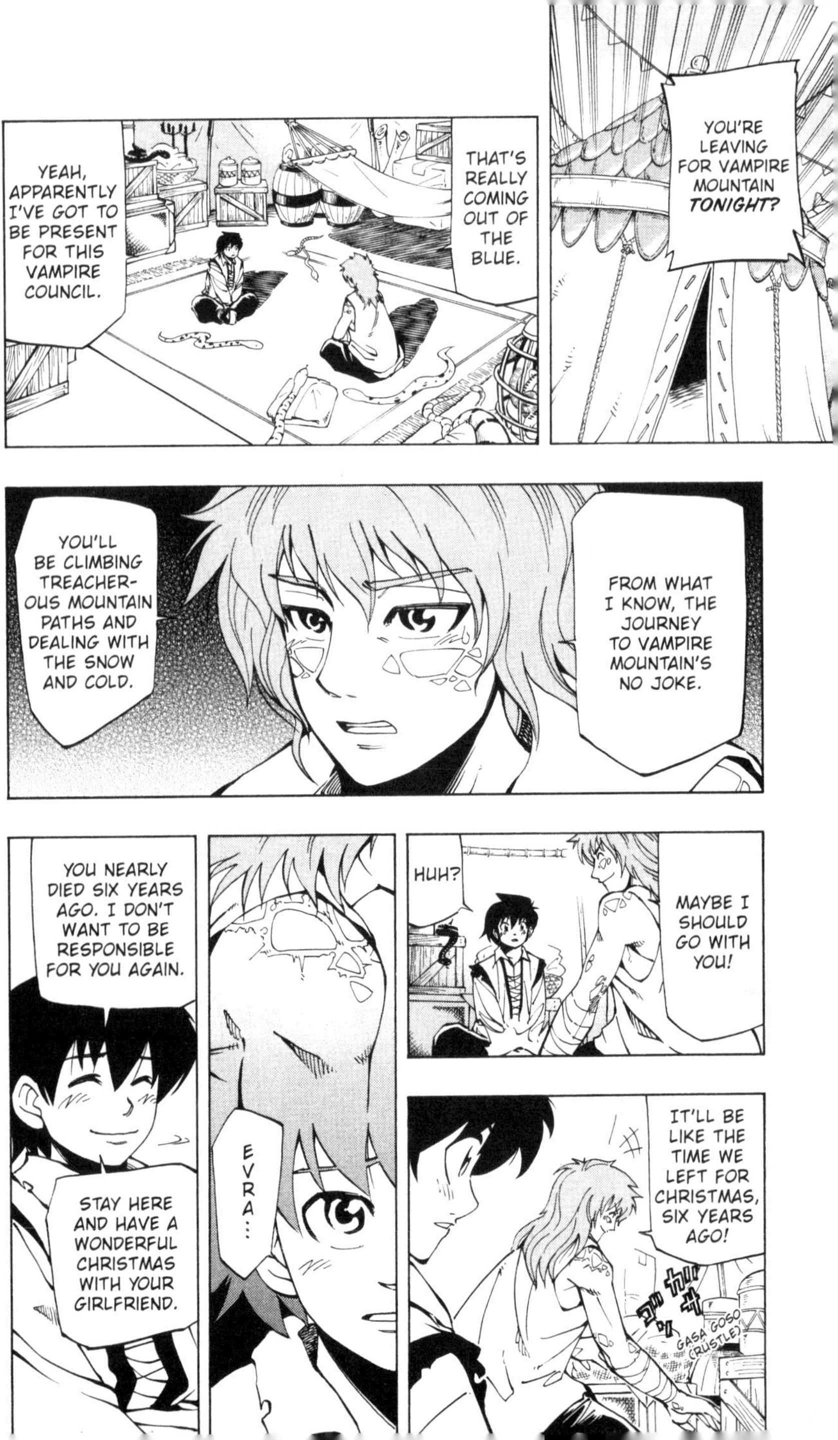
YOU'RE LEAVING FOR VAMPIRE MOUNTAIN *TONIGHT?*
THAT'S REALLY COMING OUT OF THE BLUE.
YEAH, APPARENTLY I'VE GOT TO BE PRESENT FOR THIS VAMPIRE COUNCIL.
FROM WHAT I KNOW, THE JOURNEY TO VAMPIRE MOUNTAIN'S NO JOKE.
YOU'LL BE CLIMBING TREACHER-OUS MOUNTAIN PATHS AND DEALING WITH THE SNOW AND COLD.
MAYBE I SHOULD GO WITH YOU!
HUH?
IT'LL BE LIKE THE TIME WE LEFT FOR CHRISTMAS, SIX YEARS AGO!
GASA GOSO (RUSTLE)
EVRA...
YOU NEARLY DIED SIX YEARS AGO. I DON'T WANT TO BE RESPONSIBLE FOR YOU AGAIN.
STAY HERE AND HAVE A WONDERFUL CHRISTMAS WITH YOUR GIRLFRIEND.

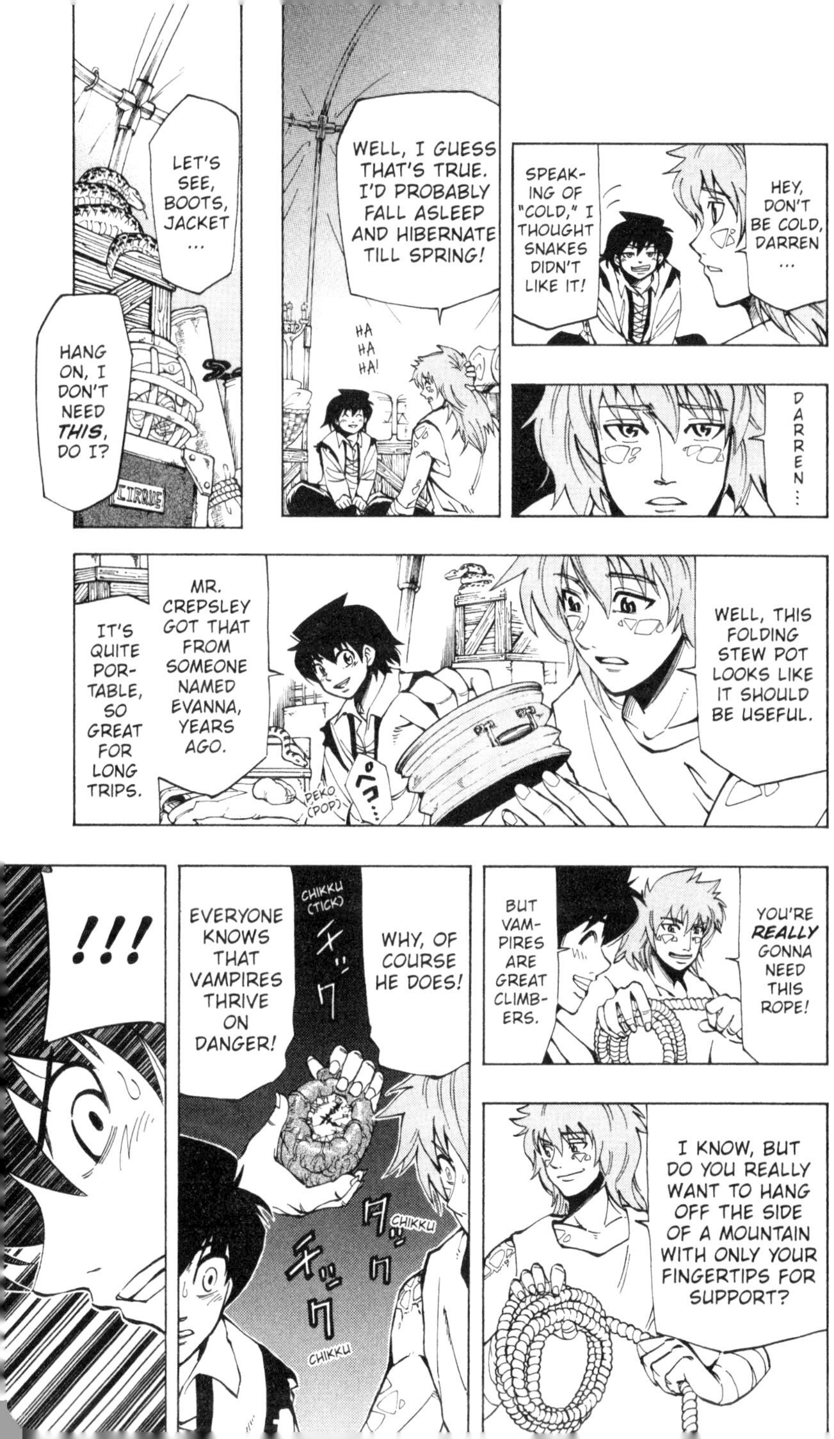
HEY, DON'T BE COLD, DARREN ...
SPEAKING OF "COLD," I THOUGHT SNAKES DIDN'T LIKE IT!
DARREN...
WELL, I GUESS THAT'S TRUE. I'D PROBABLY FALL ASLEEP AND HIBERNATE TILL SPRING!
HA HA HA!
LET'S SEE, BOOTS, JACKET ...
HANG ON, I DON'T NEED ***THIS***, DO I?
CIRQUE
WELL, THIS FOLDING STEW POT LOOKS LIKE IT SHOULD BE USEFUL.
MR. CREPSLEY GOT THAT FROM SOMEONE NAMED EVANNA, YEARS AGO.
IT'S QUITE PORTABLE, SO GREAT FOR LONG TRIPS.
PEKO (POP)
YOU'RE ***REALLY*** GONNA NEED THIS ROPE!
BUT VAMPIRES ARE GREAT CLIMBERS.
I KNOW, BUT DO YOU REALLY WANT TO HANG OFF THE SIDE OF A MOUNTAIN WITH ONLY YOUR FINGERTIPS FOR SUPPORT?
WHY, OF COURSE HE DOES!
EVERYONE KNOWS THAT VAMPIRES THRIVE ON DANGER!
CHIKKU (TICK)
CHIKKU
CHIKKU
!!!

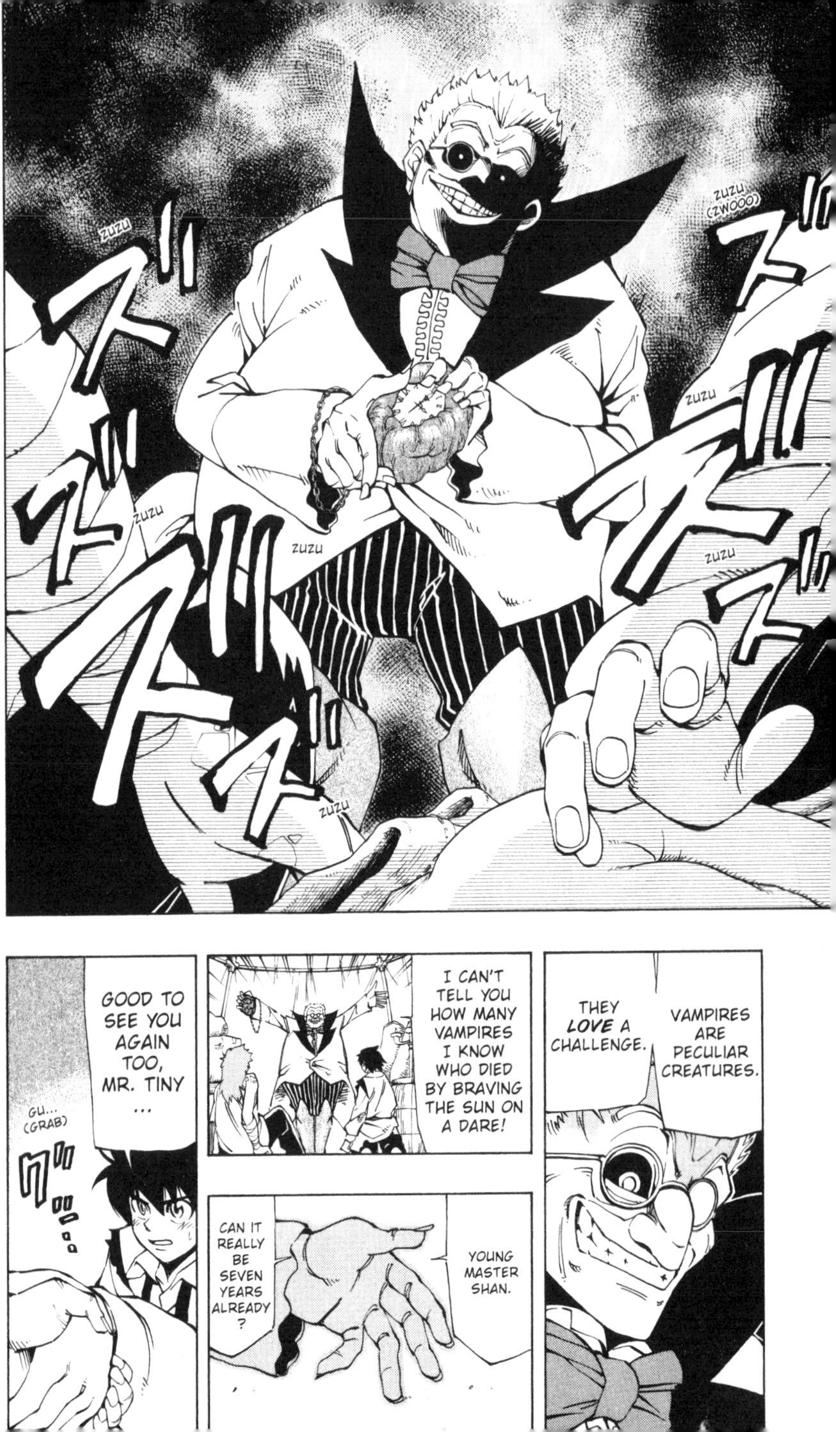
ZUZU (ZWOOO)
ZUZU
ZUZU
ZUZU
ZUZU
ZUZU
ZUZU
VAMPIRES ARE PECULIAR CREATURES.
THEY *LOVE* A CHALLENGE.
I CAN'T TELL YOU HOW MANY VAMPIRES I KNOW WHO DIED BY BRAVING THE SUN ON A DARE!
YOUNG MASTER SHAN.
CAN IT REALLY BE SEVEN YEARS ALREADY?
GOOD TO SEE YOU AGAIN TOO, MR. TINY ...
GU... (GRAB)

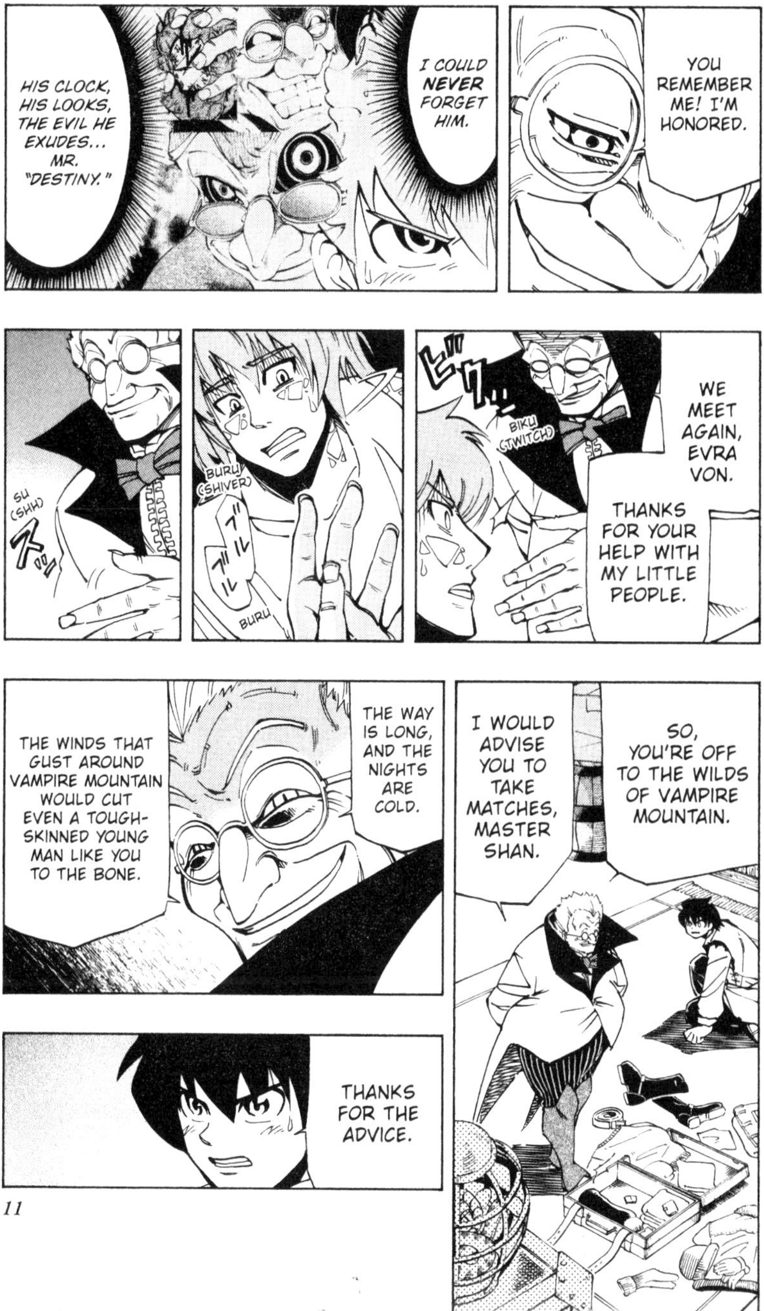
YOU REMEMBER ME! I'M HONORED.
I COULD **NEVER** FORGET HIM.
HIS CLOCK, HIS LOOKS, THE EVIL HE EXUDES... MR. "DESTINY."
BIKU (TWITCH)
WE MEET AGAIN, EVRA VON.
THANKS FOR YOUR HELP WITH MY LITTLE PEOPLE.
BURU (SHIVER)
BURU
SU (SHH)
SO, YOU'RE OFF TO THE WILDS OF VAMPIRE MOUNTAIN.
I WOULD ADVISE YOU TO TAKE MATCHES, MASTER SHAN.
THE WAY IS LONG, AND THE NIGHTS ARE COLD.
THE WINDS THAT GUST AROUND VAMPIRE MOUNTAIN WOULD CUT EVEN A TOUGH-SKINNED YOUNG MAN LIKE YOU TO THE BONE.
THANKS FOR THE ADVICE.

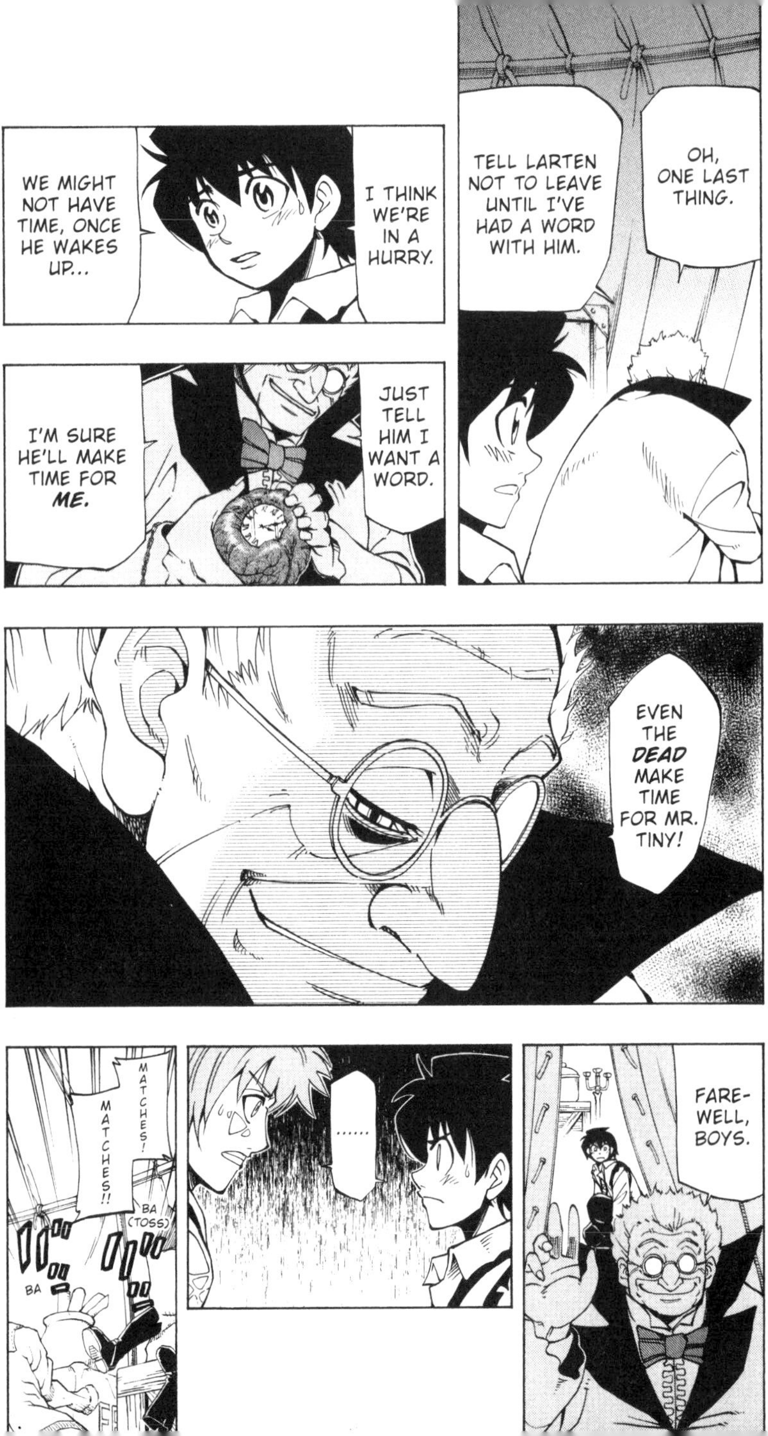
OH, ONE LAST THING.
TELL LARTEN NOT TO LEAVE UNTIL I'VE HAD A WORD WITH HIM.
I THINK WE'RE IN A HURRY.
WE MIGHT NOT HAVE TIME, ONCE HE WAKES UP...
JUST TELL HIM I WANT A WORD.
I'M SURE HE'LL MAKE TIME FOR **ME.**
EVEN THE ***DEAD*** MAKE TIME FOR MR. TINY!
FARE-WELL, BOYS.
......
MATCHES!
MATCHES!!
BA (TOSS)
BA

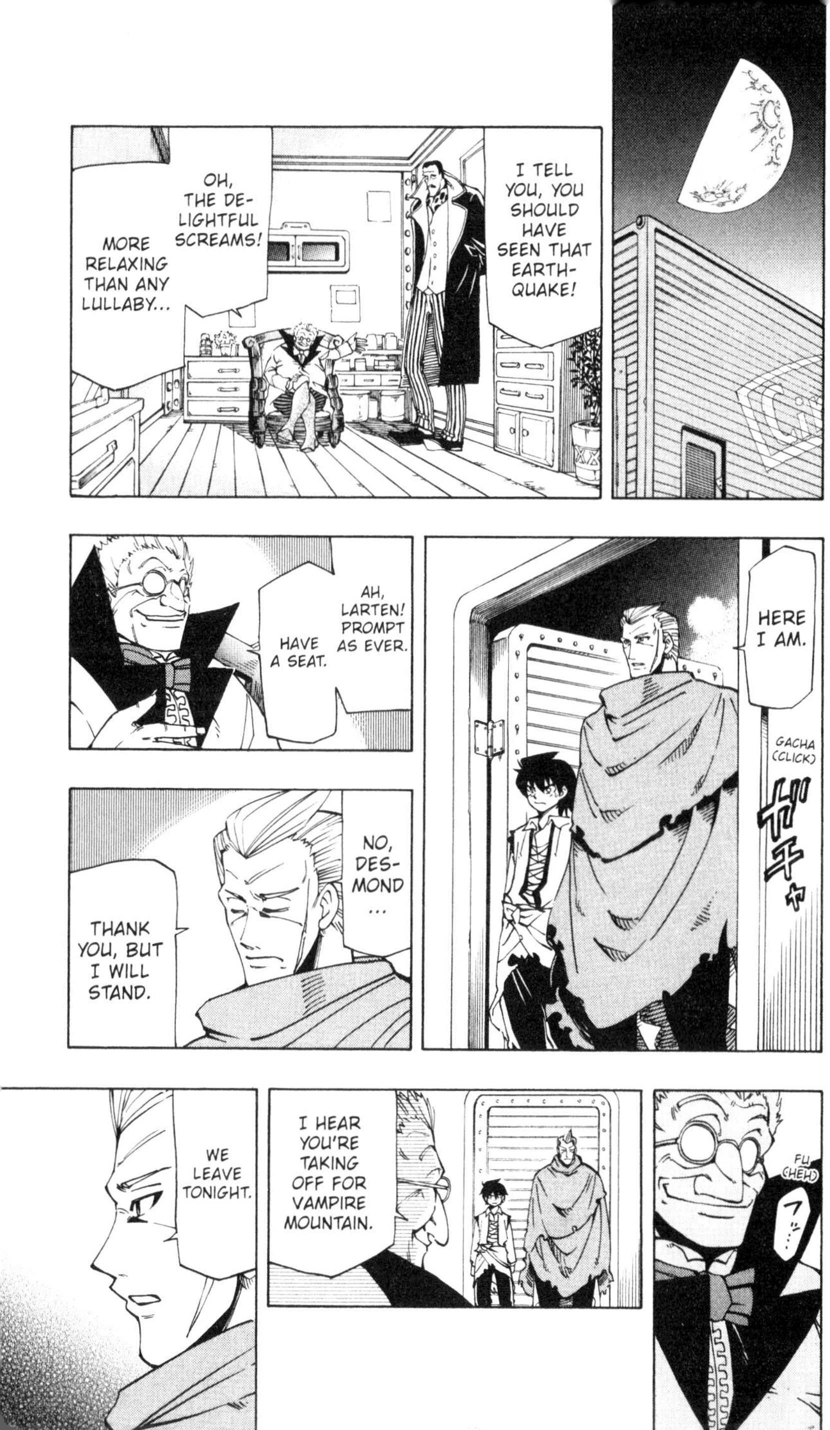
I TELL YOU, YOU SHOULD HAVE SEEN THAT EARTHQUAKE!
OH, THE DELIGHTFUL SCREAMS!
MORE RELAXING THAN ANY LULLABY...
HERE I AM.
GACHA (CLICK)
ガチャ
AH, LARTEN! PROMPT AS EVER.
HAVE A SEAT.
NO, DESMOND...
THANK YOU, BUT I WILL STAND.
FU (HEH)
フッ…
I HEAR YOU'RE TAKING OFF FOR VAMPIRE MOUNTAIN.
WE LEAVE TONIGHT.

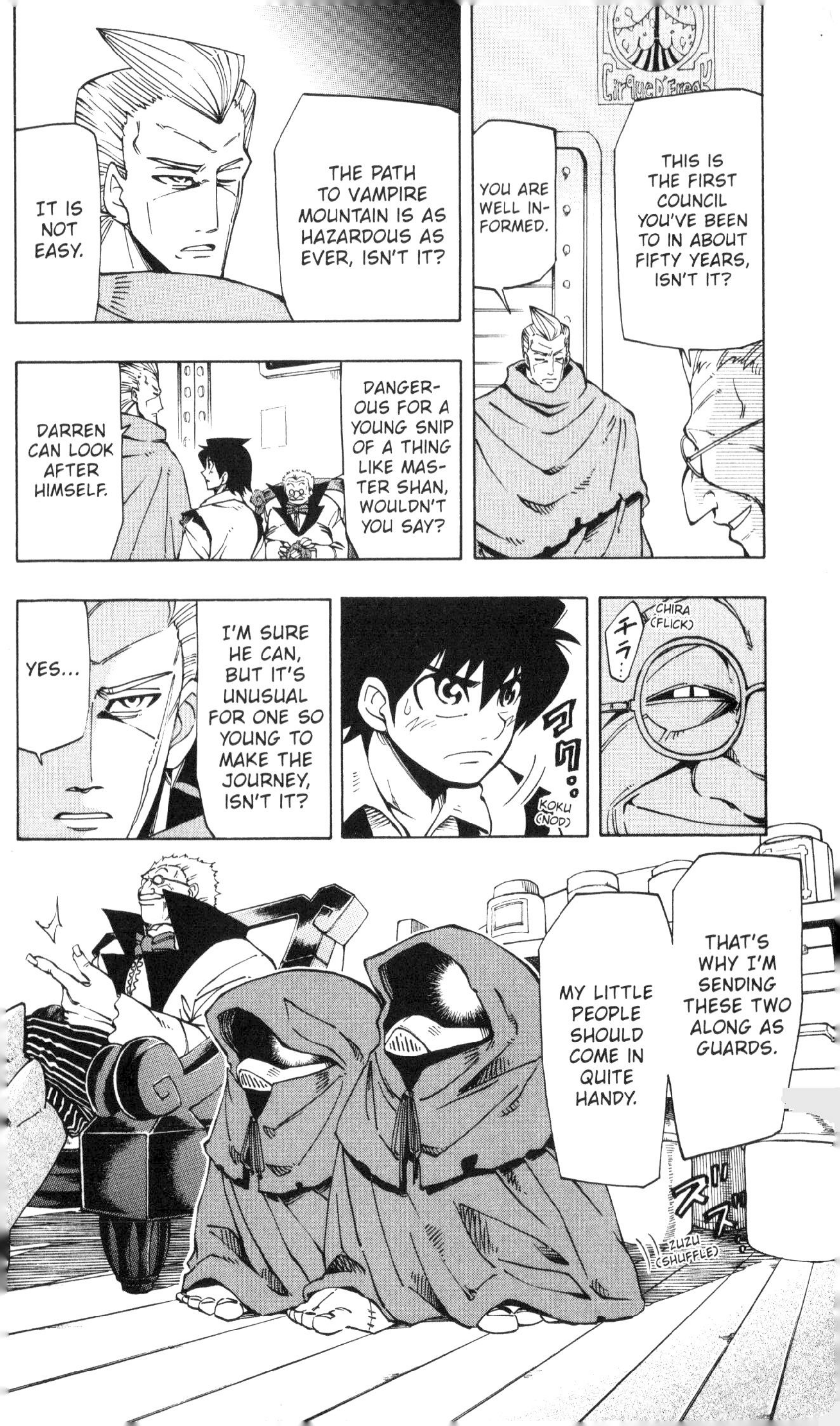

Cirque D'Freak
THIS IS THE FIRST COUNCIL YOU'VE BEEN TO IN ABOUT FIFTY YEARS, ISN'T IT?
YOU ARE WELL INFORMED.
THE PATH TO VAMPIRE MOUNTAIN IS AS HAZARDOUS AS EVER, ISN'T IT?
IT IS NOT EASY.
DANGEROUS FOR A YOUNG SNIP OF A THING LIKE MASTER SHAN, WOULDN'T YOU SAY?
DARREN CAN LOOK AFTER HIMSELF.
チラ…
CHIRA (FLICK)
コク。。
KOKU (NOD)
I'M SURE HE CAN, BUT IT'S UNUSUAL FOR ONE SO YOUNG TO MAKE THE JOURNEY, ISN'T IT?
YES...
THAT'S WHY I'M SENDING THESE TWO ALONG AS GUARDS.
MY LITTLE PEOPLE SHOULD COME IN QUITE HANDY.
ズズ
ZUZU (SHUFFLE)

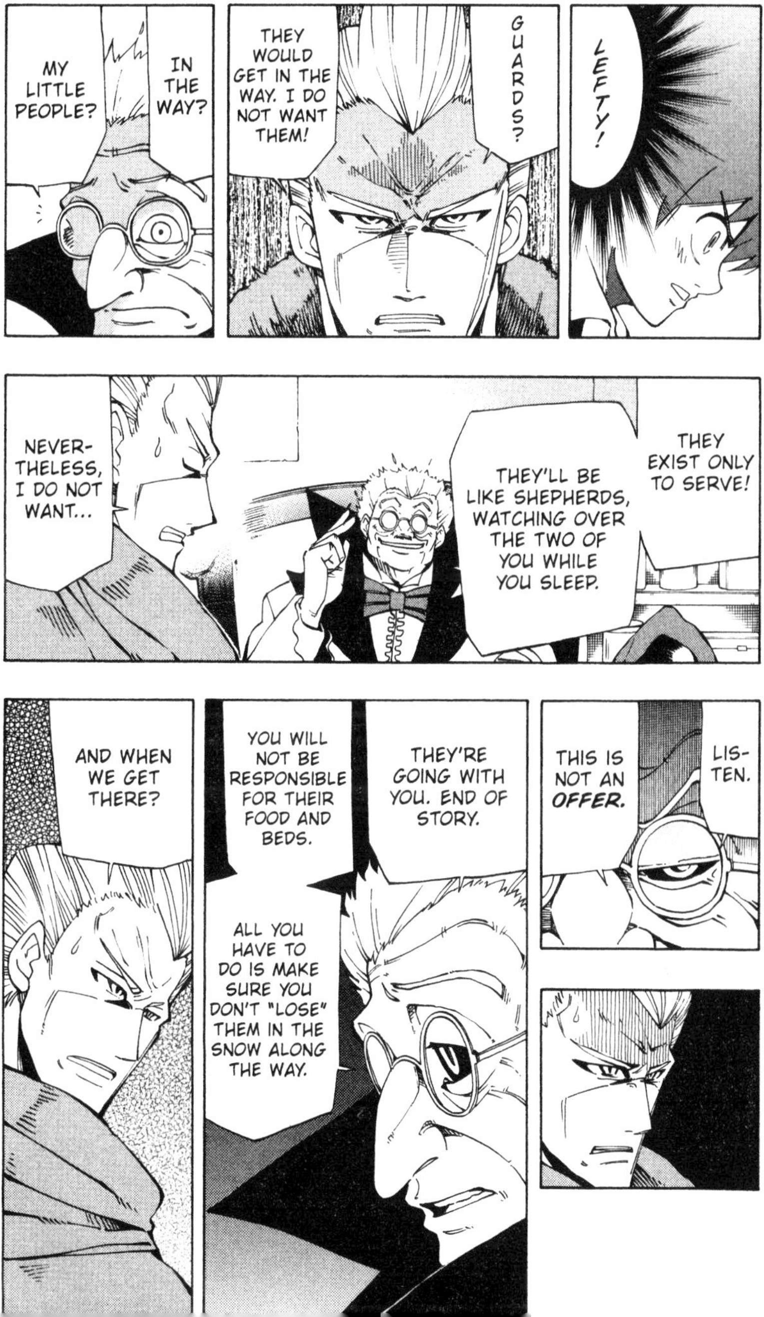
LEFTY!
GUARDS?
THEY WOULD GET IN THE WAY. I DO NOT WANT THEM!
IN THE WAY?
MY LITTLE PEOPLE?
THEY EXIST ONLY TO SERVE!
THEY'LL BE LIKE SHEPHERDS, WATCHING OVER THE TWO OF YOU WHILE YOU SLEEP.
NEVER-THELESS, I DO NOT WANT...
LIS-TEN.
THIS IS NOT AN *OFFER.*
THEY'RE GOING WITH YOU. END OF STORY.
YOU WILL NOT BE RESPONSIBLE FOR THEIR FOOD AND BEDS.
ALL YOU HAVE TO DO IS MAKE SURE YOU DON'T "LOSE" THEM IN THE SNOW ALONG THE WAY.
AND WHEN WE GET THERE?

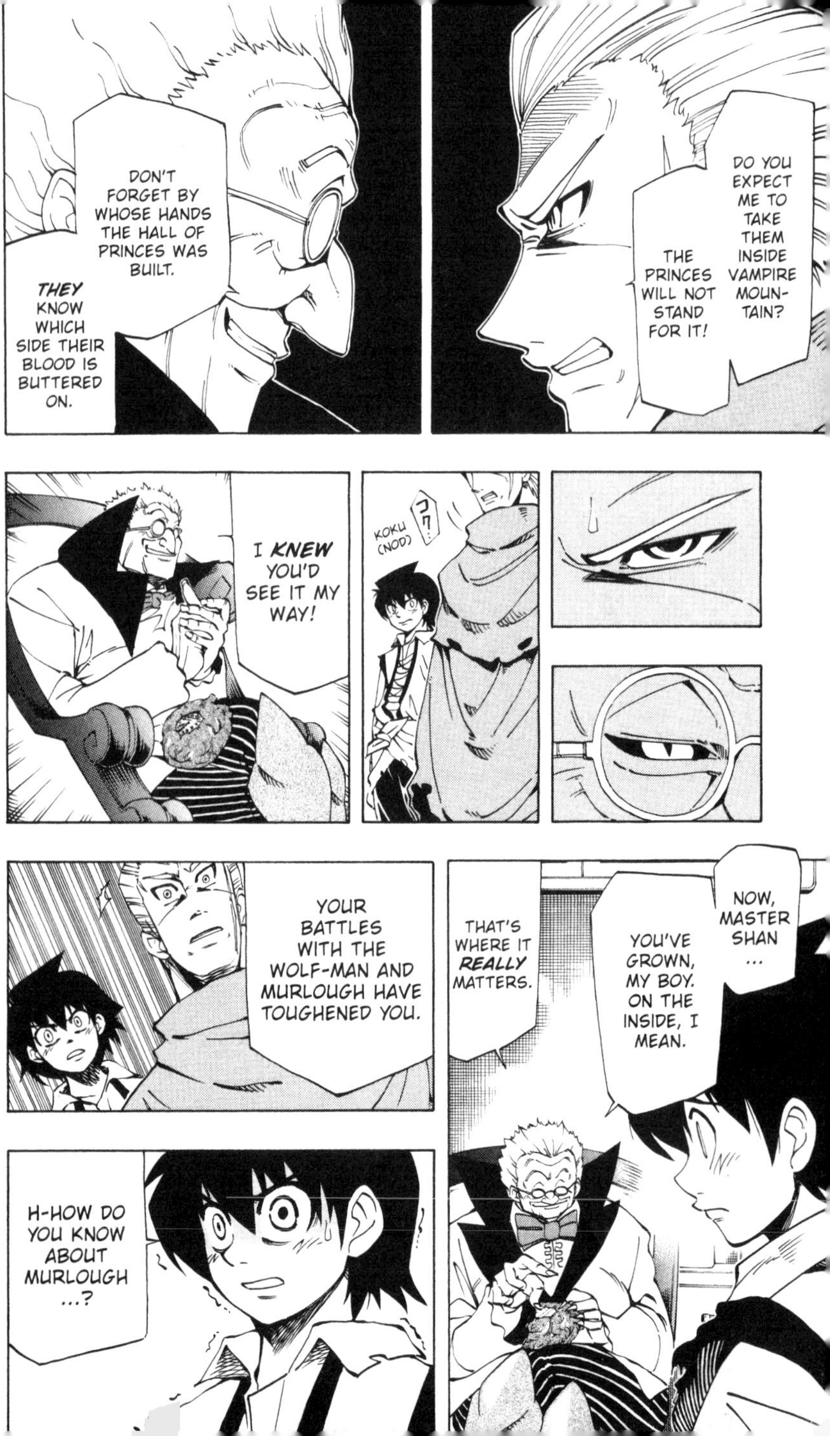
DO YOU EXPECT ME TO TAKE THEM INSIDE VAMPIRE MOUN-TAIN?
THE PRINCES WILL NOT STAND FOR IT!
DON'T FORGET BY WHOSE HANDS THE HALL OF PRINCES WAS BUILT.
THEY KNOW WHICH SIDE THEIR BLOOD IS BUTTERED ON.
コク
KOKU (NOD)
I *KNEW* YOU'D SEE IT MY WAY!
NOW, MASTER SHAN ...
YOU'VE GROWN, MY BOY. ON THE INSIDE, I MEAN.
THAT'S WHERE IT *REALLY* MATTERS.
YOUR BATTLES WITH THE WOLF-MAN AND MURLOUGH HAVE TOUGHENED YOU.
H-HOW DO YOU KNOW ABOUT MURLOUGH ...?

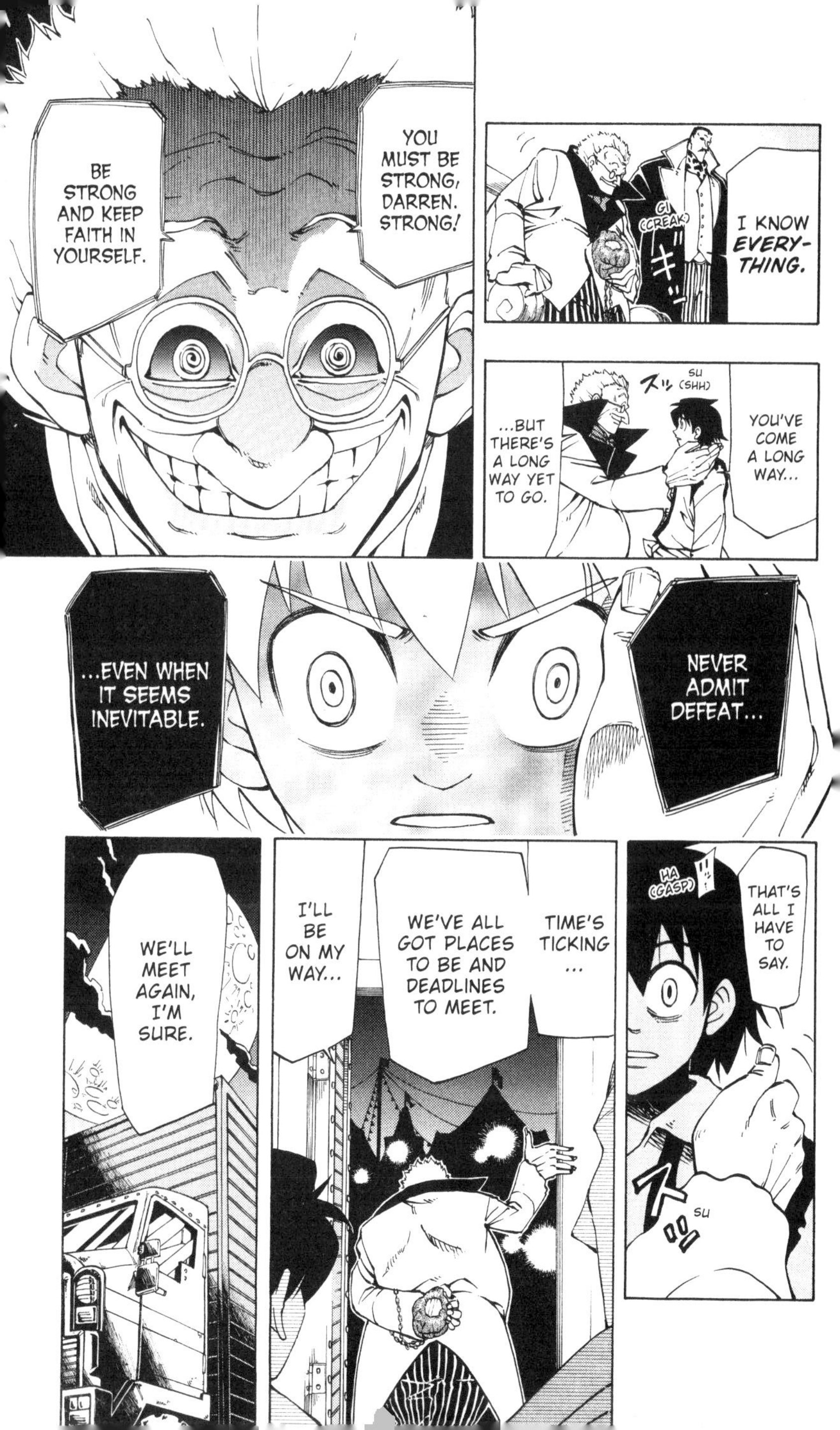

I KNOW EVERYTHING.
GI (CREAK)
YOU'VE COME A LONG WAY...
SU (SHH)
...BUT THERE'S A LONG WAY YET TO GO.
YOU MUST BE STRONG, DARREN. STRONG!
BE STRONG AND KEEP FAITH IN YOURSELF.
NEVER ADMIT DEFEAT...
...EVEN WHEN IT SEEMS INEVITABLE.
THAT'S ALL I HAVE TO SAY.
HA (GASP)
SU
TIME'S TICKING ...
WE'VE ALL GOT PLACES TO BE AND DEADLINES TO MEET.
I'LL BE ON MY WAY...
WE'LL MEET AGAIN, I'M SURE.

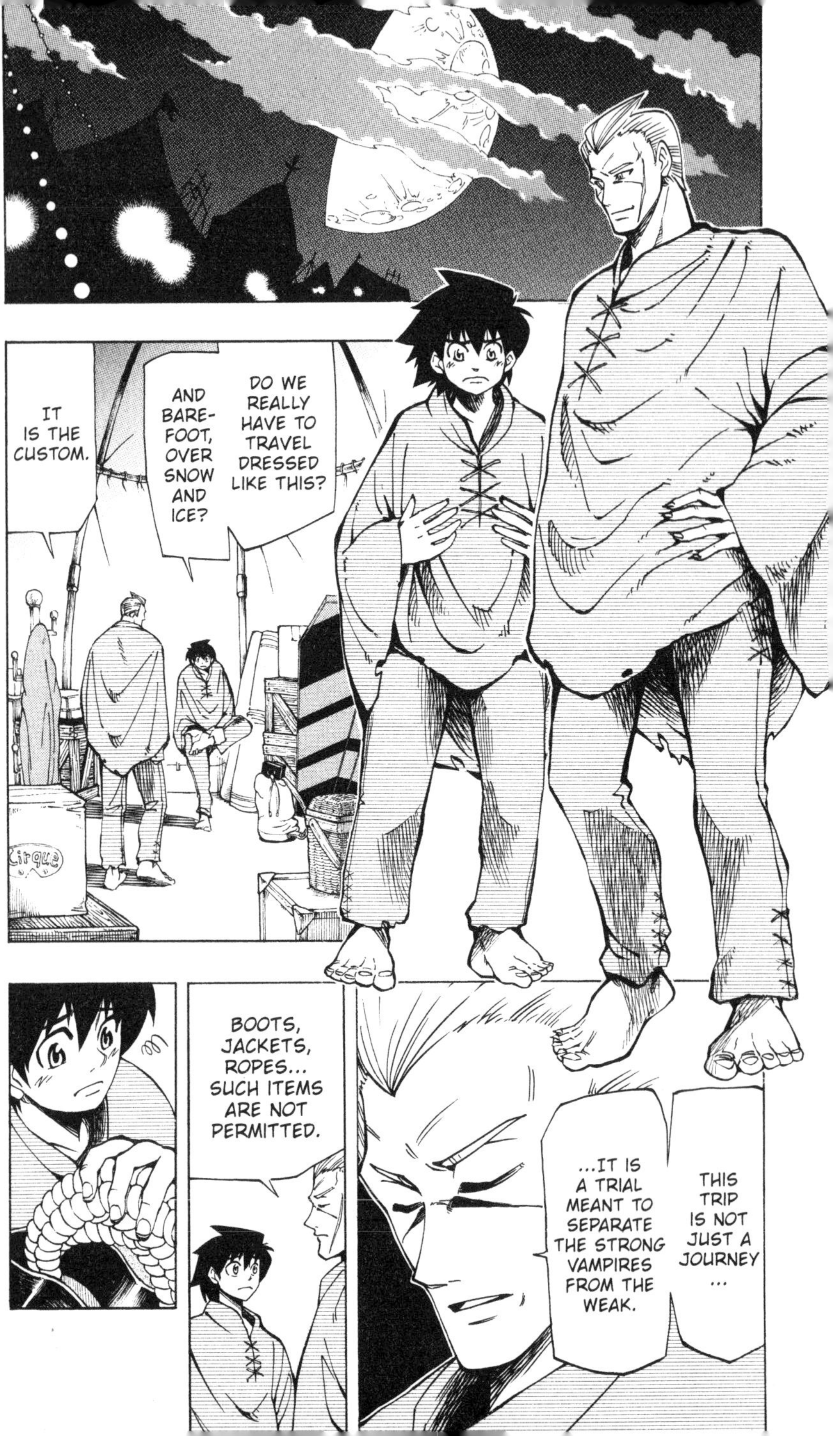
DO WE REALLY HAVE TO TRAVEL DRESSED LIKE THIS?
AND BARE-FOOT, OVER SNOW AND ICE?
IT IS THE CUSTOM.
Cirque
THIS TRIP IS NOT JUST A JOURNEY ...
...IT IS A TRIAL MEANT TO SEPARATE THE STRONG VAMPIRES FROM THE WEAK.
BOOTS, JACKETS, ROPES... SUCH ITEMS ARE NOT PERMITTED.

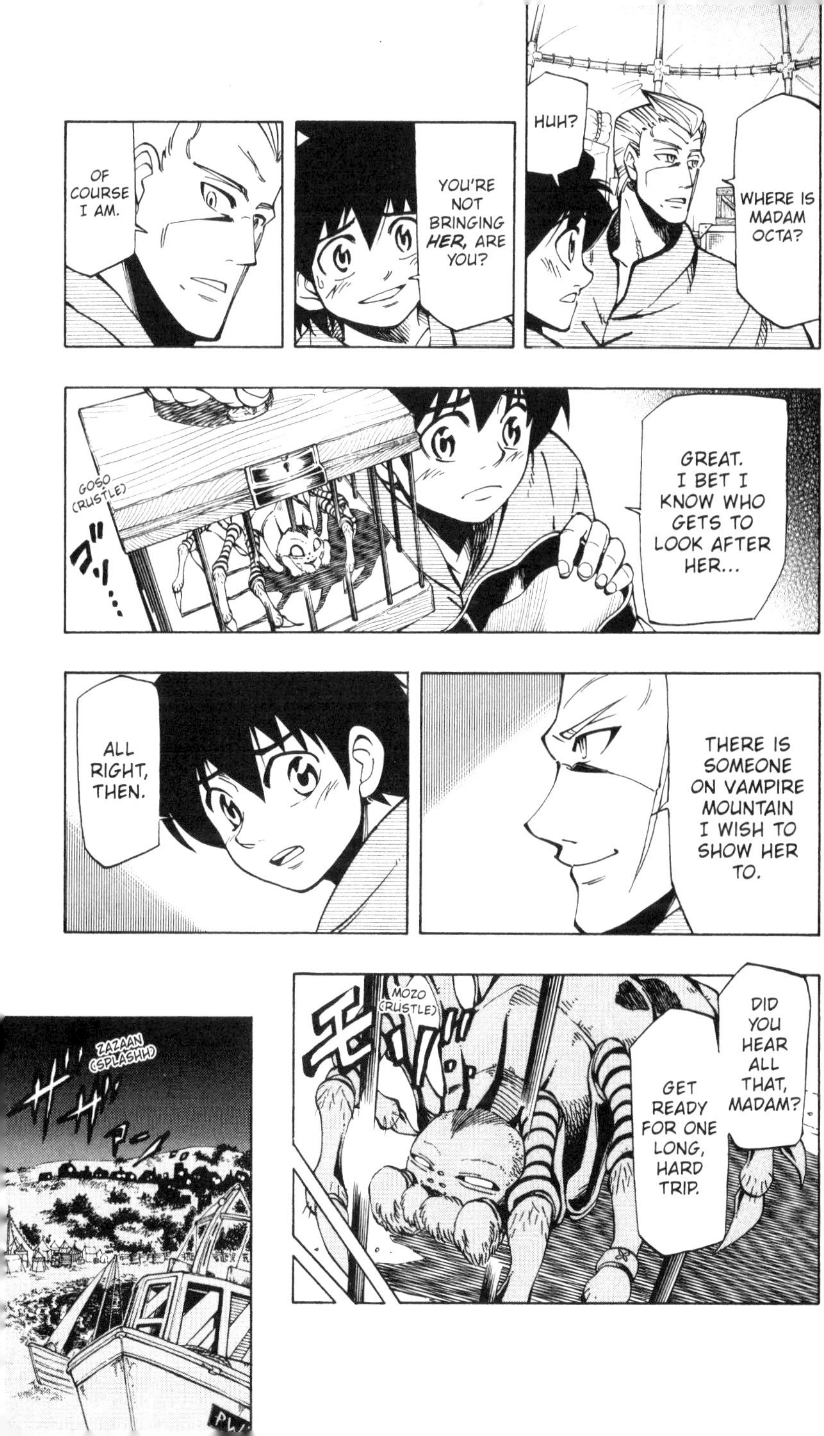

WHERE IS MADAM OCTA?
HUH?
YOU'RE NOT BRINGING *HER*, ARE YOU?
OF COURSE I AM.
GREAT. I BET I KNOW WHO GETS TO LOOK AFTER HER...
GOSO (RUSTLE)
THERE IS SOMEONE ON VAMPIRE MOUNTAIN I WISH TO SHOW HER TO.
ALL RIGHT, THEN.
DID YOU HEAR ALL THAT, MADAM?
GET READY FOR ONE LONG, HARD TRIP.
MOZO (RUSTLE)
ZAZAAN (SPLASHH)

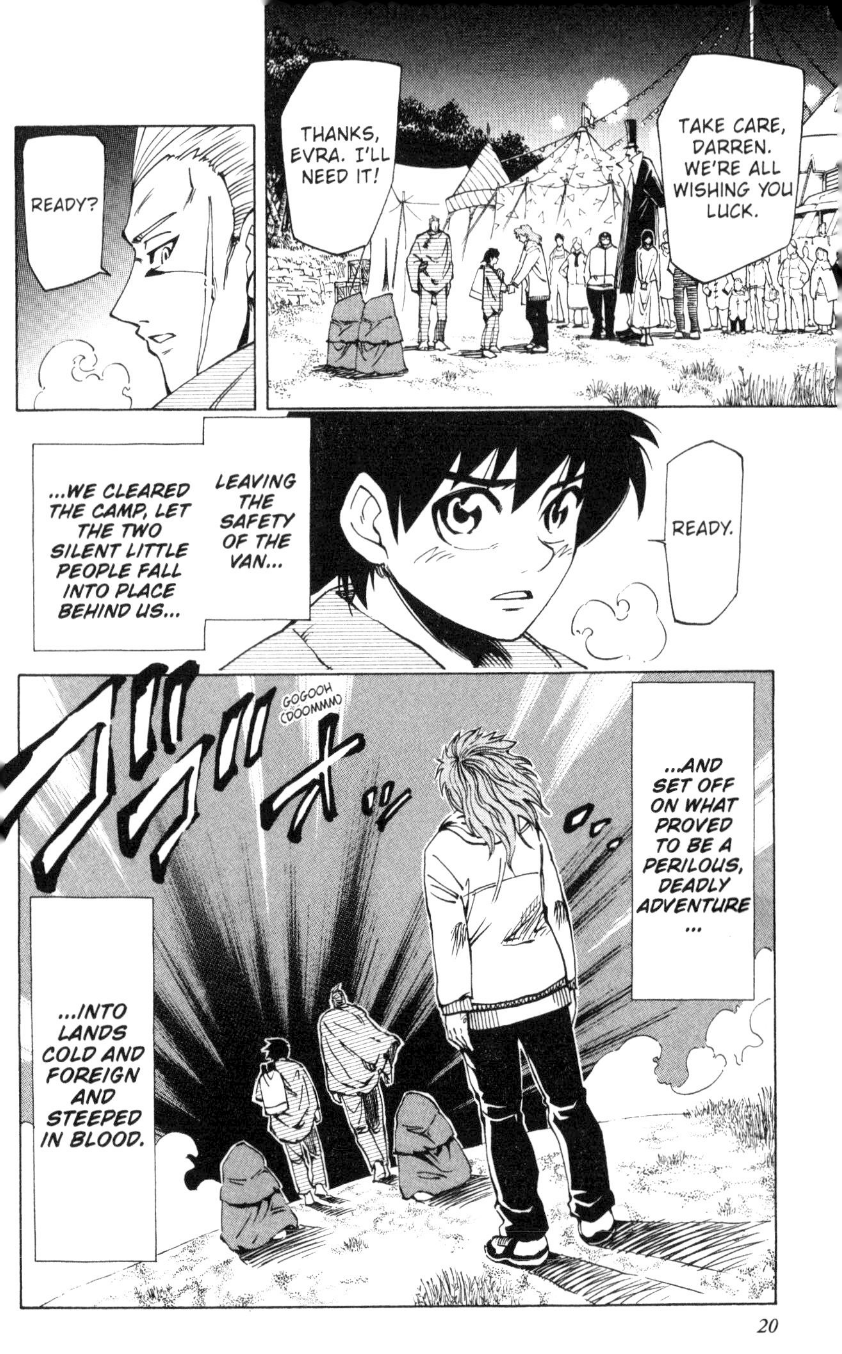
TAKE CARE, DARREN. WE'RE ALL WISHING YOU LUCK.
THANKS, EVRA. I'LL NEED IT!
READY?
READY.
LEAVING THE SAFETY OF THE VAN...
...WE CLEARED THE CAMP, LET THE TWO SILENT LITTLE PEOPLE FALL INTO PLACE BEHIND US...
...AND SET OFF ON WHAT PROVED TO BE A PERILOUS, DEADLY ADVENTURE ...
GOGOOH (DOOMMM)
...INTO LANDS COLD AND FOREIGN AND STEEPED IN BLOOD.

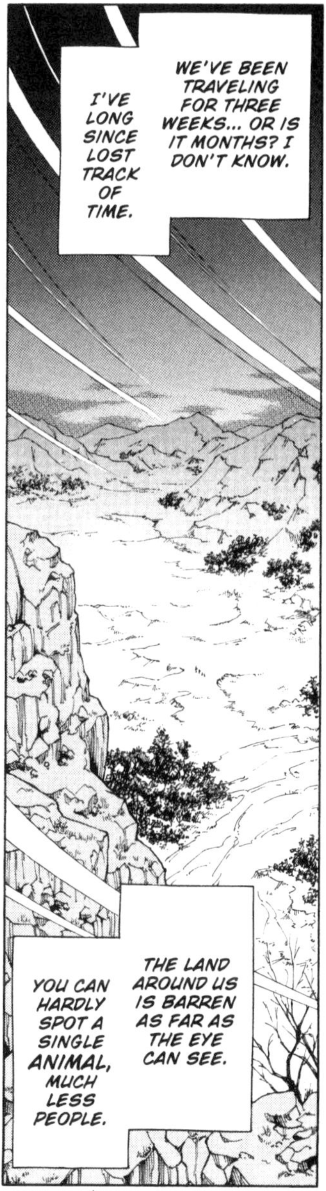
WE'VE BEEN TRAVELING FOR THREE WEEKS... OR IS IT MONTHS? I DON'T KNOW.
I'VE LONG SINCE LOST TRACK OF TIME.
THE LAND AROUND US IS BARREN AS FAR AS THE EYE CAN SEE.
YOU CAN HARDLY SPOT A SINGLE ANIMAL, MUCH LESS PEOPLE.

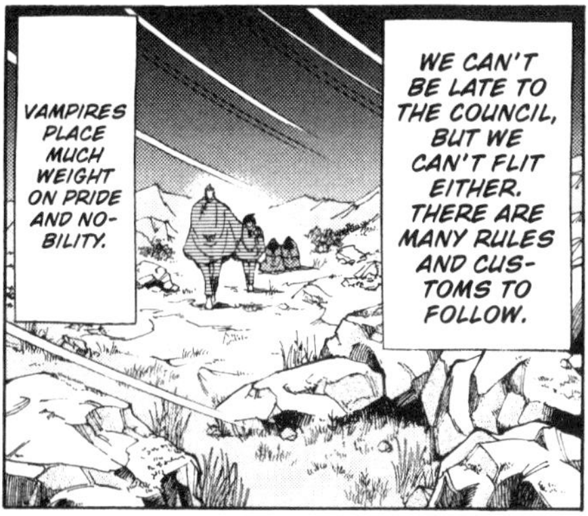
WE CAN'T BE LATE TO THE COUNCIL, BUT WE CAN'T FLIT EITHER. THERE ARE MANY RULES AND CUSTOMS TO FOLLOW.
VAMPIRES PLACE MUCH WEIGHT ON PRIDE AND NOBILITY.

CHAPTER 26: STREAK

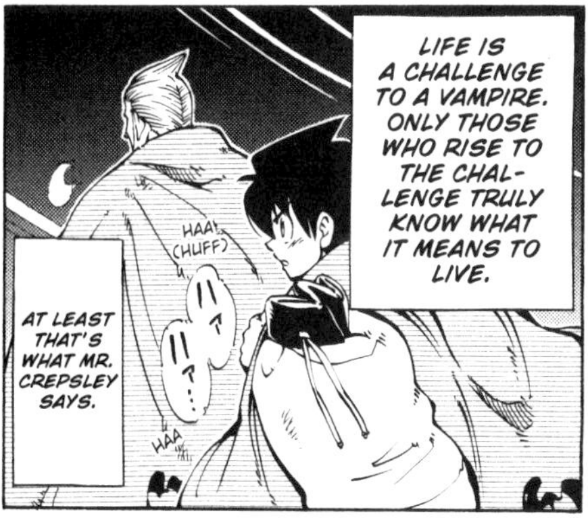
LIFE IS A CHALLENGE TO A VAMPIRE. ONLY THOSE WHO RISE TO THE CHALLENGE TRULY KNOW WHAT IT MEANS TO LIVE.
HAA (HUFF)
ハァ
ハァ…
HAA
AT LEAST THAT'S WHAT MR. CREPSLEY SAYS.

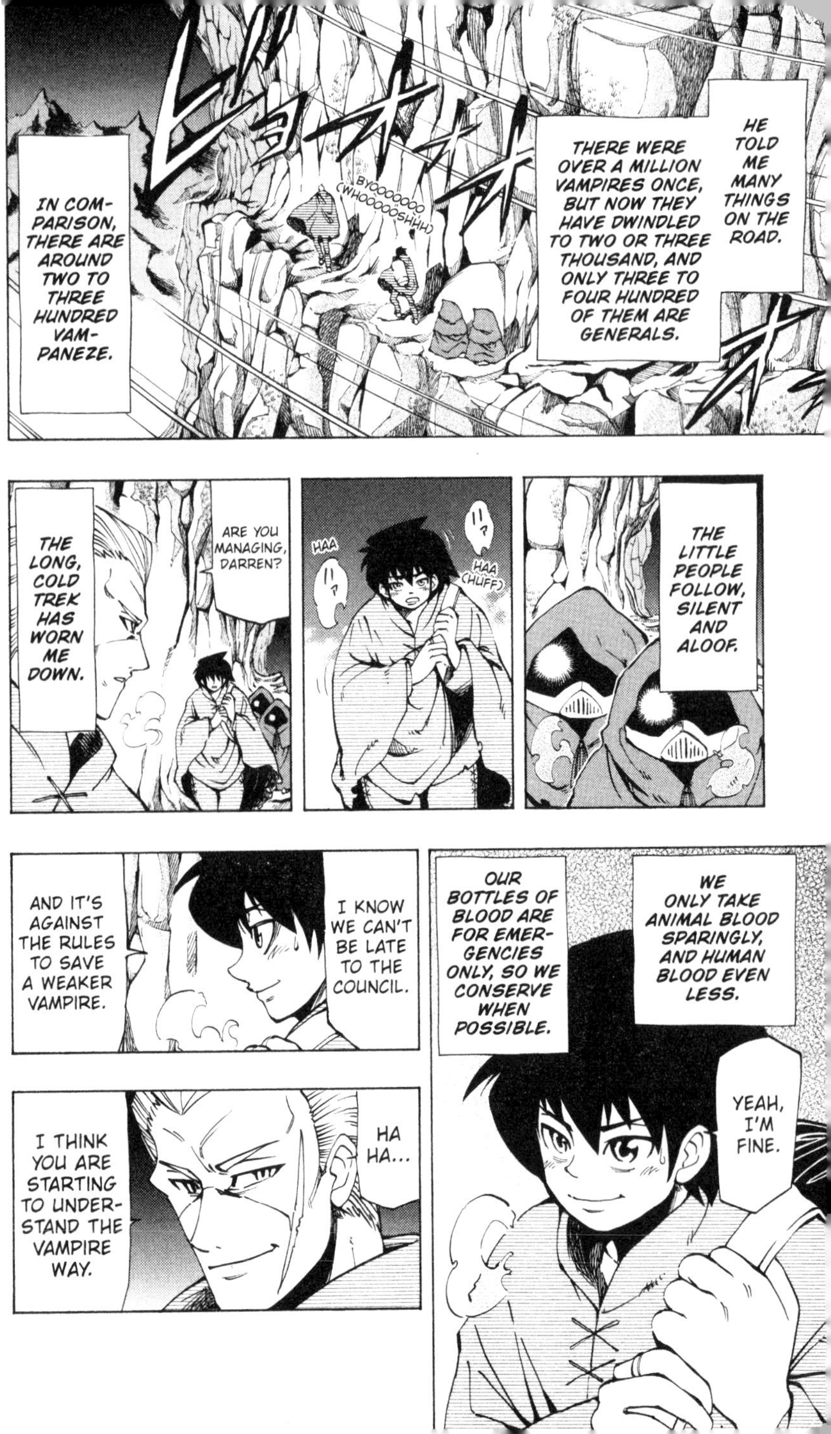
HE TOLD ME MANY THINGS ON THE ROAD.
THERE WERE OVER A MILLION VAMPIRES ONCE, BUT NOW THEY HAVE DWINDLED TO TWO OR THREE THOUSAND, AND ONLY THREE TO FOUR HUNDRED OF THEM ARE GENERALS.
BYOOOOOOO (WHOOOOOSHHH)
IN COMPARISON, THERE ARE AROUND TWO TO THREE HUNDRED VAMPANEZE.
THE LITTLE PEOPLE FOLLOW, SILENT AND ALOOF.
HAA (HUFF)
HAA
ARE YOU MANAGING, DARREN?
THE LONG, COLD TREK HAS WORN ME DOWN.
WE ONLY TAKE ANIMAL BLOOD SPARINGLY, AND HUMAN BLOOD EVEN LESS.
OUR BOTTLES OF BLOOD ARE FOR EMERGENCIES ONLY, SO WE CONSERVE WHEN POSSIBLE.
YEAH, I'M FINE.
I KNOW WE CAN'T BE LATE TO THE COUNCIL.
AND IT'S AGAINST THE RULES TO SAVE A WEAKER VAMPIRE.
HA HA...
I THINK YOU ARE STARTING TO UNDERSTAND THE VAMPIRE WAY.

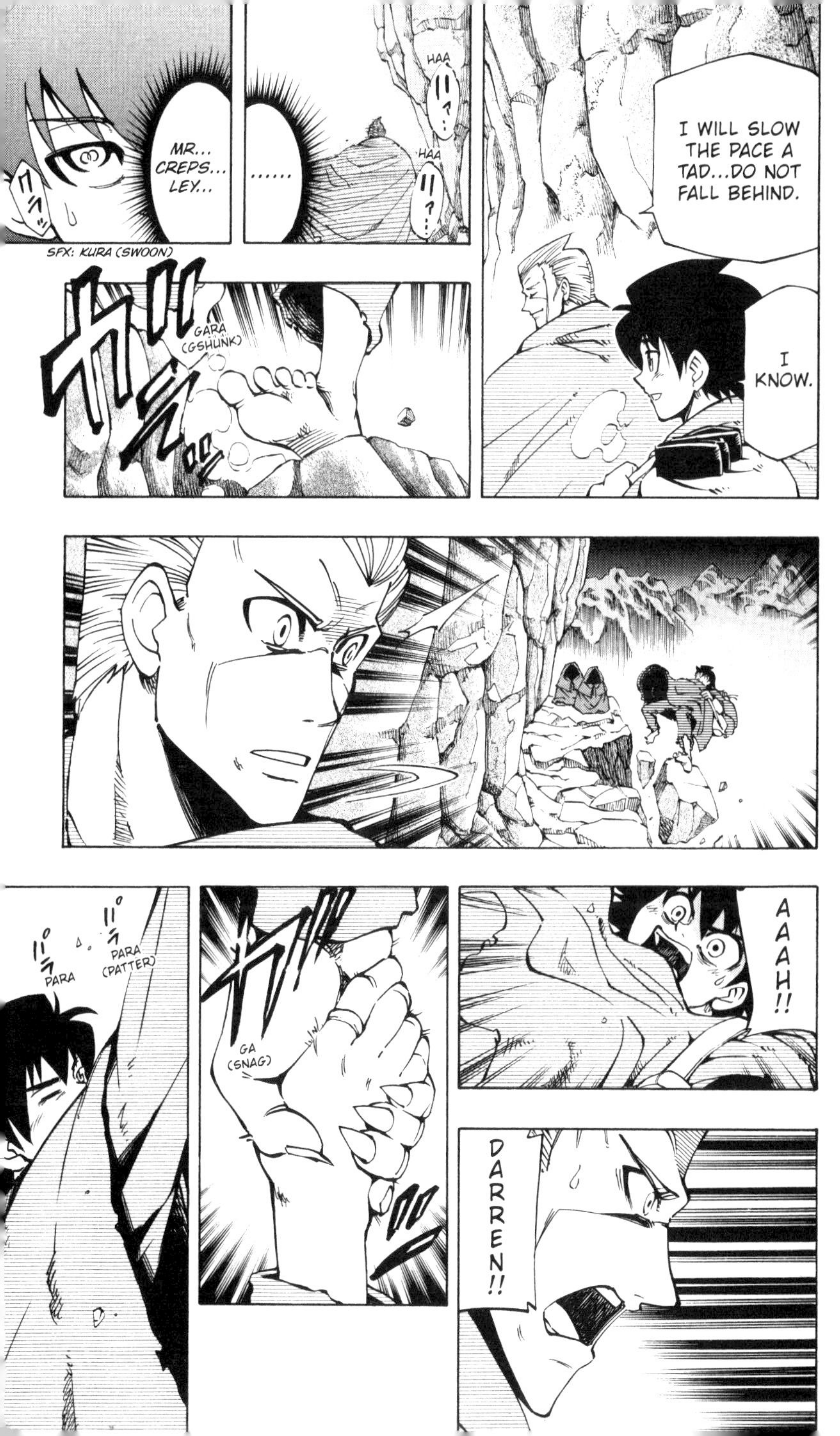

I WILL SLOW THE PACE A TAD...DO NOT FALL BEHIND.
I KNOW.
HAA
HAA
......
MR... CREPS... LEY...
SFX: KURA (SWOON)
GARA (GSHUNK)
AAAH!!
DARREN!!
GA (SNAG)
PARA (PATTER)
PARA

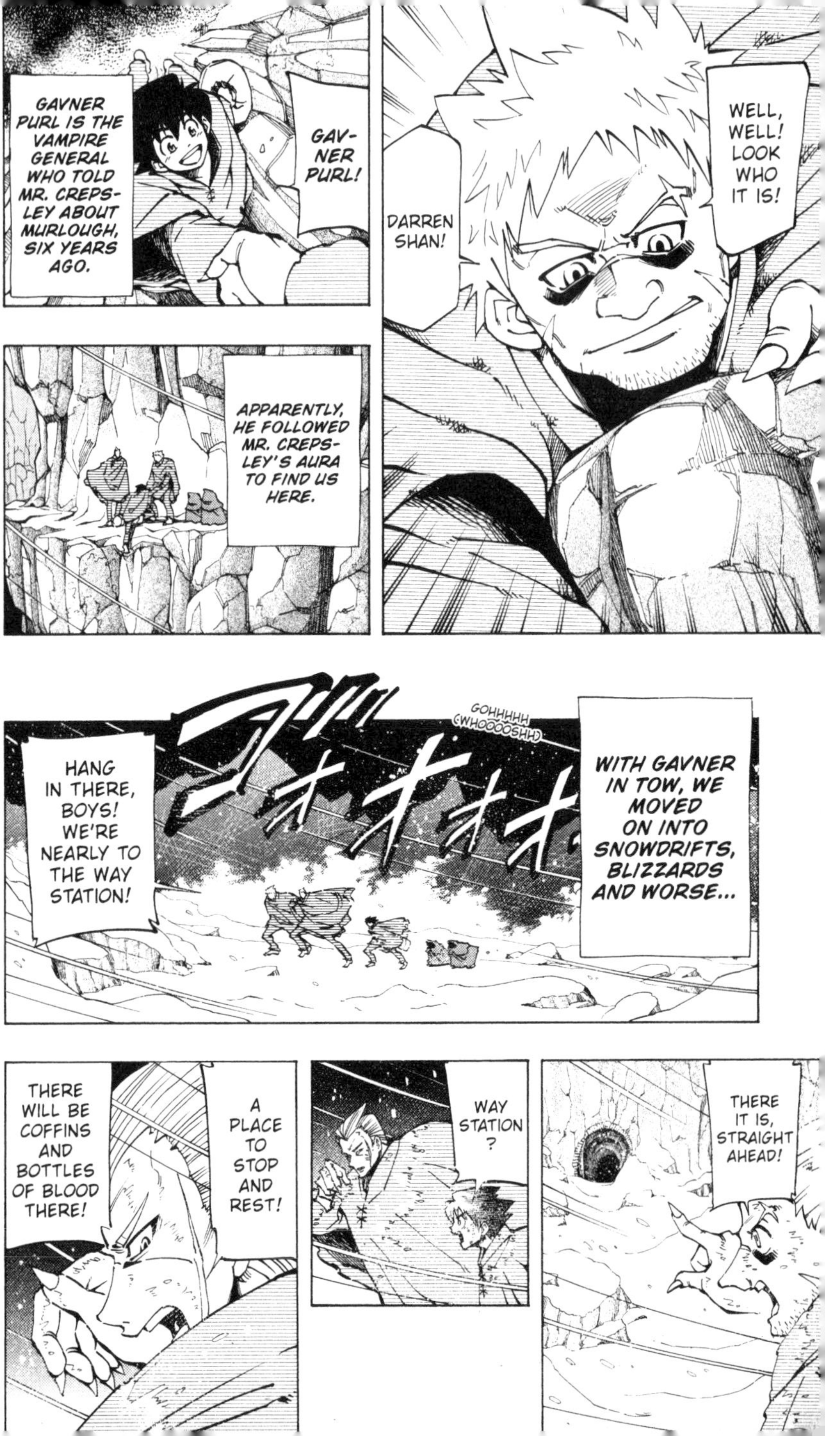
WELL, WELL! LOOK WHO IT IS!
DARREN SHAN!
GAV-NER PURL!
GAVNER PURL IS THE VAMPIRE GENERAL WHO TOLD MR. CREPS-LEY ABOUT MURLOUGH, SIX YEARS AGO.
APPARENTLY, HE FOLLOWED MR. CREPS-LEY'S AURA TO FIND US HERE.
WITH GAVNER IN TOW, WE MOVED ON INTO SNOWDRIFTS, BLIZZARDS AND WORSE...
GOHHHHH (WHOOOOSHH)
HANG IN THERE, BOYS! WE'RE NEARLY TO THE WAY STATION!
THERE IT IS, STRAIGHT AHEAD!
WAY STATION?
A PLACE TO STOP AND REST!
THERE WILL BE COFFINS AND BOTTLES OF BLOOD THERE!

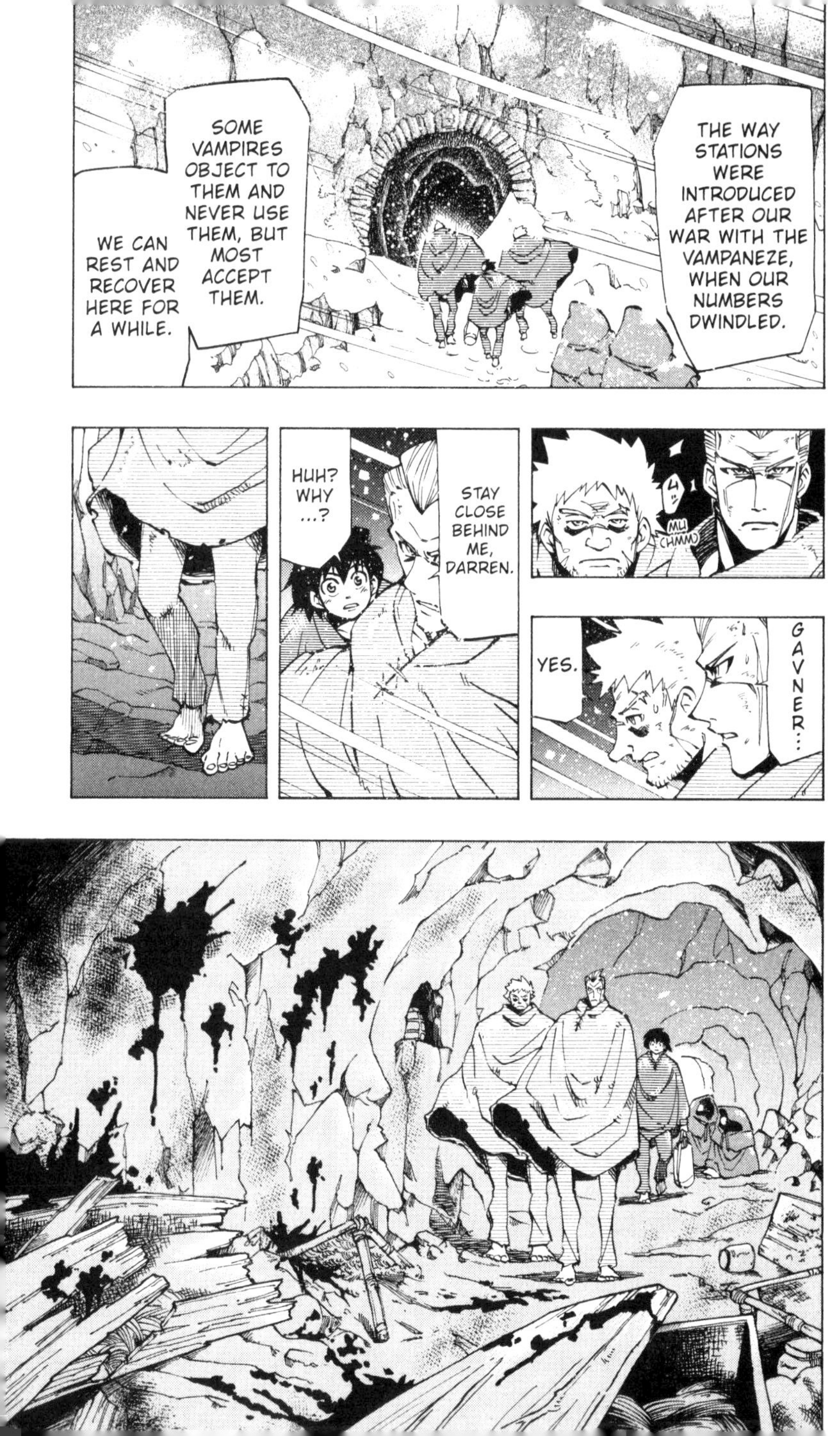
THE WAY STATIONS WERE INTRODUCED AFTER OUR WAR WITH THE VAMPANEZE, WHEN OUR NUMBERS DWINDLED.
SOME VAMPIRES OBJECT TO THEM AND NEVER USE THEM, BUT MOST ACCEPT THEM.
WE CAN REST AND RECOVER HERE FOR A WHILE.
MU (HMM)
GAVNER...
YES.
STAY CLOSE BEHIND ME, DARREN.
HUH? WHY ...?

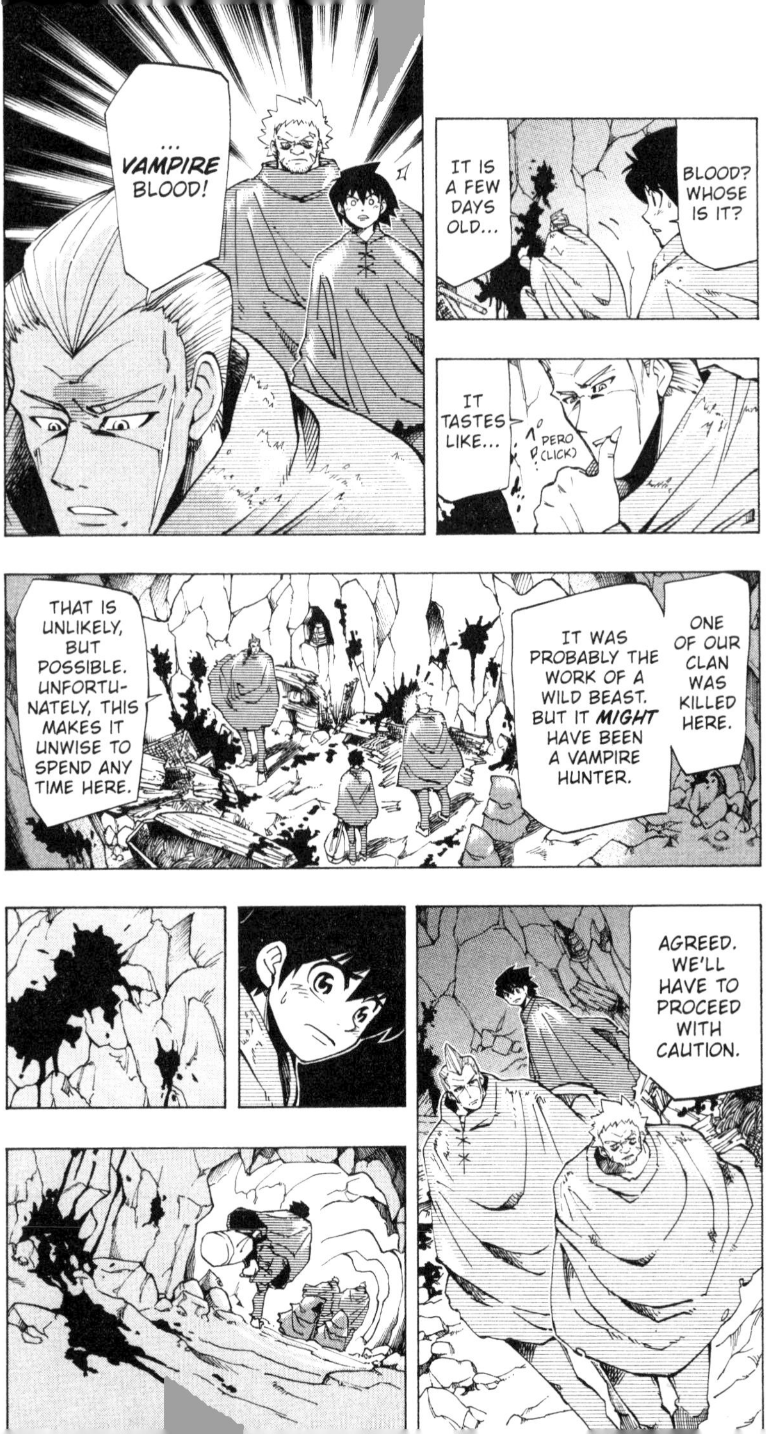
BLOOD? WHOSE IS IT?
IT IS A FEW DAYS OLD...
IT TASTES LIKE...
PERO (CLICK)
... VAMPIRE BLOOD!
ONE OF OUR CLAN WAS KILLED HERE.
IT WAS PROBABLY THE WORK OF A WILD BEAST. BUT IT MIGHT HAVE BEEN A VAMPIRE HUNTER.
THAT IS UNLIKELY, BUT POSSIBLE. UNFORTU-NATELY, THIS MAKES IT UNWISE TO SPEND ANY TIME HERE.
AGREED. WE'LL HAVE TO PROCEED WITH CAUTION.

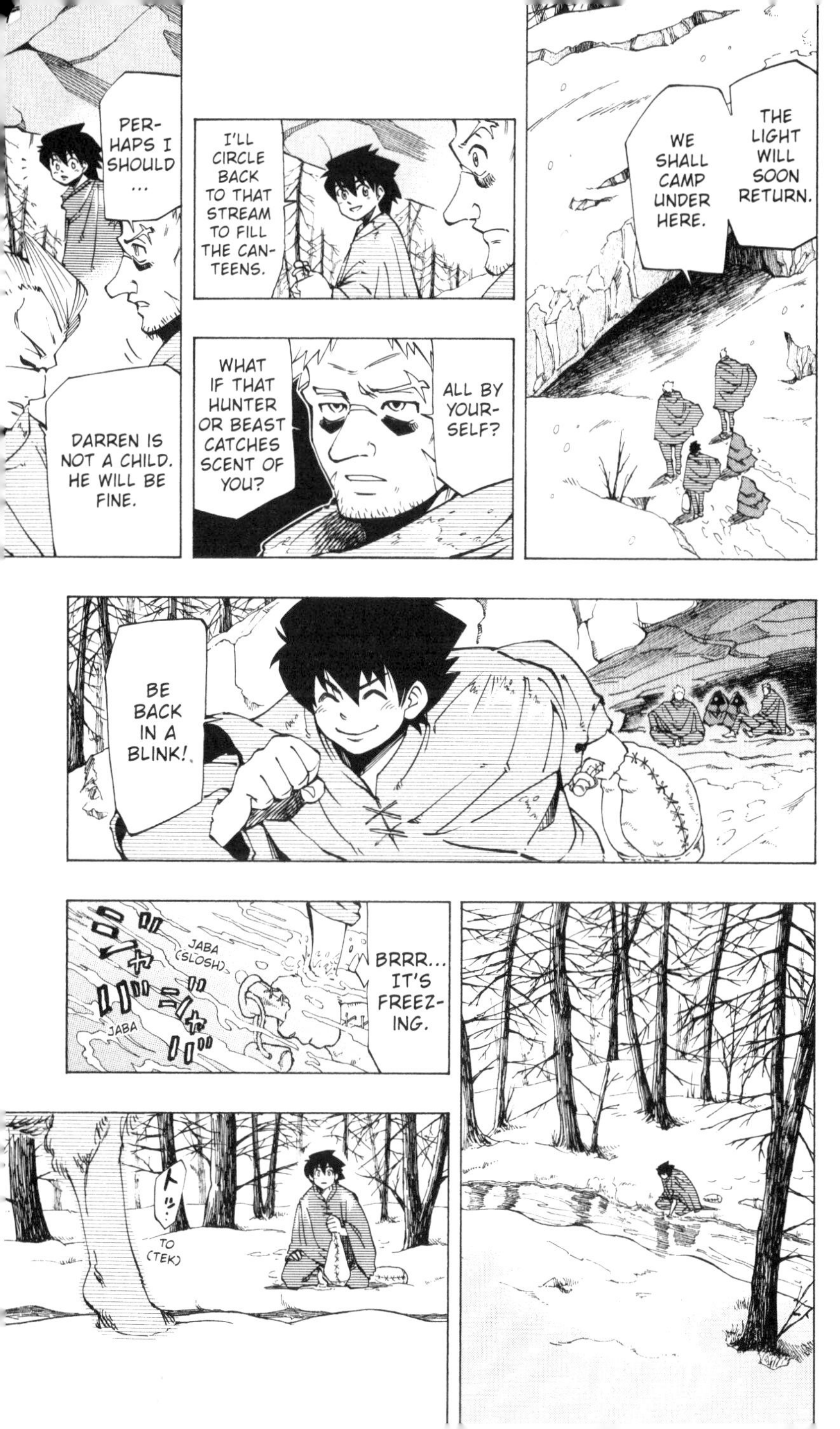
THE LIGHT WILL SOON RETURN.
WE SHALL CAMP UNDER HERE.
I'LL CIRCLE BACK TO THAT STREAM TO FILL THE CANTEENS.
ALL BY YOURSELF?
WHAT IF THAT HUNTER OR BEAST CATCHES SCENT OF YOU?
PERHAPS I SHOULD ...
DARREN IS NOT A CHILD. HE WILL BE FINE.
BE BACK IN A BLINK!
BRRR... IT'S FREEZING.
JABA (SLOSH)
JABA
TO (TEK)

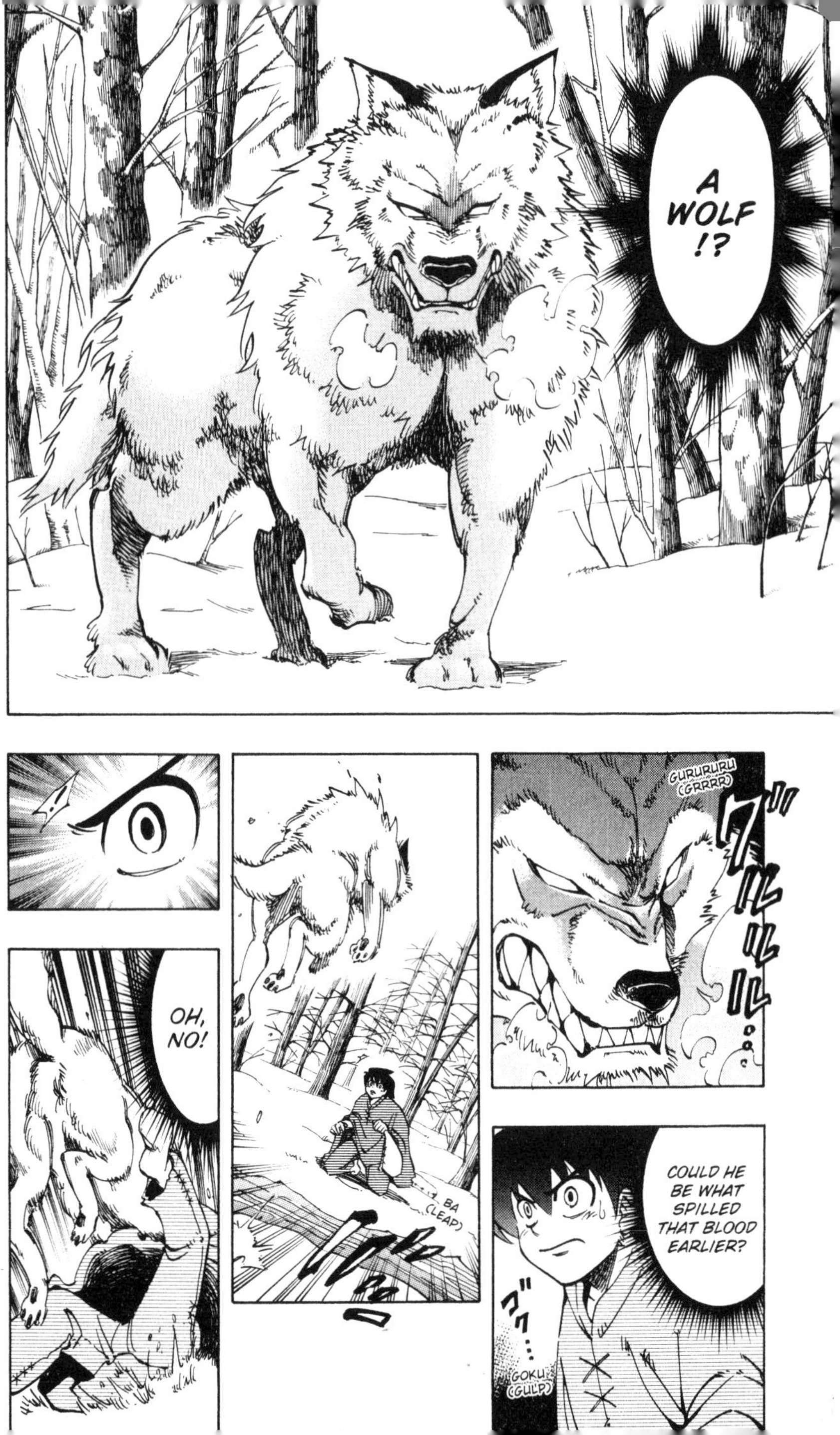
A WOLF !?
GURURURU (GRRRR)
COULD HE BE WHAT SPILLED THAT BLOOD EARLIER?
GOKU (GULP)
BA (LEAP)
OH, NO!

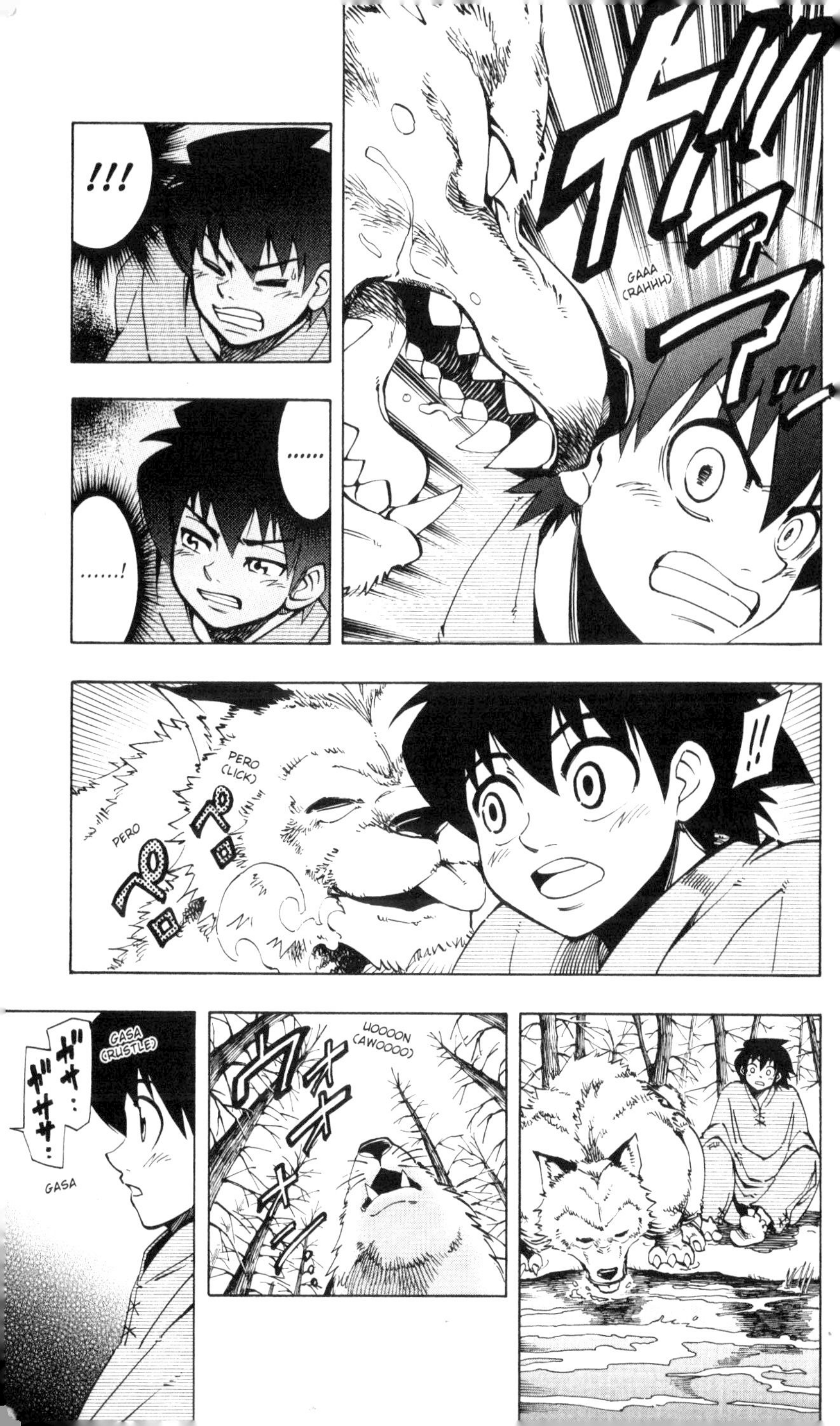

GAAA (RAHHH)
!!!
......
......!
!!
PERO (LICK)
PERO
UOOOON (AWOOOO)
GASA (RUSTLE)
ガサ.. ガササ..
GASA

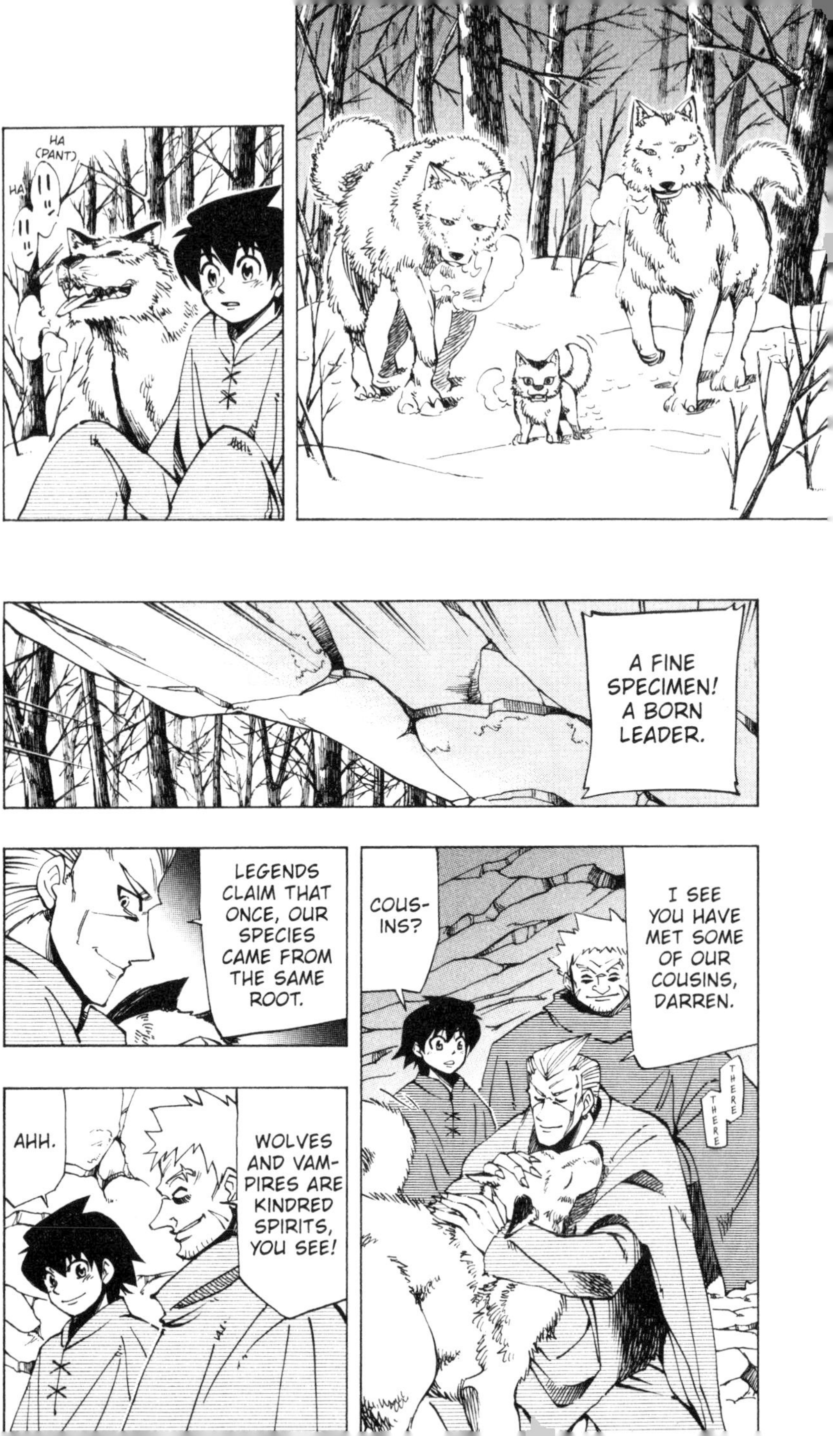
HA (PANT) HA
A FINE SPECIMEN! A BORN LEADER.
I SEE YOU HAVE MET SOME OF OUR COUSINS, DARREN.
THERE THERE
COUS-INS?
LEGENDS CLAIM THAT ONCE, OUR SPECIES CAME FROM THE SAME ROOT.
WOLVES AND VAM-PIRES ARE KINDRED SPIRITS, YOU SEE!
AHH.

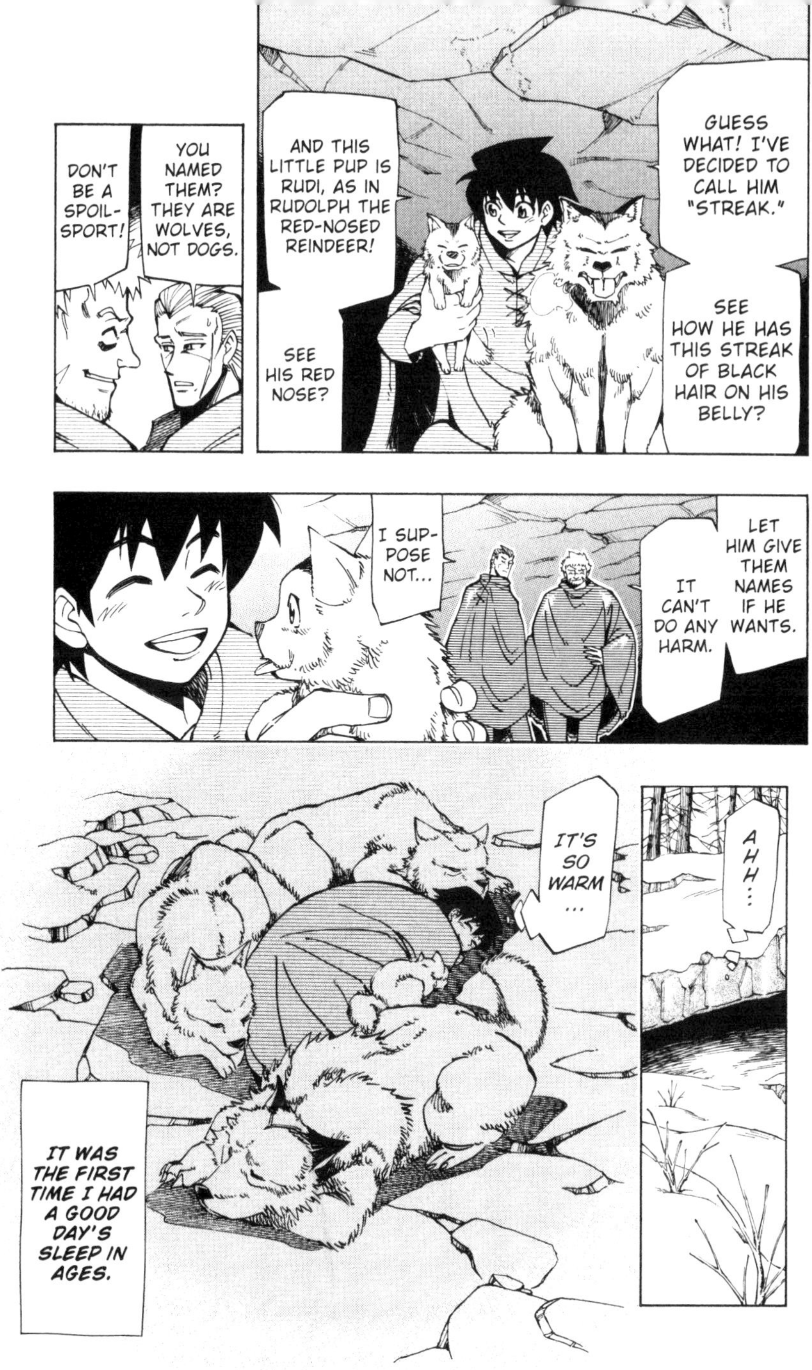
GUESS WHAT! I'VE DECIDED TO CALL HIM "STREAK."
SEE HOW HE HAS THIS STREAK OF BLACK HAIR ON HIS BELLY?
AND THIS LITTLE PUP IS RUDI, AS IN RUDOLPH THE RED-NOSED REINDEER!
SEE HIS RED NOSE?
YOU NAMED THEM? THEY ARE WOLVES, NOT DOGS.
DON'T BE A SPOIL-SPORT!
LET HIM GIVE THEM NAMES IF HE WANTS.
IT CAN'T DO ANY HARM.
I SUP-POSE NOT...
AHH...
IT'S SO WARM...
IT WAS THE FIRST TIME I HAD A GOOD DAY'S SLEEP IN AGES.

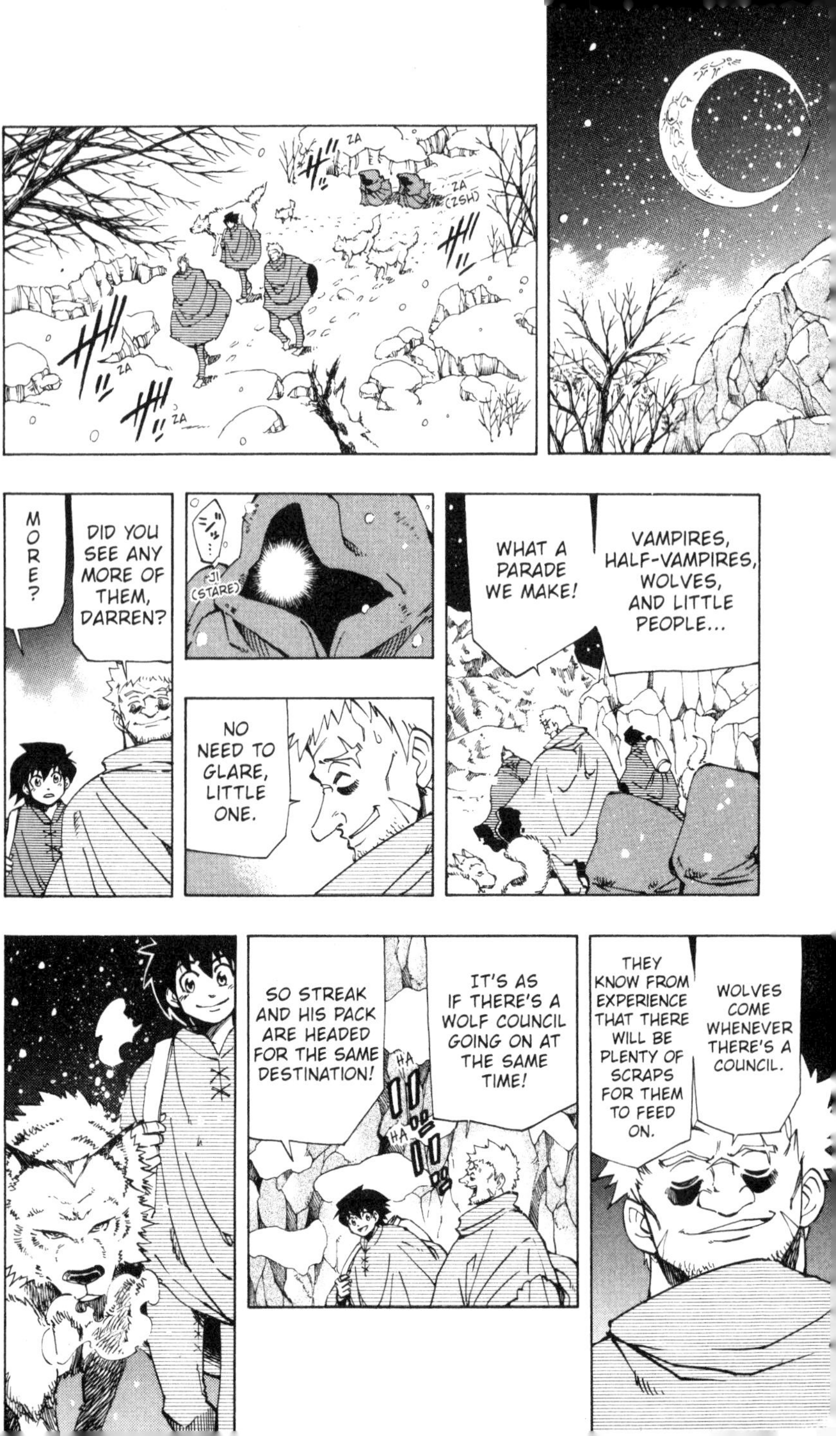
ZA
ZA (ZSH)
ZA
ZA
VAMPIRES, HALF-VAMPIRES, WOLVES, AND LITTLE PEOPLE...
WHAT A PARADE WE MAKE!
JI (STARE)
NO NEED TO GLARE, LITTLE ONE.
DID YOU SEE ANY MORE OF THEM, DARREN?
MORE?
WOLVES COME WHENEVER THERE'S A COUNCIL.
THEY KNOW FROM EXPERIENCE THAT THERE WILL BE PLENTY OF SCRAPS FOR THEM TO FEED ON.
IT'S AS IF THERE'S A WOLF COUNCIL GOING ON AT THE SAME TIME!
SO STREAK AND HIS PACK ARE HEADED FOR THE SAME DESTINATION!
HA
HA

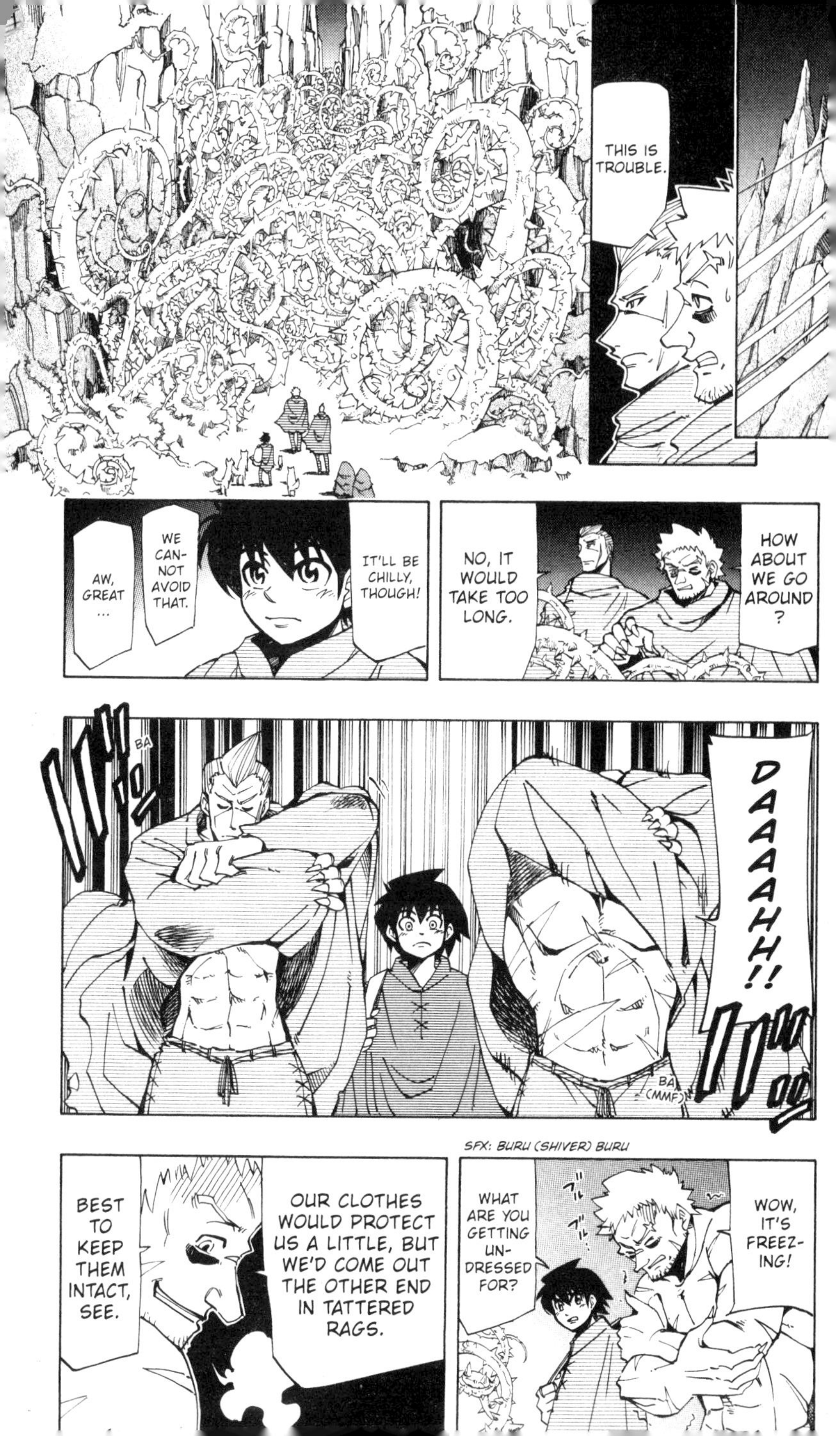
THIS IS TROUBLE.
HOW ABOUT WE GO AROUND?
NO, IT WOULD TAKE TOO LONG.
IT'LL BE CHILLY, THOUGH!
WE CANNOT AVOID THAT.
AW, GREAT...
DAAAAAHH!!
BA
BA (MMF)
SFX: BURU (SHIVER) BURU
WOW, IT'S FREEZING!
WHAT ARE YOU GETTING UNDRESSED FOR?
OUR CLOTHES WOULD PROTECT US A LITTLE, BUT WE'D COME OUT THE OTHER END IN TATTERED RAGS.
BEST TO KEEP THEM INTACT, SEE.

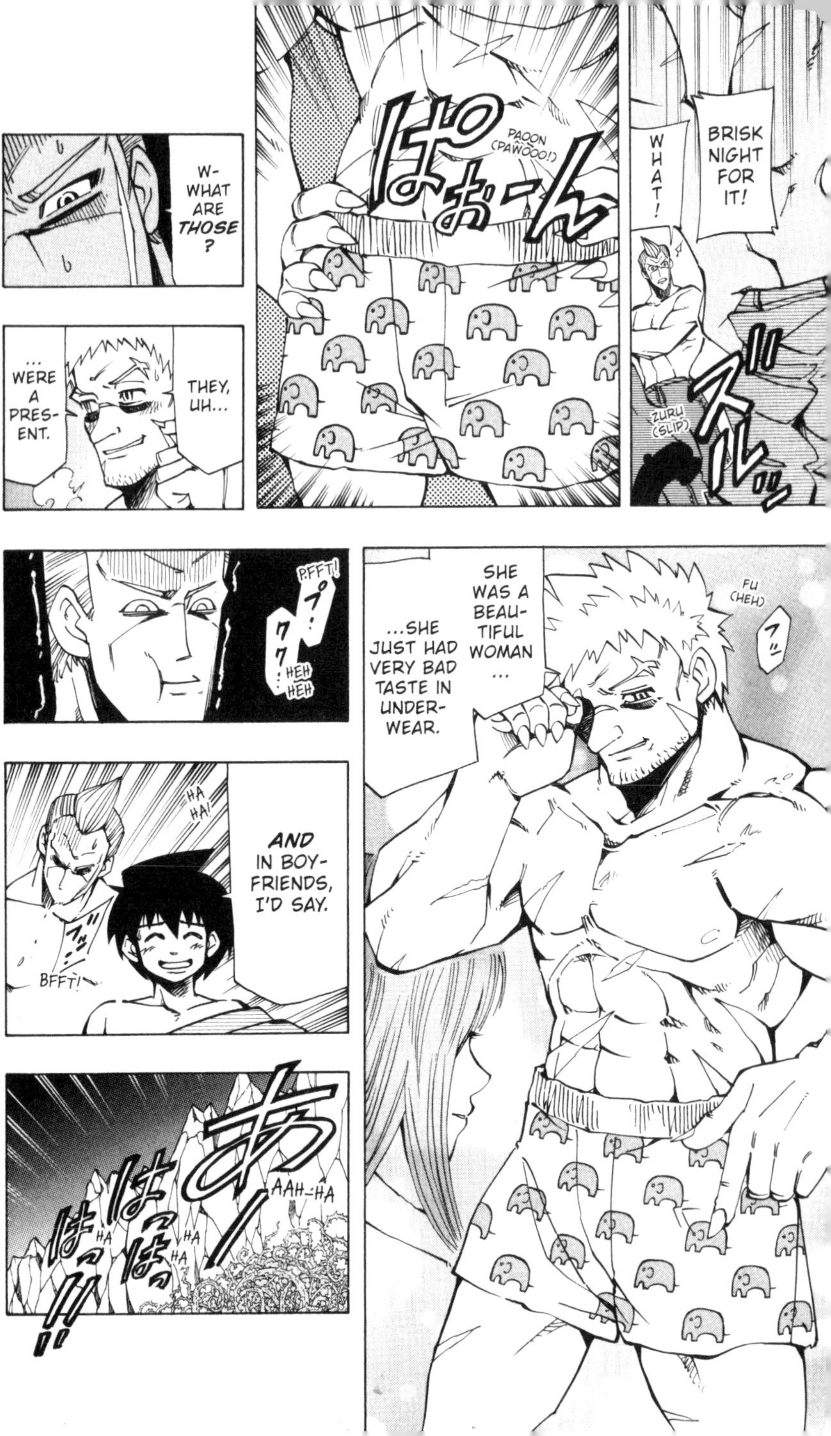
BRISK NIGHT FOR IT!
WHAT!
ZURU (SLIP)
ズルッ
PAOON (PAWOOO!)
ぱおーん
W-WHAT ARE THOSE?
THEY, UH...
...WERE A PRESENT.
FU (HEH)
フッ
SHE WAS A BEAUTIFUL WOMAN...
...SHE JUST HAD VERY BAD TASTE IN UNDERWEAR.
PFFT!
プッ
ククッ
HEH HEH
HA HA!
AND IN BOYFRIENDS, I'D SAY.
BFFT!
あーはっはっはっ!!
AAH-HA
HA
HA
HA

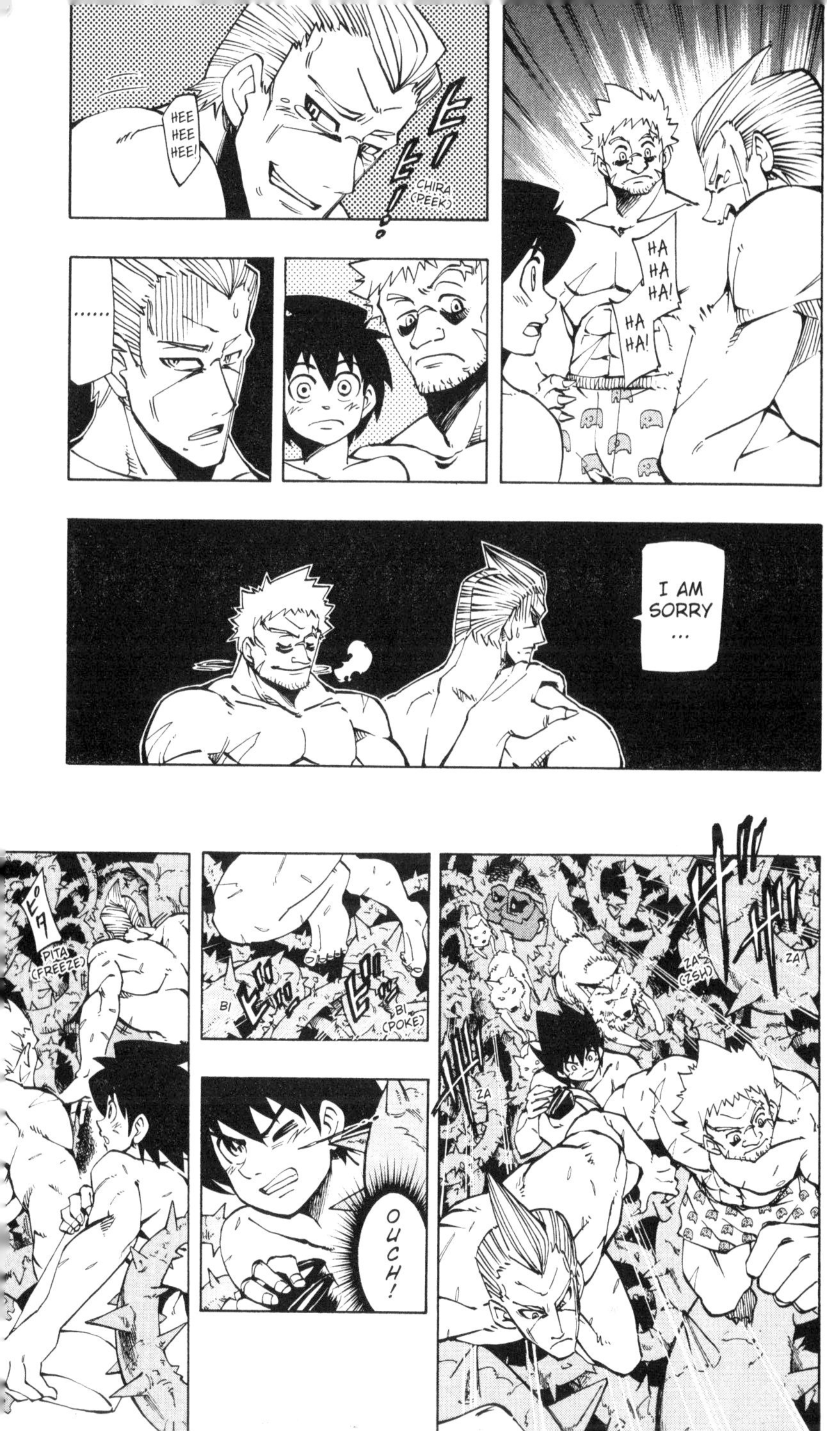
HA HA HA!
HA HA!
HEE HEE HEE!
CHIRA (PEEK)
......
I AM SORRY ...
ZA
ZAS (ZSH)
ZA!
BI
BI (POKE)
OUCH!
PITA (FREEZE)

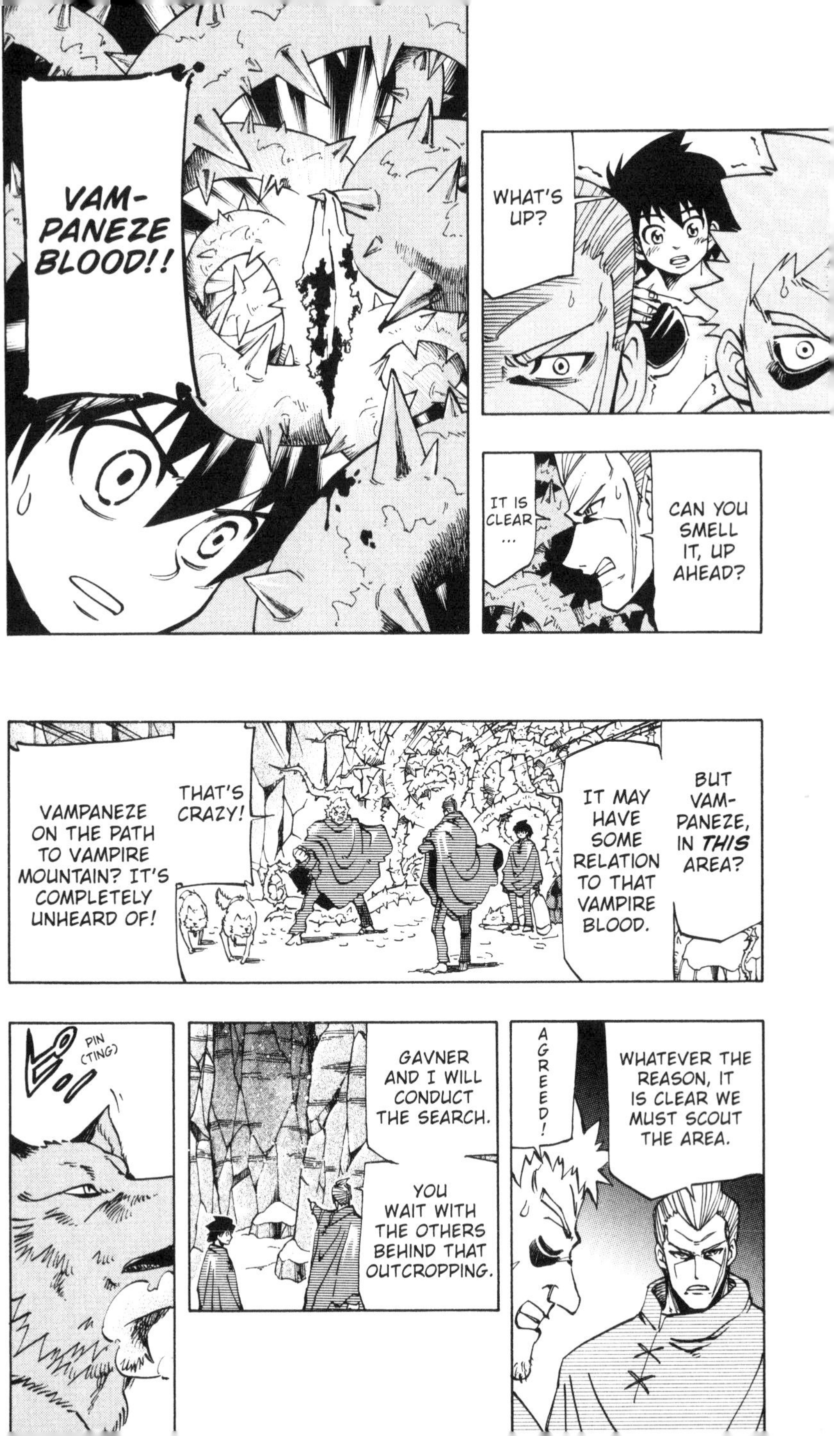
WHAT'S UP?
CAN YOU SMELL IT, UP AHEAD?
IT IS CLEAR…
VAM-PANEZE BLOOD!!
BUT VAM-PANEZE, IN *THIS* AREA?
IT MAY HAVE SOME RELATION TO THAT VAMPIRE BLOOD.
THAT'S CRAZY!
VAMPANEZE ON THE PATH TO VAMPIRE MOUNTAIN? IT'S COMPLETELY UNHEARD OF!
WHATEVER THE REASON, IT IS CLEAR WE MUST SCOUT THE AREA.
AGREED!
GAVNER AND I WILL CONDUCT THE SEARCH.
YOU WAIT WITH THE OTHERS BEHIND THAT OUTCROPPING.
PIN (TING)

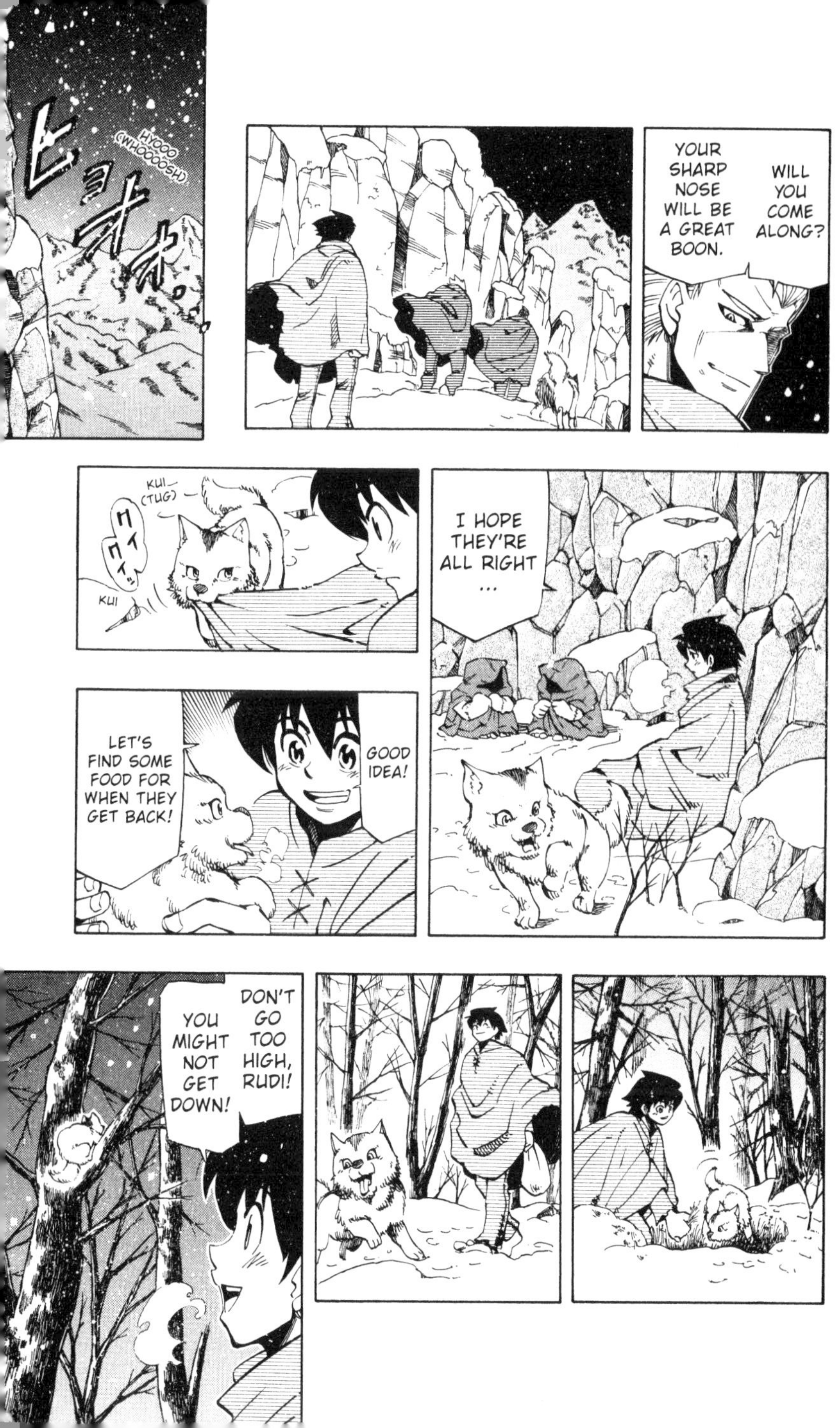
WILL YOU COME ALONG?
YOUR SHARP NOSE WILL BE A GREAT BOON.
HYOOO (WHOOOOSH)
I HOPE THEY'RE ALL RIGHT ...
KUI (TUG)
KUI
GOOD IDEA!
LET'S FIND SOME FOOD FOR WHEN THEY GET BACK!
DON'T GO TOO HIGH, RUDI!
YOU MIGHT NOT GET DOWN!

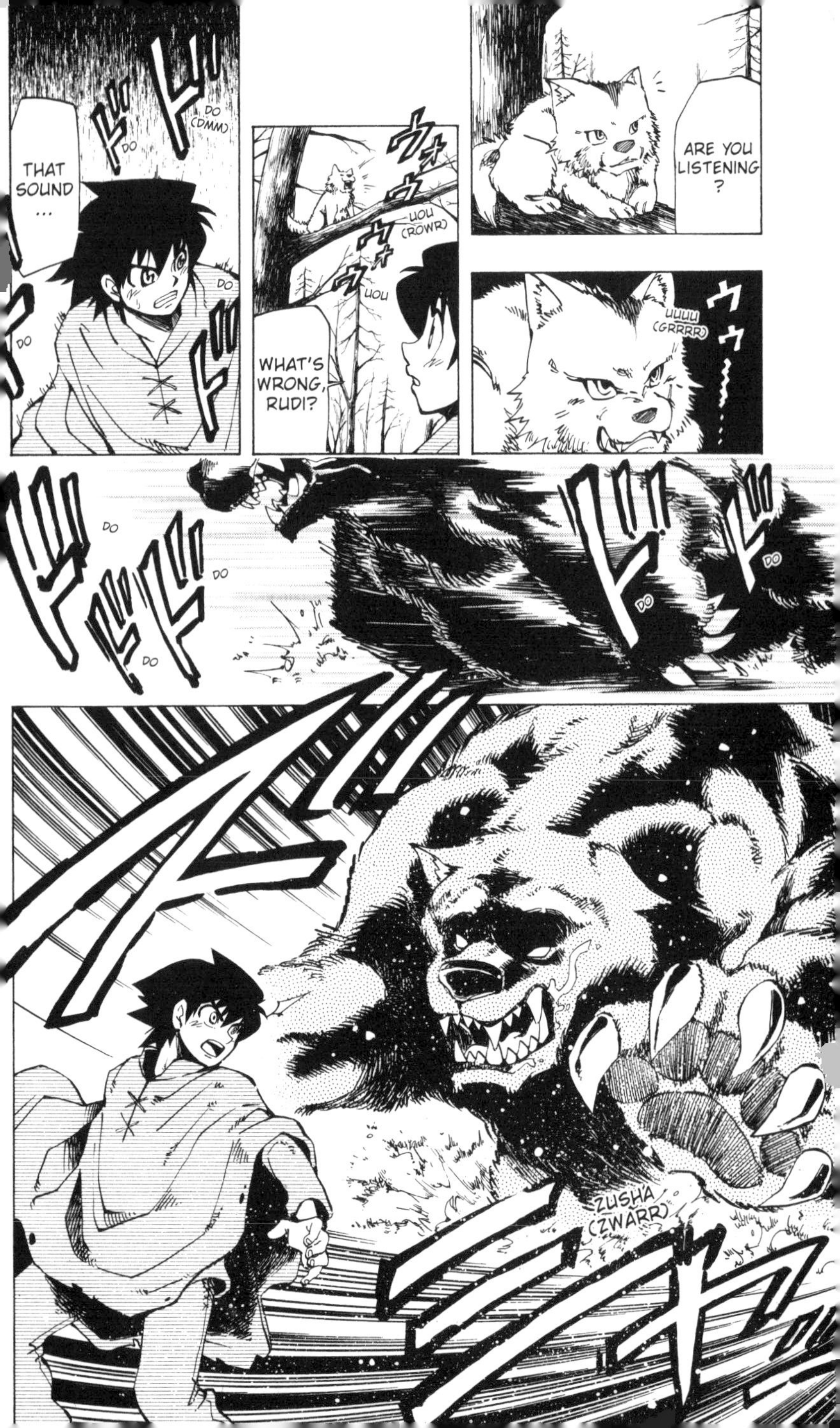
ARE YOU LISTENING ?
UUUU (GRRRR)
UOU (ROWR)
UOU
WHAT'S WRONG, RUDI?
DO (DMM)
DO
THAT SOUND ...
DO
DO
DO
DO
DO
DO
DO
ZUSHA (ZWARR)

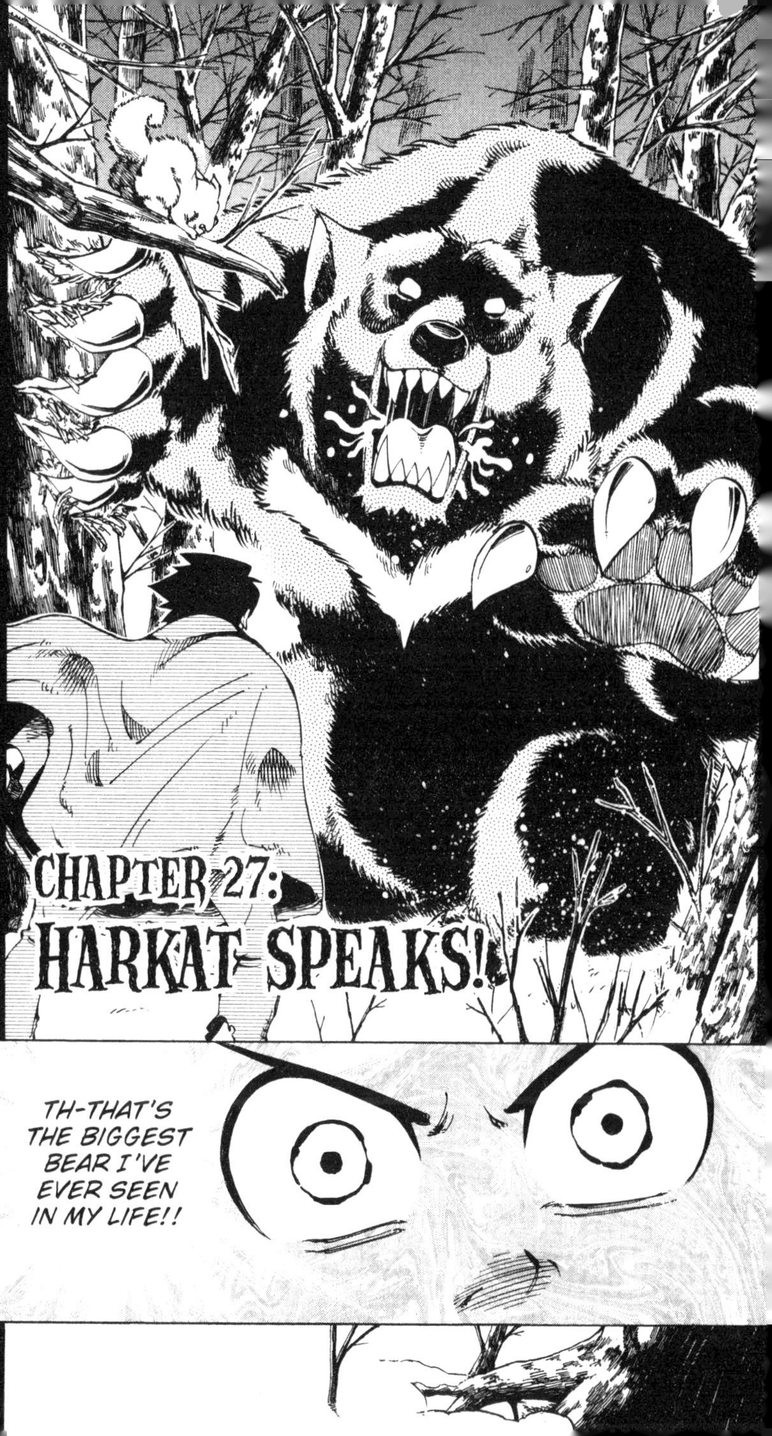
CHAPTER 27:
HARKAT SPEAKS!
TH-THAT'S THE BIGGEST BEAR I'VE EVER SEEN IN MY LIFE!!

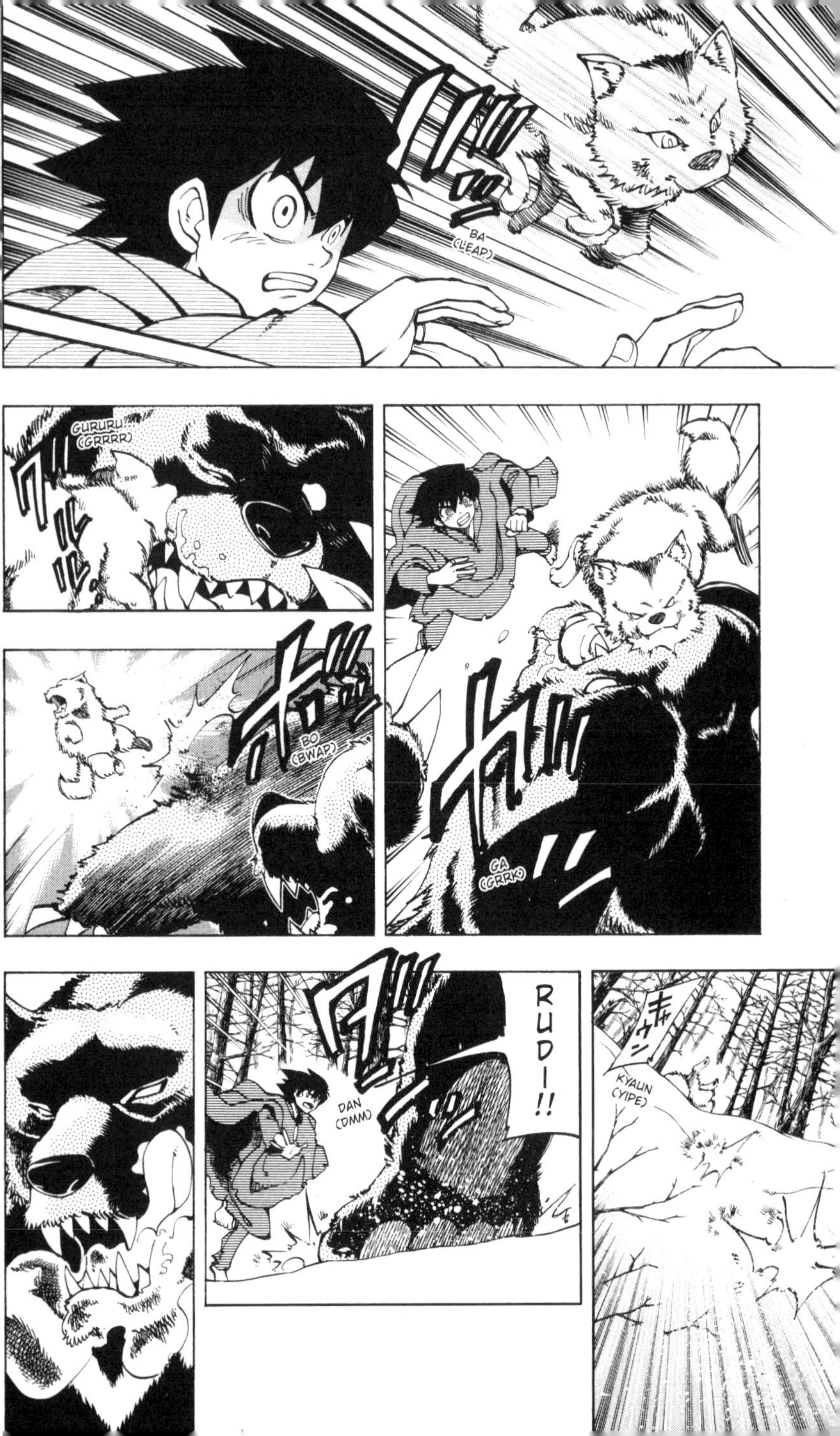
BA
(LEAP)
GA
(GRRK)
GURURU
(GRRRR)
BO
(BWAP)
キャウン
KYAUN
(YIPE)
RUDI!!
DAN
(DMM)

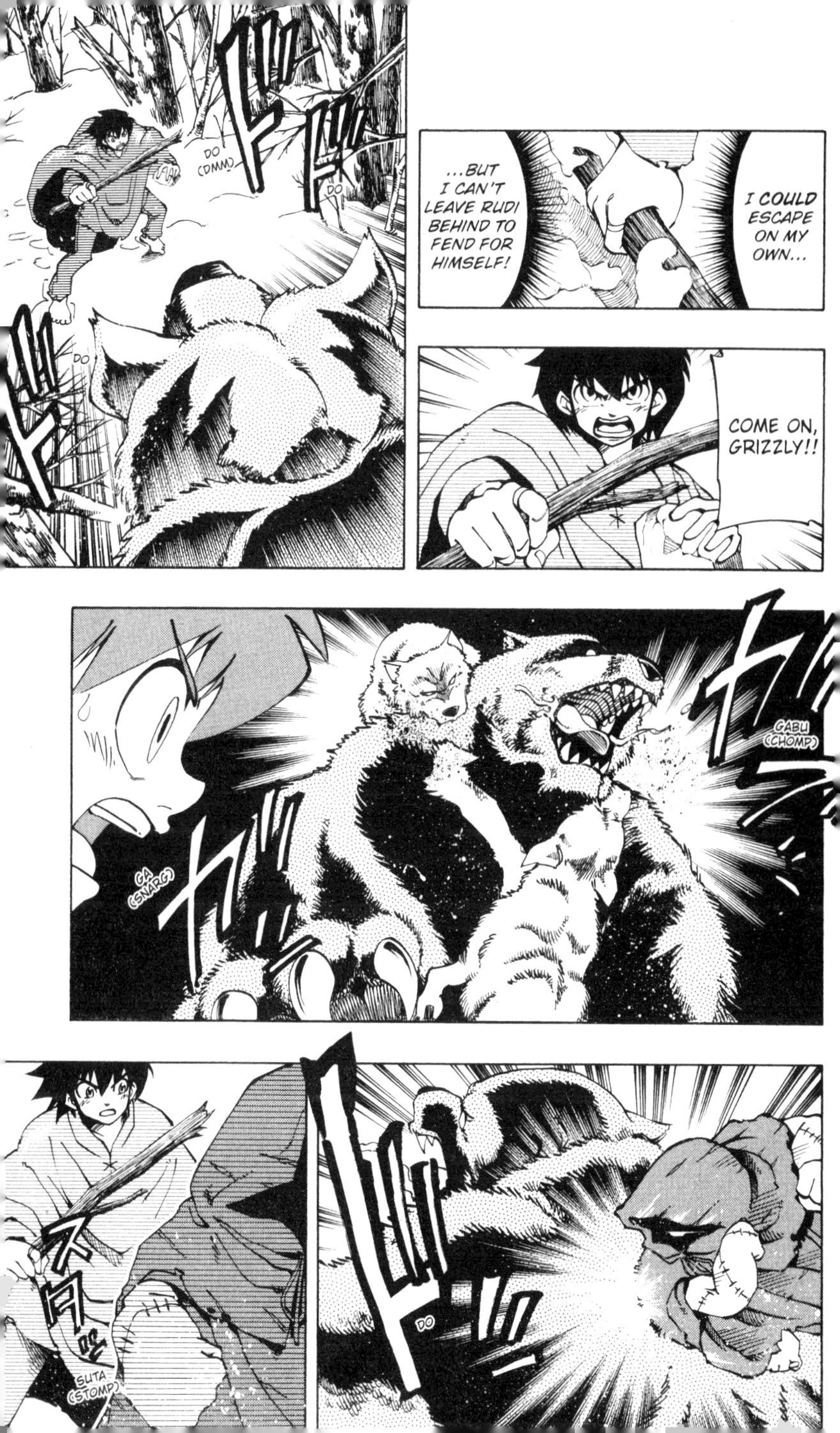
I COULD ESCAPE ON MY OWN...
...BUT I CAN'T LEAVE RUDI BEHIND TO FEND FOR HIMSELF!
COME ON, GRIZZLY!!
DO (DMM)
DO
DO
GABU (CHOMP)
GA (SNARG)
DO
SUTA (STOMP)

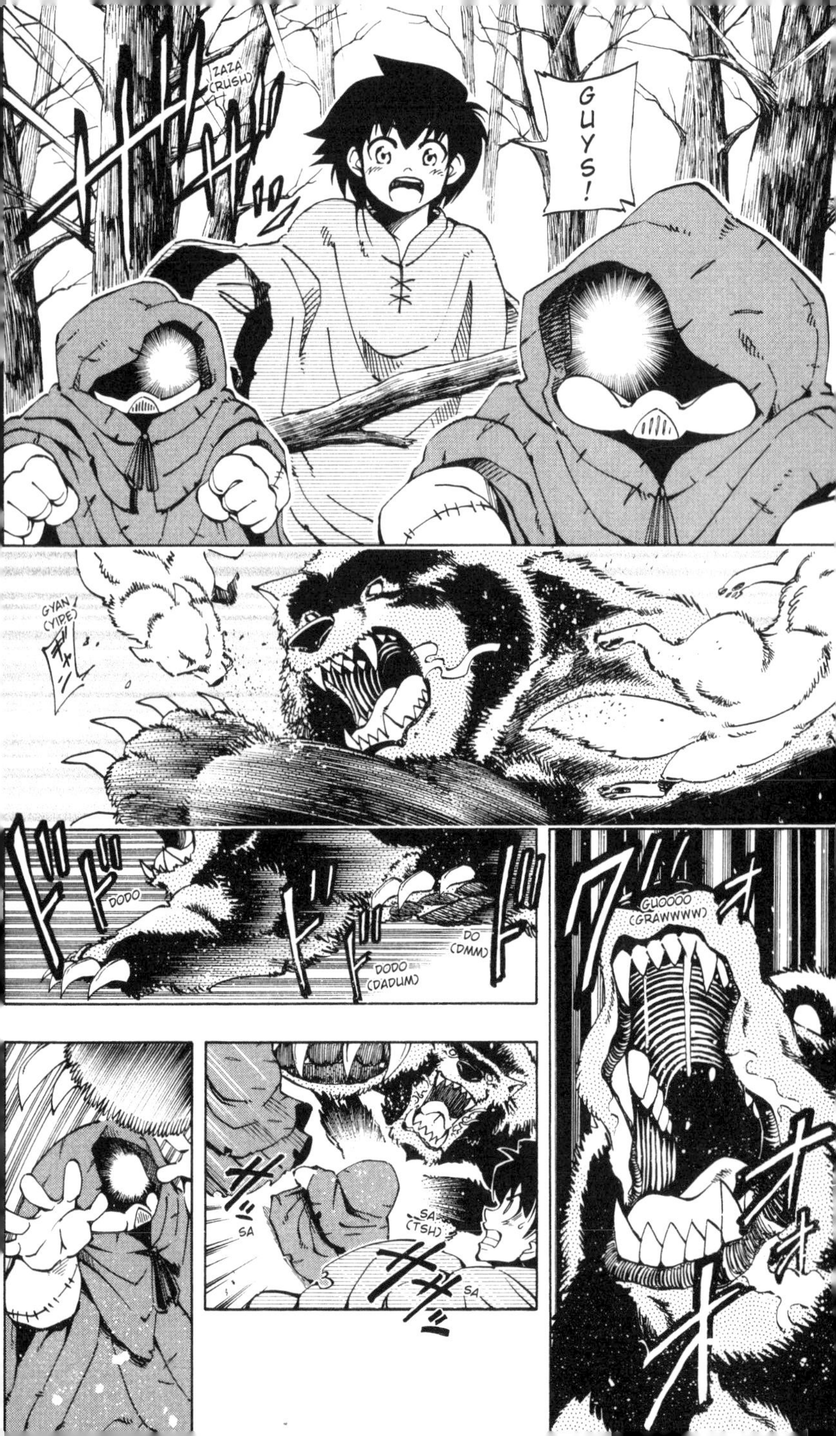
GUYS!
ZAZA (RUSH)
GYAN (YIPE)
GUOOOO (GRAWWWW)
DO (DMM)
DODO (DADUM)
DODO
SA (TSH)
SA
SA

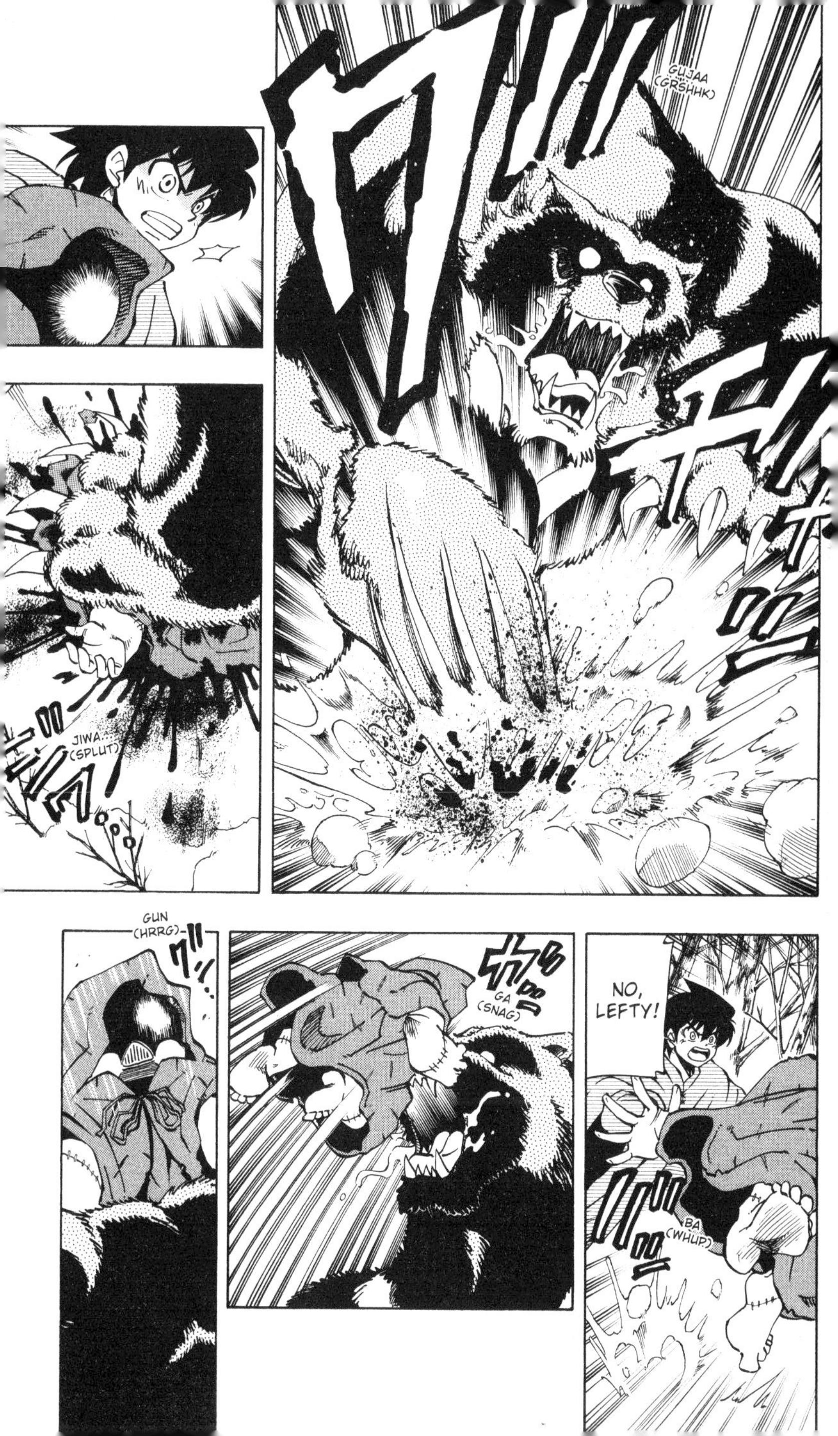
GUJAA (GRSHHK)
JIWA... (SPLUT)
NO, LEFTY!
BA (WHUP)
GA (SNAG)
GUN (HRRG)

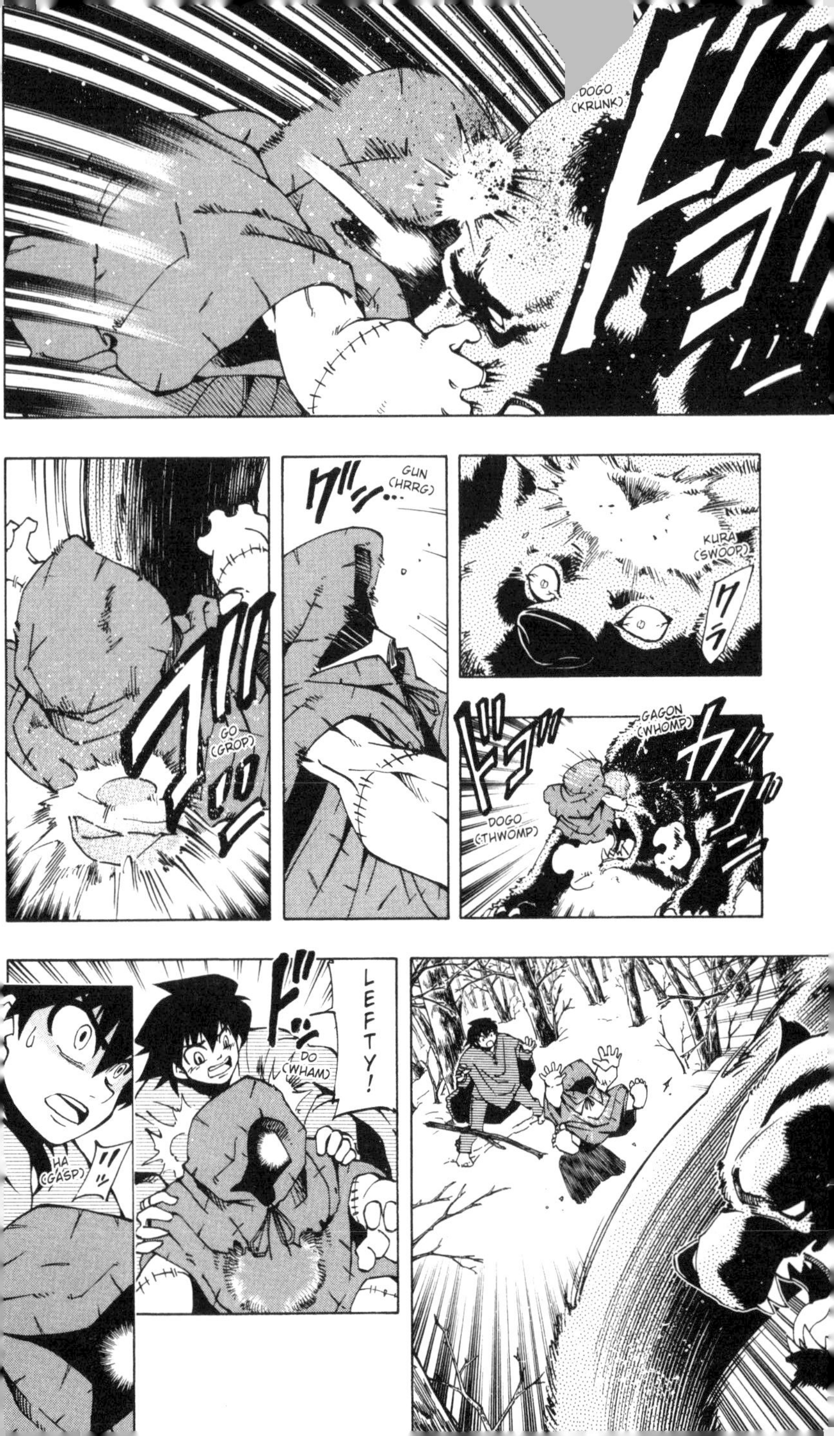
DOGO (KRUNK)
KURA (SWOOP)
GAGON (WHOMP)
DOGO (THWOMP)
GUN (HRRG)
GO (GROP)
DO (WHAM)
LEFTY!
HA (GASP)

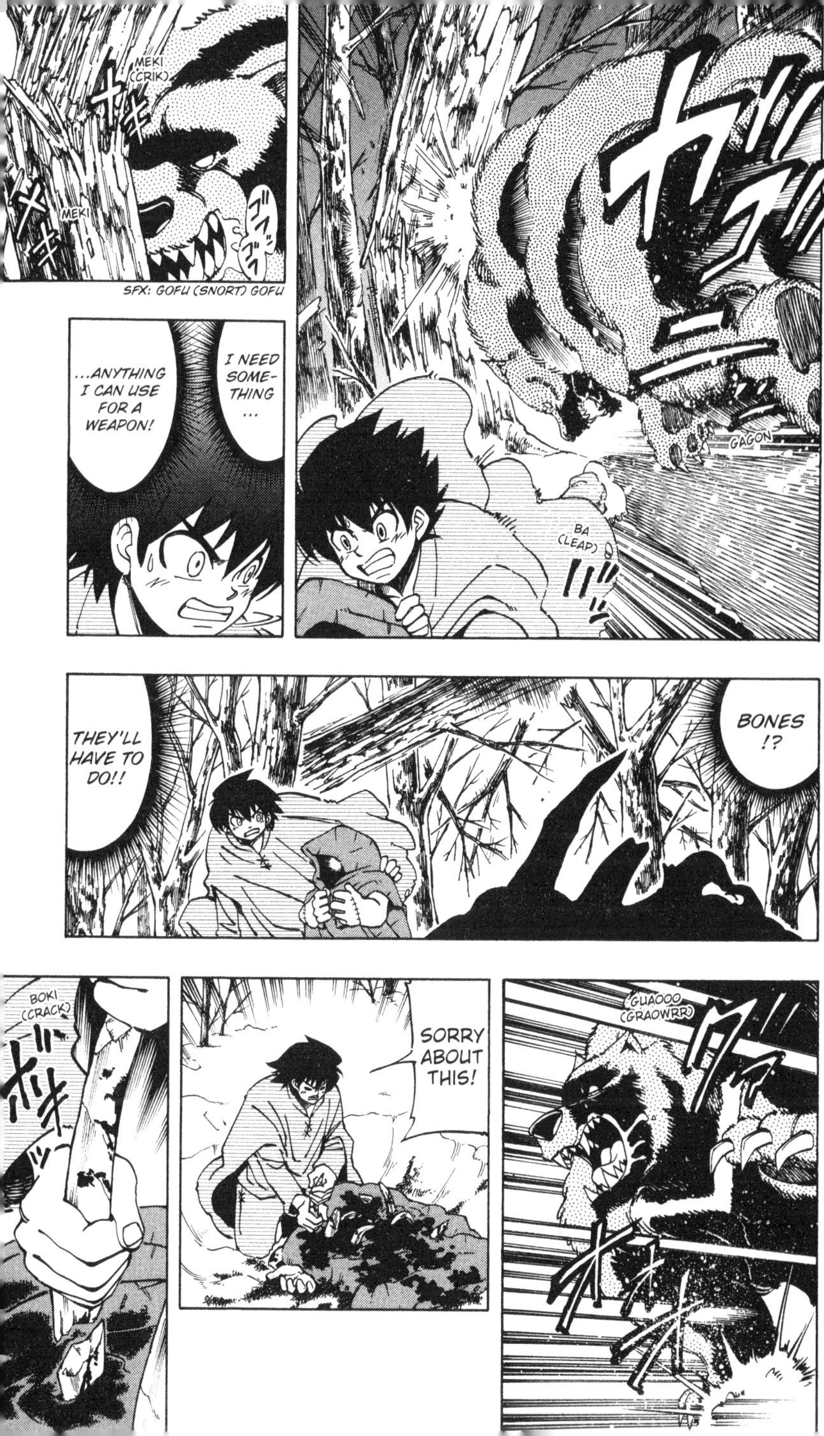
GAGON
BA (LEAP)
MEKI (CRIK)
MEKI
SFX: GOFU (SNORT) GOFU
I NEED SOME-THING ...
...ANYTHING I CAN USE FOR A WEAPON!
BONES !?
THEY'LL HAVE TO DO!!
GUAOOO (GRAOWRR)
SORRY ABOUT THIS!
BOKI (CRACK)

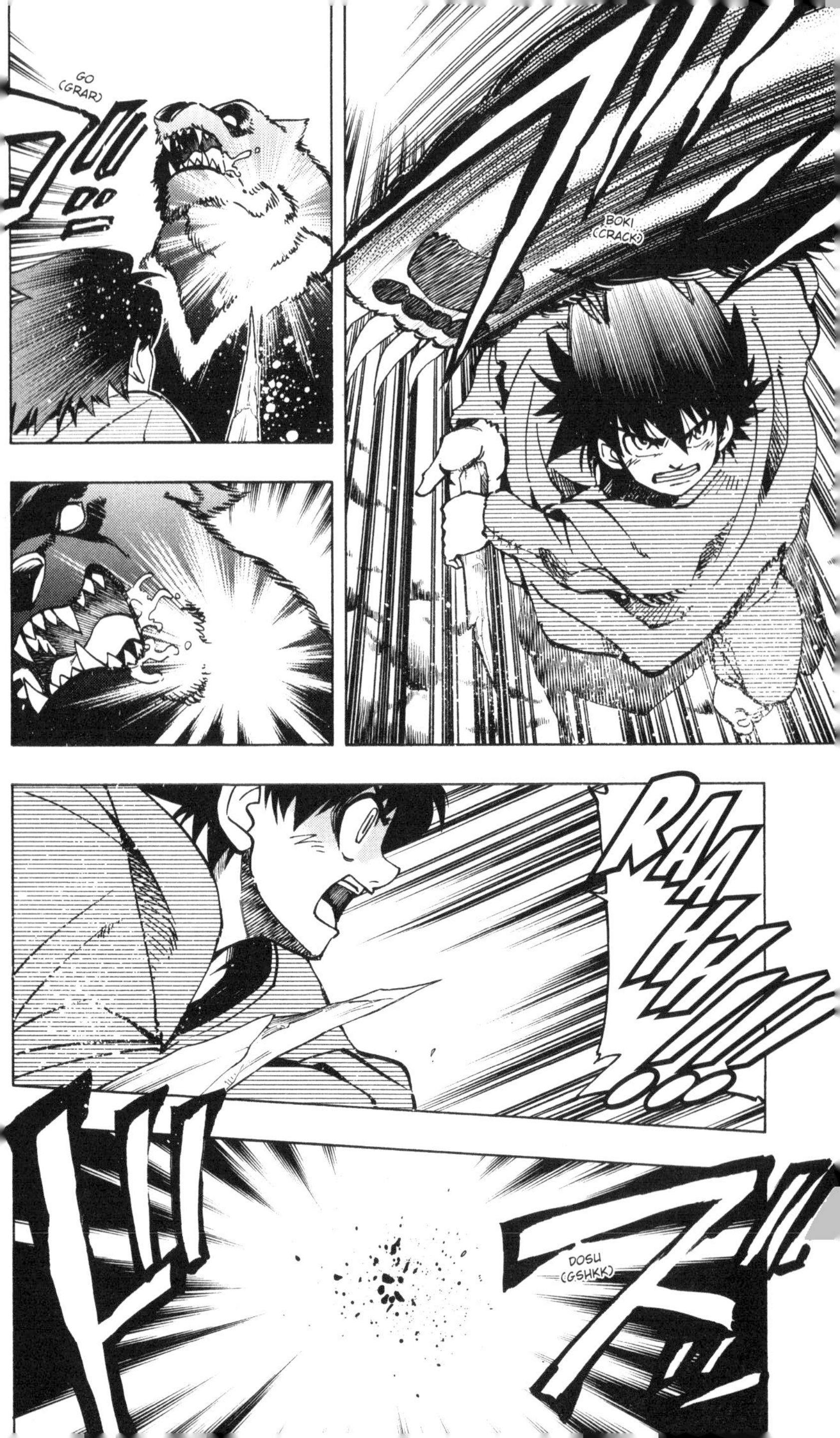
BOKI
(CRACK)
GO
(GRAR)
DOSU
(GSHKK)

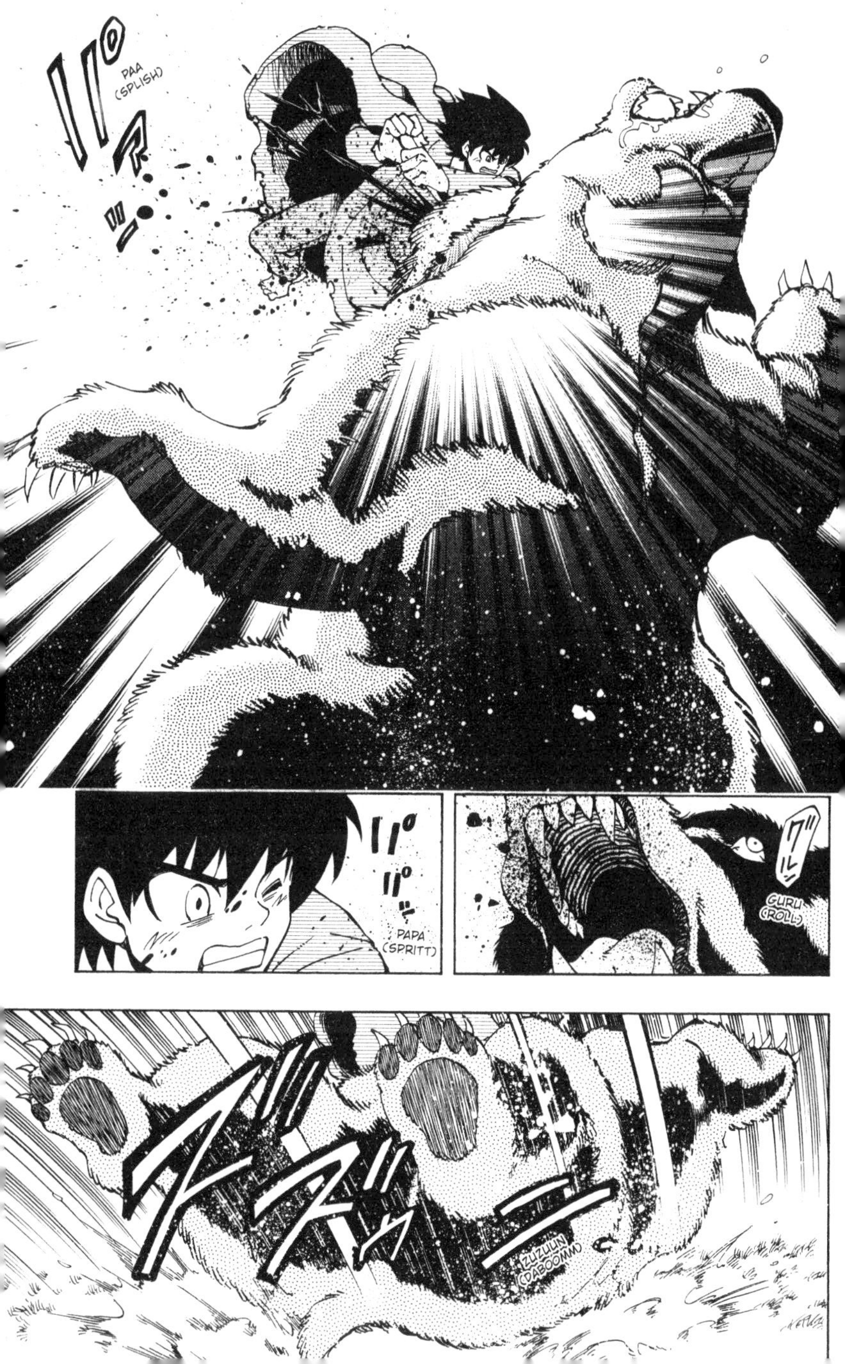
PAA
(SPLISH)
GURU
(ROLL)
PAPA
(SPRITT)
ZUZUUN
(DABOOMM)

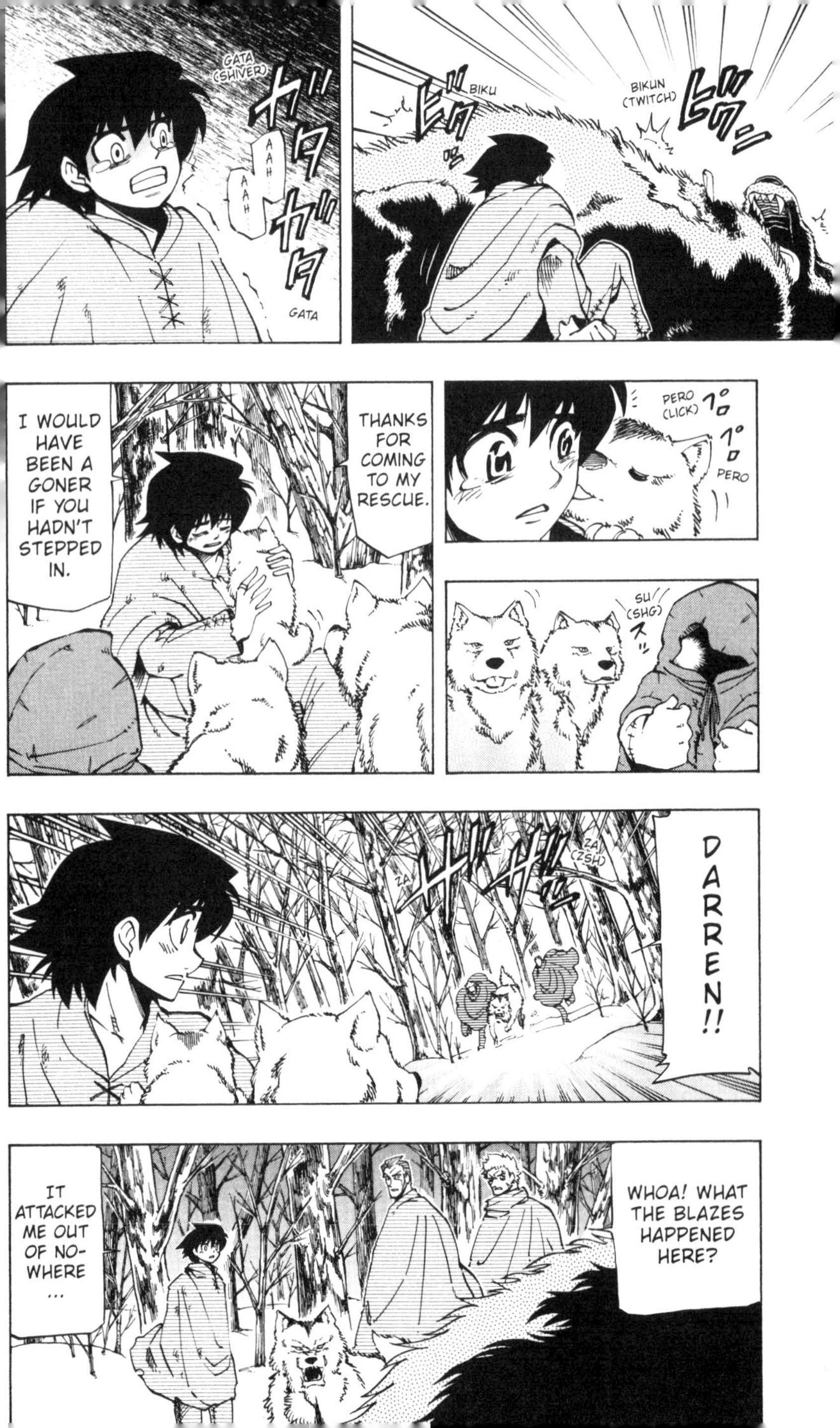
BIKUN (TWITCH)
BIKU
GATA (SHIVER)
AAH... AAH...
GATA
PERO (LICK)
PERO
SU (SHG)
THANKS FOR COMING TO MY RESCUE.
I WOULD HAVE BEEN A GONER IF YOU HADN'T STEPPED IN.
DARREN!!
ZA (ZSH)
ZA
WHOA! WHAT THE BLAZES HAPPENED HERE?
IT ATTACKED ME OUT OF NO-WHERE...

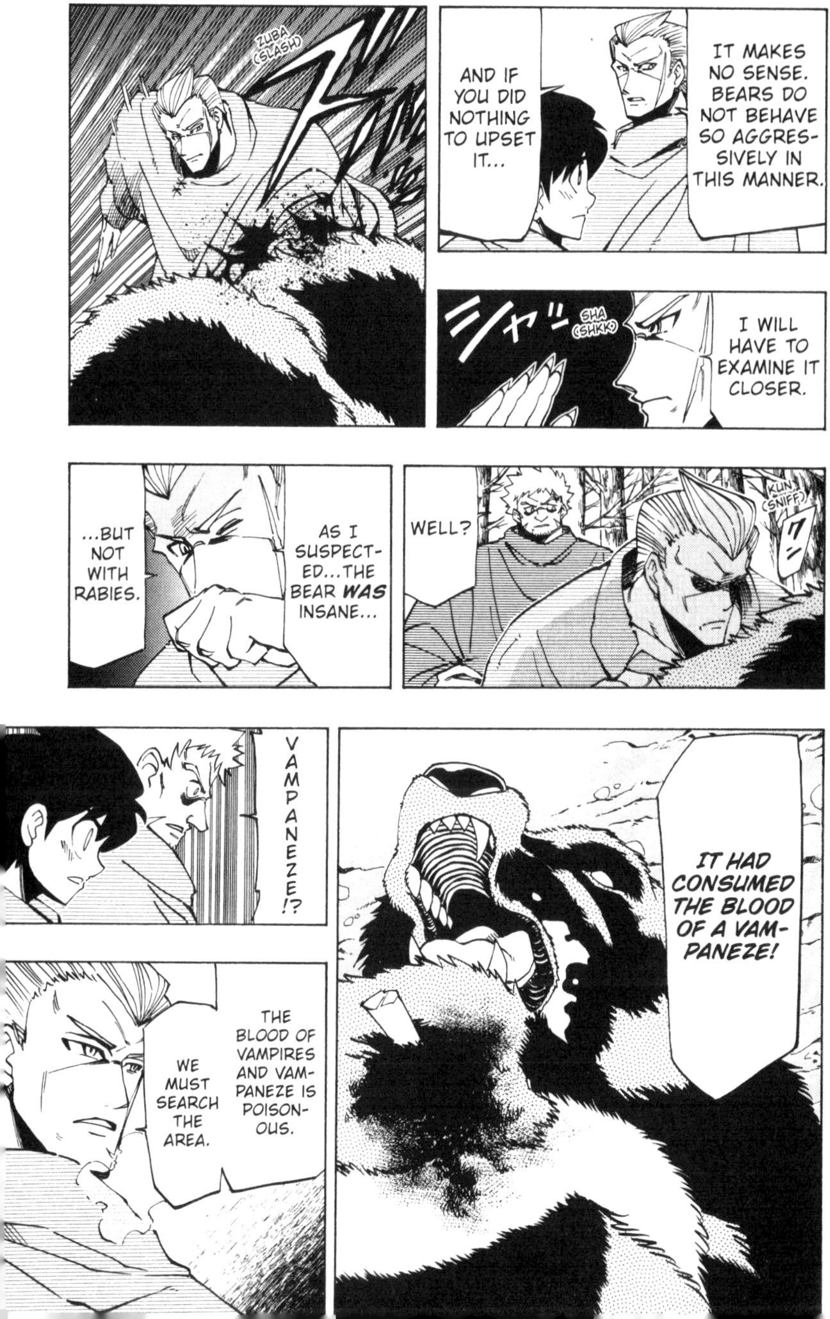
IT MAKES NO SENSE. BEARS DO NOT BEHAVE SO AGGRES-SIVELY IN THIS MANNER.
AND IF YOU DID NOTHING TO UPSET IT...
ZUBA (SLASH)
I WILL HAVE TO EXAMINE IT CLOSER.
SHA (SHKK)
KUN (SNIFF)
WELL?
AS I SUSPECT-ED...THE BEAR **WAS** INSANE...
...BUT NOT WITH RABIES.
IT HAD CONSUMED THE BLOOD OF A VAM-PANEZE!
VAMPANEZE!?
THE BLOOD OF VAMPIRES AND VAM-PANEZE IS POISON-OUS.
WE MUST SEARCH THE AREA.

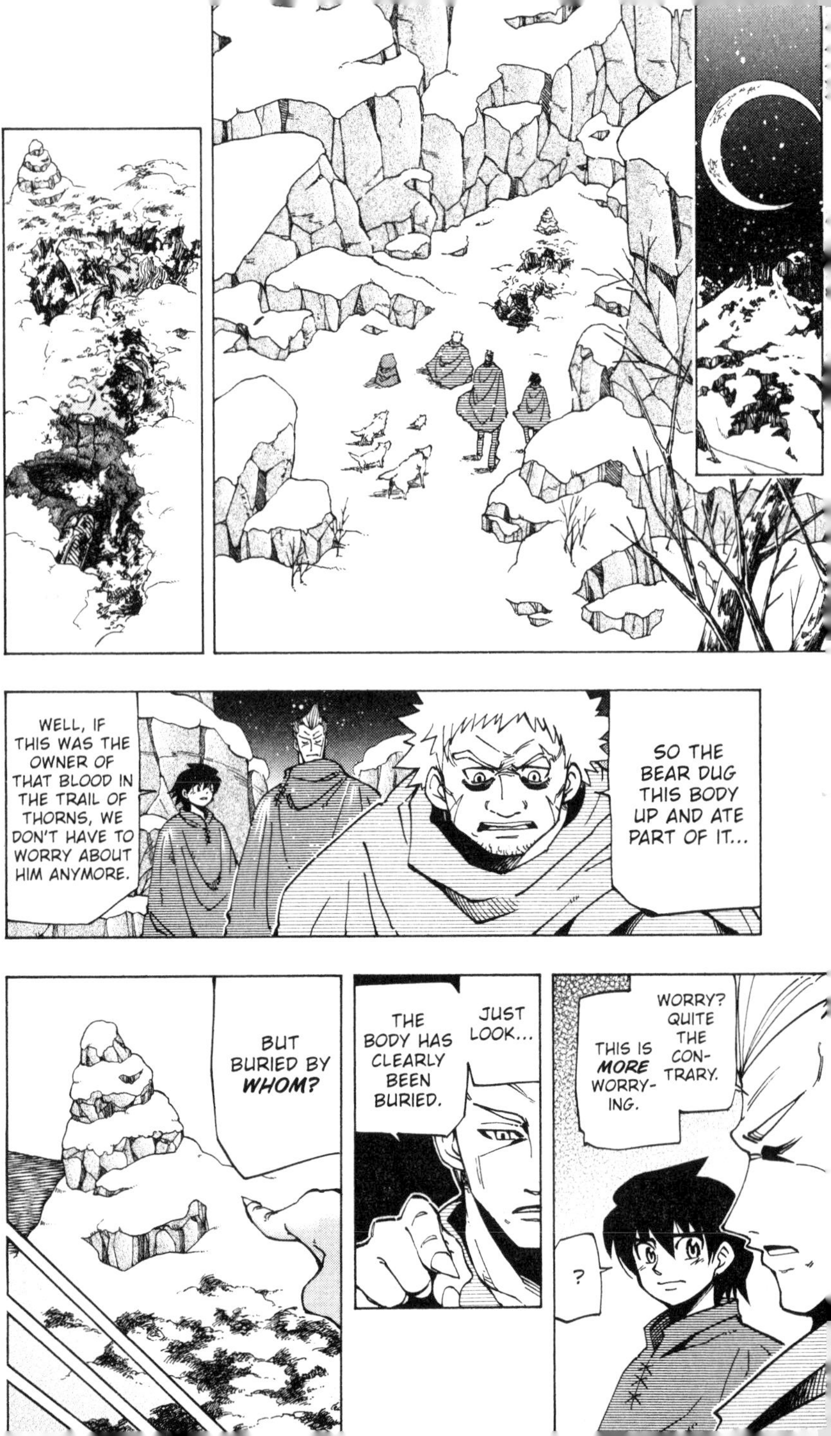
SO THE BEAR DUG THIS BODY UP AND ATE PART OF IT...
WELL, IF THIS WAS THE OWNER OF THAT BLOOD IN THE TRAIL OF THORNS, WE DON'T HAVE TO WORRY ABOUT HIM ANYMORE.
WORRY? QUITE THE CONTRARY.
THIS IS *MORE* WORRYING.
?
JUST LOOK...
THE BODY HAS CLEARLY BEEN BURIED.
BUT BURIED BY *WHOM?*

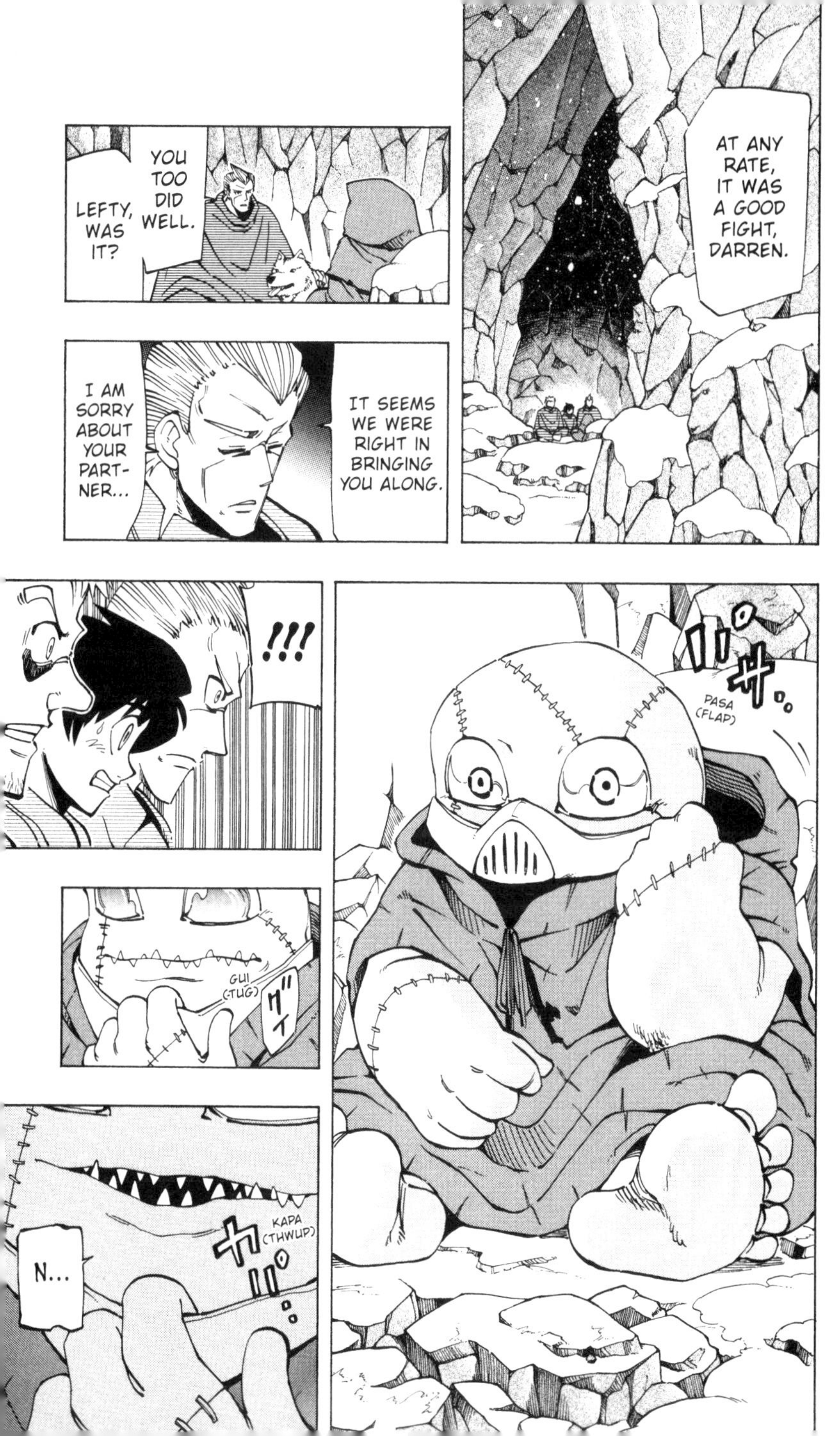
AT ANY RATE, IT WAS A GOOD FIGHT, DARREN.
YOU TOO DID WELL.
LEFTY, WAS IT?
IT SEEMS WE WERE RIGHT IN BRINGING YOU ALONG.
I AM SORRY ABOUT YOUR PARTNER...
パサ
PASA (FLAP)
!!!
グイ
GUI (TUG)
カパ
KAPA (THWUP)
N...

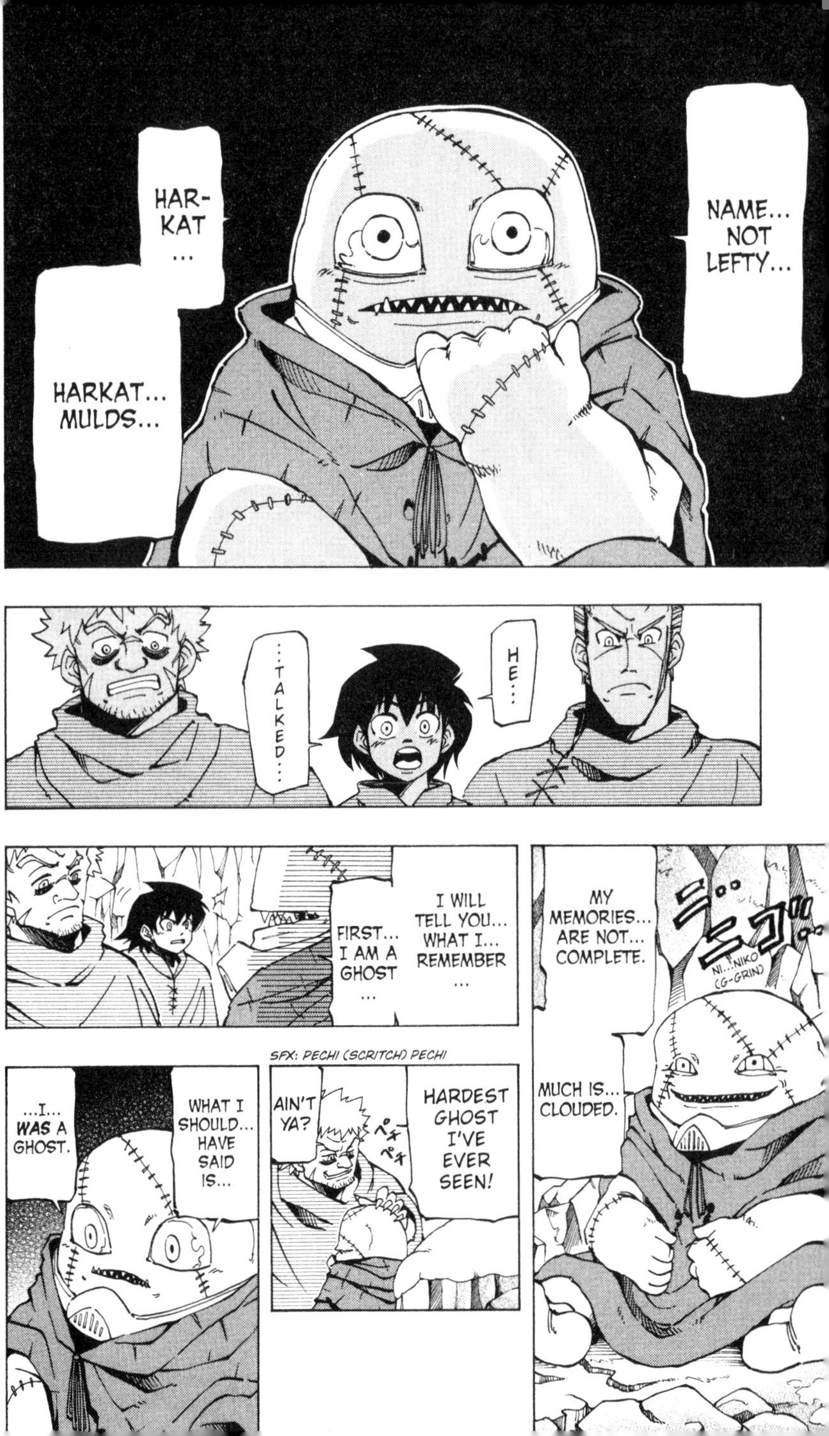
NAME... NOT LEFTY...
HAR-KAT ...
HARKAT... MULDS...
HE...
...TALKED...
MY MEMORIES... ARE NOT... COMPLETE.
NI...NIKO (G-GRIN)
MUCH IS... CLOUDED.
I WILL TELL YOU... WHAT I... REMEMBER ...
FIRST... I AM A GHOST ...
SFX: PECHI (SCRITCH) PECHI
HARDEST GHOST I'VE EVER SEEN!
AIN'T YA?
WHAT I SHOULD... HAVE SAID IS...
...I... **WAS** A GHOST.

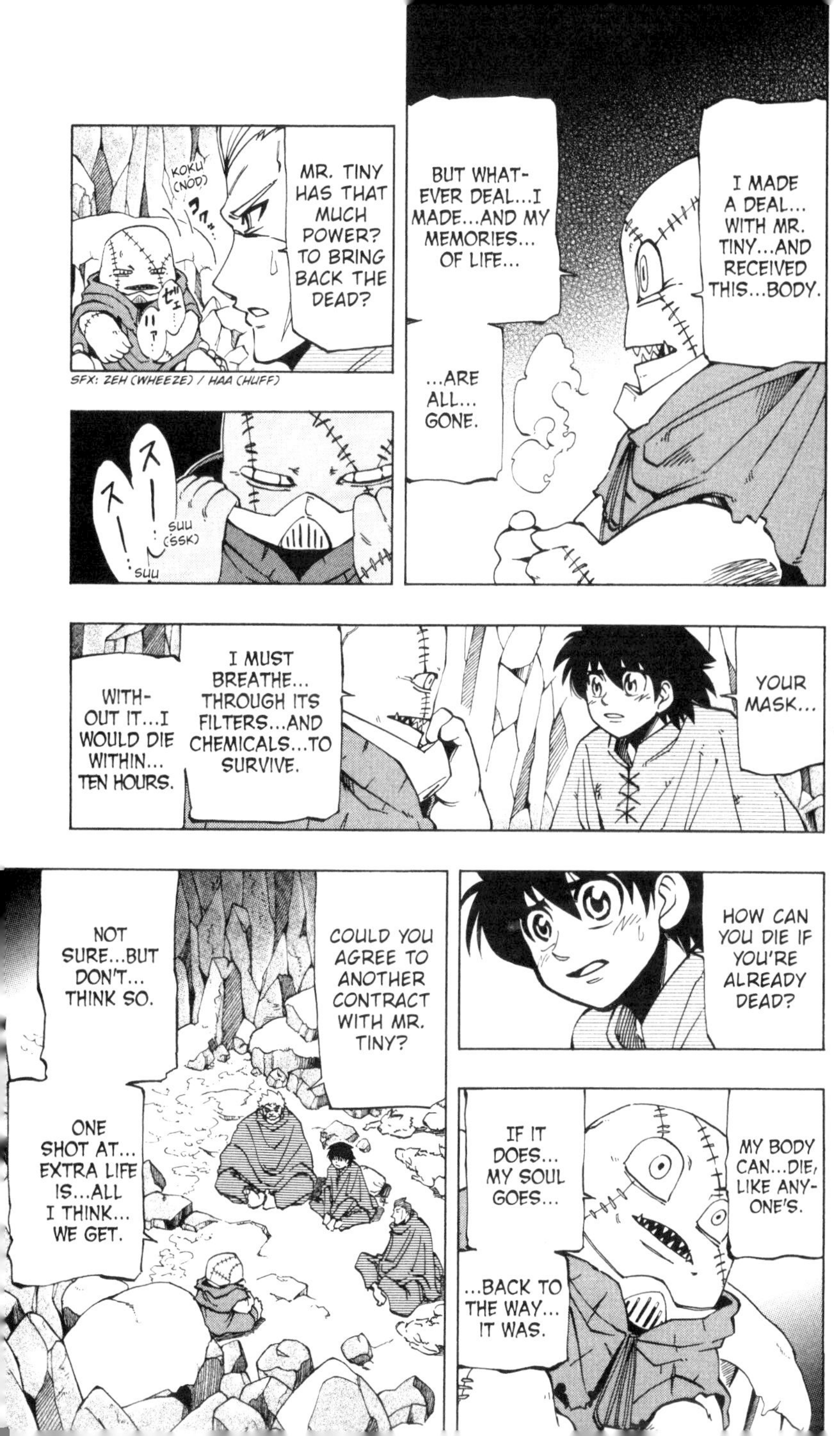
I MADE A DEAL... WITH MR. TINY...AND RECEIVED THIS...BODY.
BUT WHATEVER DEAL...I MADE...AND MY MEMORIES... OF LIFE...
...ARE ALL... GONE.
MR. TINY HAS THAT MUCH POWER? TO BRING BACK THE DEAD?
KOKU (NOD)
SFX: ZEH (WHEEZE) / HAA (HUFF)
SUU (SSK)
SUU
YOUR MASK...
I MUST BREATHE... THROUGH ITS FILTERS...AND CHEMICALS...TO SURVIVE.
WITHOUT IT...I WOULD DIE WITHIN... TEN HOURS.
HOW CAN YOU DIE IF YOU'RE ALREADY DEAD?
MY BODY CAN...DIE, LIKE ANYONE'S.
IF IT DOES... MY SOUL GOES...
...BACK TO THE WAY... IT WAS.
COULD YOU AGREE TO ANOTHER CONTRACT WITH MR. TINY?
NOT SURE...BUT DON'T... THINK SO.
ONE SHOT AT... EXTRA LIFE IS...ALL I THINK... WE GET.

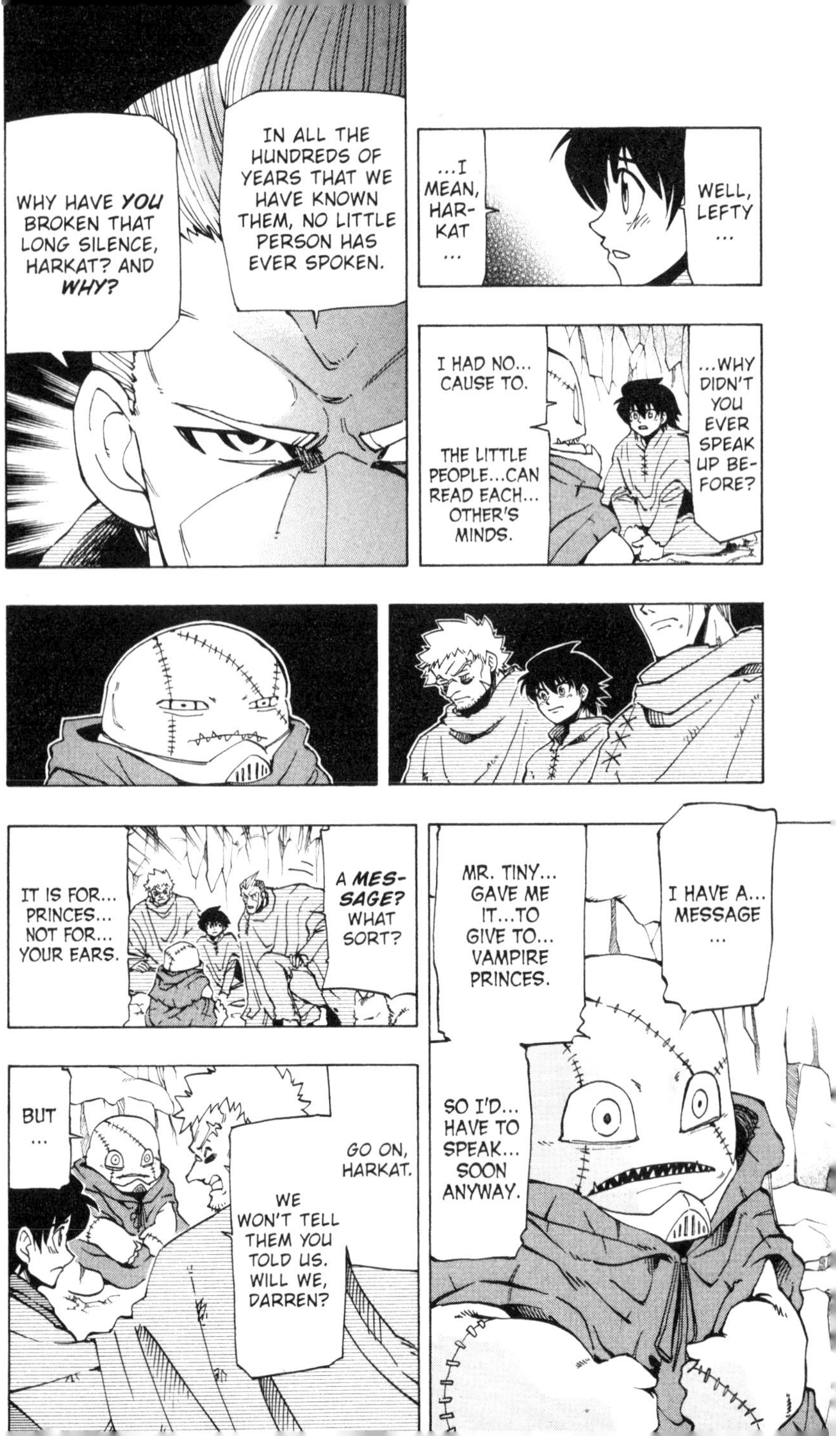
WELL, LEFTY ...
...I MEAN, HAR-KAT ...
...WHY DIDN'T YOU EVER SPEAK UP BE-FORE?
I HAD NO... CAUSE TO.
THE LITTLE PEOPLE...CAN READ EACH... OTHER'S MINDS.
IN ALL THE HUNDREDS OF YEARS THAT WE HAVE KNOWN THEM, NO LITTLE PERSON HAS EVER SPOKEN.
WHY HAVE ***YOU*** BROKEN THAT LONG SILENCE, HARKAT? AND ***WHY?***
I HAVE A... MESSAGE ...
MR. TINY... GAVE ME IT...TO GIVE TO... VAMPIRE PRINCES.
SO I'D... HAVE TO SPEAK... SOON ANYWAY.
A ***MES-SAGE?*** WHAT SORT?
IT IS FOR... PRINCES... NOT FOR... YOUR EARS.
GO ON, HARKAT.
WE WON'T TELL THEM YOU TOLD US. WILL WE, DARREN?
BUT ...

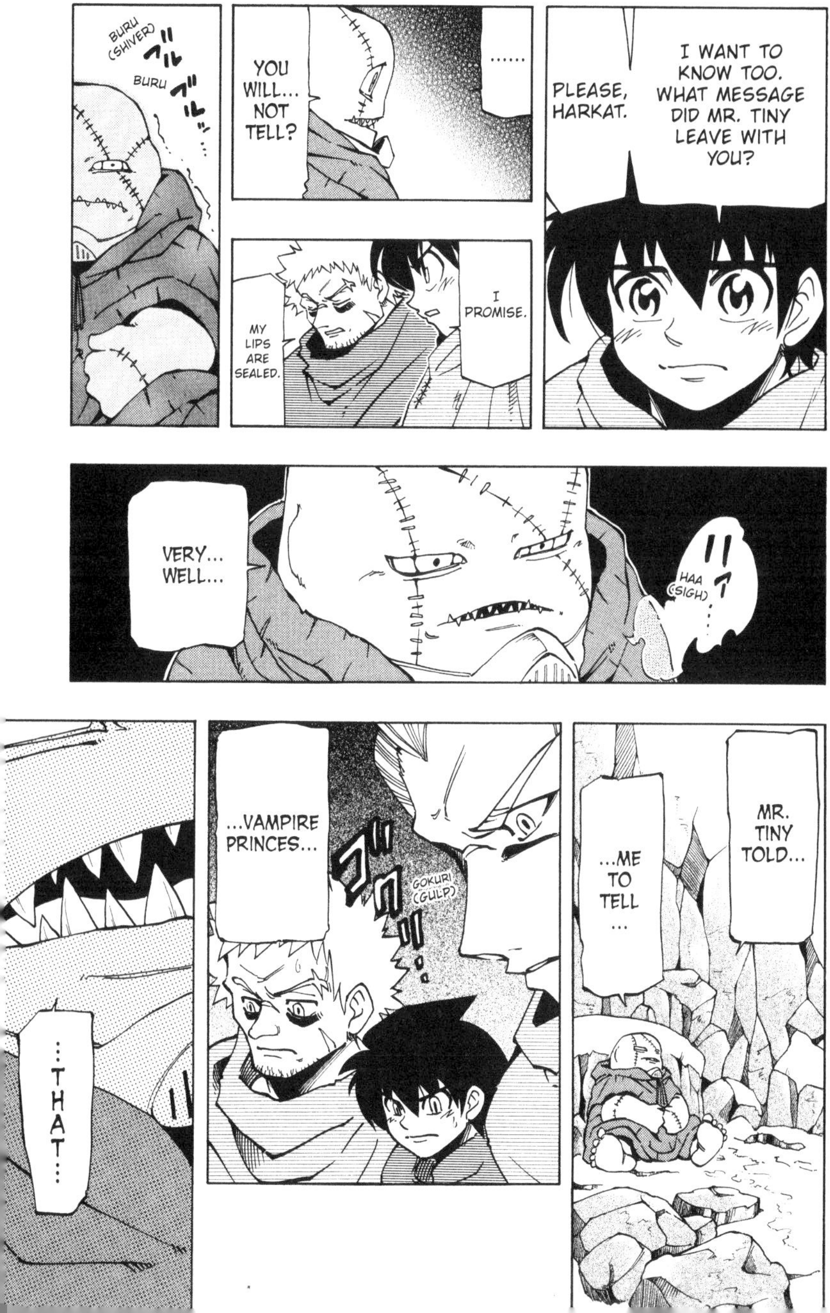
I WANT TO KNOW TOO. WHAT MESSAGE DID MR. TINY LEAVE WITH YOU?
PLEASE, HARKAT.
......
YOU WILL... NOT TELL?
I PROMISE.
MY LIPS ARE SEALED.
BURU (SHIVER)
ブル
BURU
ブルッ...
HAA (SIGH)
ハァ...
VERY... WELL...
MR. TINY TOLD...
...ME TO TELL ...
...VAMPIRE PRINCES...
GOKURI (GULP)
ゴクッ...
...THAT...

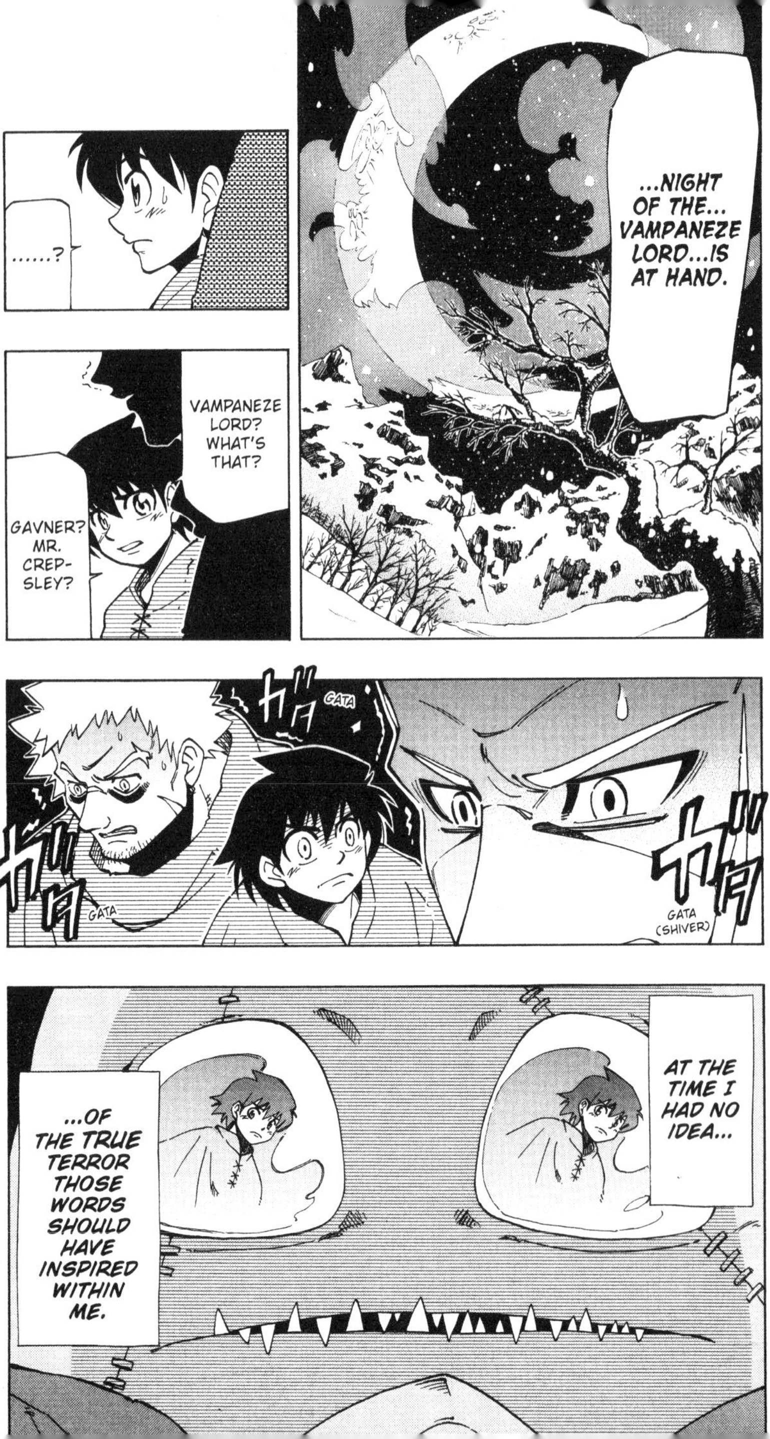
...NIGHT OF THE... VAMPANEZE LORD...IS AT HAND.
......?
VAMPANEZE LORD? WHAT'S THAT?
GAVNER? MR. CREPSLEY?
GATA (SHIVER)
GATA
GATA
AT THE TIME I HAD NO IDEA...
...OF THE TRUE TERROR THOSE WORDS SHOULD HAVE INSPIRED WITHIN ME.

INTO THE HALLS

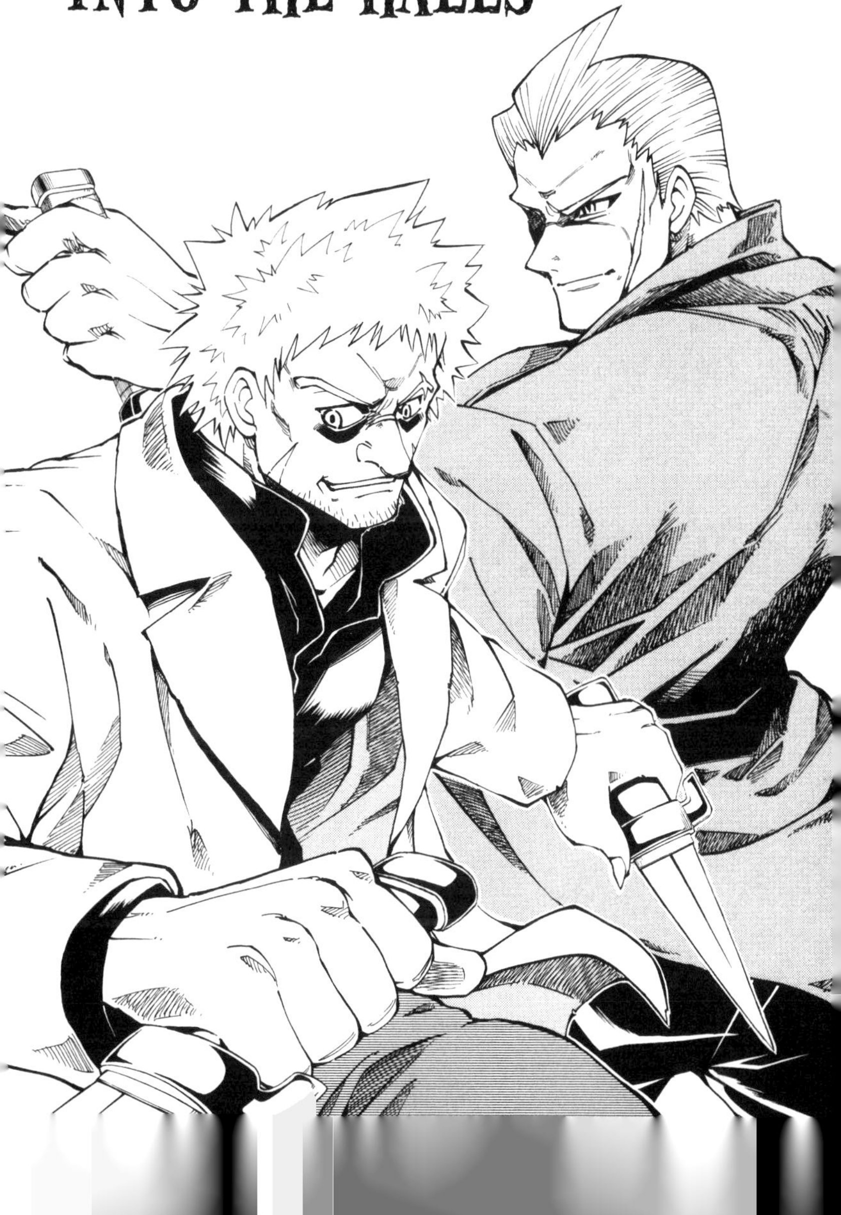

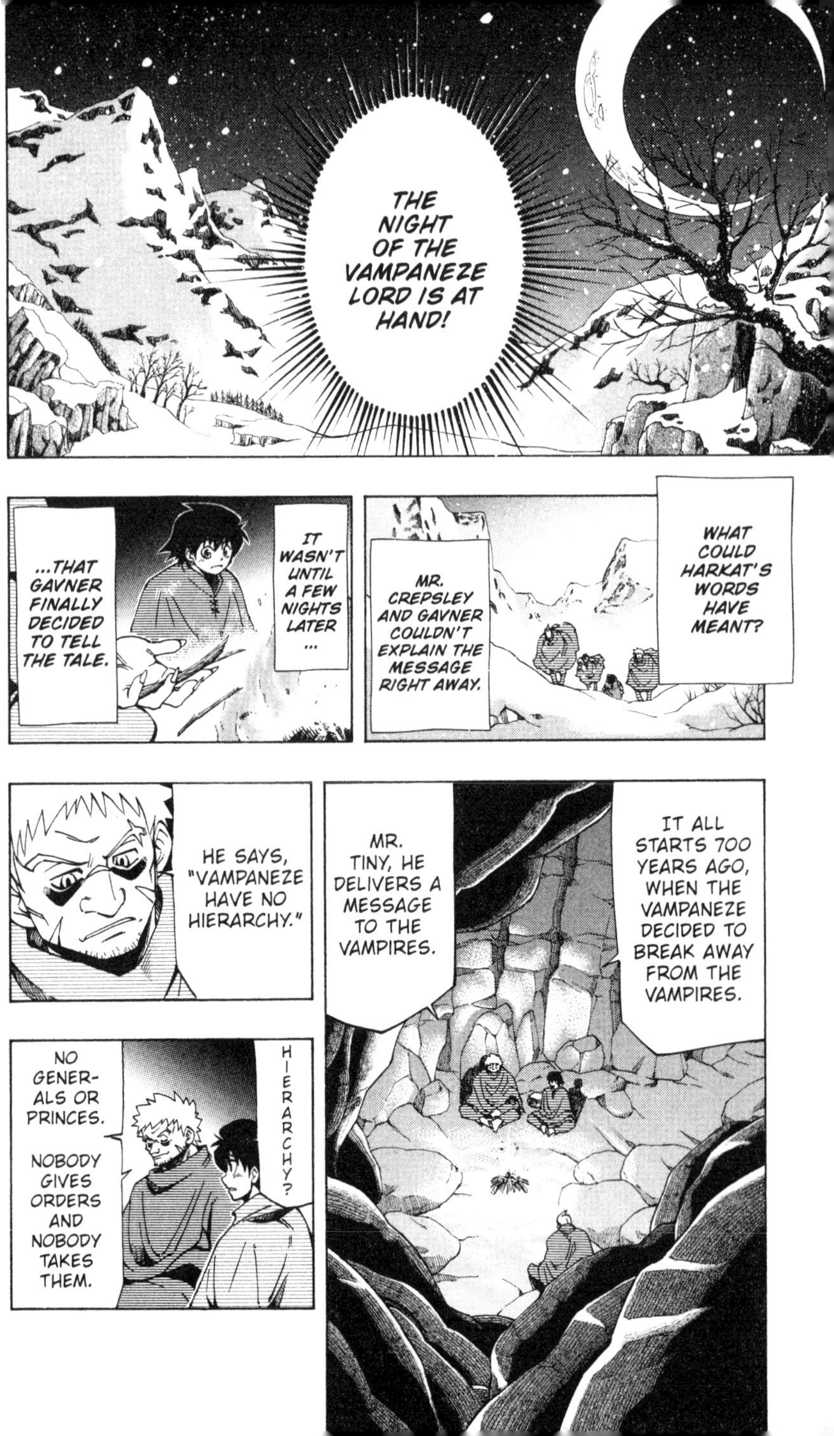
THE NIGHT OF THE VAMPANEZE LORD IS AT HAND!
WHAT COULD HARKAT'S WORDS HAVE MEANT?
MR. CREPSLEY AND GAVNER COULDN'T EXPLAIN THE MESSAGE RIGHT AWAY.
IT WASN'T UNTIL A FEW NIGHTS LATER ...
...THAT GAVNER FINALLY DECIDED TO TELL THE TALE.
IT ALL STARTS 700 YEARS AGO, WHEN THE VAMPANEZE DECIDED TO BREAK AWAY FROM THE VAMPIRES.
MR. TINY, HE DELIVERS A MESSAGE TO THE VAMPIRES.
HE SAYS, "VAMPANEZE HAVE NO HIERARCHY."
HIERARCHY?
NO GENER-ALS OR PRINCES.
NOBODY GIVES ORDERS AND NOBODY TAKES THEM.

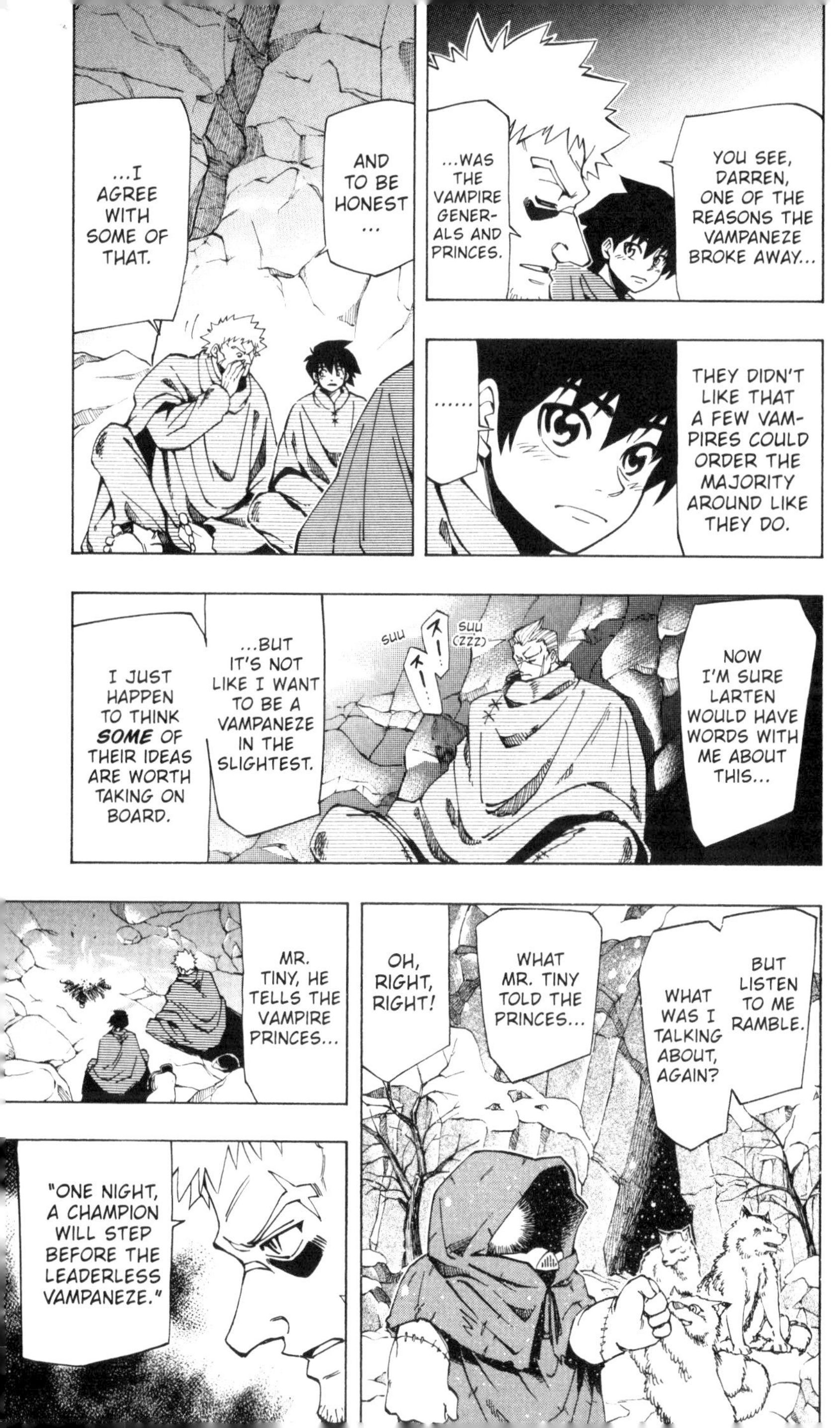
YOU SEE, DARREN, ONE OF THE REASONS THE VAMPANEZE BROKE AWAY...
...WAS THE VAMPIRE GENERALS AND PRINCES.
THEY DIDN'T LIKE THAT A FEW VAMPIRES COULD ORDER THE MAJORITY AROUND LIKE THEY DO.
......
AND TO BE HONEST...
...I AGREE WITH SOME OF THAT.
NOW I'M SURE LARTEN WOULD HAVE WORDS WITH ME ABOUT THIS...
SUU (ZZZ)
スー...
スー...
SUU
...BUT IT'S NOT LIKE I WANT TO BE A VAMPANEZE IN THE SLIGHTEST.
I JUST HAPPEN TO THINK ***SOME*** OF THEIR IDEAS ARE WORTH TAKING ON BOARD.
BUT LISTEN TO ME RAMBLE.
WHAT WAS I TALKING ABOUT, AGAIN?
WHAT MR. TINY TOLD THE PRINCES...
OH, RIGHT, RIGHT!
MR. TINY, HE TELLS THE VAMPIRE PRINCES...
"ONE NIGHT, A CHAMPION WILL STEP BEFORE THE LEADERLESS VAMPANEZE."

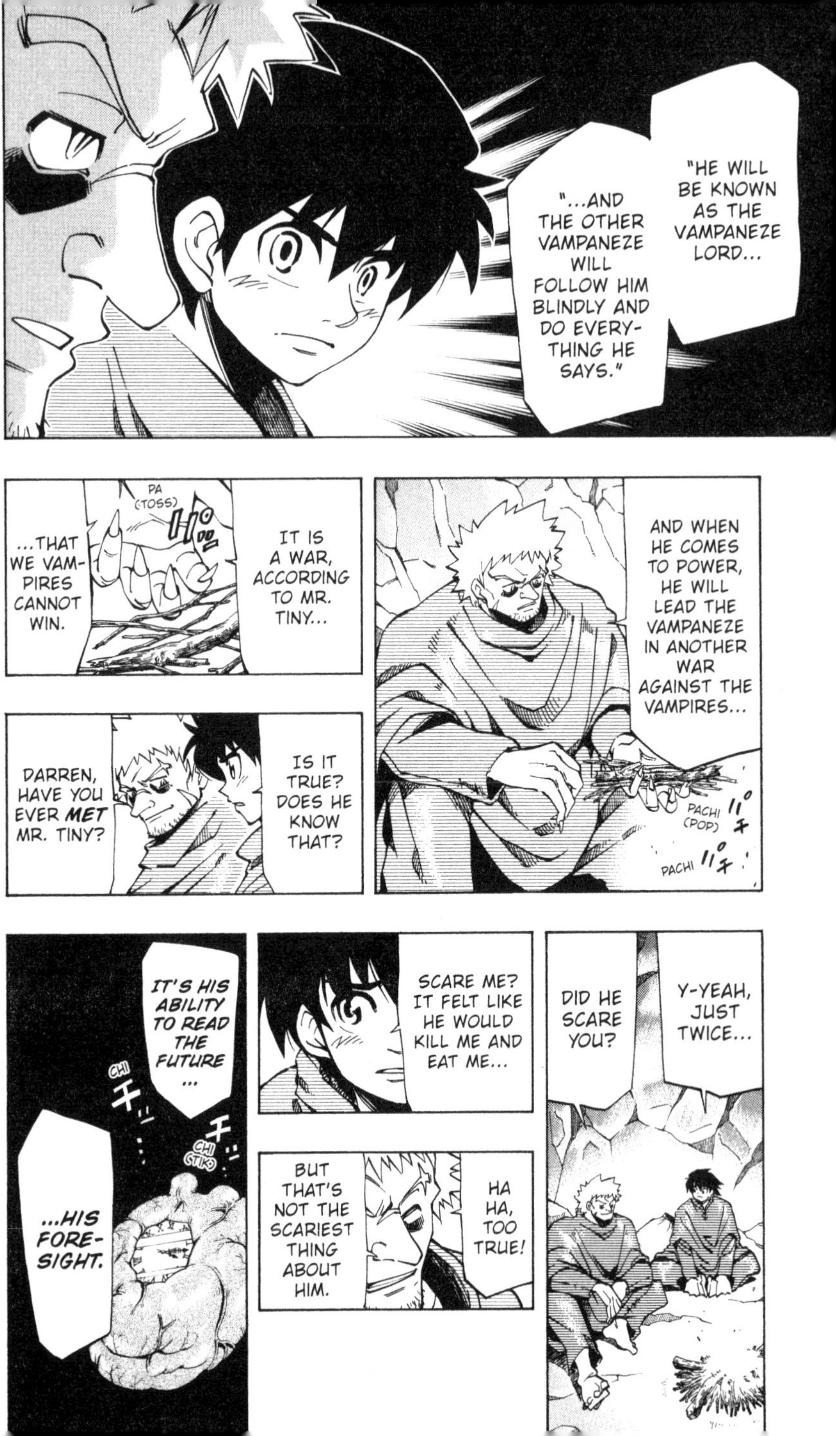
"HE WILL BE KNOWN AS THE VAMPANEZE LORD...
"...AND THE OTHER VAMPANEZE WILL FOLLOW HIM BLINDLY AND DO EVERYTHING HE SAYS."
AND WHEN HE COMES TO POWER, HE WILL LEAD THE VAMPANEZE IN ANOTHER WAR AGAINST THE VAMPIRES...
PACHI (POP)
PACHI
IT IS A WAR, ACCORDING TO MR. TINY...
PA (TOSS)
...THAT WE VAMPIRES CANNOT WIN.
IS IT TRUE? DOES HE KNOW THAT?
DARREN, HAVE YOU EVER *MET* MR. TINY?
Y-YEAH, JUST TWICE...
DID HE SCARE YOU?
SCARE ME? IT FELT LIKE HE WOULD KILL ME AND EAT ME...
HA HA, TOO TRUE!
BUT THAT'S NOT THE SCARIEST THING ABOUT HIM.
IT'S HIS ABILITY TO READ THE FUTURE...
CHI
CHI (TIK)
...HIS FORESIGHT.

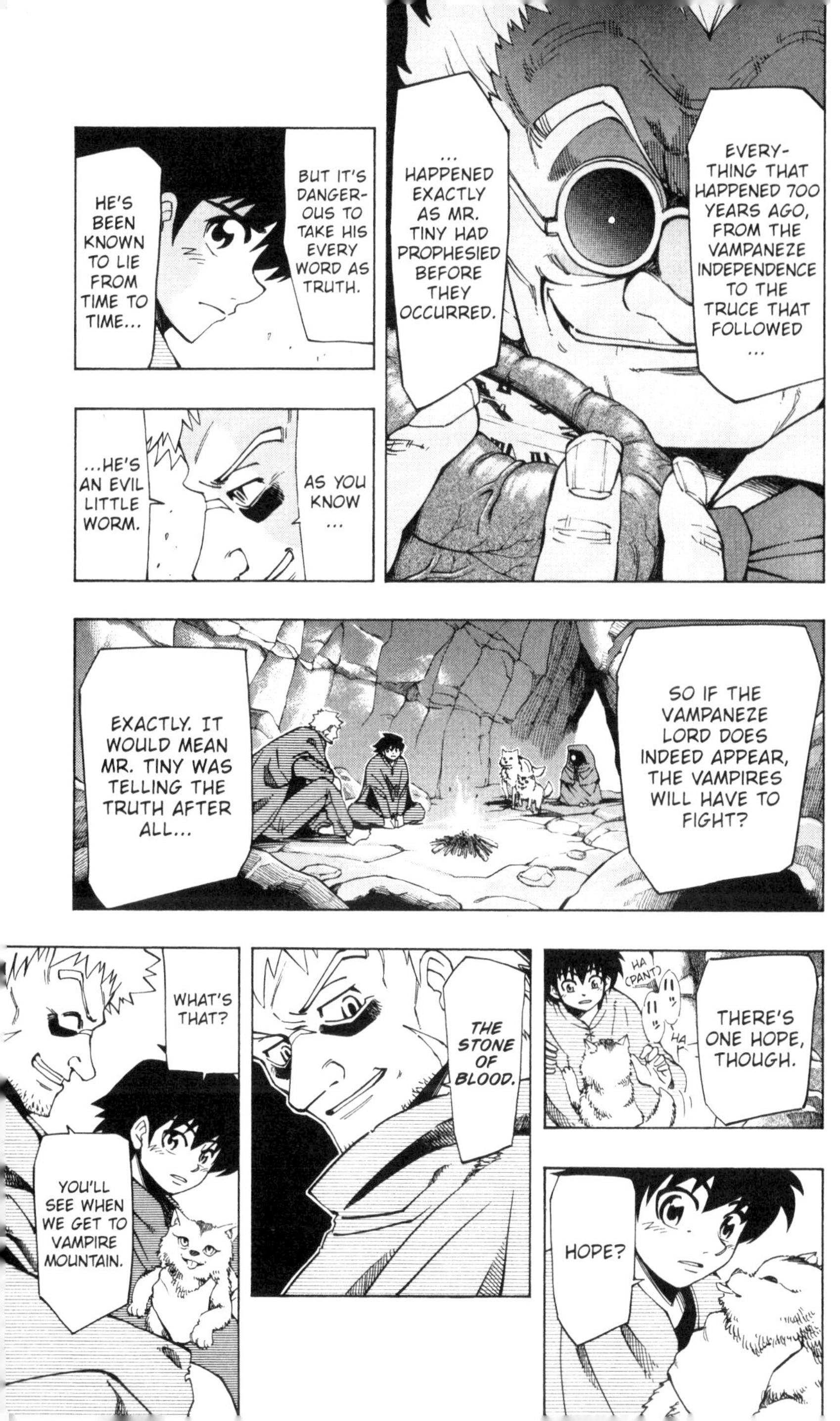
EVERY-THING THAT HAPPENED 700 YEARS AGO, FROM THE VAMPANEZE INDEPENDENCE TO THE TRUCE THAT FOLLOWED ...
... HAPPENED EXACTLY AS MR. TINY HAD PROPHESIED BEFORE THEY OCCURRED.
BUT IT'S DANGER-OUS TO TAKE HIS EVERY WORD AS TRUTH.
HE'S BEEN KNOWN TO LIE FROM TIME TO TIME...
AS YOU KNOW ...
...HE'S AN EVIL LITTLE WORM.
SO IF THE VAMPANEZE LORD DOES INDEED APPEAR, THE VAMPIRES WILL HAVE TO FIGHT?
EXACTLY. IT WOULD MEAN MR. TINY WAS TELLING THE TRUTH AFTER ALL...
THERE'S ONE HOPE, THOUGH.
HA (PANT) HA
HOPE?
THE STONE OF BLOOD.
WHAT'S THAT?
YOU'LL SEE WHEN WE GET TO VAMPIRE MOUNTAIN.

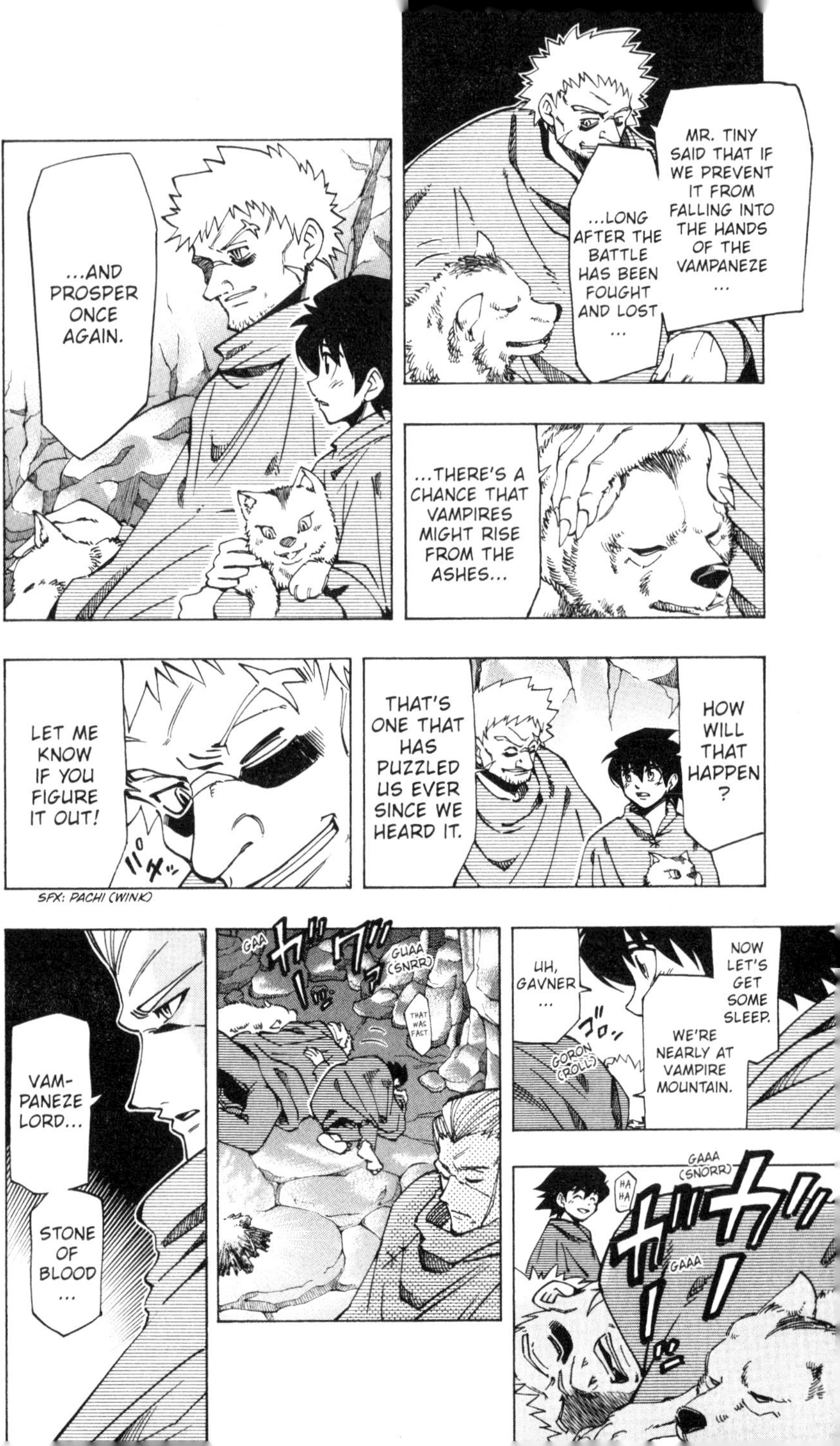
MR. TINY SAID THAT IF WE PREVENT IT FROM FALLING INTO THE HANDS OF THE VAMPANEZE ...
...LONG AFTER THE BATTLE HAS BEEN FOUGHT AND LOST ...
...THERE'S A CHANCE THAT VAMPIRES MIGHT RISE FROM THE ASHES...
...AND PROSPER ONCE AGAIN.
HOW WILL THAT HAPPEN ?
THAT'S ONE THAT HAS PUZZLED US EVER SINCE WE HEARD IT.
LET ME KNOW IF YOU FIGURE IT OUT!
SFX: PACHI (WINK)
NOW LET'S GET SOME SLEEP.
WE'RE NEARLY AT VAMPIRE MOUNTAIN.
UH, GAVNER ...
GORON (ROLL)
GAAA (SNORR)
HA HA
GAAA
GAA
GUAA (SNRR)
THAT WAS FAST.
VAM-PANEZE LORD...
STONE OF BLOOD ...

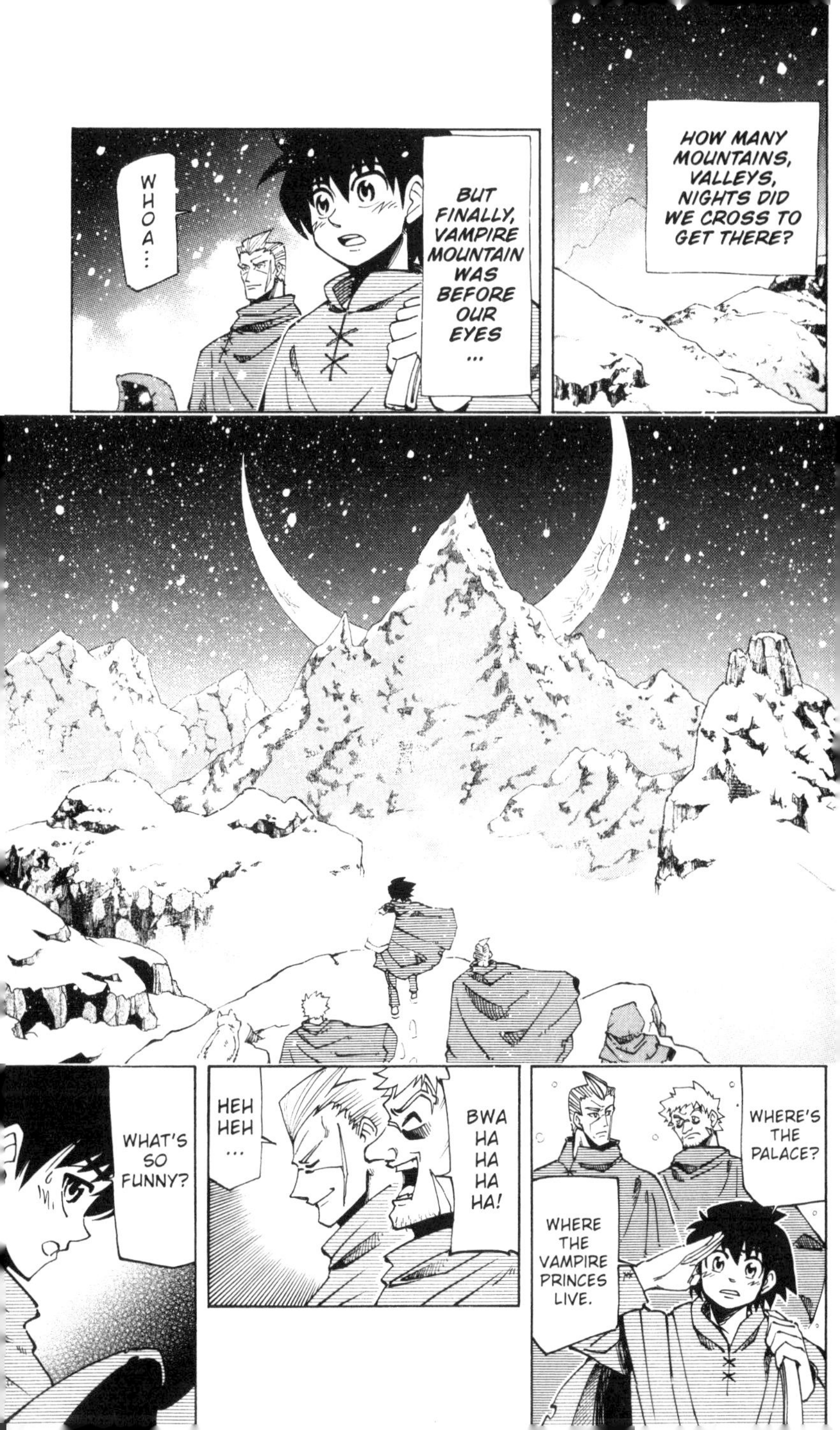
HOW MANY MOUNTAINS, VALLEYS, NIGHTS DID WE CROSS TO GET THERE?
BUT FINALLY, VAMPIRE MOUNTAIN WAS BEFORE OUR EYES ...
WHOA...
WHERE'S THE PALACE?
WHERE THE VAMPIRE PRINCES LIVE.
BWA HA HA HA HA!
HEH HEH ...
WHAT'S SO FUNNY?

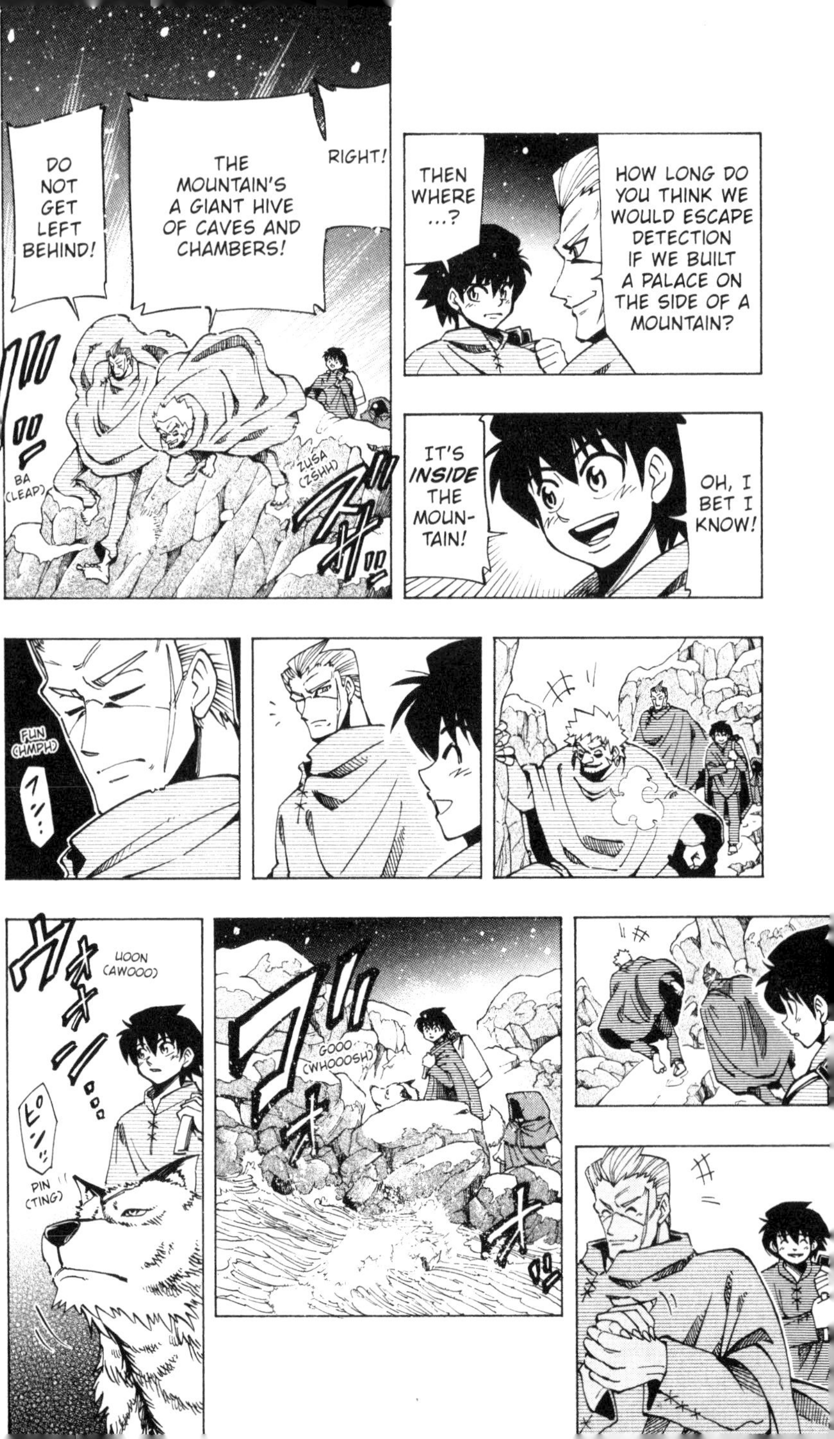
HOW LONG DO YOU THINK WE WOULD ESCAPE DETECTION IF WE BUILT A PALACE ON THE SIDE OF A MOUNTAIN?
THEN WHERE ...?
OH, I BET I KNOW!
IT'S *INSIDE* THE MOUN-TAIN!
RIGHT!
THE MOUNTAIN'S A GIANT HIVE OF CAVES AND CHAMBERS!
DO NOT GET LEFT BEHIND!
ZUSA (ZSHH)
BA (LEAP)
FUN (HMPH)
GOOO (WHOOOSH)
UOON (AWOOO)
PIN (TING)

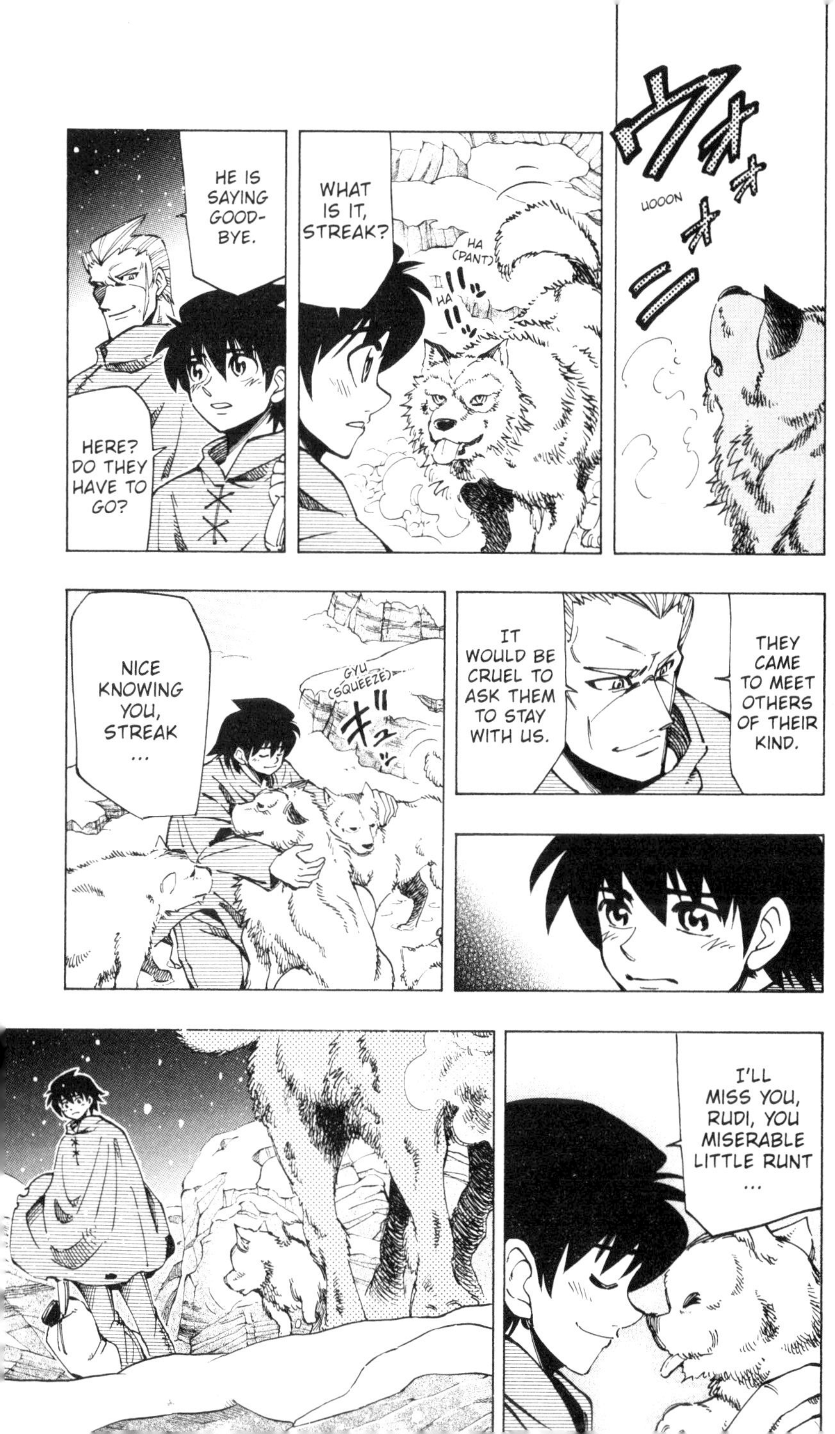
ウォォォン
UOOON
WHAT IS IT, STREAK?
HA (PANT)
ハッ ハッ
HE IS SAYING GOOD-BYE.
HERE? DO THEY HAVE TO GO?
THEY CAME TO MEET OTHERS OF THEIR KIND.
IT WOULD BE CRUEL TO ASK THEM TO STAY WITH US.
GYU (SQUEEZE)
ギュッ
NICE KNOWING YOU, STREAK ...
I'LL MISS YOU, RUDI, YOU MISERABLE LITTLE RUNT ...

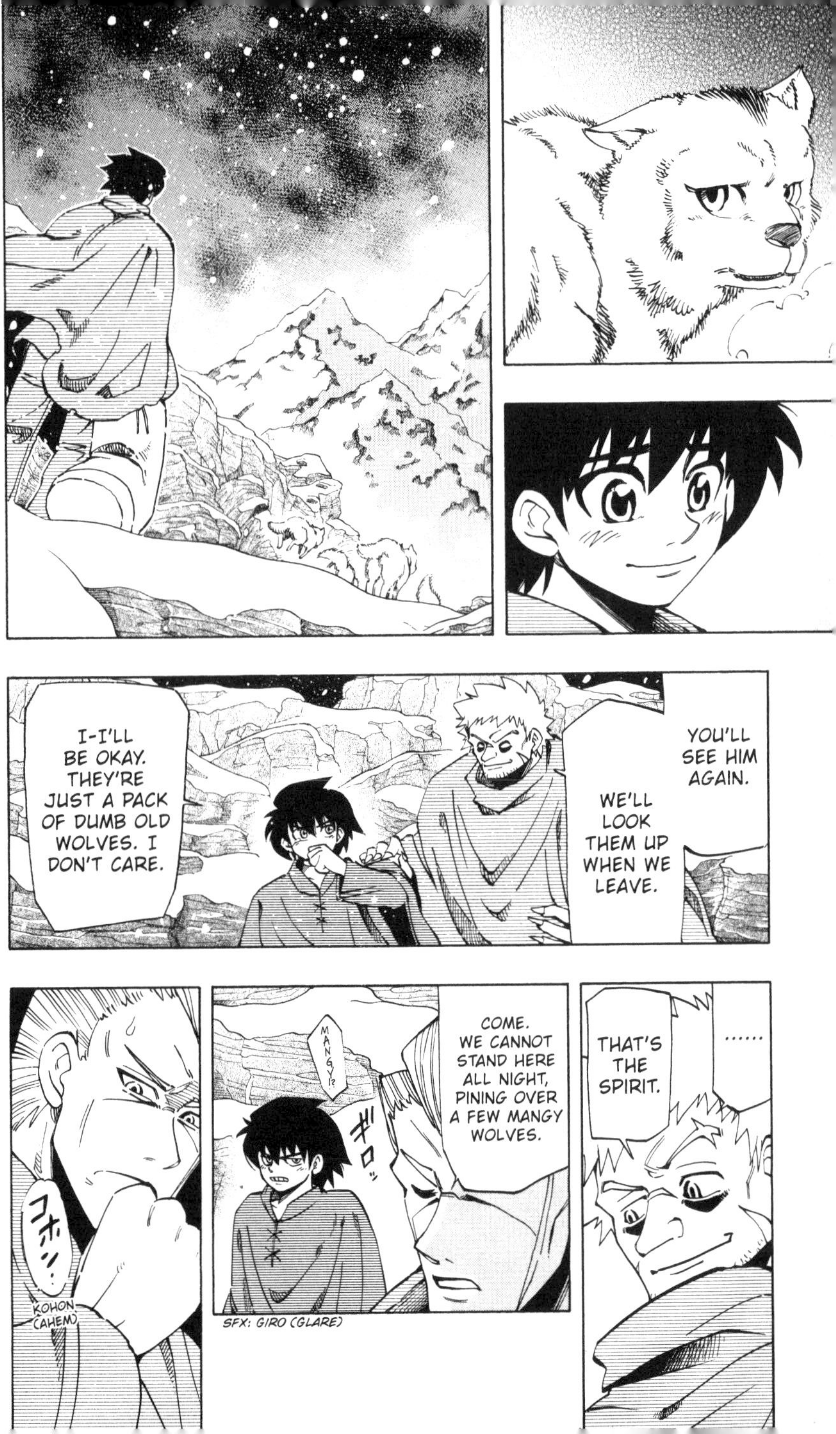
YOU'LL SEE HIM AGAIN.
WE'LL LOOK THEM UP WHEN WE LEAVE.
I-I'LL BE OKAY. THEY'RE JUST A PACK OF DUMB OLD WOLVES. I DON'T CARE.
......
THAT'S THE SPIRIT.
COME. WE CANNOT STAND HERE ALL NIGHT, PINING OVER A FEW MANGY WOLVES.
MANGY!?
ギロッ
SFX: GIRO (GLARE)
コホン
KOHON (AHEM)

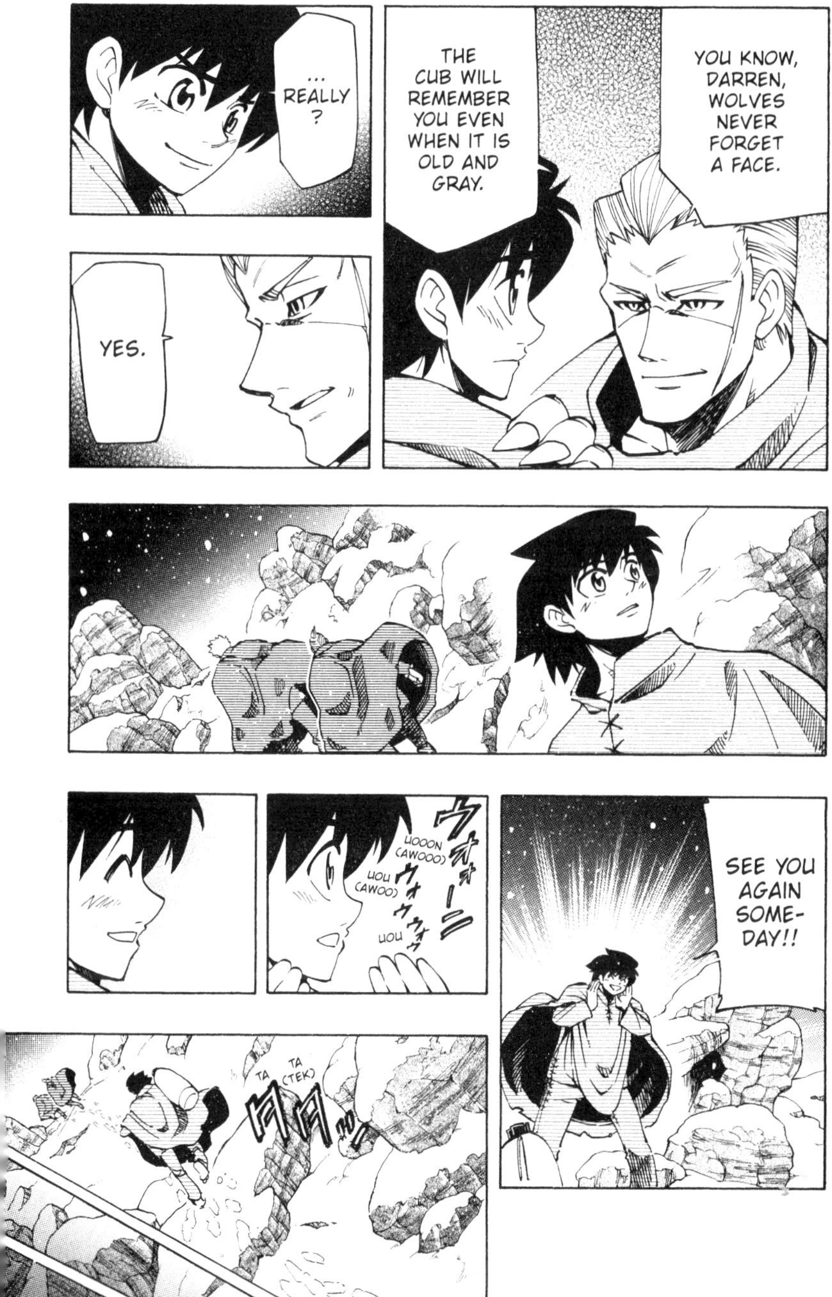
YOU KNOW, DARREN, WOLVES NEVER FORGET A FACE.
THE CUB WILL REMEMBER YOU EVEN WHEN IT IS OLD AND GRAY.
... REALLY ?
YES.
SEE YOU AGAIN SOME-DAY!!
UOOON (AWOOO)
UOU (AWOO)
UOU
TA TA (TEK)

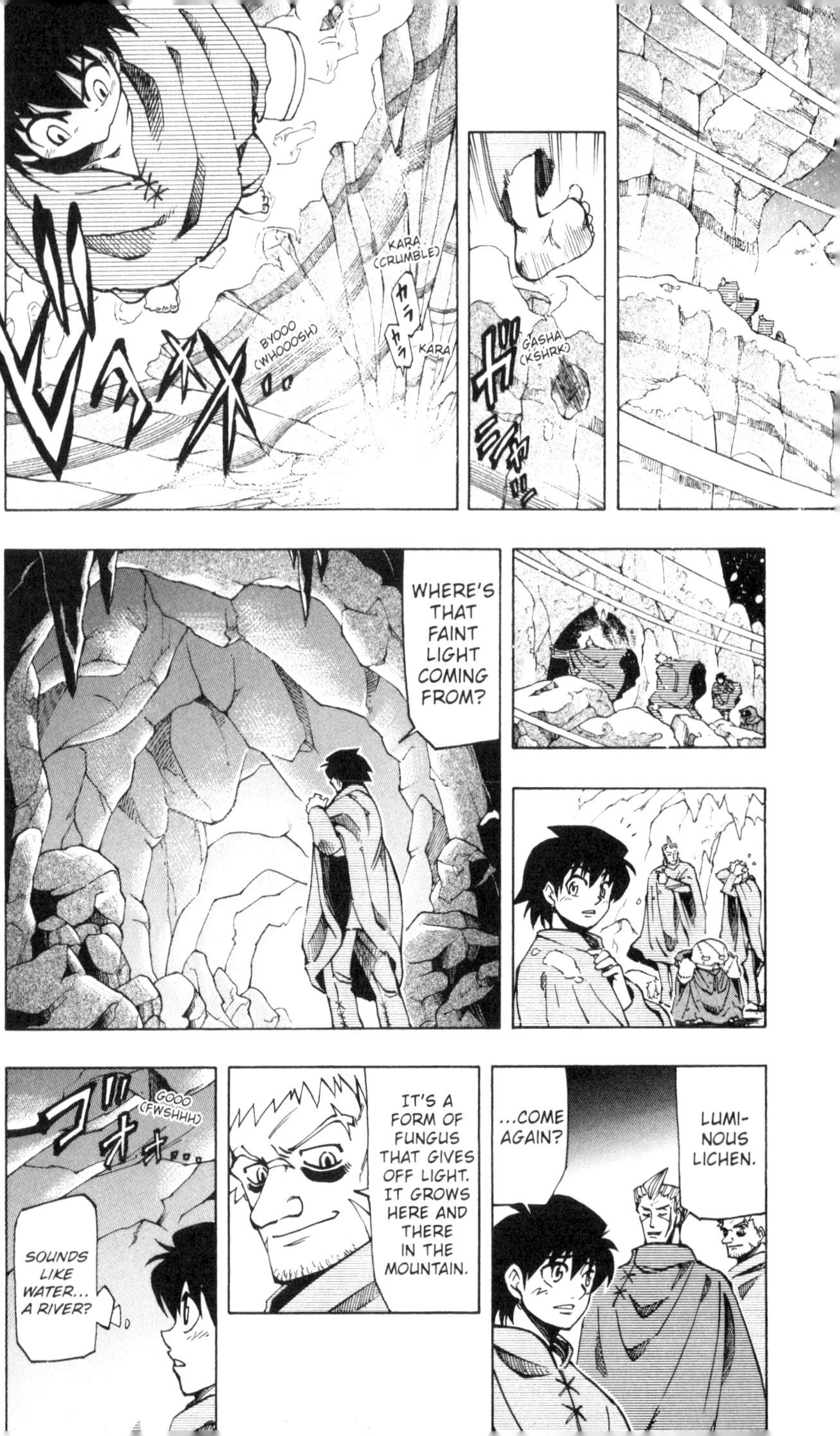
GASHA (KSHRK)
KARA (CRUMBLE)
カラ
カラ
KARA
BYOOO (WHOOOSH)
WHERE'S THAT FAINT LIGHT COMING FROM?
LUMI-NOUS LICHEN.
...COME AGAIN?
IT'S A FORM OF FUNGUS THAT GIVES OFF LIGHT. IT GROWS HERE AND THERE IN THE MOUNTAIN.
GOOO (FWSHHH)
SOUNDS LIKE WATER... A RIVER?

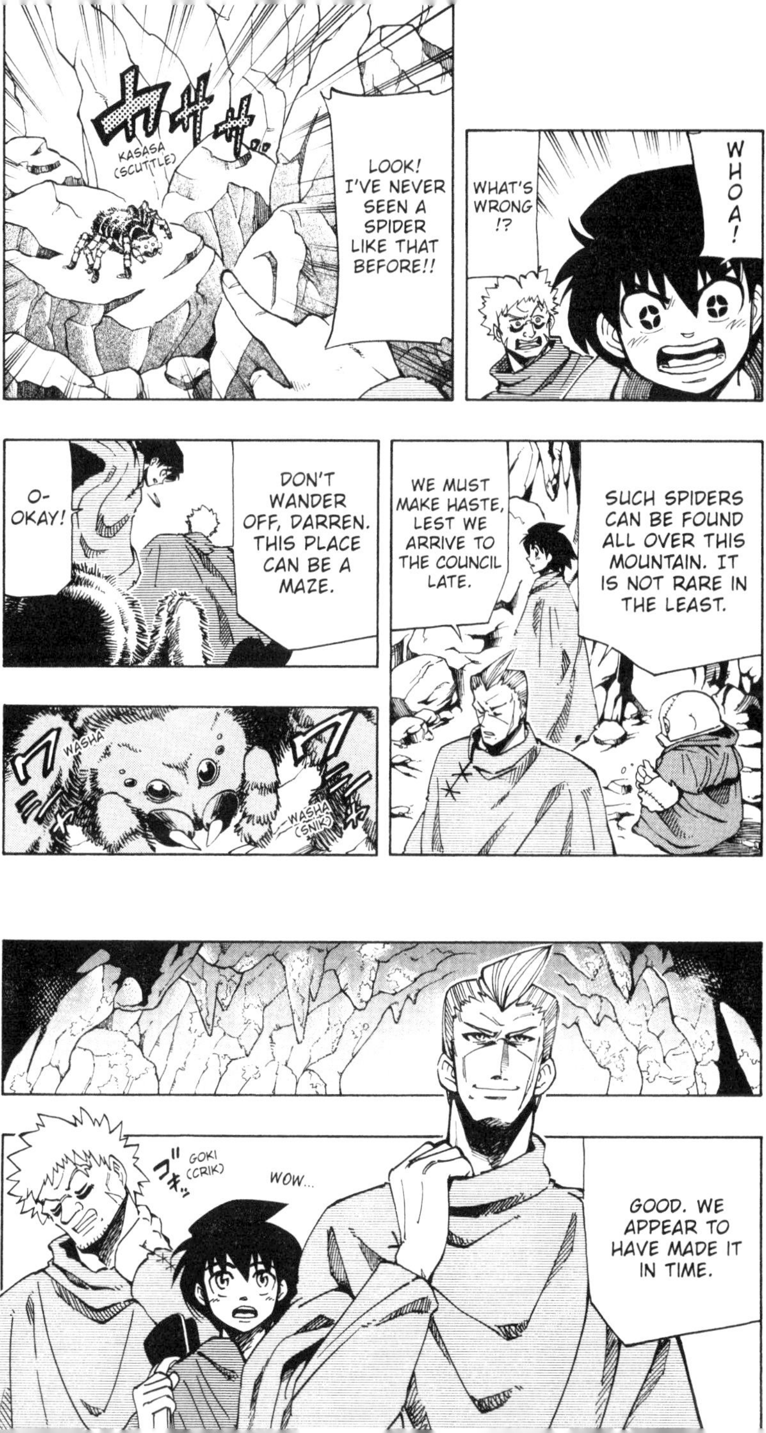
WHOA!
WHAT'S WRONG!?
LOOK! I'VE NEVER SEEN A SPIDER LIKE THAT BEFORE!!
KASASA (SCUTTLE)
SUCH SPIDERS CAN BE FOUND ALL OVER THIS MOUNTAIN. IT IS NOT RARE IN THE LEAST.
WE MUST MAKE HASTE, LEST WE ARRIVE TO THE COUNCIL LATE.
DON'T WANDER OFF, DARREN. THIS PLACE CAN BE A MAZE.
O-OKAY!
WASHA
WASHA (SNIK)
GOOD. WE APPEAR TO HAVE MADE IT IN TIME.
WOW...
GOKI (CRIK)

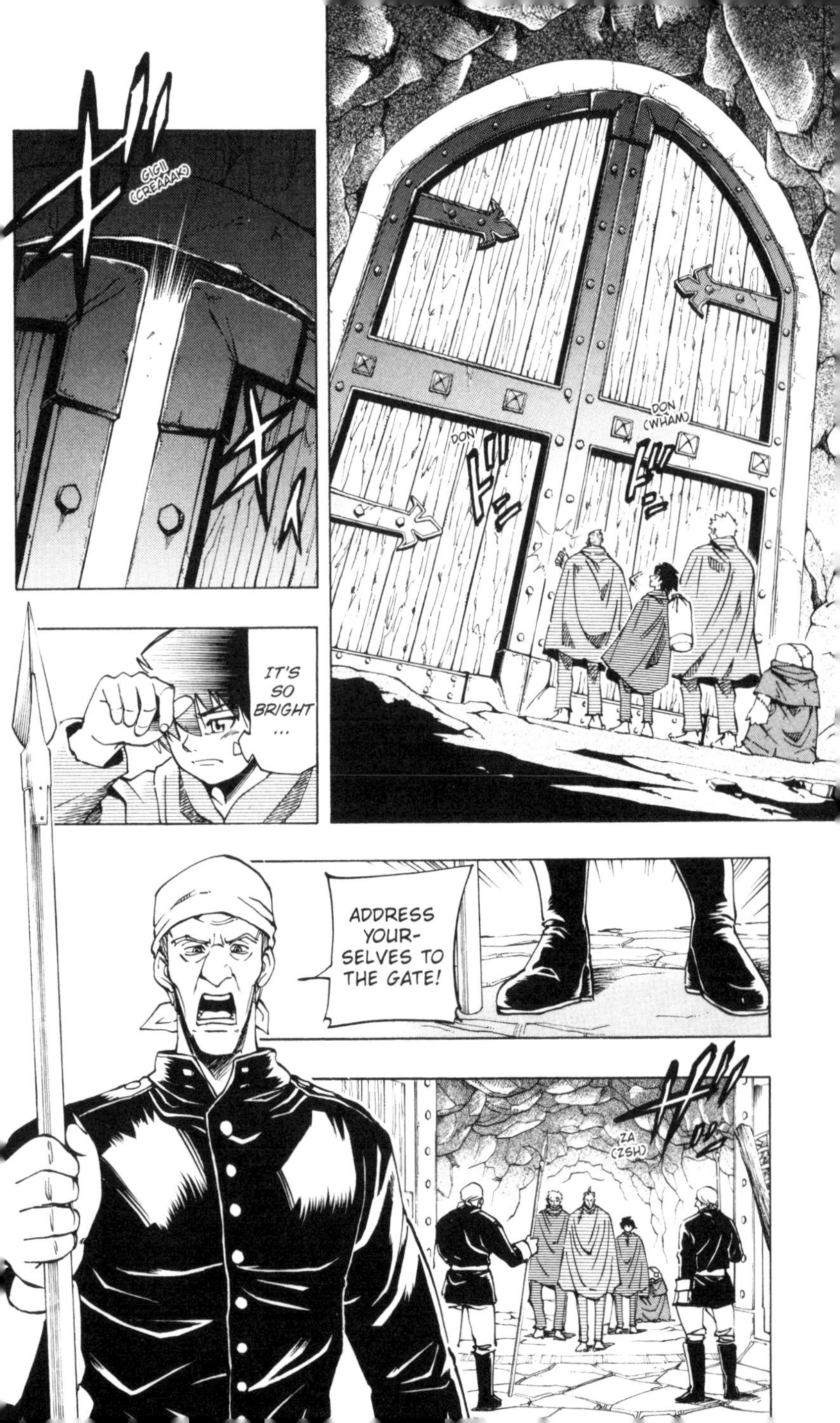
DON! (WHAM)
DON
GIGII (CREAAAK)
IT'S SO BRIGHT ...
ADDRESS YOUR-SELVES TO THE GATE!
ZA (ZSH)

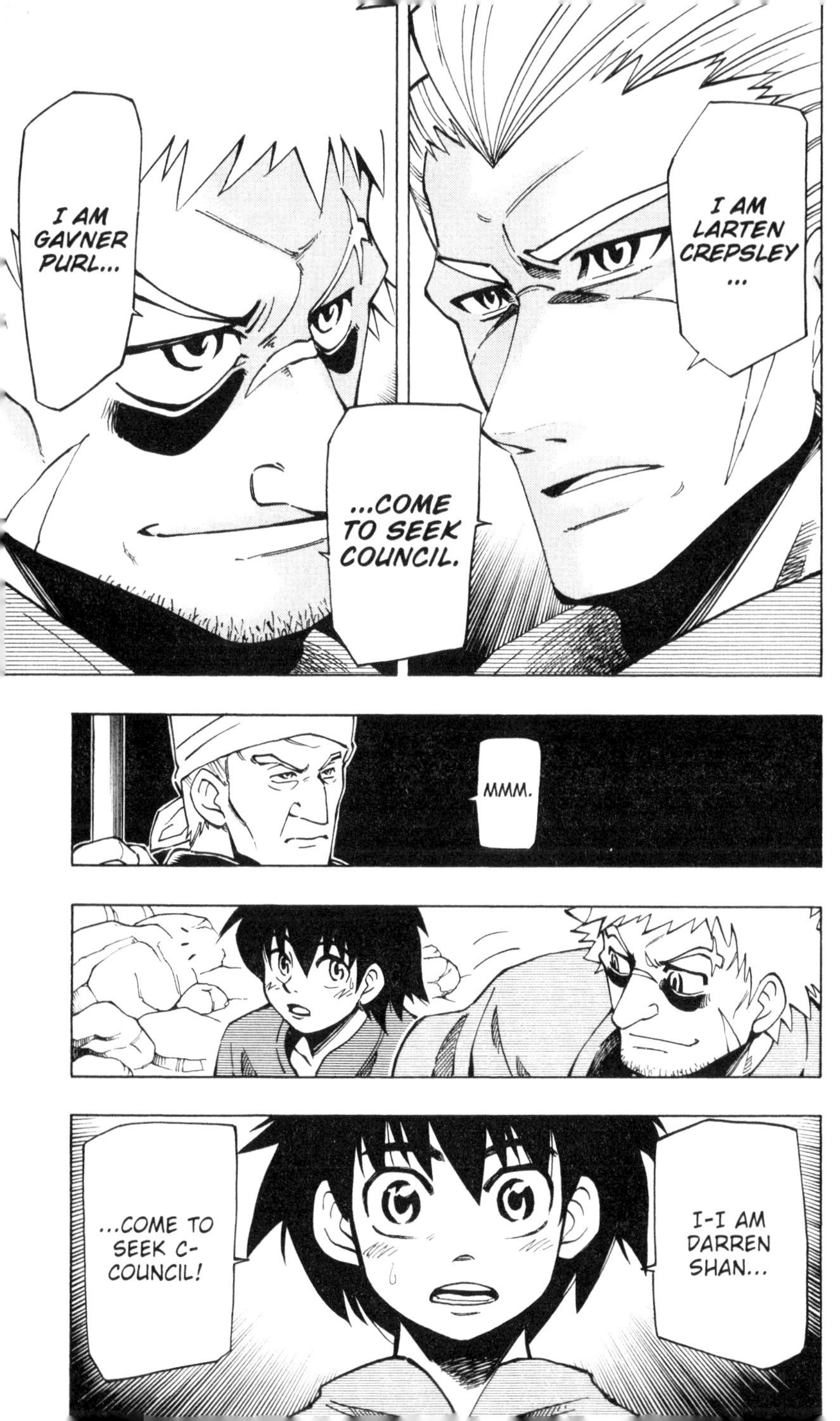
I AM LARTEN CREPSLEY ...
I AM GAVNER PURL...
...COME TO SEEK COUNCIL.
MMM.
I-I AM DARREN SHAN...
...COME TO SEEK C-COUNCIL!

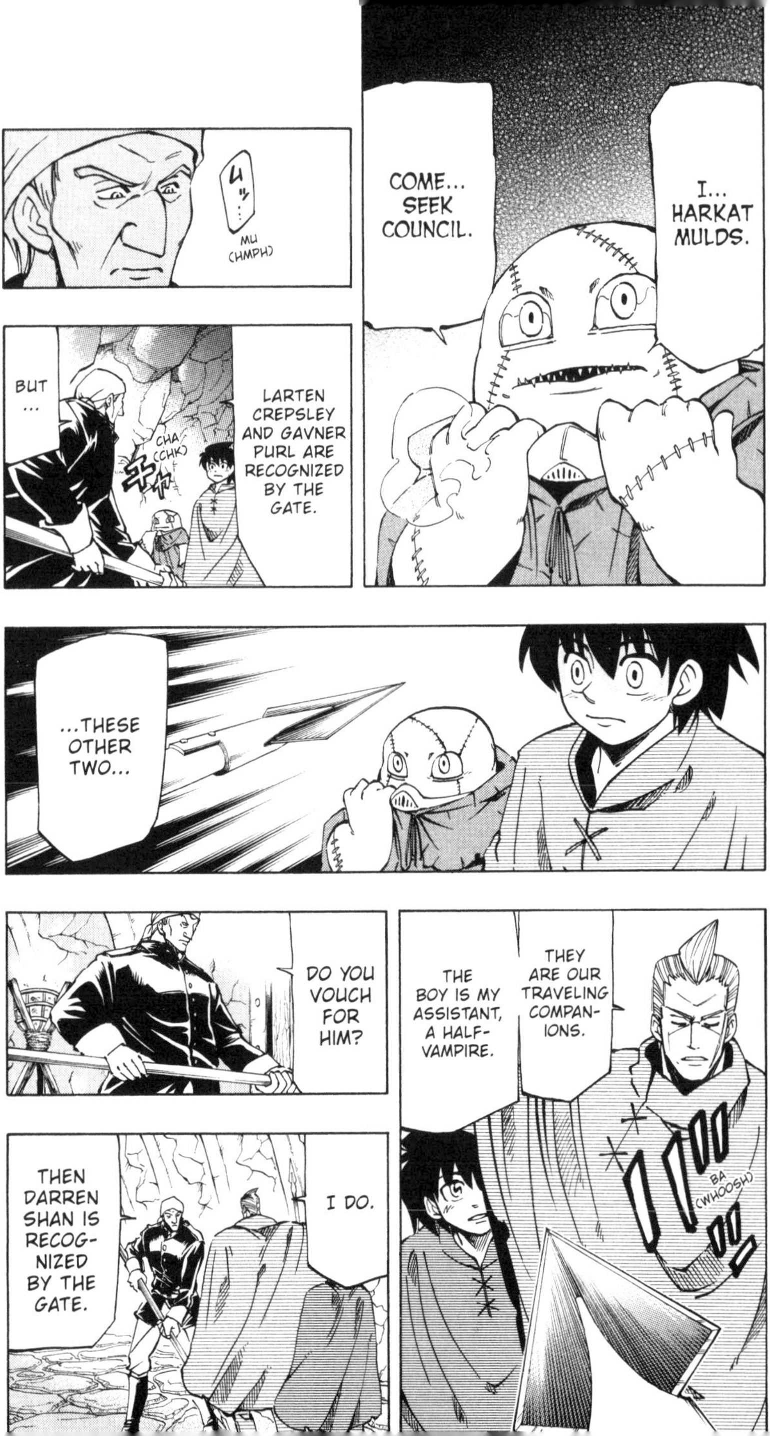
I... HARKAT MULDS.
COME... SEEK COUNCIL.
ムッ…
MU (HMPH)
LARTEN CREPSLEY AND GAVNER PURL ARE RECOGNIZED BY THE GATE.
BUT ...
チャ
CHA (CHK)
...THESE OTHER TWO...
THEY ARE OUR TRAVELING COMPAN- IONS.
THE BOY IS MY ASSISTANT, A HALF- VAMPIRE.
BA (WHOOSH)
DO YOU VOUCH FOR HIM?
I DO.
THEN DARREN SHAN IS RECOG- NIZED BY THE GATE.

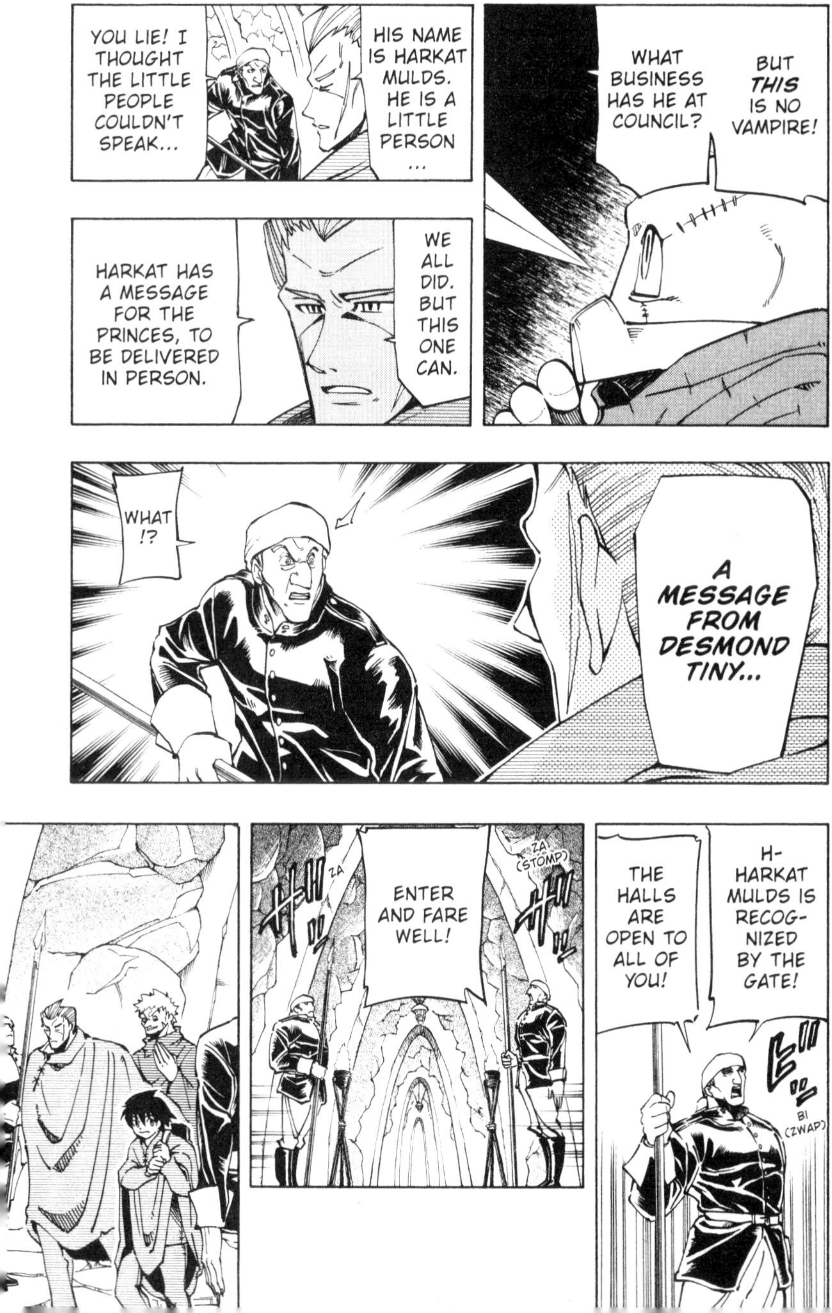
BUT THIS IS NO VAMPIRE!
WHAT BUSINESS HAS HE AT COUNCIL?
HIS NAME IS HARKAT MULDS. HE IS A LITTLE PERSON...
YOU LIE! I THOUGHT THE LITTLE PEOPLE COULDN'T SPEAK...
WE ALL DID. BUT THIS ONE CAN.
HARKAT HAS A MESSAGE FOR THE PRINCES, TO BE DELIVERED IN PERSON.
A MESSAGE FROM DESMOND TINY...
WHAT !?
H-HARKAT MULDS IS RECOG-NIZED BY THE GATE!
THE HALLS ARE OPEN TO ALL OF YOU!
BI (ZWAP)
ZA (STOMP)
ENTER AND FARE WELL!
ZA

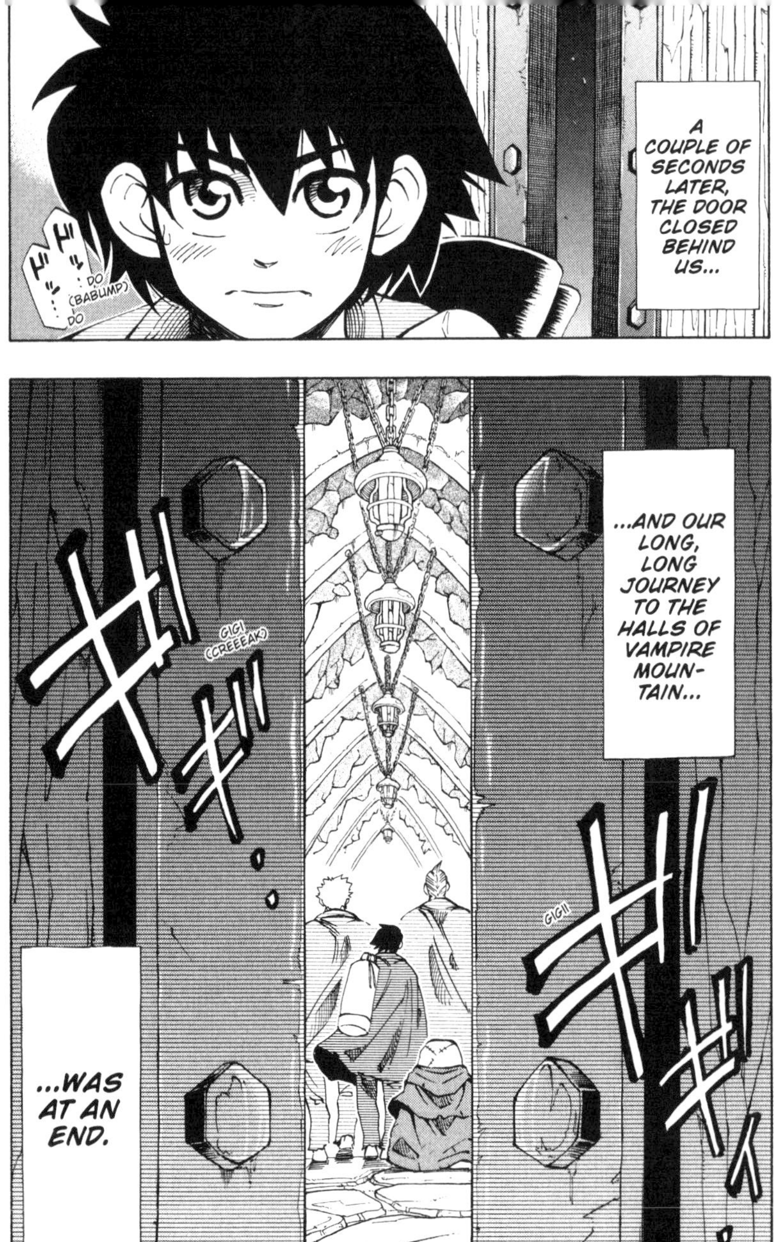
A COUPLE OF SECONDS LATER, THE DOOR CLOSED BEHIND US...
DO (BABUMP) DO
...AND OUR LONG, LONG JOURNEY TO THE HALLS OF VAMPIRE MOUN-TAIN...
GIGI
GIGI (CREEEAK)
...WAS AT AN END.

CHAPTER 29: QUARTERMASTER SEBA NILE

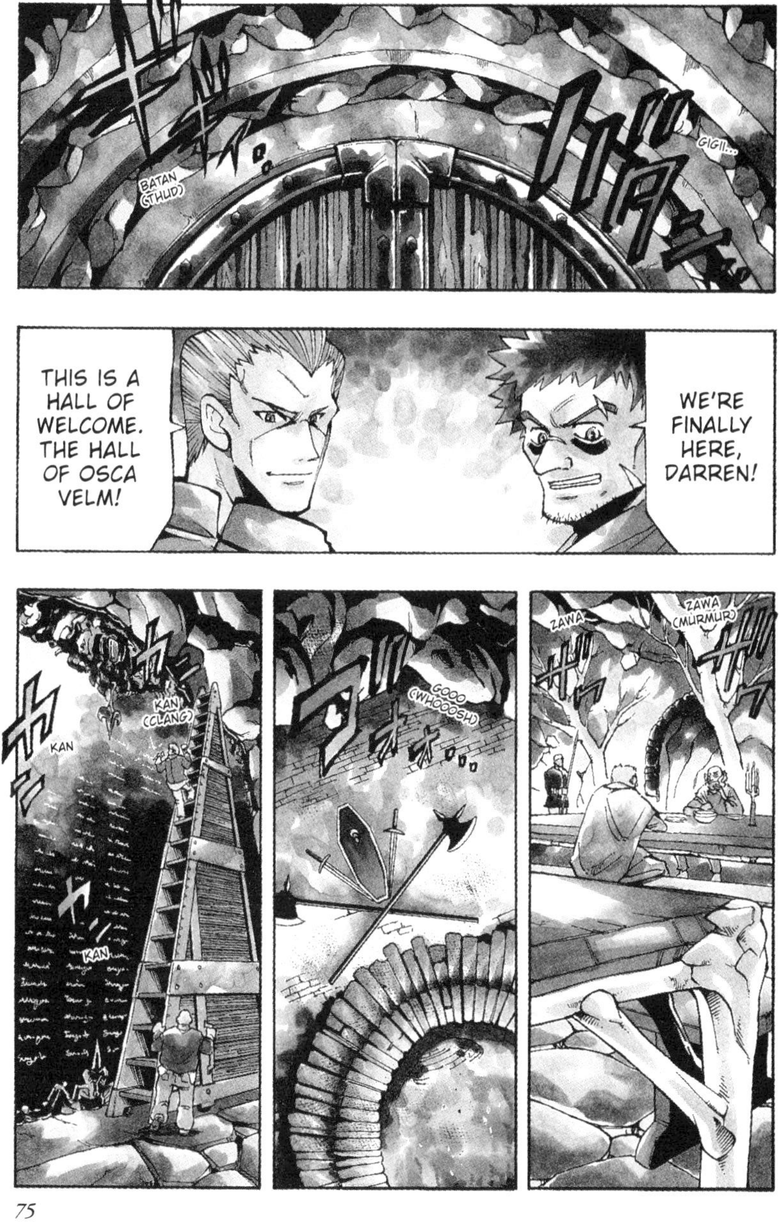
GIGII...
BATAN (THUD)
WE'RE FINALLY HERE, DARREN!
THIS IS A HALL OF WELCOME. THE HALL OF OSCA VELM!
ZAWA (MURMUR)
ZAWA
GOOO (WHOOOSH)
KAN (CLANG)
KAN
KAN

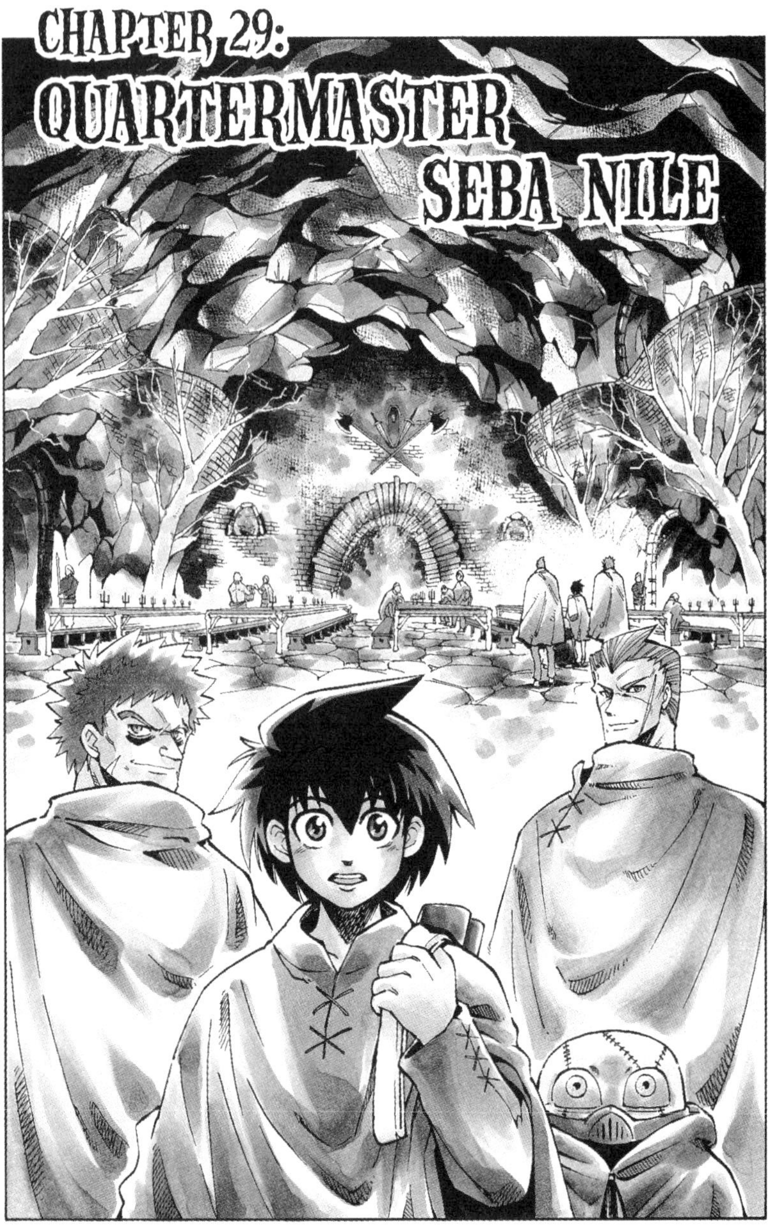
CHAPTER 29:
QUARTERMASTER
SEBA NILE

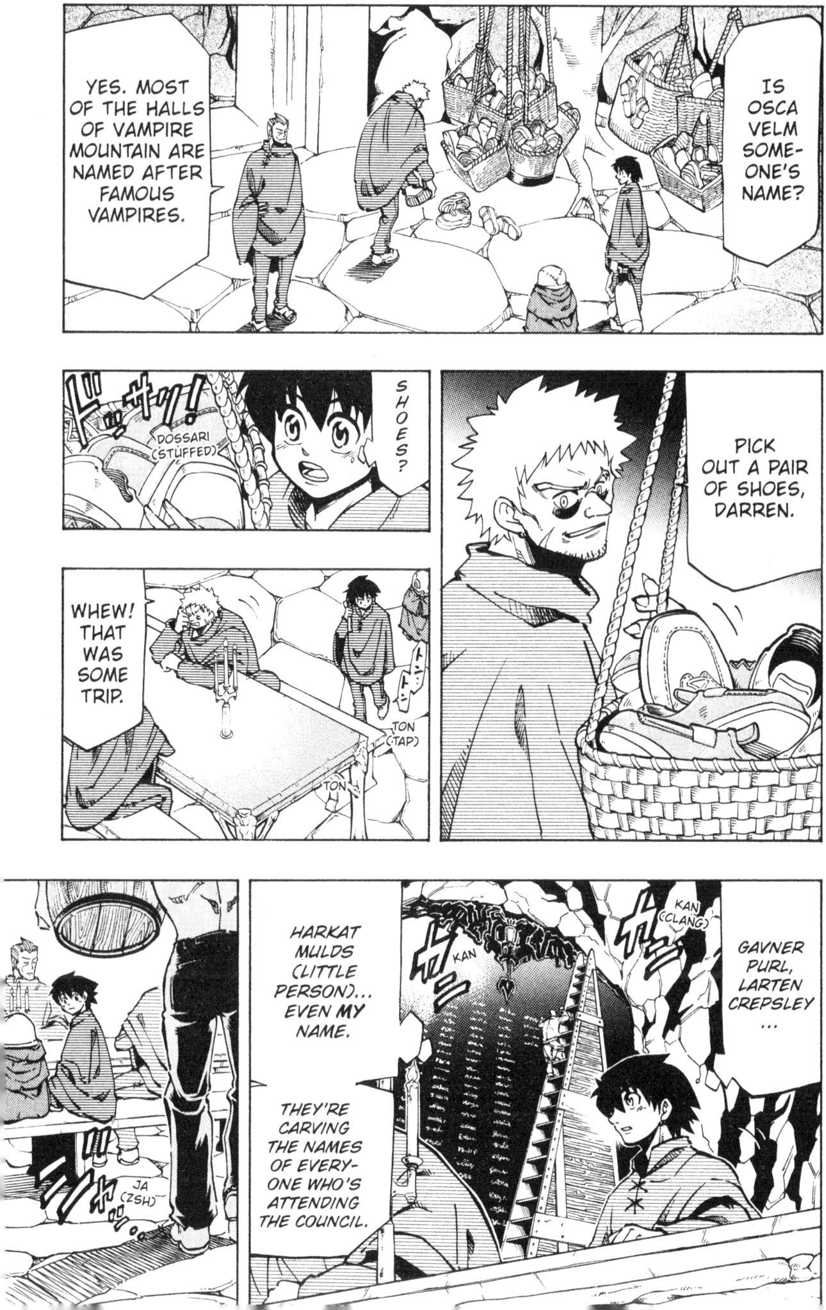
IS OSCA VELM SOME-ONE'S NAME?
YES. MOST OF THE HALLS OF VAMPIRE MOUNTAIN ARE NAMED AFTER FAMOUS VAMPIRES.
PICK OUT A PAIR OF SHOES, DARREN.
SHOES?
DOSSARI (STUFFED)
WHEW! THAT WAS SOME TRIP.
TON (TAP)
TON
GAVNER PURL, LARTEN CREPSLEY ...
KAN (CLANG)
KAN
HARKAT MULDS (LITTLE PERSON)... EVEN MY NAME.
THEY'RE CARVING THE NAMES OF EVERY-ONE WHO'S ATTENDING THE COUNCIL.
JA (ZSH)

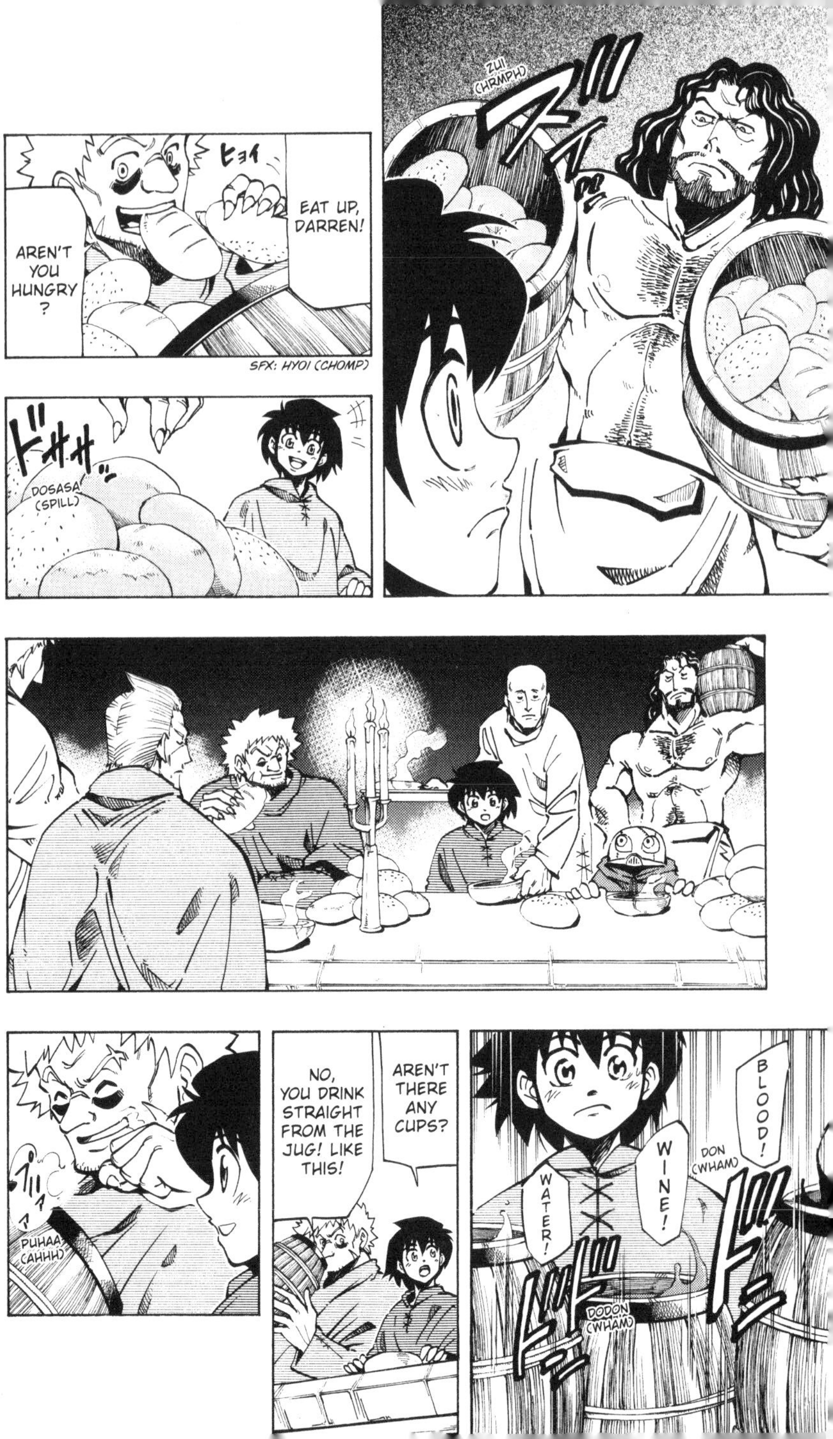
ZUI (HRMPH)
ヒョイ
EAT UP, DARREN!
AREN'T YOU HUNGRY?
SFX: HYOI (CHOMP)
DOSASA (SPILL)
BLOOD!
WINE!
WATER!
DON (WHAM)
DODON (WHAM)
AREN'T THERE ANY CUPS?
NO, YOU DRINK STRAIGHT FROM THE JUG! LIKE THIS!
PUHAA (AHHH)

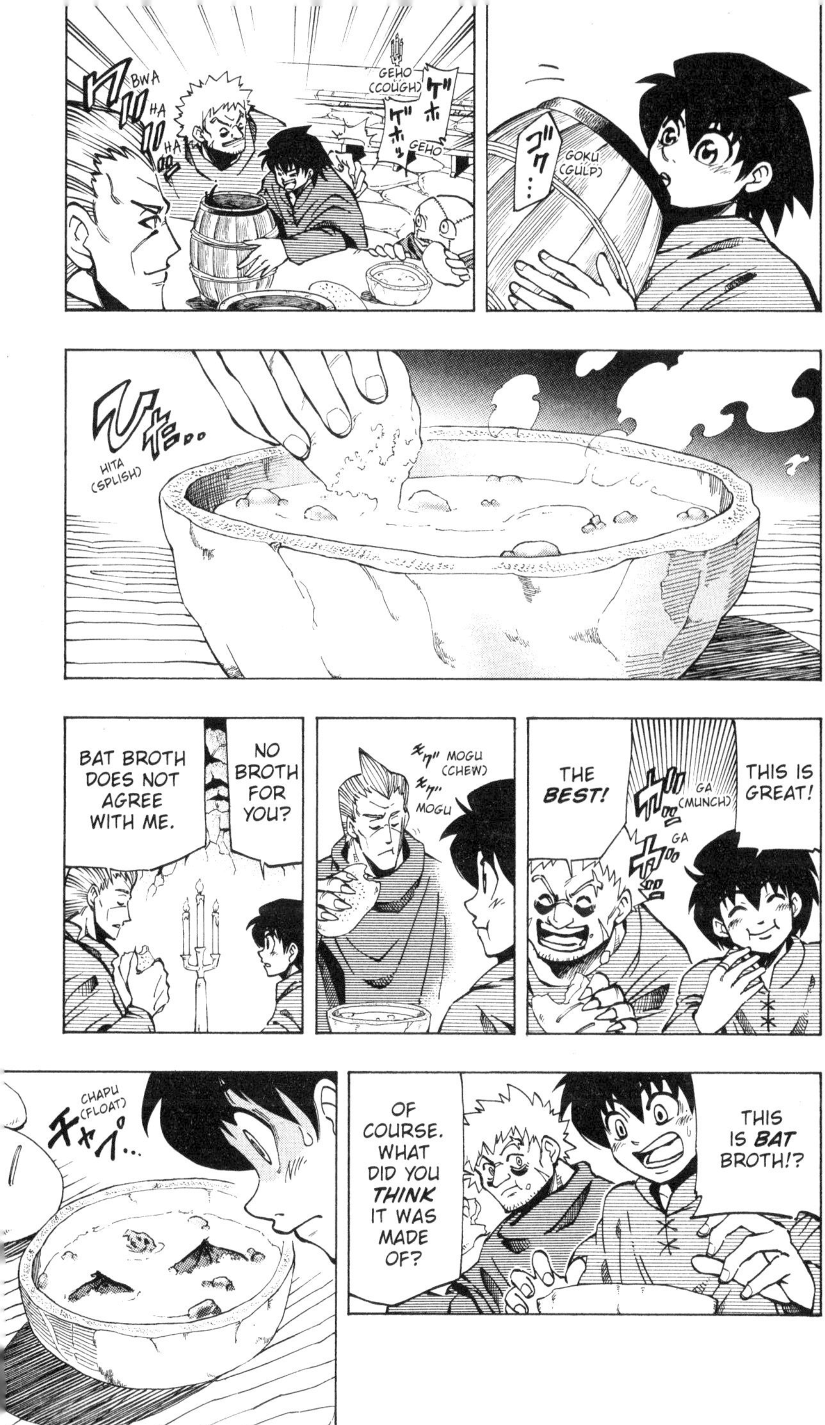
ゴク…
GOKU (GULP)
ゲホ
GEHO (COUGH)
ゲホッ
GEHO
BWA HA HA
HITA (SPLISH)
THIS IS GREAT!
GA (MUNCH)
GA
THE BEST!
MOGU (CHEW)
MOGU
NO BROTH FOR YOU?
BAT BROTH DOES NOT AGREE WITH ME.
THIS IS BAT BROTH!?
OF COURSE. WHAT DID YOU THINK IT WAS MADE OF?
CHAPU (FLOAT)
チャプ…

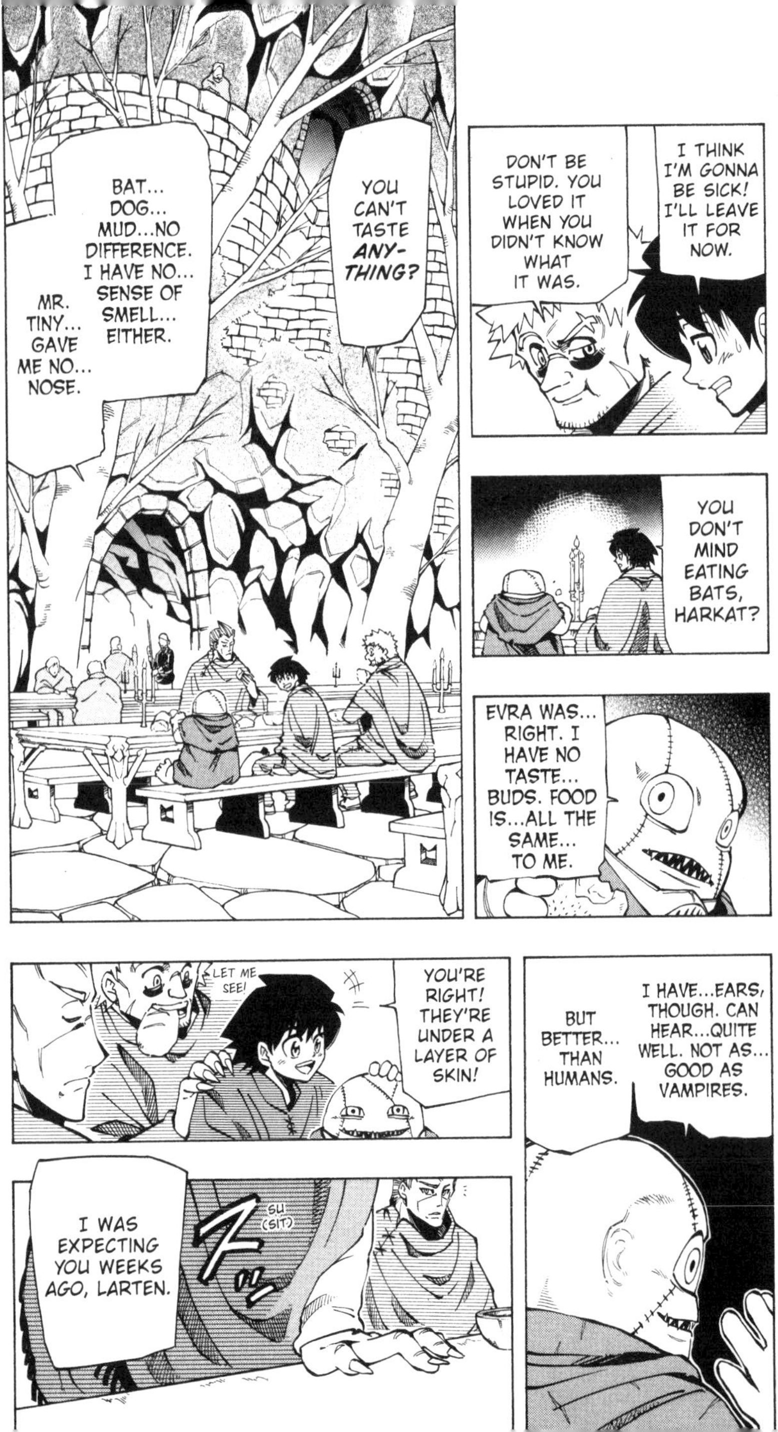
I THINK I'M GONNA BE SICK! I'LL LEAVE IT FOR NOW.
DON'T BE STUPID. YOU LOVED IT WHEN YOU DIDN'T KNOW WHAT IT WAS.
YOU DON'T MIND EATING BATS, HARKAT?
EVRA WAS... RIGHT. I HAVE NO TASTE... BUDS. FOOD IS...ALL THE SAME... TO ME.
YOU CAN'T TASTE *ANYTHING?*
BAT... DOG... MUD...NO DIFFERENCE. I HAVE NO... SENSE OF SMELL... EITHER.
MR. TINY... GAVE ME NO... NOSE.
I HAVE...EARS, THOUGH. CAN HEAR...QUITE WELL. NOT AS... GOOD AS VAMPIRES.
BUT BETTER... THAN HUMANS.
YOU'RE RIGHT! THEY'RE UNDER A LAYER OF SKIN!
LET ME SEE!
SU (SIT)
I WAS EXPECTING YOU WEEKS AGO, LARTEN.

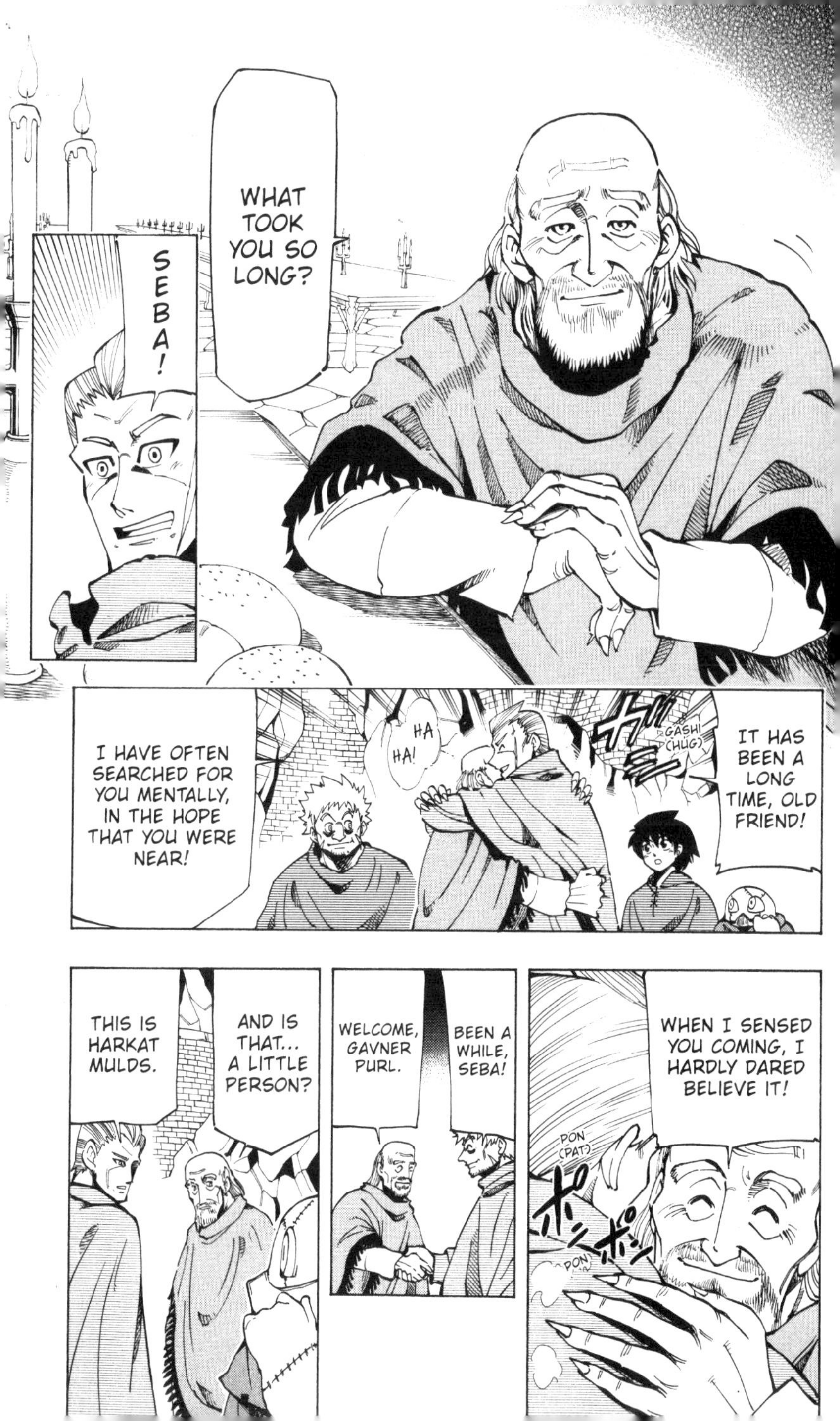
WHAT TOOK YOU SO LONG?
SEBA!
IT HAS BEEN A LONG TIME, OLD FRIEND!
GASHI (HUG)
HA HA!
I HAVE OFTEN SEARCHED FOR YOU MENTALLY, IN THE HOPE THAT YOU WERE NEAR!
WHEN I SENSED YOU COMING, I HARDLY DARED BELIEVE IT!
PON (PAT)
PON
BEEN A WHILE, SEBA!
WELCOME, GAVNER PURL.
AND IS THAT... A LITTLE PERSON?
THIS IS HARKAT MULDS.

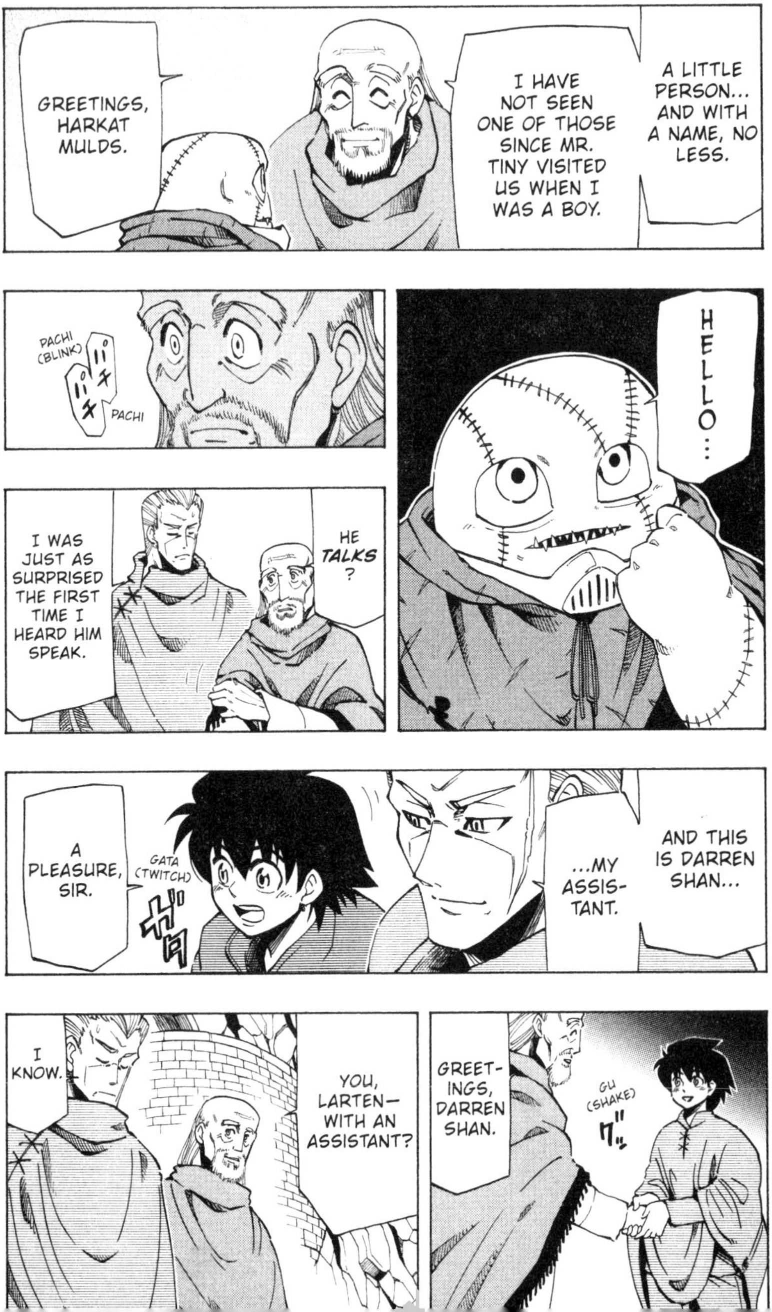
A LITTLE PERSON... AND WITH A NAME, NO LESS.
I HAVE NOT SEEN ONE OF THOSE SINCE MR. TINY VISITED US WHEN I WAS A BOY.
GREETINGS, HARKAT MULDS.
HELLO...
PACHI (BLINK)
PACHI
HE *TALKS*?
I WAS JUST AS SURPRISED THE FIRST TIME I HEARD HIM SPEAK.
AND THIS IS DARREN SHAN...
...MY ASSISTANT.
GATA (TWITCH)
A PLEASURE, SIR.
GREETINGS, DARREN SHAN.
GU (SHAKE)
YOU, LARTEN—WITH AN ASSISTANT?
I KNOW.

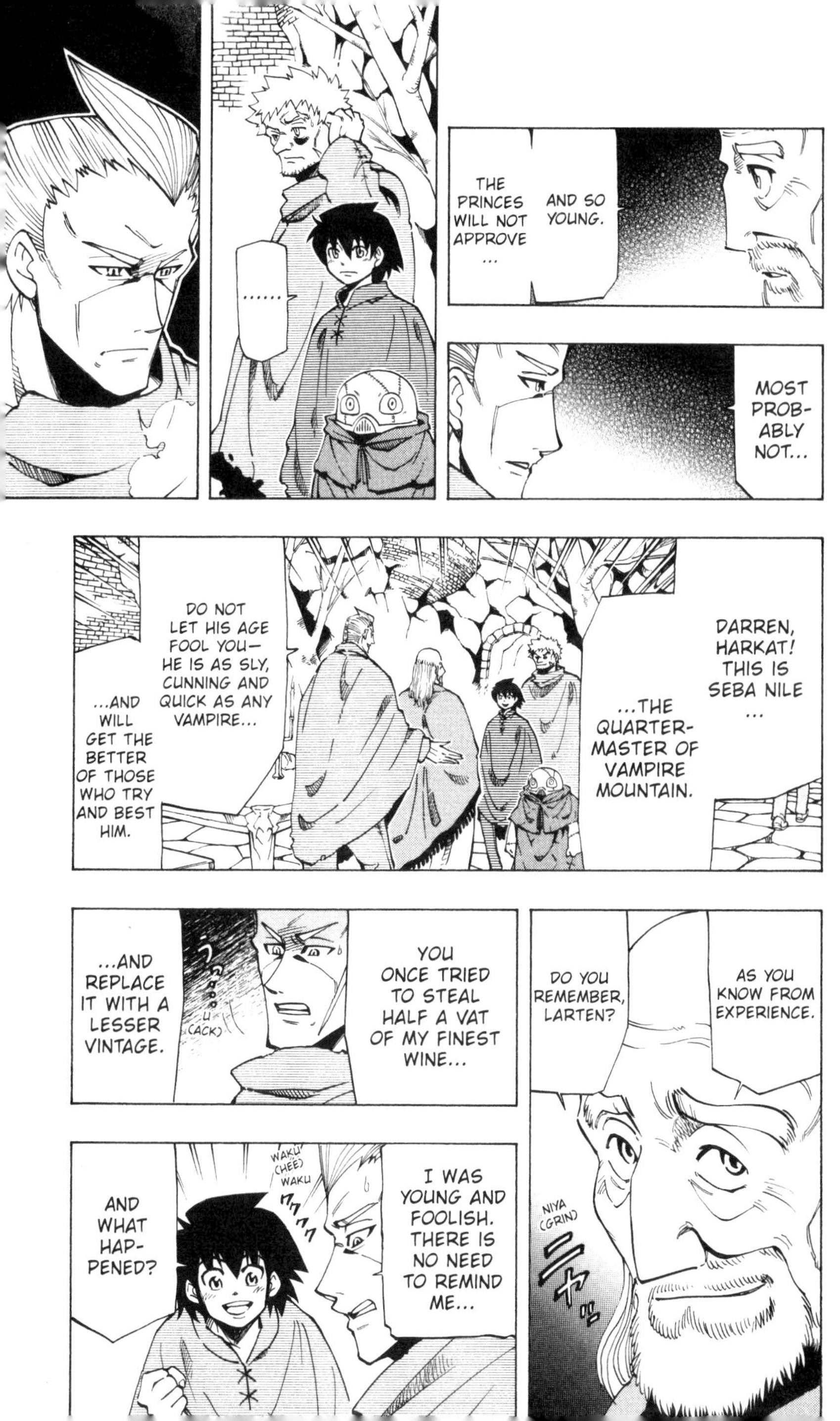
AND SO YOUNG.
THE PRINCES WILL NOT APPROVE ...
MOST PROB-ABLY NOT...
......
DARREN, HARKAT! THIS IS SEBA NILE ...
...THE QUARTER-MASTER OF VAMPIRE MOUNTAIN.
DO NOT LET HIS AGE FOOL YOU— HE IS AS SLY, CUNNING AND QUICK AS ANY VAMPIRE...
...AND WILL GET THE BETTER OF THOSE WHO TRY AND BEST HIM.
AS YOU KNOW FROM EXPERIENCE.
DO YOU REMEMBER, LARTEN?
NIYA (GRIN)
YOU ONCE TRIED TO STEAL HALF A VAT OF MY FINEST WINE...
U (ACK)
...AND REPLACE IT WITH A LESSER VINTAGE.
I WAS YOUNG AND FOOLISH. THERE IS NO NEED TO REMIND ME...
WAKU (HEE) WAKU
AND WHAT HAP-PENED?

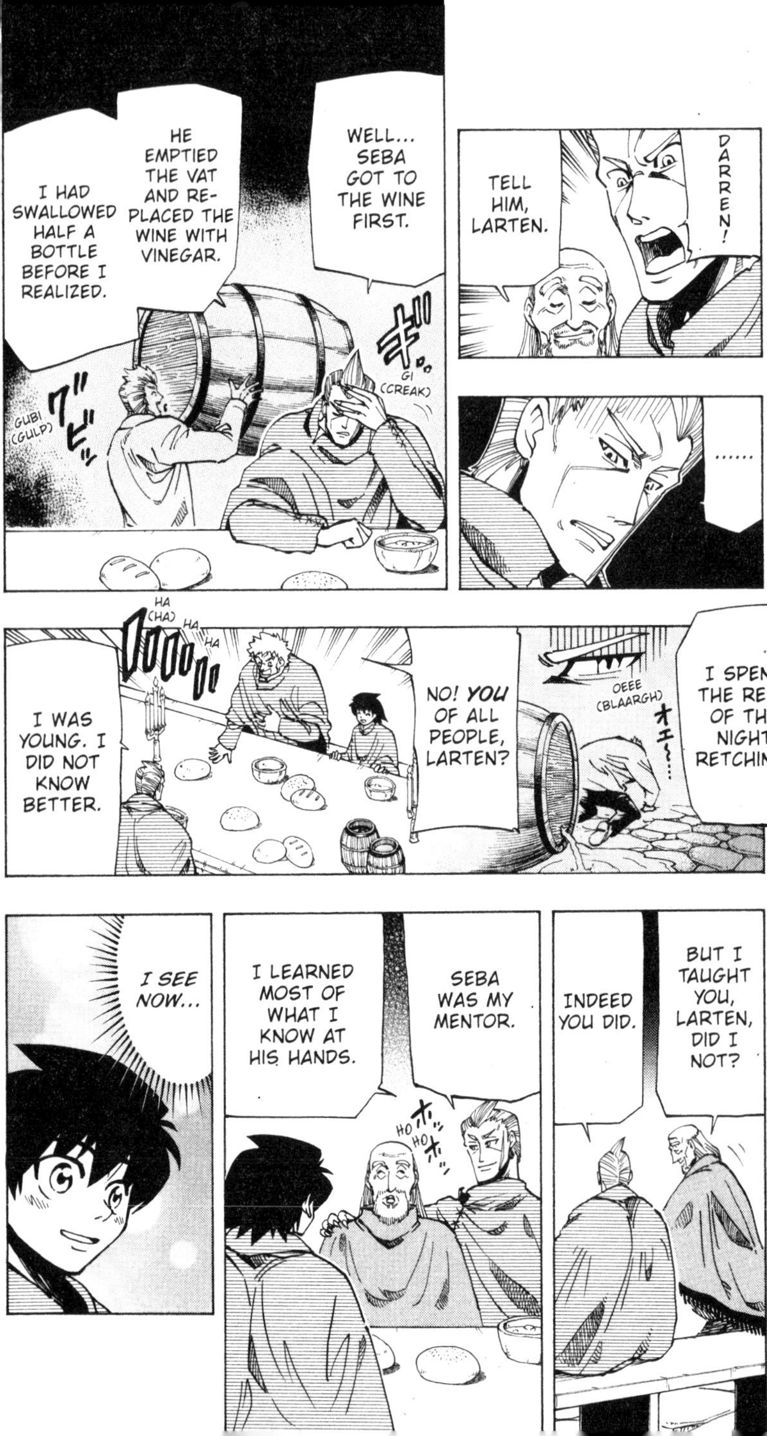
DARREN!
TELL HIM, LARTEN.
......
WELL... SEBA GOT TO THE WINE FIRST.
HE EMPTIED THE VAT AND RE-PLACED THE WINE WITH VINEGAR.
I HAD SWALLOWED HALF A BOTTLE BEFORE I REALIZED.
GI (CREAK)
GUBI (GULP)
I SPENT THE REST OF THE NIGHT RETCHING.
OEEE (BLAARGH)
NO! *YOU* OF ALL PEOPLE, LARTEN?
HA (HA) HA HA
I WAS YOUNG. I DID NOT KNOW BETTER.
BUT I TAUGHT YOU, LARTEN, DID I NOT?
INDEED YOU DID.
SEBA WAS MY MENTOR.
I LEARNED MOST OF WHAT I KNOW AT HIS HANDS.
HO HO
I SEE NOW...

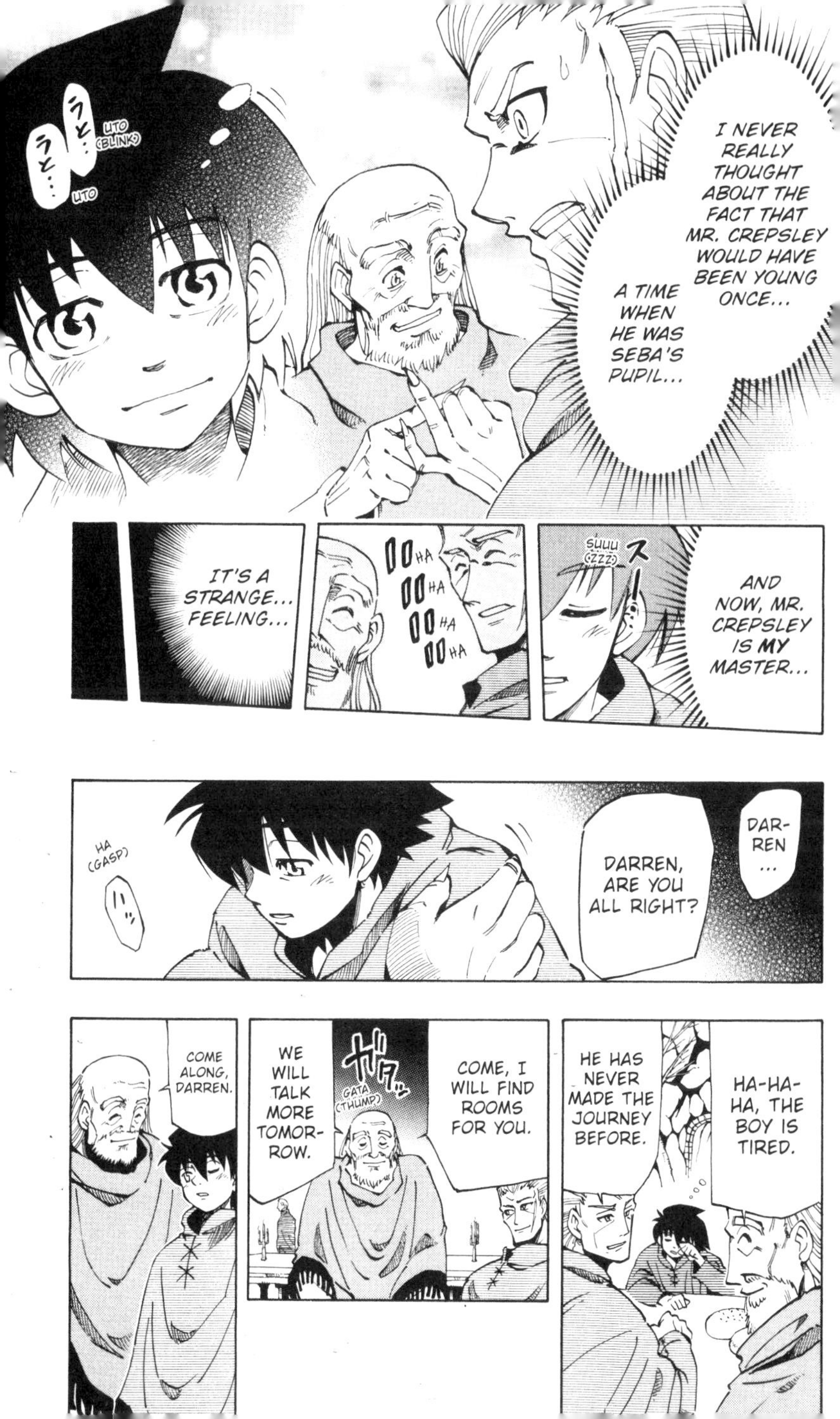
I NEVER REALLY THOUGHT ABOUT THE FACT THAT MR. CREPSLEY WOULD HAVE BEEN YOUNG ONCE...
A TIME WHEN HE WAS SEBA'S PUPIL...
ウと…
UTO (BLINK)
ウと…
UTO
AND NOW, MR. CREPSLEY IS MY MASTER...
ス
SUUU (ZZZ)
HA HA HA HA
IT'S A STRANGE... FEELING...
DAR-REN...
DARREN, ARE YOU ALL RIGHT?
HA (GASP)
HA-HA-HA, THE BOY IS TIRED.
HE HAS NEVER MADE THE JOURNEY BEFORE.
COME, I WILL FIND ROOMS FOR YOU.
ガタッ
GATA (THUMP)
WE WILL TALK MORE TOMORROW.
COME ALONG, DARREN.

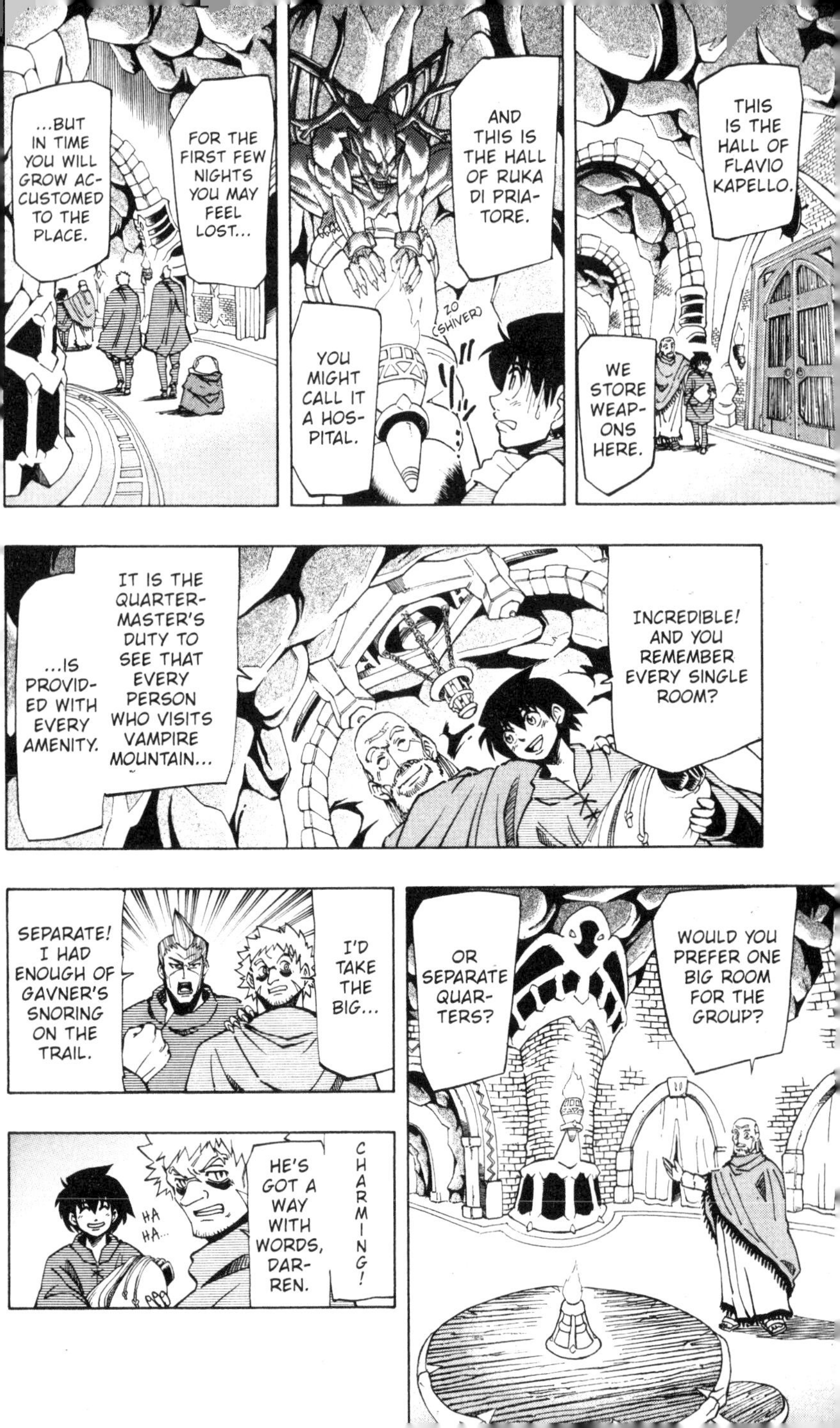
THIS IS THE HALL OF FLAVIO KAPELLO.
WE STORE WEAPONS HERE.
AND THIS IS THE HALL OF RUKA DI PRIATORE.
ZO (SHIVER)
YOU MIGHT CALL IT A HOSPITAL.
FOR THE FIRST FEW NIGHTS YOU MAY FEEL LOST...
...BUT IN TIME YOU WILL GROW ACCUSTOMED TO THE PLACE.
INCREDIBLE! AND YOU REMEMBER EVERY SINGLE ROOM?
IT IS THE QUARTERMASTER'S DUTY TO SEE THAT EVERY PERSON WHO VISITS VAMPIRE MOUNTAIN...
...IS PROVIDED WITH EVERY AMENITY.
WOULD YOU PREFER ONE BIG ROOM FOR THE GROUP?
OR SEPARATE QUARTERS?
I'D TAKE THE BIG...
SEPARATE! I HAD ENOUGH OF GAVNER'S SNORING ON THE TRAIL.
CHARMING!
HE'S GOT A WAY WITH WORDS, DARREN.
HA HA...

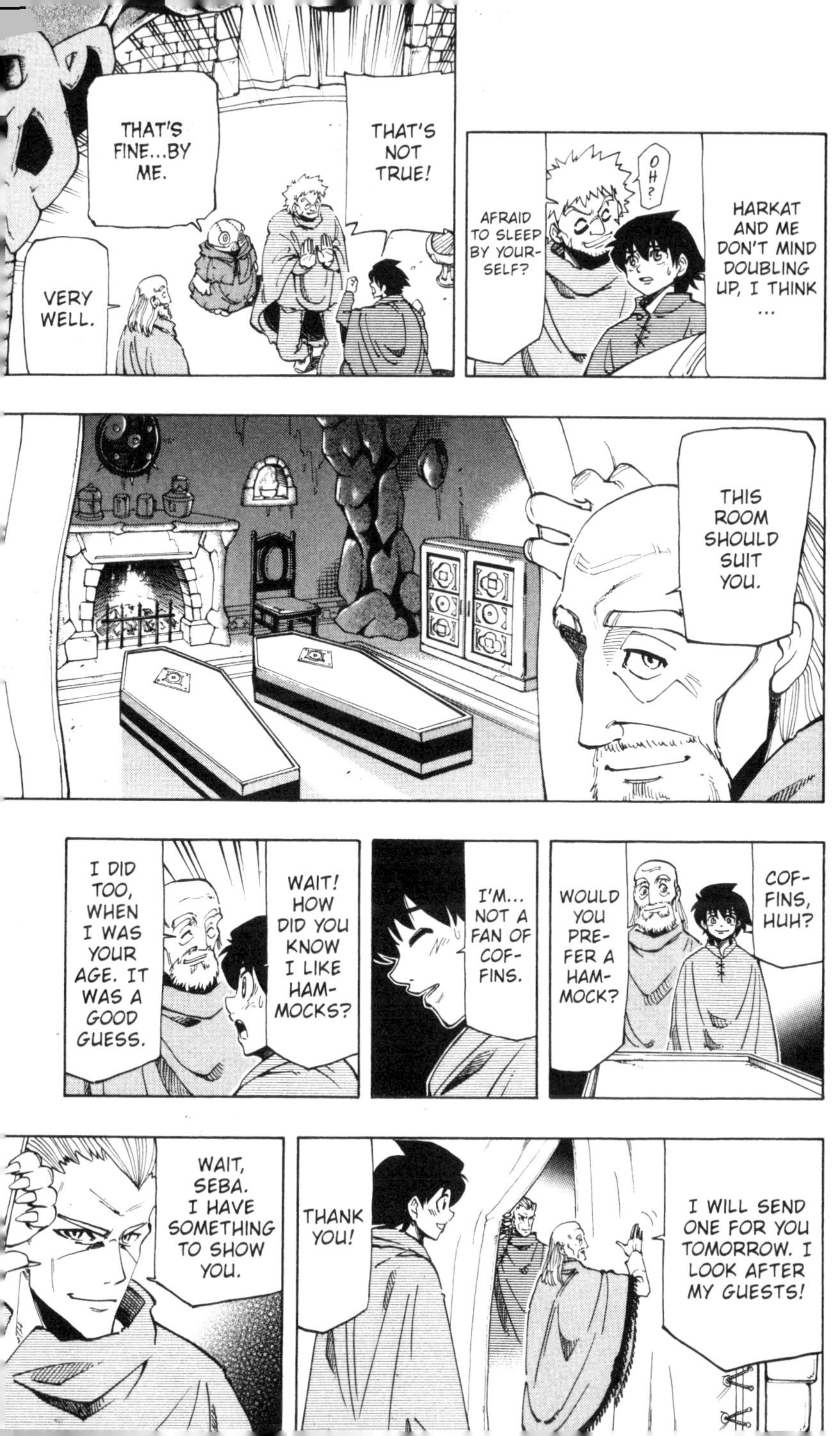
HARKAT AND ME DON'T MIND DOUBLING UP, I THINK ...
OH?
AFRAID TO SLEEP BY YOURSELF?
THAT'S NOT TRUE!
THAT'S FINE...BY ME.
VERY WELL.
THIS ROOM SHOULD SUIT YOU.
COFFINS, HUH?
WOULD YOU PREFER A HAMMOCK?
I'M... NOT A FAN OF COFFINS.
WAIT! HOW DID YOU KNOW I LIKE HAMMOCKS?
I DID TOO, WHEN I WAS YOUR AGE. IT WAS A GOOD GUESS.
I WILL SEND ONE FOR YOU TOMORROW. I LOOK AFTER MY GUESTS!
THANK YOU!
WAIT, SEBA. I HAVE SOMETHING TO SHOW YOU.

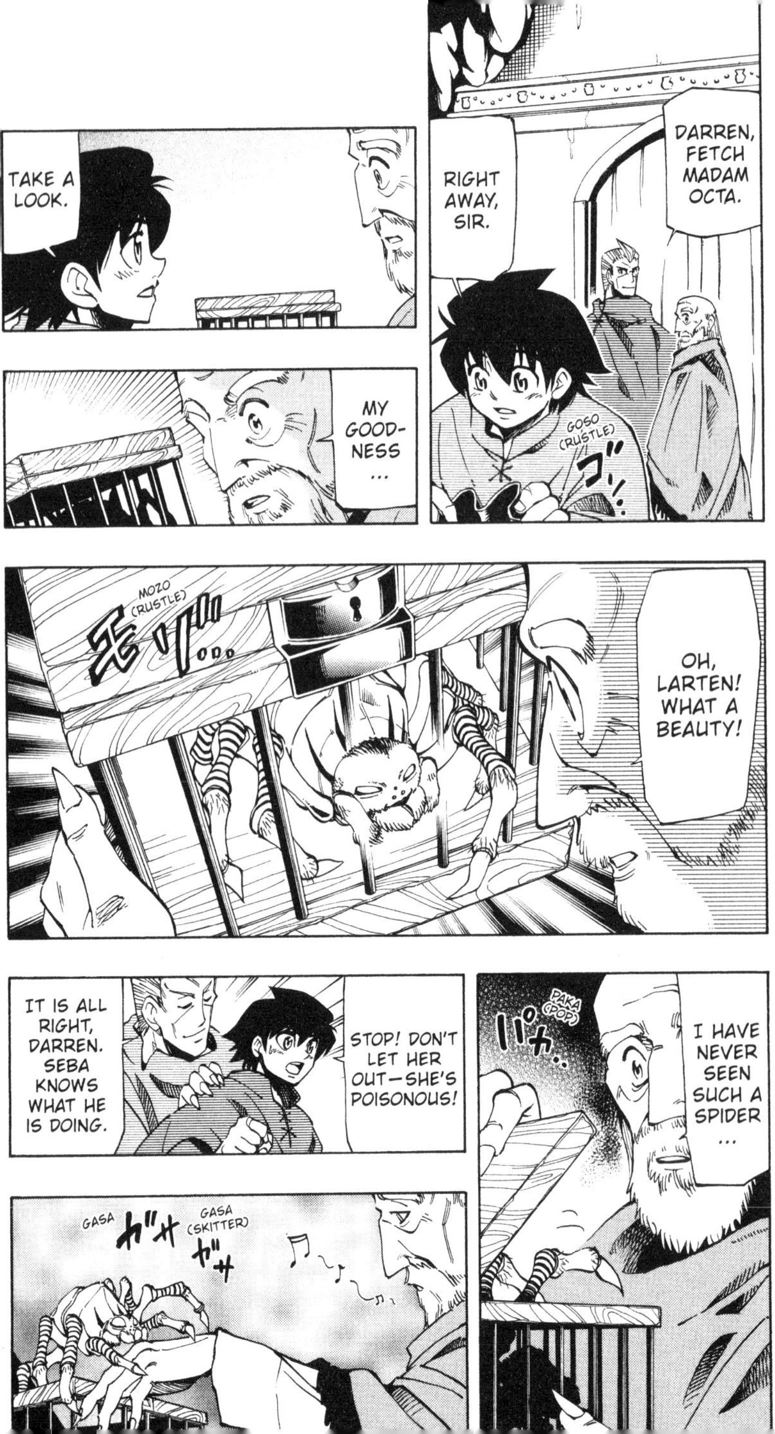
DARREN, FETCH MADAM OCTA.
RIGHT AWAY, SIR.
GOSO (RUSTLE)
TAKE A LOOK.
MY GOODNESS ...
OH, LARTEN! WHAT A BEAUTY!
MOZO (RUSTLE)
I HAVE NEVER SEEN SUCH A SPIDER ...
PAKA (POP)
STOP! DON'T LET HER OUT—SHE'S POISONOUS!
IT IS ALL RIGHT, DARREN. SEBA KNOWS WHAT HE IS DOING.
GASA
GASA (SKITTER)

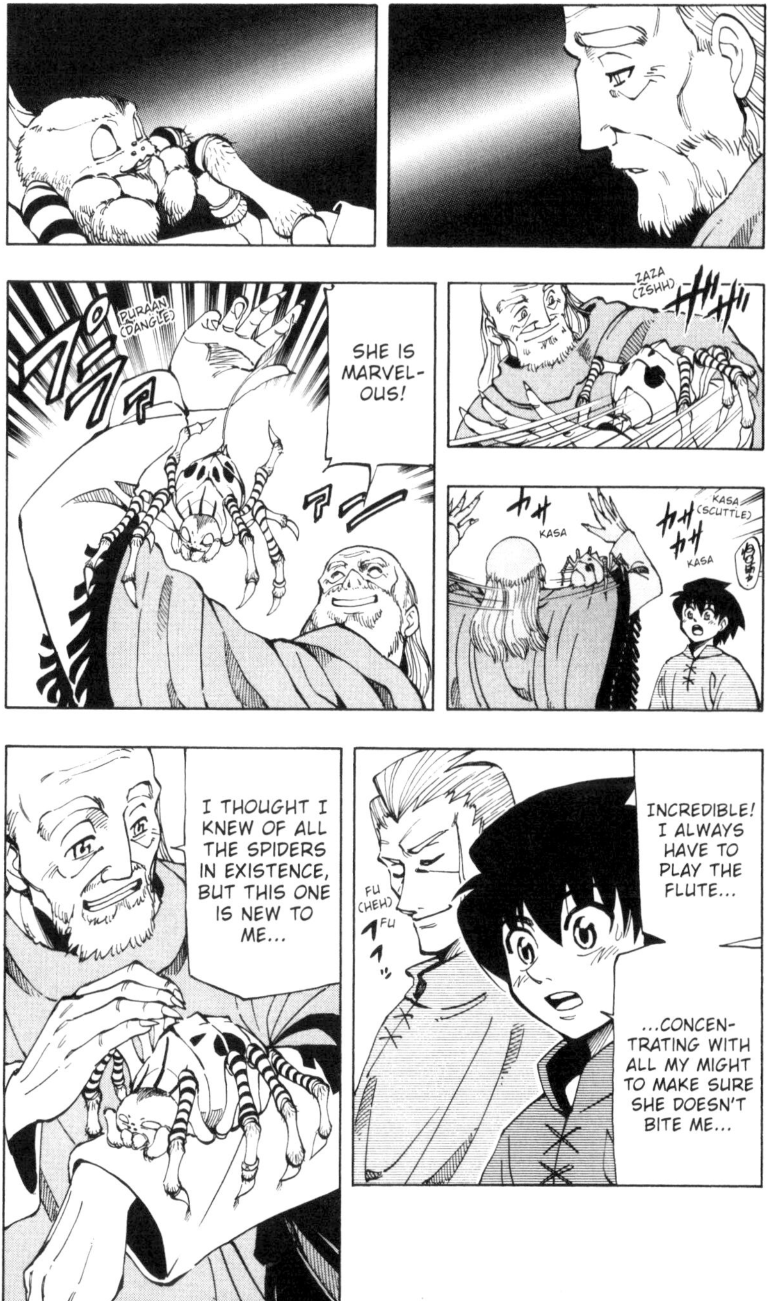
ZAZA (ZSHH)
KASA (SCUTTLE)
KASA
KASA
PURAAN (DANGLE)
SHE IS MARVEL-OUS!
INCREDIBLE! I ALWAYS HAVE TO PLAY THE FLUTE...
...CONCEN-TRATING WITH ALL MY MIGHT TO MAKE SURE SHE DOESN'T BITE ME...
FU (HEH) FU
I THOUGHT I KNEW OF ALL THE SPIDERS IN EXISTENCE, BUT THIS ONE IS NEW TO ME...

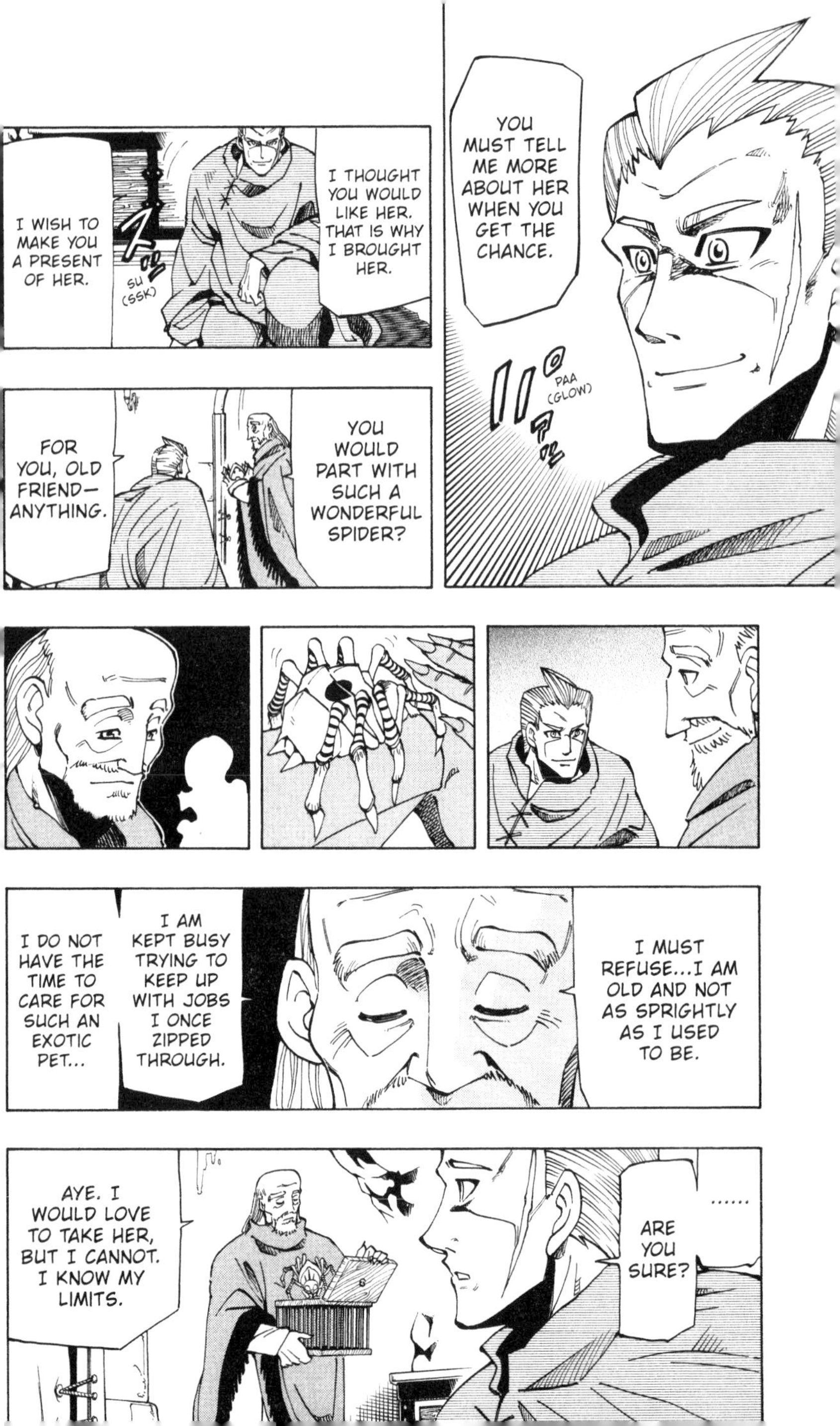

YOU MUST TELL ME MORE ABOUT HER WHEN YOU GET THE CHANCE.
PAA (GLOW)
I THOUGHT YOU WOULD LIKE HER. THAT IS WHY I BROUGHT HER.
SU (SSK)
I WISH TO MAKE YOU A PRESENT OF HER.
YOU WOULD PART WITH SUCH A WONDERFUL SPIDER?
FOR YOU, OLD FRIEND—ANYTHING.
I MUST REFUSE...I AM OLD AND NOT AS SPRIGHTLY AS I USED TO BE.
I AM KEPT BUSY TRYING TO KEEP UP WITH JOBS I ONCE ZIPPED THROUGH.
I DO NOT HAVE THE TIME TO CARE FOR SUCH AN EXOTIC PET...
......
ARE YOU SURE?
AYE. I WOULD LOVE TO TAKE HER, BUT I CANNOT. I KNOW MY LIMITS.

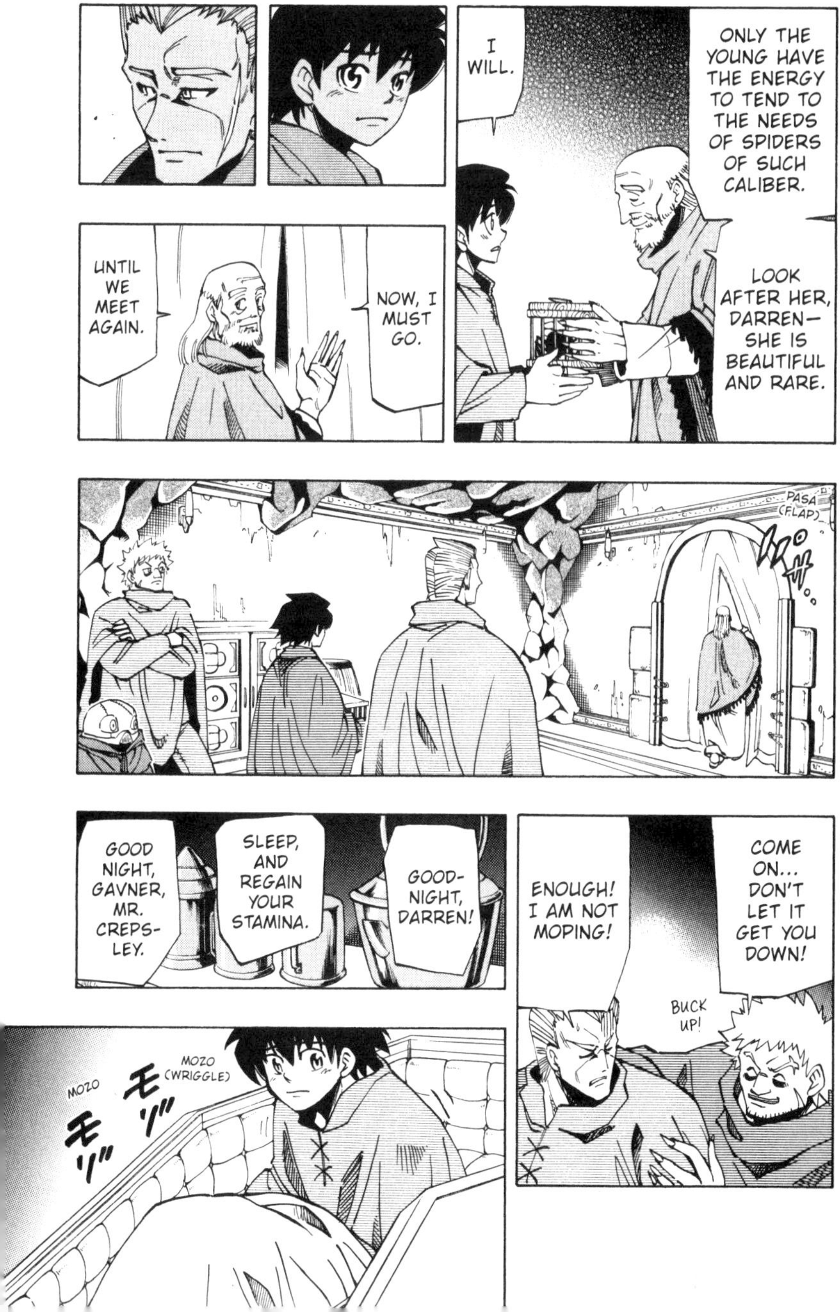
ONLY THE YOUNG HAVE THE ENERGY TO TEND TO THE NEEDS OF SPIDERS OF SUCH CALIBER.
LOOK AFTER HER, DARREN— SHE IS BEAUTIFUL AND RARE.
I WILL.
NOW, I MUST GO.
UNTIL WE MEET AGAIN.
PASA (FLAP)
COME ON... DON'T LET IT GET YOU DOWN!
ENOUGH! I AM NOT MOPING!
BUCK UP!
GOOD-NIGHT, DARREN!
SLEEP, AND REGAIN YOUR STAMINA.
GOOD NIGHT, GAVNER, MR. CREPS-LEY.
MOZO (WRIGGLE)
MOZO

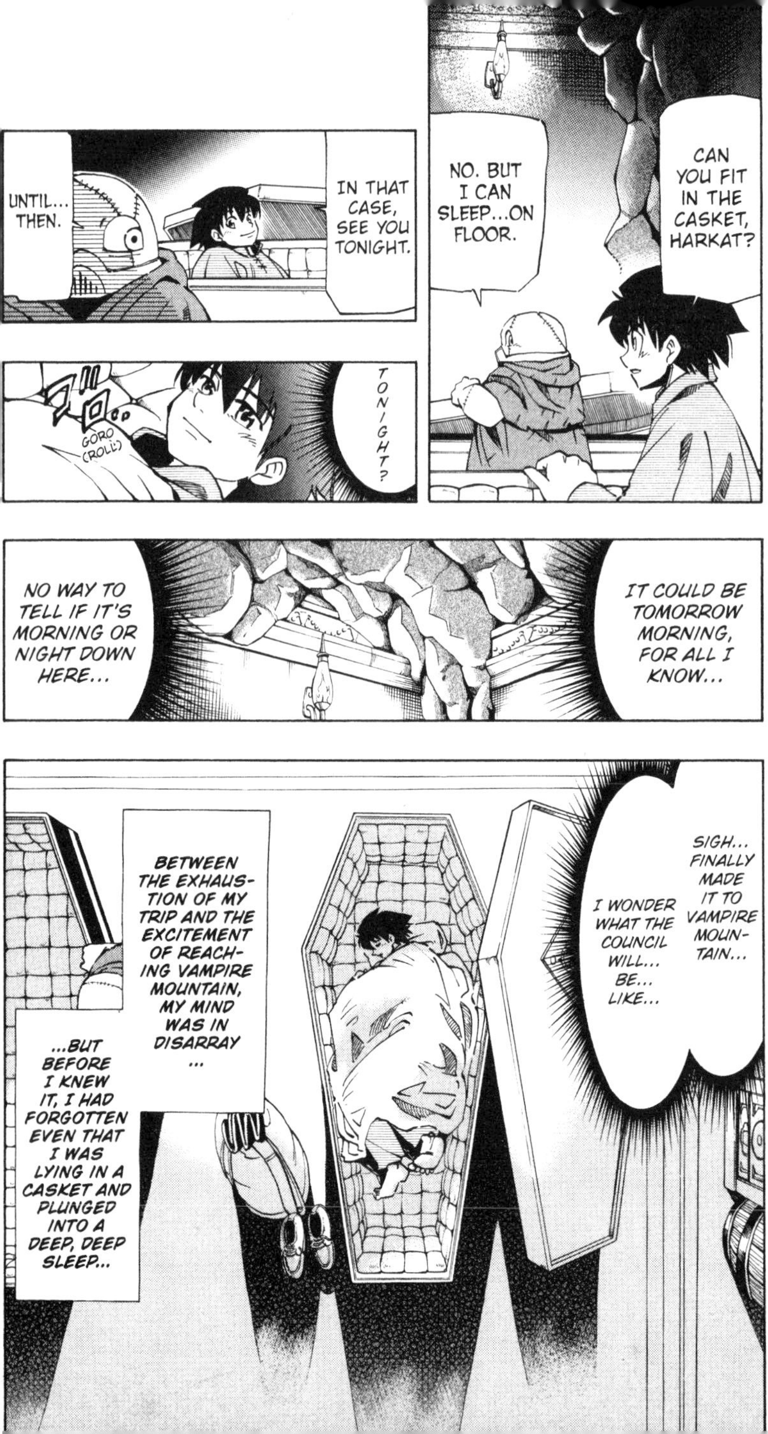
CAN YOU FIT IN THE CASKET, HARKAT?
NO. BUT I CAN SLEEP...ON FLOOR.
IN THAT CASE, SEE YOU TONIGHT.
UNTIL... THEN.
TONIGHT?
GORO (ROLL)
IT COULD BE TOMORROW MORNING, FOR ALL I KNOW...
NO WAY TO TELL IF IT'S MORNING OR NIGHT DOWN HERE...
SIGH... FINALLY MADE IT TO VAMPIRE MOUN-TAIN...
I WONDER WHAT THE COUNCIL WILL... BE... LIKE...
BETWEEN THE EXHAUS-TION OF MY TRIP AND THE EXCITEMENT OF REACH-ING VAMPIRE MOUNTAIN, MY MIND WAS IN DISARRAY ...
...BUT BEFORE I KNEW IT, I HAD FORGOTTEN EVEN THAT I WAS LYING IN A CASKET AND PLUNGED INTO A DEEP, DEEP SLEEP...

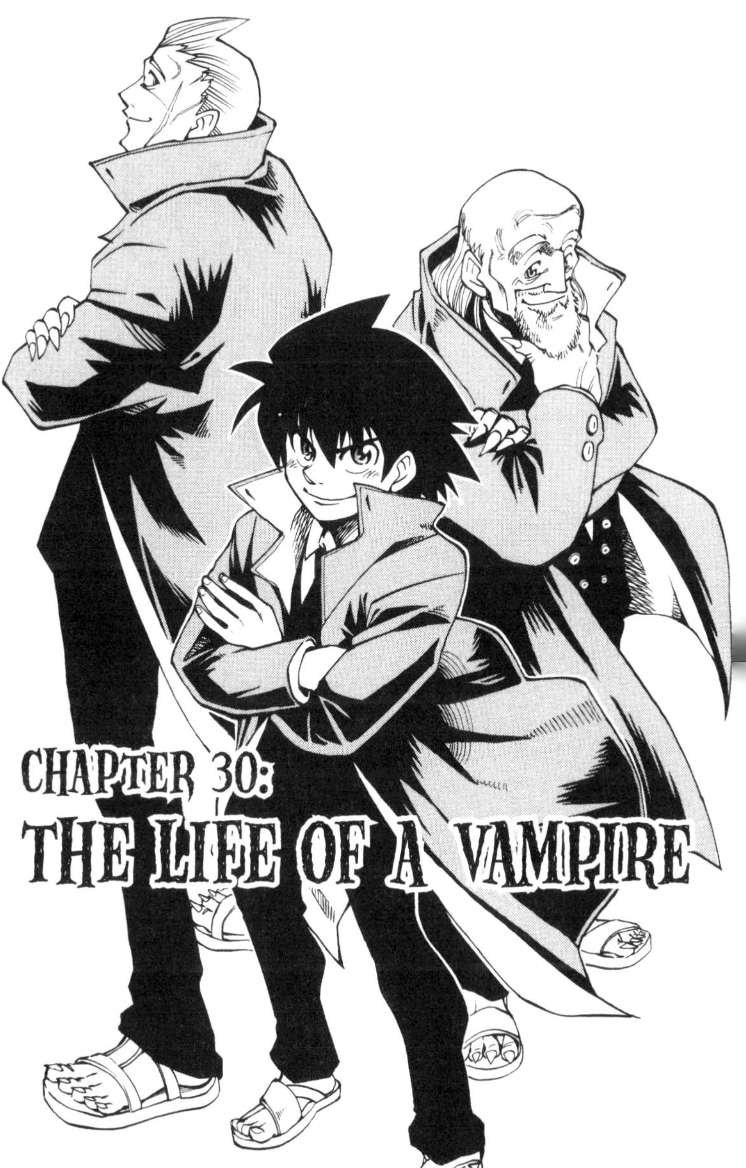
CHAPTER 30:
THE LIFE OF A VAMPIRE

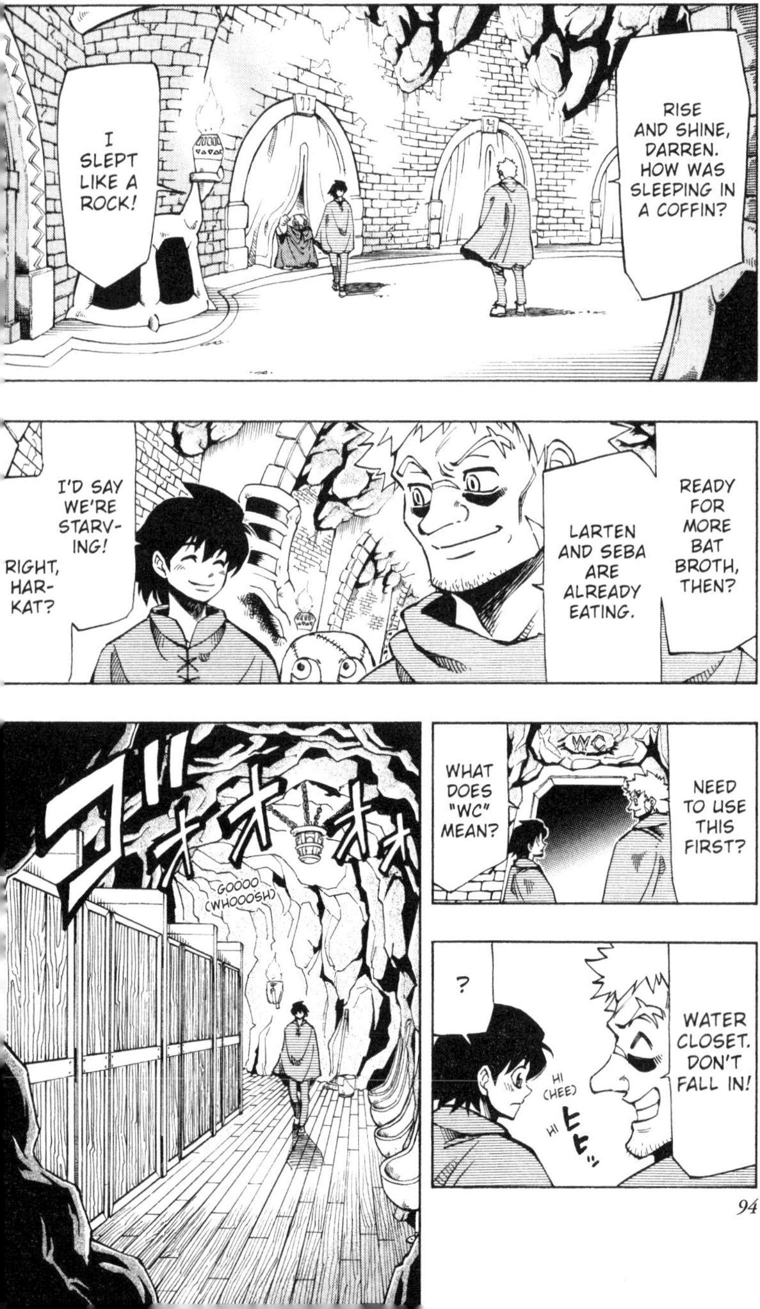

RISE AND SHINE, DARREN. HOW WAS SLEEPING IN A COFFIN?
I SLEPT LIKE A ROCK!
READY FOR MORE BAT BROTH, THEN?
LARTEN AND SEBA ARE ALREADY EATING.
I'D SAY WE'RE STARV-ING!
RIGHT, HAR-KAT?
NEED TO USE THIS FIRST?
WC
WHAT DOES "WC" MEAN?
WATER CLOSET. DON'T FALL IN!
?
HI HI (HEE)
GOOOO (WHOOOSH)

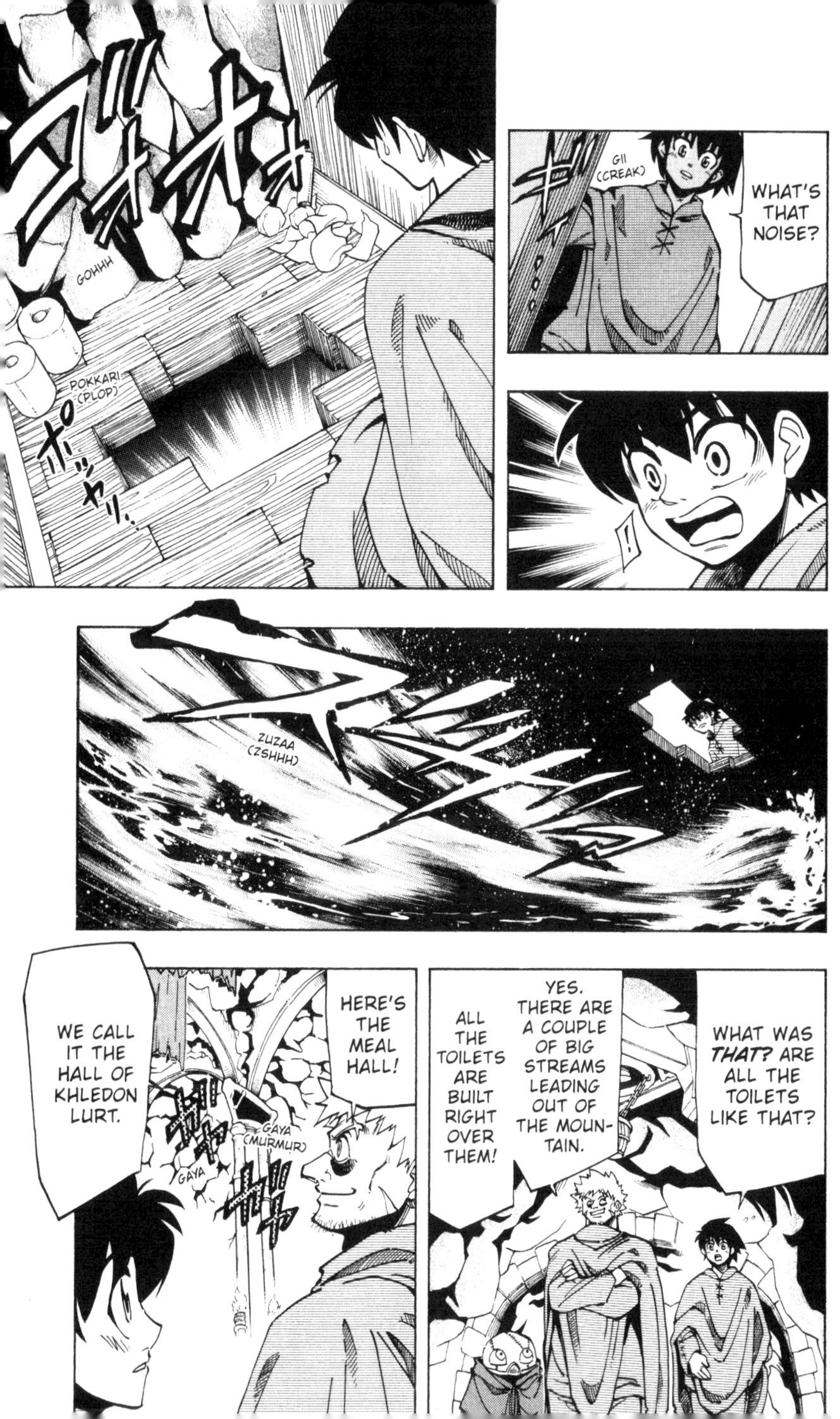
GII (CREAK)
WHAT'S THAT NOISE?
!
GOHHH
POKKARI (PLOP)
ZUZAA (ZSHHH)
WHAT WAS *THAT?* ARE ALL THE TOILETS LIKE THAT?
YES. THERE ARE A COUPLE OF BIG STREAMS LEADING OUT OF THE MOUN-TAIN.
ALL THE TOILETS ARE BUILT RIGHT OVER THEM!
HERE'S THE MEAL HALL!
GAYA (MURMUR)
GAYA
WE CALL IT THE HALL OF KHLEDON LURT.

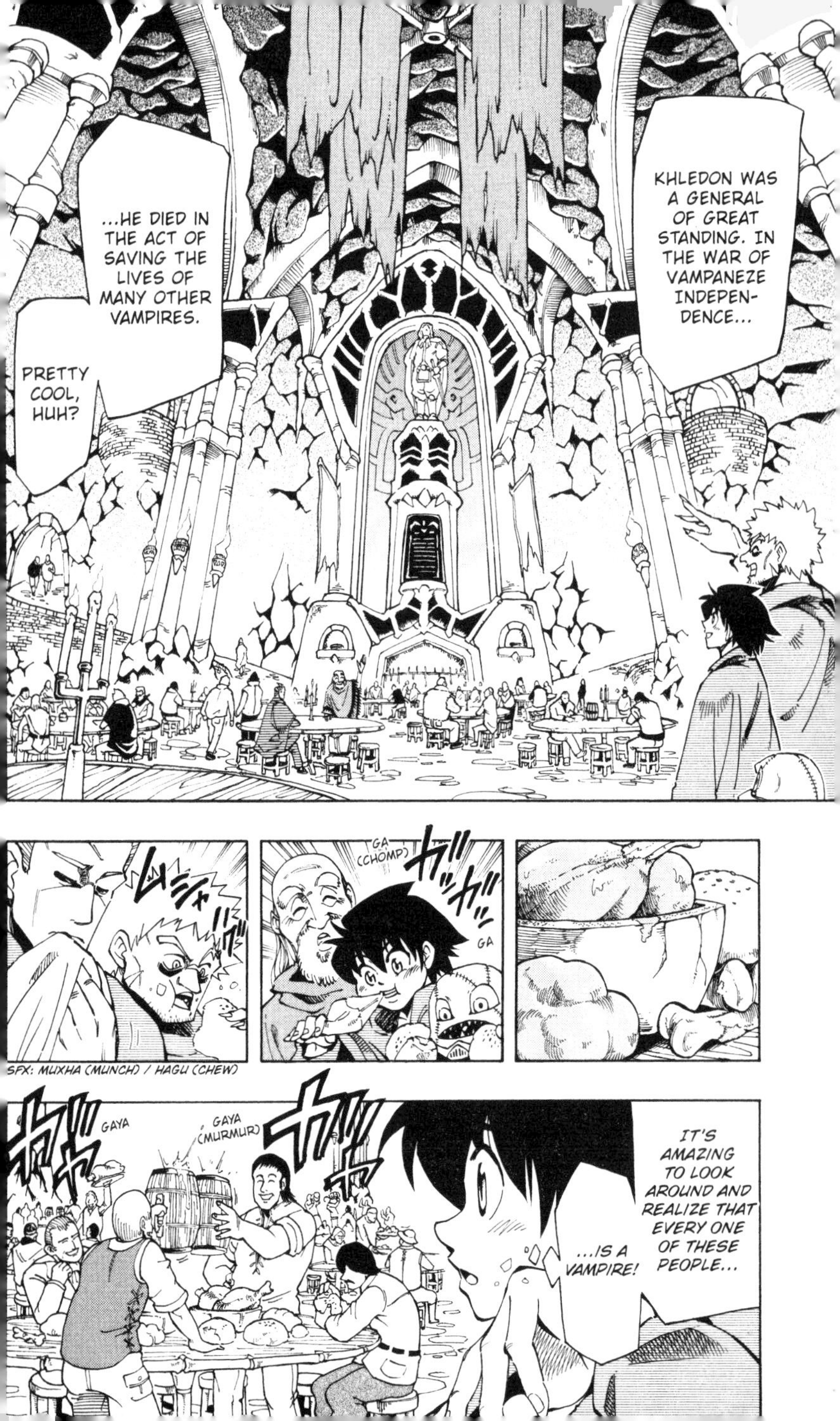
KHLEDON WAS A GENERAL OF GREAT STANDING. IN THE WAR OF VAMPANEZE INDEPEN-DENCE...
...HE DIED IN THE ACT OF SAVING THE LIVES OF MANY OTHER VAMPIRES.
PRETTY COOL, HUH?
GA (CHOMP)
GA
SFX: MUXHA (MUNCH) / HAGU (CHEW)
IT'S AMAZING TO LOOK AROUND AND REALIZE THAT EVERY ONE OF THESE PEOPLE...
...IS A VAMPIRE!
GAYA (MURMUR)
GAYA

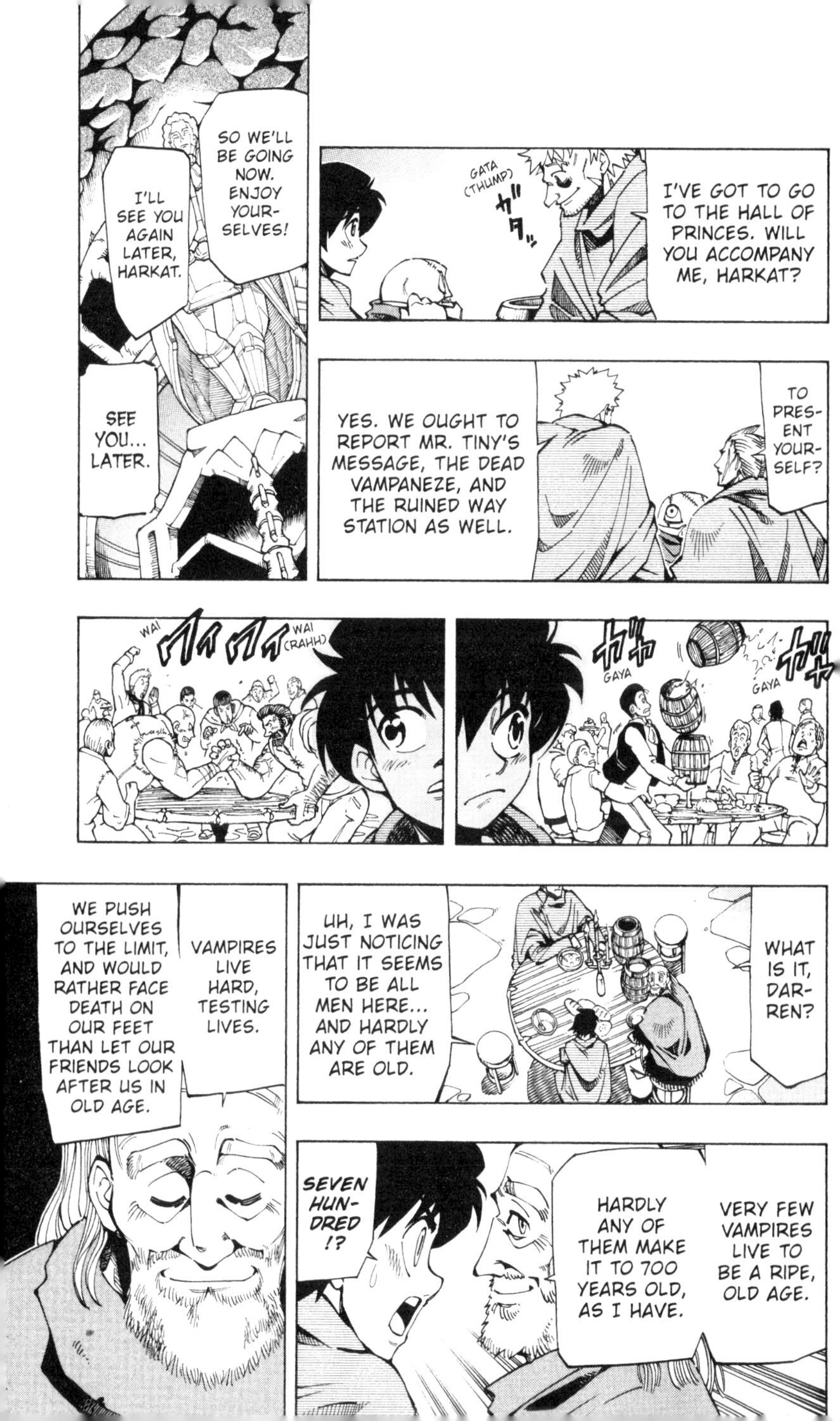
I'VE GOT TO GO TO THE HALL OF PRINCES. WILL YOU ACCOMPANY ME, HARKAT?
GATA (THUMP)
TO PRESENT YOURSELF?
YES. WE OUGHT TO REPORT MR. TINY'S MESSAGE, THE DEAD VAMPANEZE, AND THE RUINED WAY STATION AS WELL.
SO WE'LL BE GOING NOW. ENJOY YOURSELVES!
I'LL SEE YOU AGAIN LATER, HARKAT.
SEE YOU... LATER.
GAYA
GAYA
WAI
WAI (RAHH)
WHAT IS IT, DARREN?
UH, I WAS JUST NOTICING THAT IT SEEMS TO BE ALL MEN HERE... AND HARDLY ANY OF THEM ARE OLD.
VERY FEW VAMPIRES LIVE TO BE A RIPE, OLD AGE.
HARDLY ANY OF THEM MAKE IT TO 700 YEARS OLD, AS I HAVE.
SEVEN HUNDRED!?
VAMPIRES LIVE HARD, TESTING LIVES.
WE PUSH OURSELVES TO THE LIMIT, AND WOULD RATHER FACE DEATH ON OUR FEET THAN LET OUR FRIENDS LOOK AFTER US IN OLD AGE.

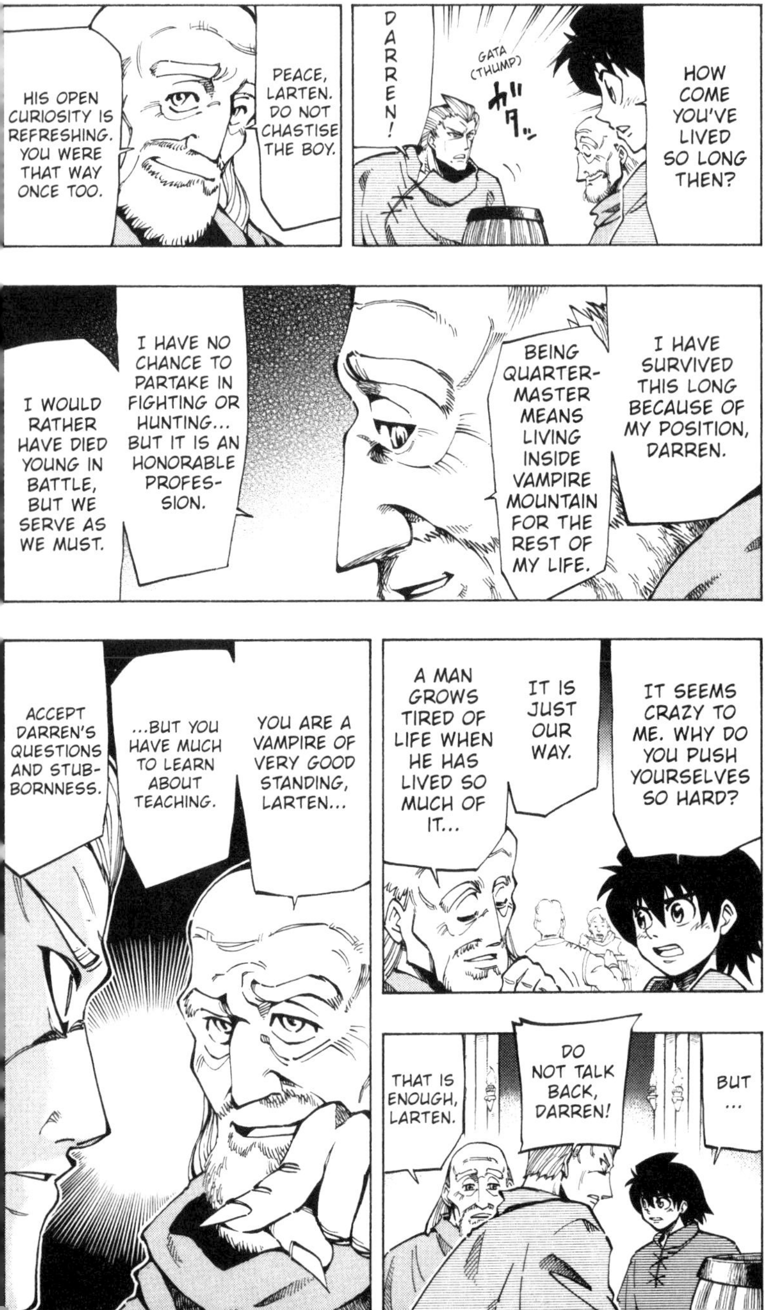
HOW COME YOU'VE LIVED SO LONG THEN?
GATA (THUMP)
ガタッ
DARREN!
PEACE, LARTEN. DO NOT CHASTISE THE BOY.
HIS OPEN CURIOSITY IS REFRESHING. YOU WERE THAT WAY ONCE TOO.
I HAVE SURVIVED THIS LONG BECAUSE OF MY POSITION, DARREN.
BEING QUARTER-MASTER MEANS LIVING INSIDE VAMPIRE MOUNTAIN FOR THE REST OF MY LIFE.
I HAVE NO CHANCE TO PARTAKE IN FIGHTING OR HUNTING... BUT IT IS AN HONORABLE PROFESSION.
I WOULD RATHER HAVE DIED YOUNG IN BATTLE, BUT WE SERVE AS WE MUST.
IT SEEMS CRAZY TO ME. WHY DO YOU PUSH YOURSELVES SO HARD?
IT IS JUST OUR WAY.
A MAN GROWS TIRED OF LIFE WHEN HE HAS LIVED SO MUCH OF IT...
BUT...
DO NOT TALK BACK, DARREN!
THAT IS ENOUGH, LARTEN.
YOU ARE A VAMPIRE OF VERY GOOD STANDING, LARTEN...
...BUT YOU HAVE MUCH TO LEARN ABOUT TEACHING.
ACCEPT DARREN'S QUESTIONS AND STUBBORNNESS.

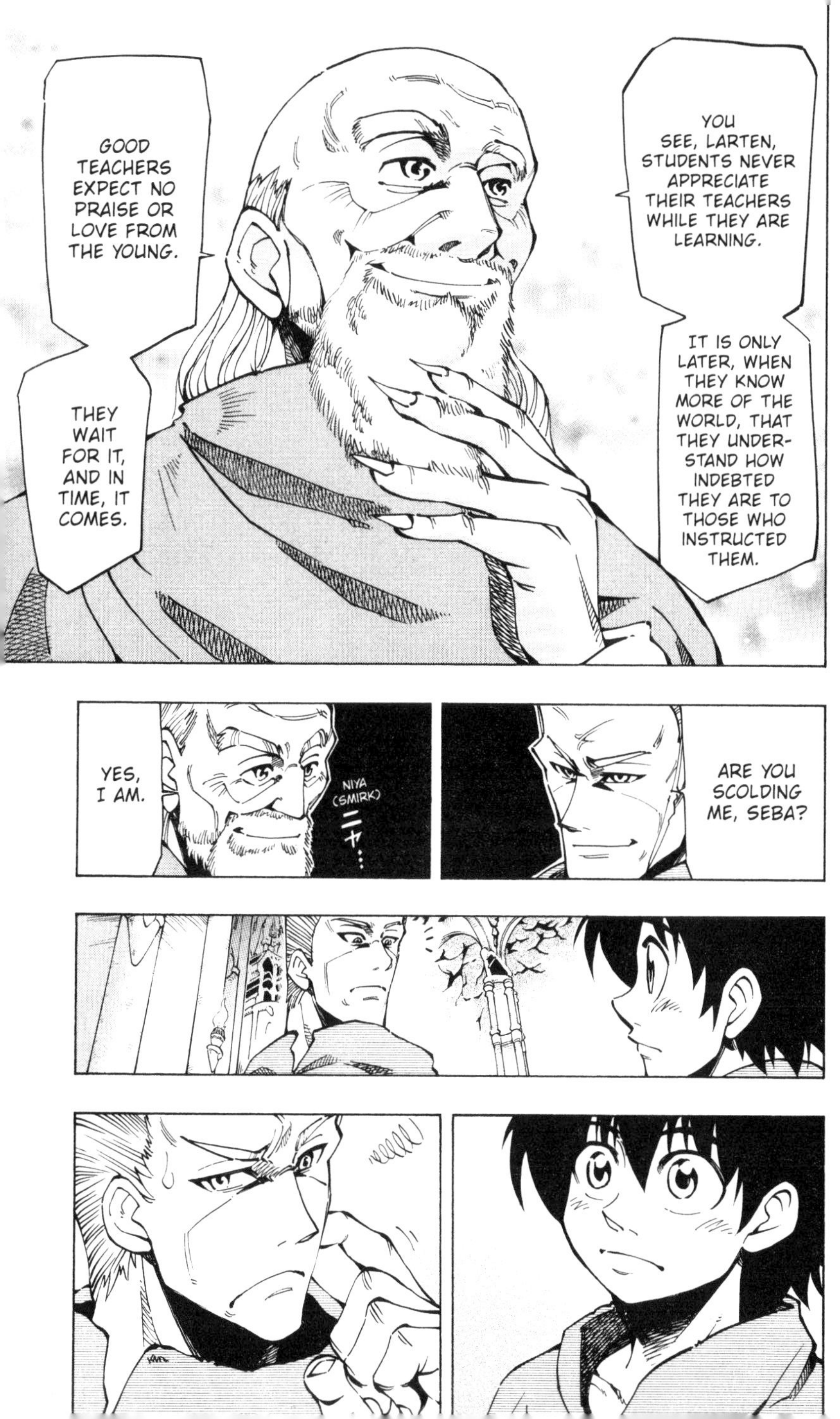
YOU SEE, LARTEN, STUDENTS NEVER APPRECIATE THEIR TEACHERS WHILE THEY ARE LEARNING.
IT IS ONLY LATER, WHEN THEY KNOW MORE OF THE WORLD, THAT THEY UNDER-STAND HOW INDEBTED THEY ARE TO THOSE WHO INSTRUCTED THEM.
GOOD TEACHERS EXPECT NO PRAISE OR LOVE FROM THE YOUNG.
THEY WAIT FOR IT, AND IN TIME, IT COMES.
ARE YOU SCOLDING ME, SEBA?
NIYA (SMIRK)
ニヤ…
YES, I AM.

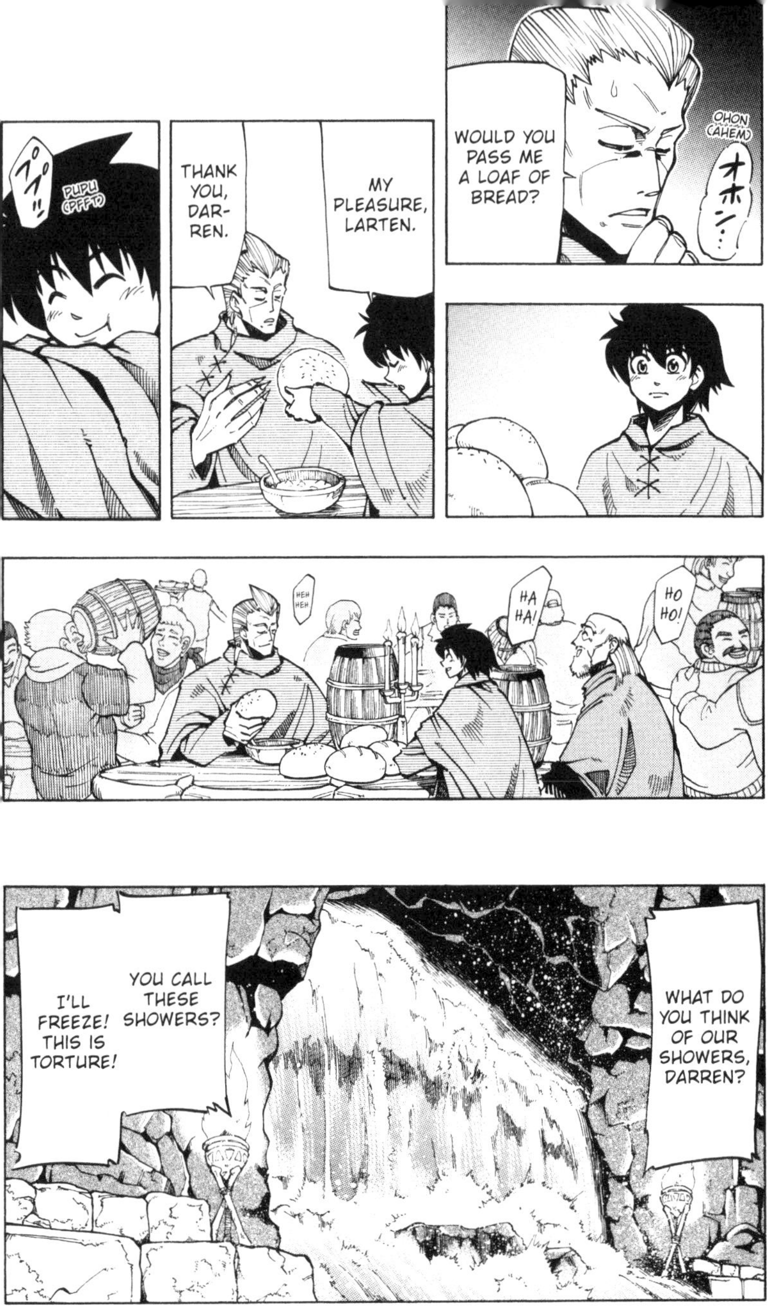
WOULD YOU PASS ME A LOAF OF BREAD?
OHON (AHEM)
オホン…
THANK YOU, DARREN.
MY PLEASURE, LARTEN.
ププ!!
PUPU (PFFT)
HO HO!
HA HA!
HEH HEH
WHAT DO YOU THINK OF OUR SHOWERS, DARREN?
YOU CALL THESE SHOWERS?
I'LL FREEZE! THIS IS TORTURE!

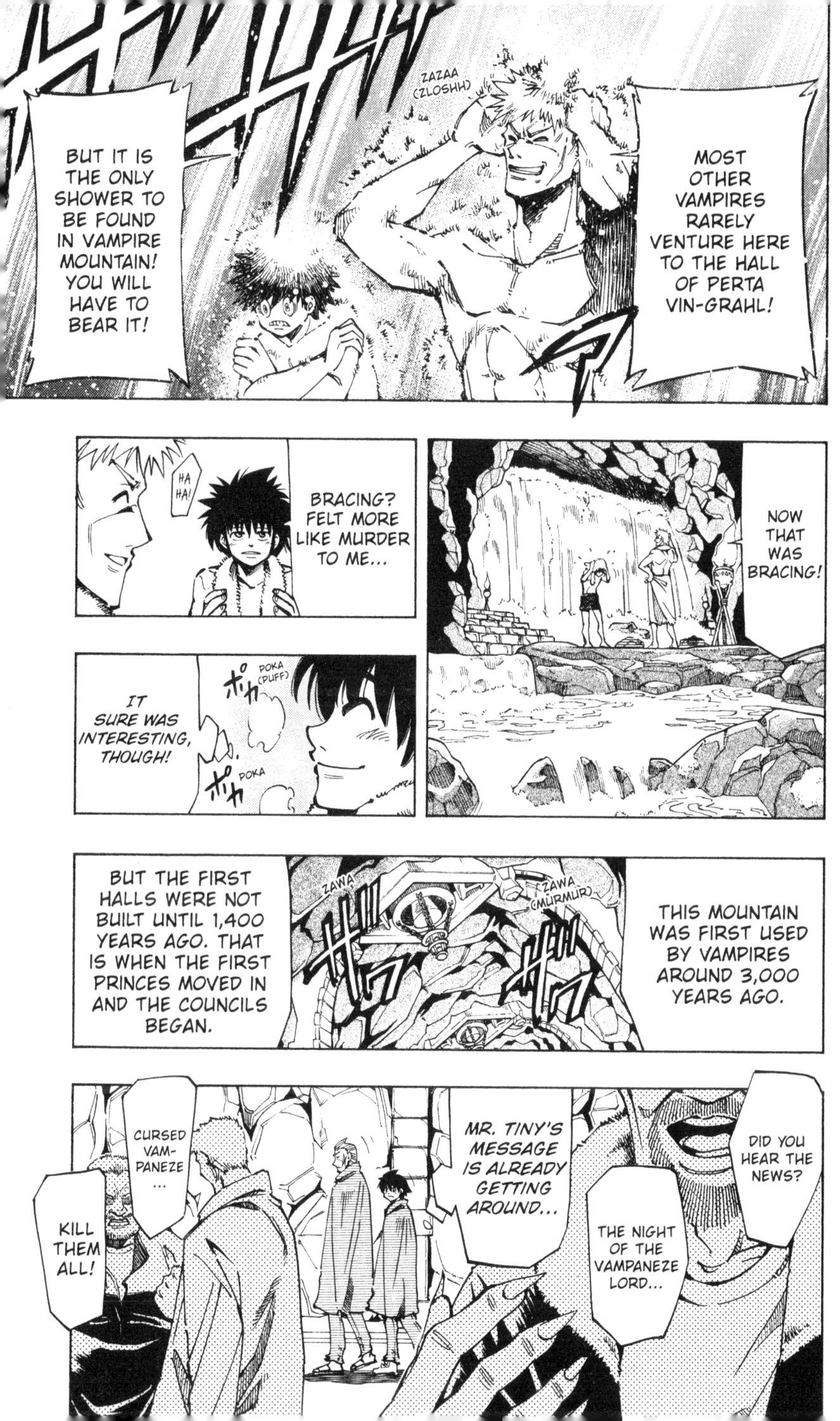
MOST OTHER VAMPIRES RARELY VENTURE HERE TO THE HALL OF PERTA VIN-GRAHL!
ZAZAA (ZLOSHH)
BUT IT IS THE ONLY SHOWER TO BE FOUND IN VAMPIRE MOUNTAIN! YOU WILL HAVE TO BEAR IT!
NOW THAT WAS BRACING!
BRACING? FELT MORE LIKE MURDER TO ME...
HA HA!
POKA (PUFF)
IT SURE WAS INTERESTING, THOUGH!
POKA
THIS MOUNTAIN WAS FIRST USED BY VAMPIRES AROUND 3,000 YEARS AGO.
ZAWA (MURMUR)
ZAWA
BUT THE FIRST HALLS WERE NOT BUILT UNTIL 1,400 YEARS AGO. THAT IS WHEN THE FIRST PRINCES MOVED IN AND THE COUNCILS BEGAN.
DID YOU HEAR THE NEWS?
THE NIGHT OF THE VAMPANEZE LORD...
MR. TINY'S MESSAGE IS ALREADY GETTING AROUND...
CURSED VAMPANEZE...
KILL THEM ALL!

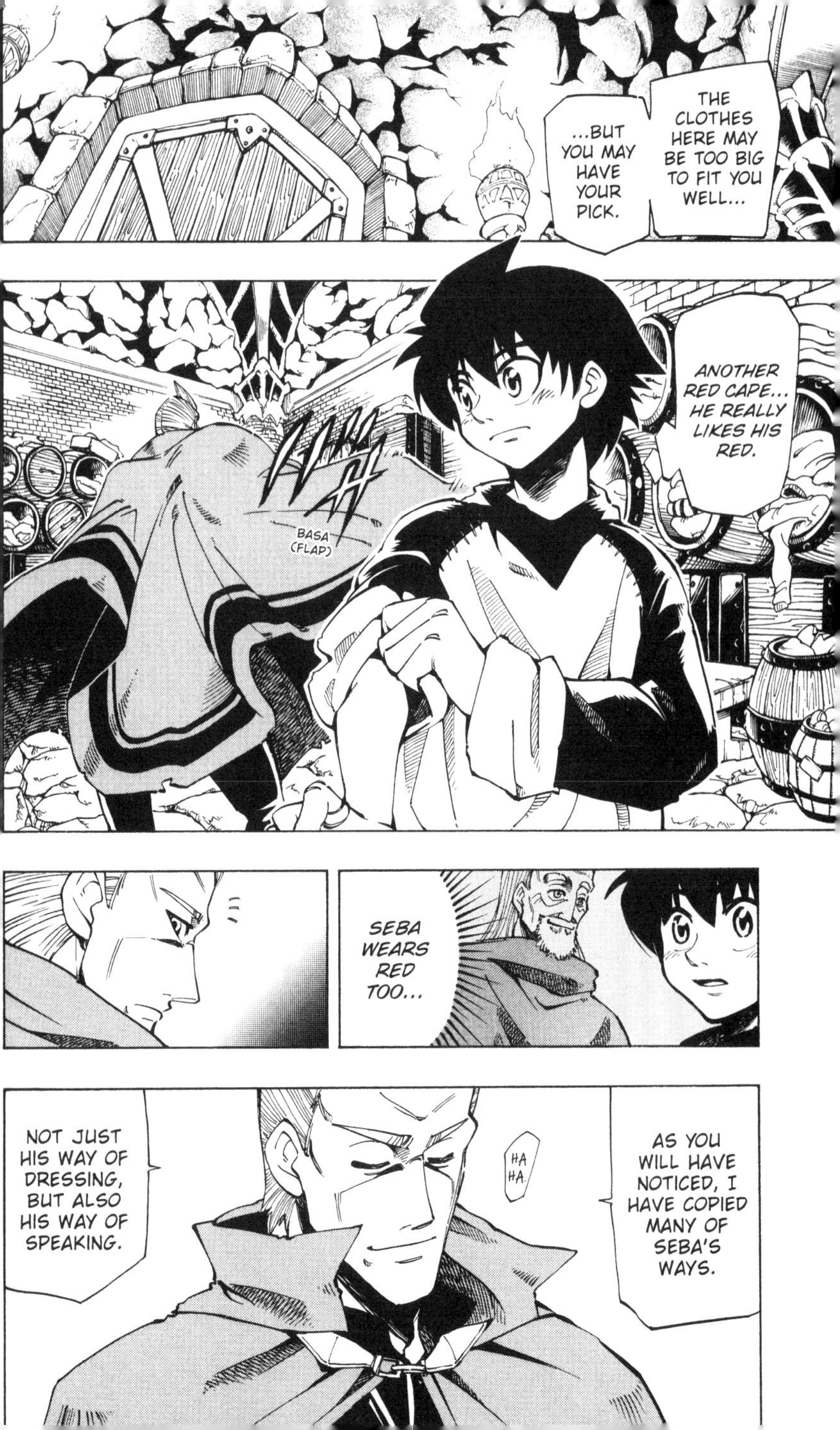
THE CLOTHES HERE MAY BE TOO BIG TO FIT YOU WELL...
...BUT YOU MAY HAVE YOUR PICK.
ANOTHER RED CAPE... HE REALLY LIKES HIS RED.
BASA (FLAP)
SEBA WEARS RED TOO...
AS YOU WILL HAVE NOTICED, I HAVE COPIED MANY OF SEBA'S WAYS.
HA HA.
NOT JUST HIS WAY OF DRESSING, BUT ALSO HIS WAY OF SPEAKING.

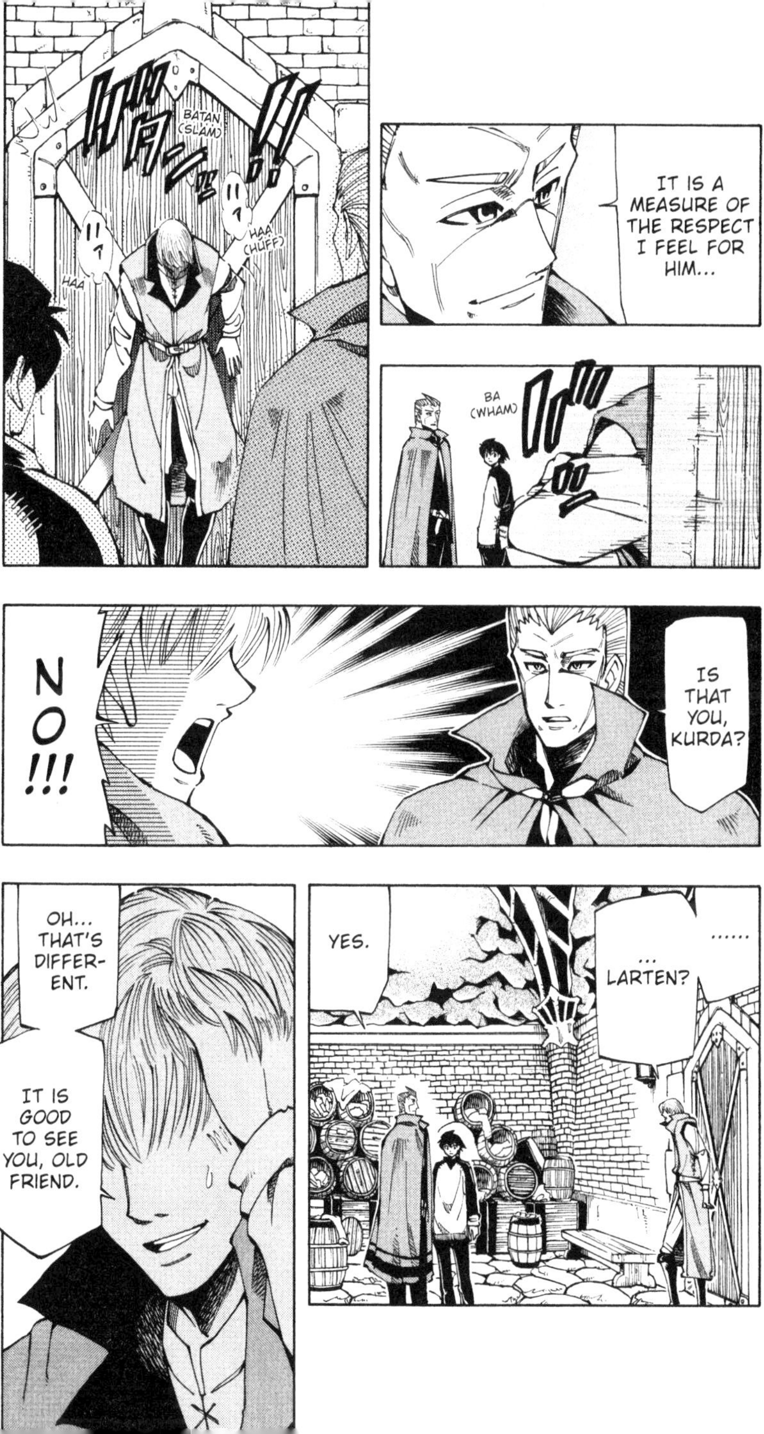
IT IS A MEASURE OF THE RESPECT I FEEL FOR HIM...
BA (WHAM)
BATAN (SLAM)
HAA (HUFF)
HAA
IS THAT YOU, KURDA?
NO!!!
......
...LARTEN?
YES.
OH... THAT'S DIFFER-ENT.
IT IS GOOD TO SEE YOU, OLD FRIEND.

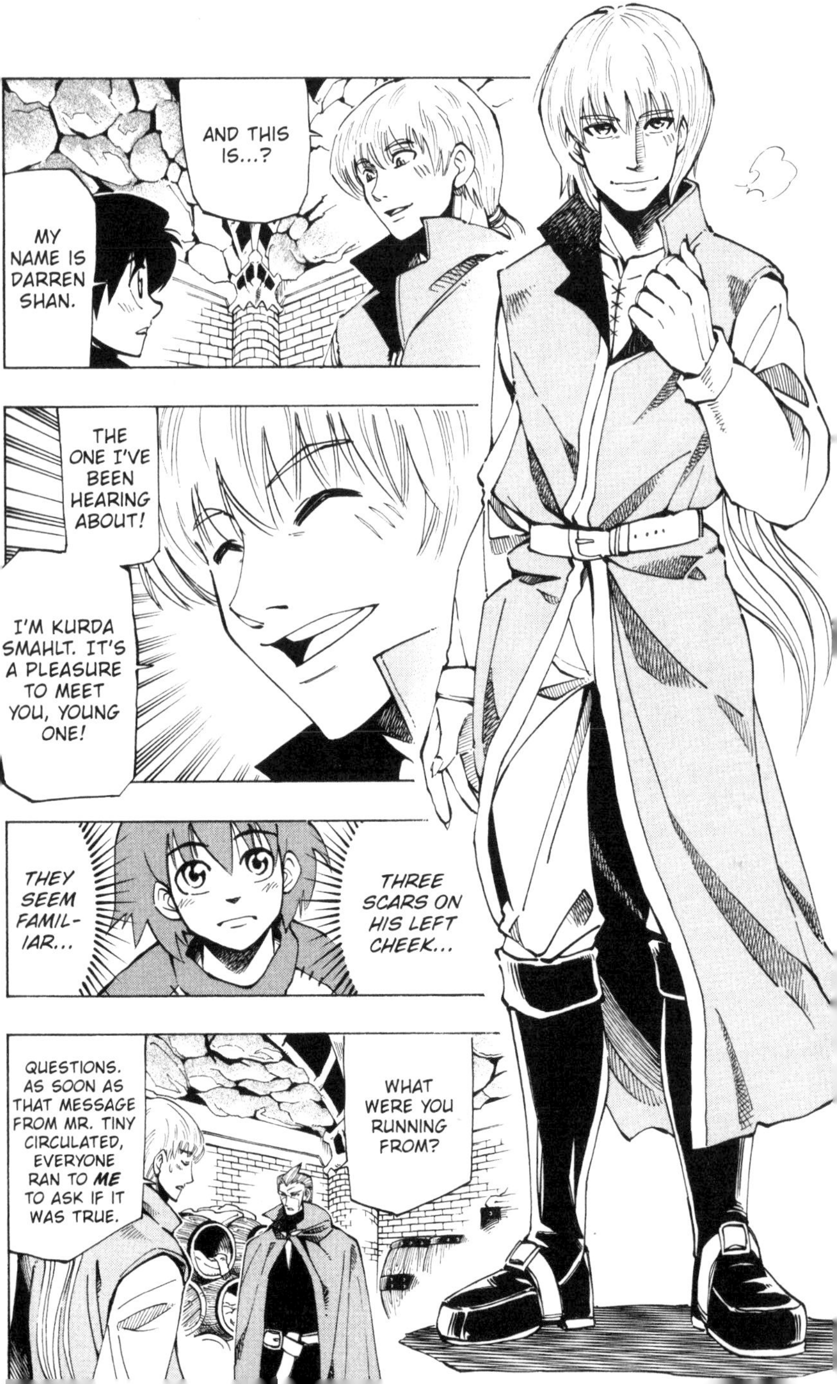
AND THIS IS...?
MY NAME IS DARREN SHAN.
THE ONE I'VE BEEN HEARING ABOUT!
I'M KURDA SMAHLT. IT'S A PLEASURE TO MEET YOU, YOUNG ONE!
THREE SCARS ON HIS LEFT CHEEK...
THEY SEEM FAMILIAR...
WHAT WERE YOU RUNNING FROM?
QUESTIONS. AS SOON AS THAT MESSAGE FROM MR. TINY CIRCULATED, EVERYONE RAN TO *ME* TO ASK IF IT WAS TRUE.

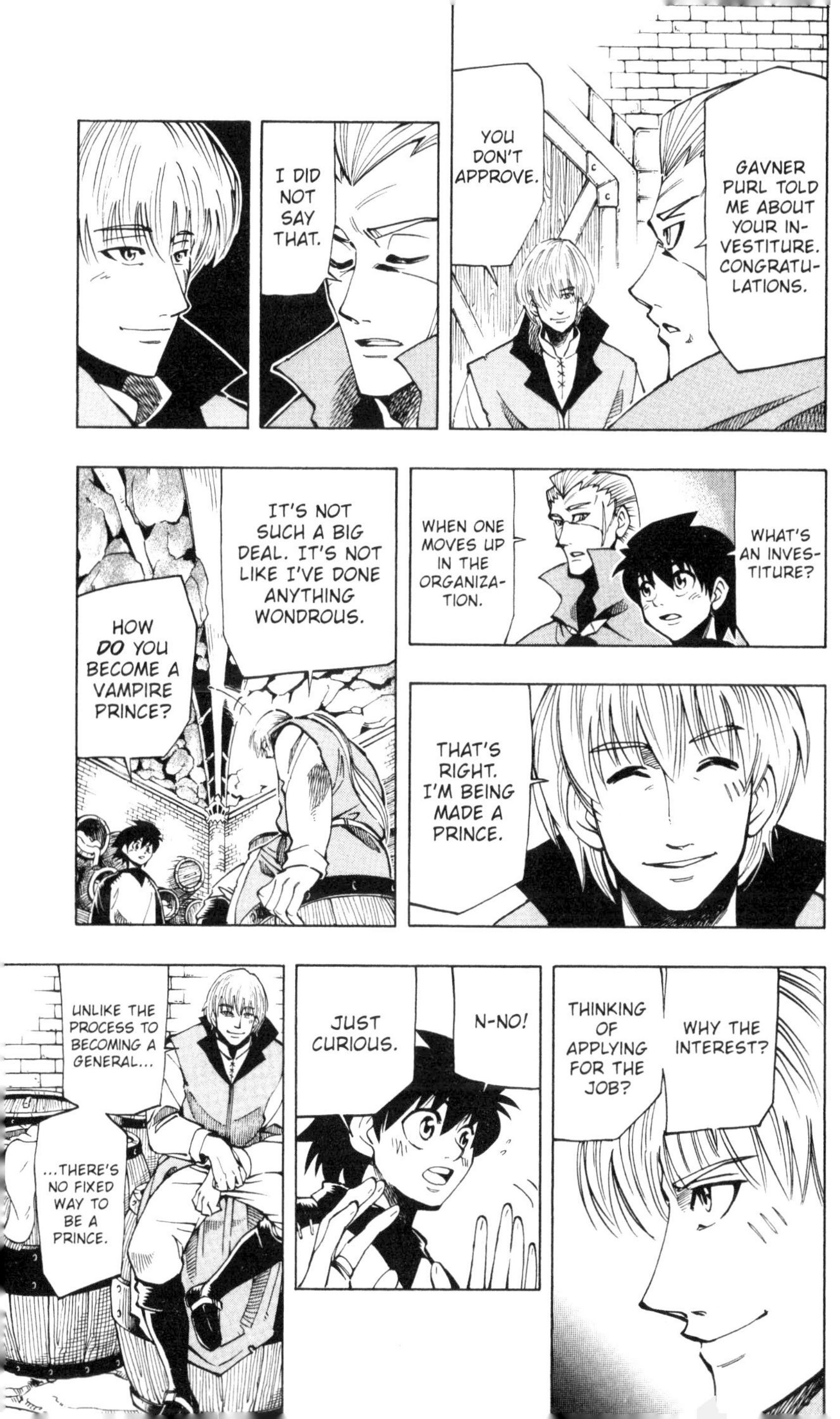
GAVNER PURL TOLD ME ABOUT YOUR INVESTITURE. CONGRATULATIONS.
YOU DON'T APPROVE.
I DID NOT SAY THAT.
WHAT'S AN INVESTITURE?
WHEN ONE MOVES UP IN THE ORGANIZATION.
THAT'S RIGHT. I'M BEING MADE A PRINCE.
IT'S NOT SUCH A BIG DEAL. IT'S NOT LIKE I'VE DONE ANYTHING WONDROUS.
HOW ***DO*** YOU BECOME A VAMPIRE PRINCE?
WHY THE INTEREST?
THINKING OF APPLYING FOR THE JOB?
N-NO!
JUST CURIOUS.
UNLIKE THE PROCESS TO BECOMING A GENERAL...
...THERE'S NO FIXED WAY TO BE A PRINCE.

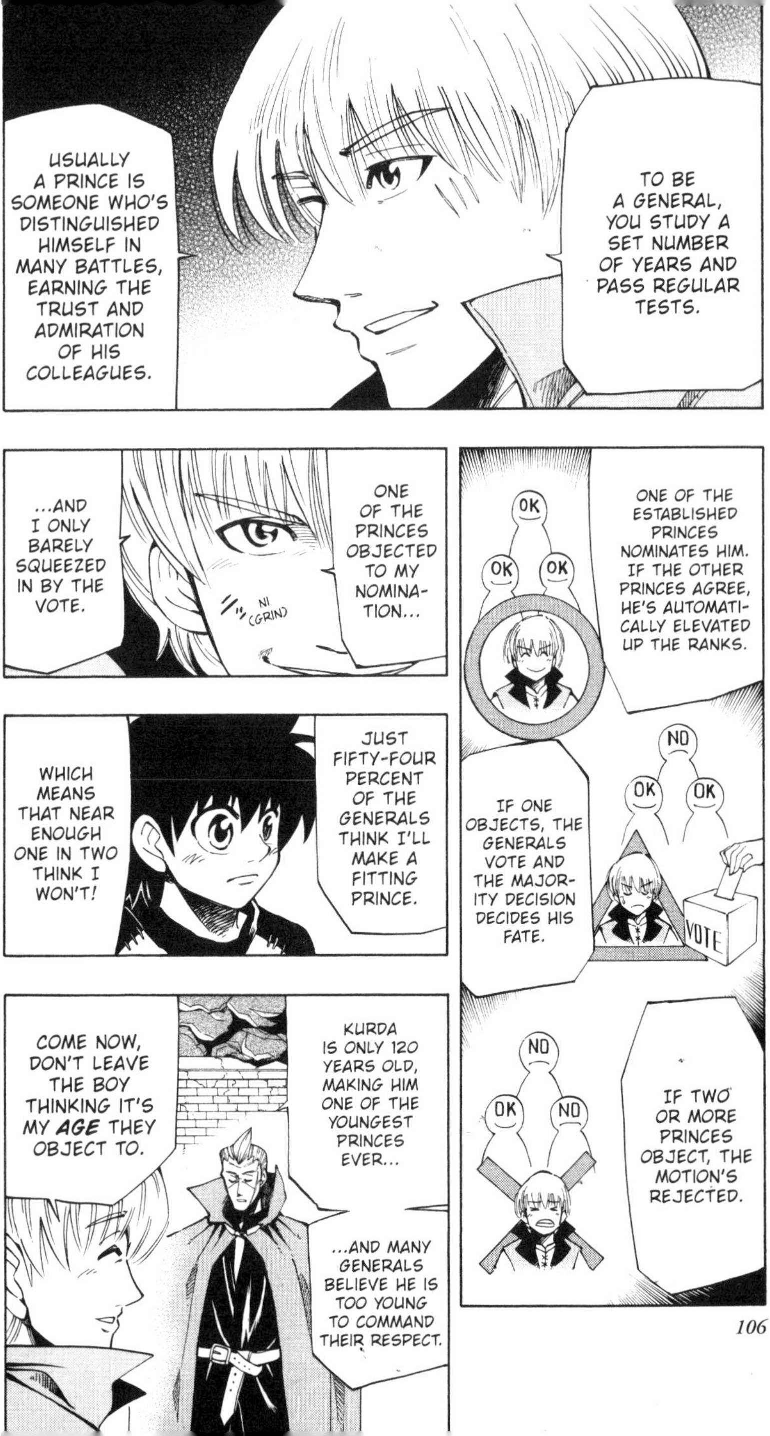
TO BE A GENERAL, YOU STUDY A SET NUMBER OF YEARS AND PASS REGULAR TESTS.
USUALLY A PRINCE IS SOMEONE WHO'S DISTINGUISHED HIMSELF IN MANY BATTLES, EARNING THE TRUST AND ADMIRATION OF HIS COLLEAGUES.
ONE OF THE ESTABLISHED PRINCES NOMINATES HIM. IF THE OTHER PRINCES AGREE, HE'S AUTOMATICALLY ELEVATED UP THE RANKS.
OK
OK
OK
NO
OK
OK
IF ONE OBJECTS, THE GENERALS VOTE AND THE MAJORITY DECISION DECIDES HIS FATE.
VOTE
IF TWO OR MORE PRINCES OBJECT, THE MOTION'S REJECTED.
NO
OK
NO
ONE OF THE PRINCES OBJECTED TO MY NOMINATION...
NI (GRIN)
...AND I ONLY BARELY SQUEEZED IN BY THE VOTE.
JUST FIFTY-FOUR PERCENT OF THE GENERALS THINK I'LL MAKE A FITTING PRINCE.
WHICH MEANS THAT NEAR ENOUGH ONE IN TWO THINK I WON'T!
KURDA IS ONLY 120 YEARS OLD, MAKING HIM ONE OF THE YOUNGEST PRINCES EVER...
...AND MANY GENERALS BELIEVE HE IS TOO YOUNG TO COMMAND THEIR RESPECT.
COME NOW, DON'T LEAVE THE BOY THINKING IT'S MY AGE THEY OBJECT TO.

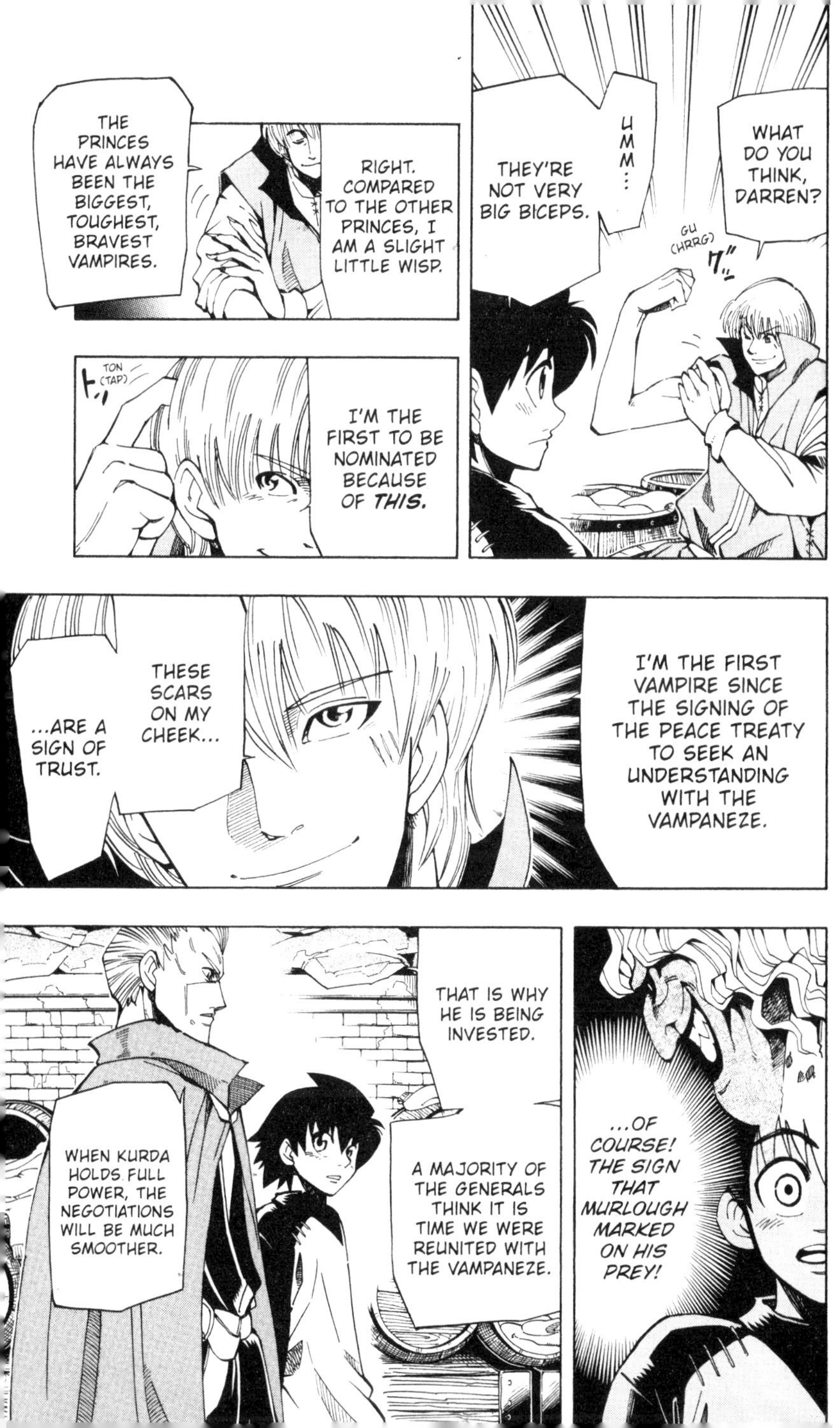
WHAT DO YOU THINK, DARREN?
GU (HRRG)
UMM...
THEY'RE NOT VERY BIG BICEPS.
RIGHT. COMPARED TO THE OTHER PRINCES, I AM A SLIGHT LITTLE WISP.
THE PRINCES HAVE ALWAYS BEEN THE BIGGEST, TOUGHEST, BRAVEST VAMPIRES.
TON (TAP)
I'M THE FIRST TO BE NOMINATED BECAUSE OF *THIS.*
I'M THE FIRST VAMPIRE SINCE THE SIGNING OF THE PEACE TREATY TO SEEK AN UNDERSTANDING WITH THE VAMPANEZE.
THESE SCARS ON MY CHEEK...
...ARE A SIGN OF TRUST.
...OF COURSE! THE SIGN THAT MURLOUGH MARKED ON HIS PREY!
THAT IS WHY HE IS BEING INVESTED.
A MAJORITY OF THE GENERALS THINK IT IS TIME WE WERE REUNITED WITH THE VAMPANEZE.
WHEN KURDA HOLDS FULL POWER, THE NEGOTIATIONS WILL BE MUCH SMOOTHER.

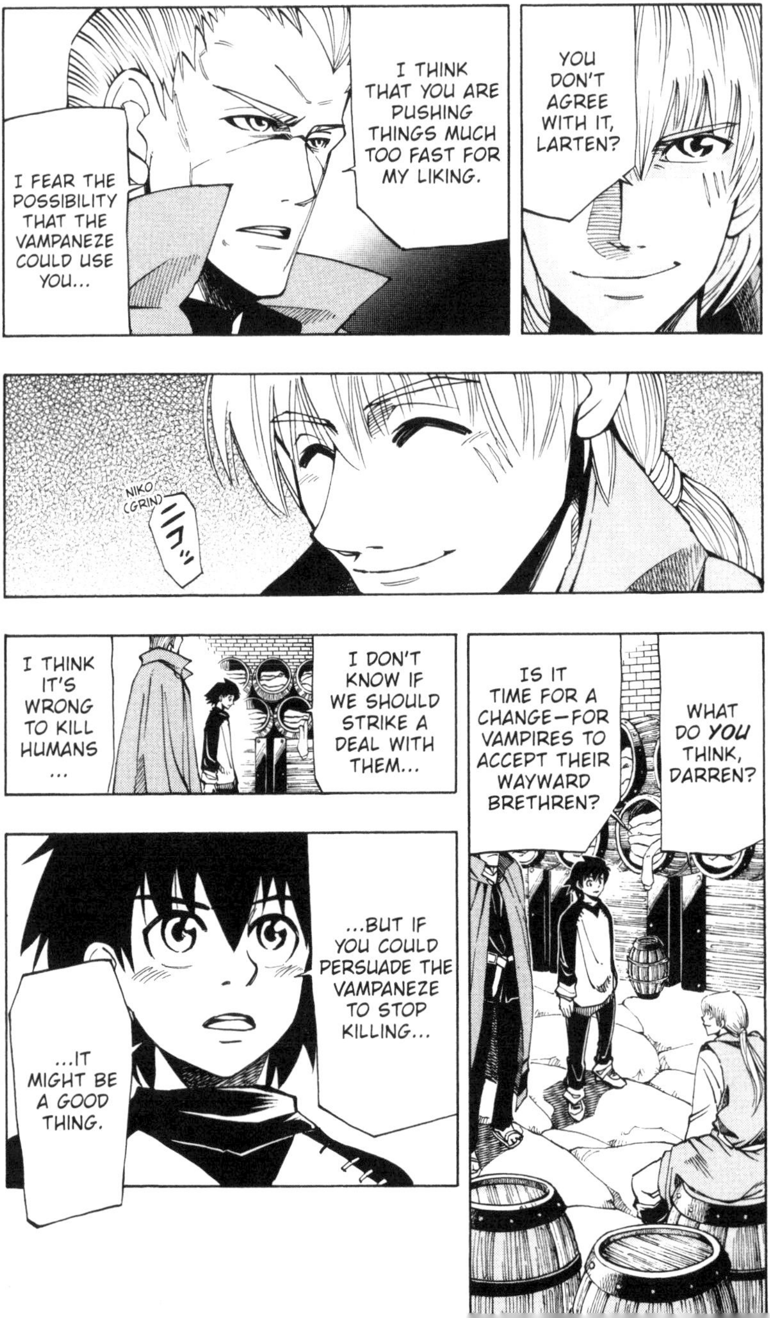
YOU DON'T AGREE WITH IT, LARTEN?
I THINK THAT YOU ARE PUSHING THINGS MUCH TOO FAST FOR MY LIKING.
I FEAR THE POSSIBILITY THAT THE VAMPANEZE COULD USE YOU...
NIKO (GRIN)
ニコッ
IS IT TIME FOR A CHANGE—FOR VAMPIRES TO ACCEPT THEIR WAYWARD BRETHREN?
WHAT DO ***YOU*** THINK, DARREN?
I DON'T KNOW IF WE SHOULD STRIKE A DEAL WITH THEM...
I THINK IT'S WRONG TO KILL HUMANS...
...BUT IF YOU COULD PERSUADE THE VAMPANEZE TO STOP KILLING...
...IT MIGHT BE A GOOD THING.

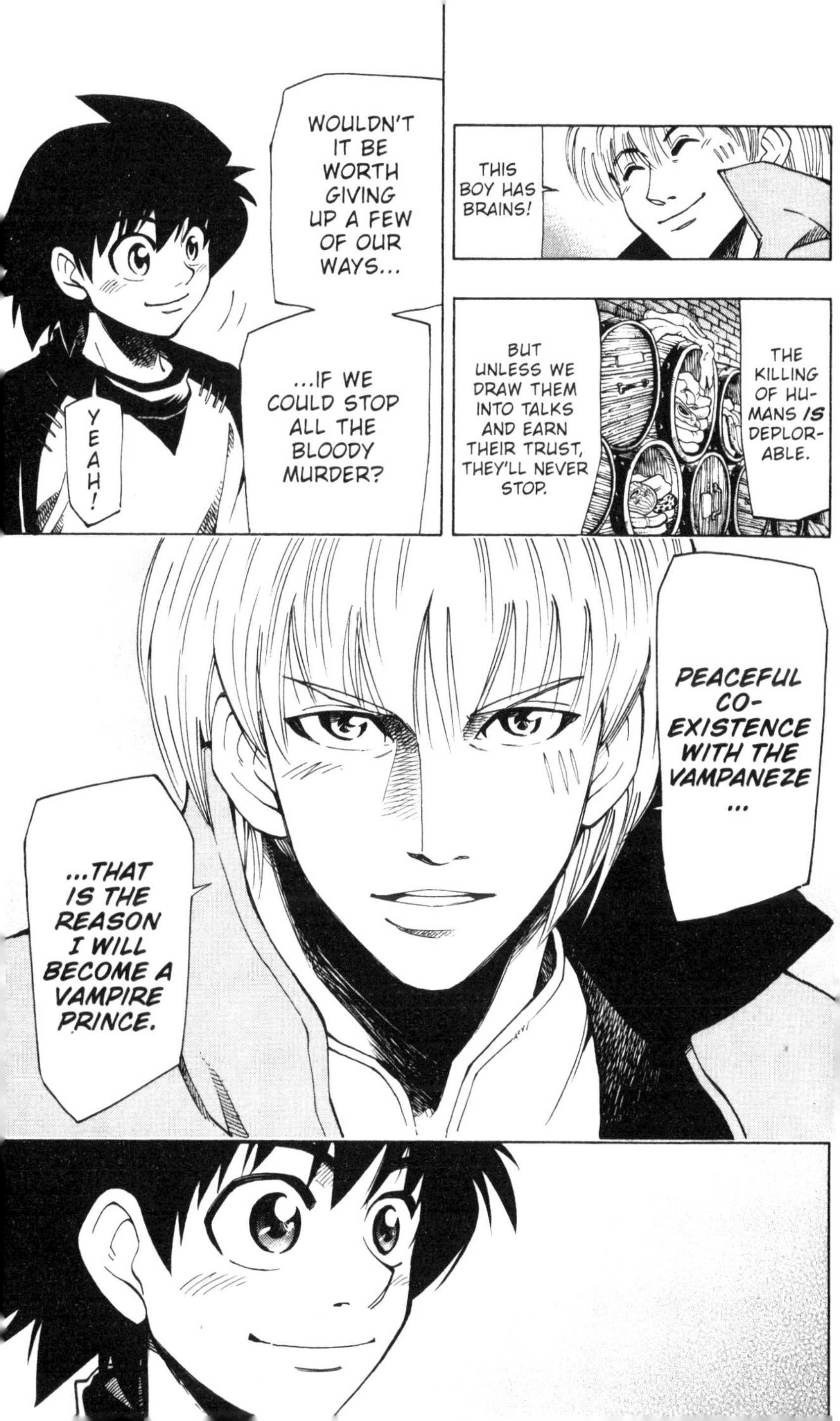
THIS BOY HAS BRAINS!
THE KILLING OF HUMANS *IS* DEPLORABLE.
BUT UNLESS WE DRAW THEM INTO TALKS AND EARN THEIR TRUST, THEY'LL NEVER STOP.
WOULDN'T IT BE WORTH GIVING UP A FEW OF OUR WAYS...
...IF WE COULD STOP ALL THE BLOODY MURDER?
YEAH!
PEACEFUL CO-EXISTENCE WITH THE VAMPANEZE...
...THAT IS THE REASON I WILL BECOME A VAMPIRE PRINCE.

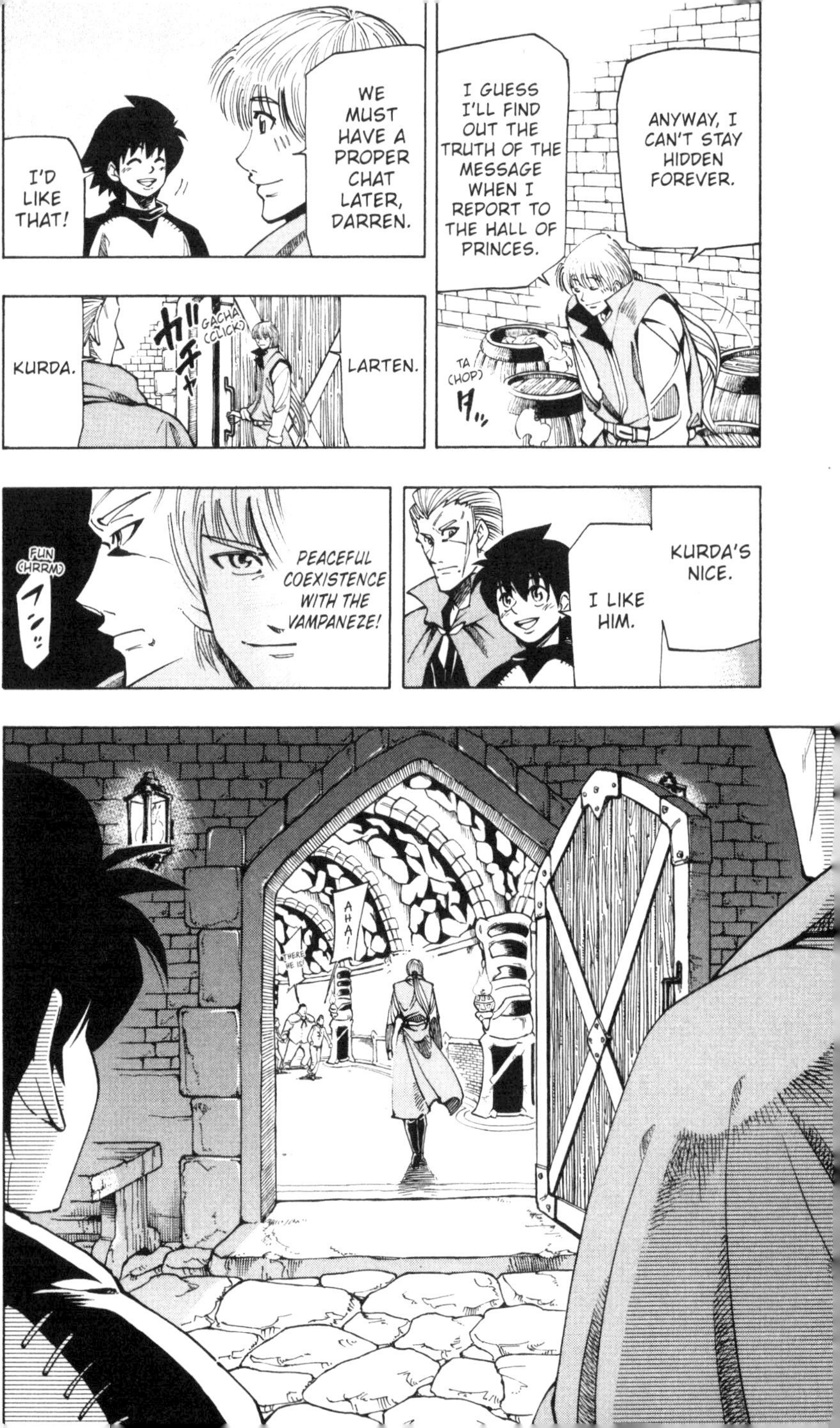
ANYWAY, I CAN'T STAY HIDDEN FOREVER.
I GUESS I'LL FIND OUT THE TRUTH OF THE MESSAGE WHEN I REPORT TO THE HALL OF PRINCES.
TA (HOP)
WE MUST HAVE A PROPER CHAT LATER, DARREN.
I'D LIKE THAT!
LARTEN.
GACHA (CLICK)
KURDA.
KURDA'S NICE.
I LIKE HIM.
PEACEFUL COEXISTENCE WITH THE VAMPANEZE!
FUN (HRRM)
AHA!
THERE HE IS!

CHAPTER 31: THE HALL OF DEATH

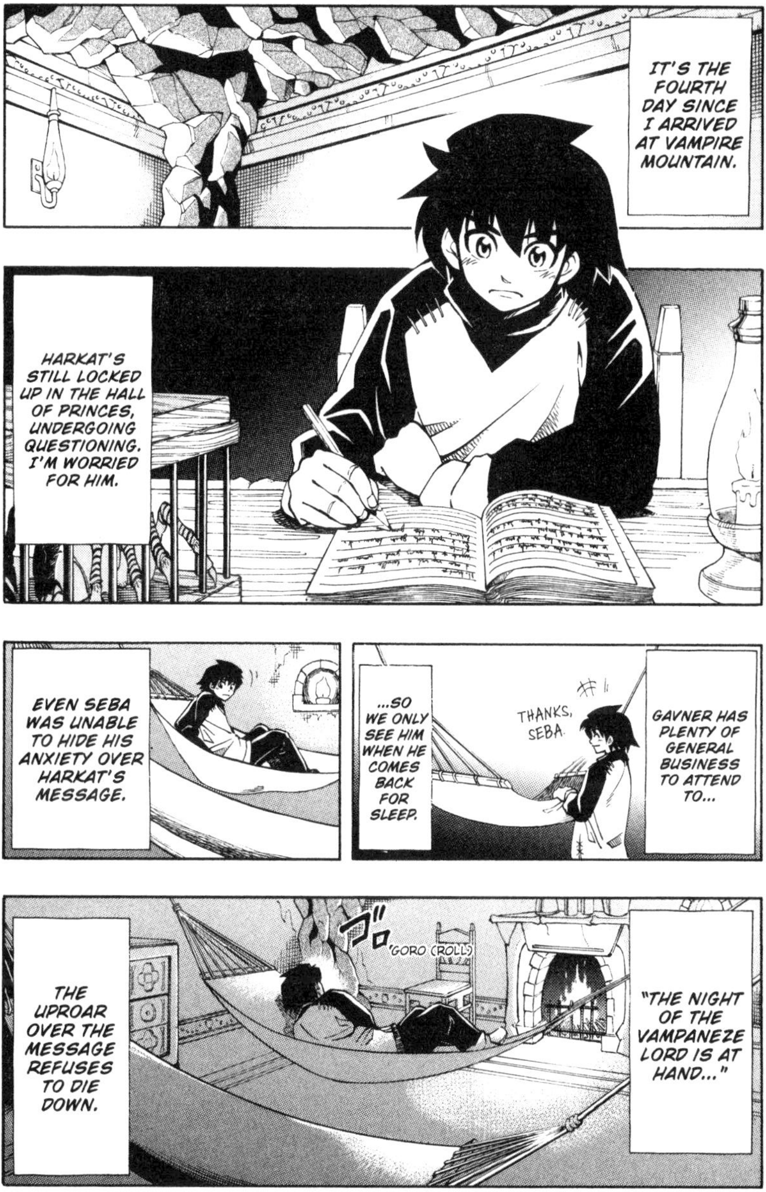
IT'S THE FOURTH DAY SINCE I ARRIVED AT VAMPIRE MOUNTAIN.
HARKAT'S STILL LOCKED UP IN THE HALL OF PRINCES, UNDERGOING QUESTIONING. I'M WORRIED FOR HIM.
GAVNER HAS PLENTY OF GENERAL BUSINESS TO ATTEND TO...
THANKS, SEBA.
...SO WE ONLY SEE HIM WHEN HE COMES BACK FOR SLEEP.
EVEN SEBA WAS UNABLE TO HIDE HIS ANXIETY OVER HARKAT'S MESSAGE.
"THE NIGHT OF THE VAMPANEZE LORD IS AT HAND..."
ゴロ
GORO (ROLL)
THE UPROAR OVER THE MESSAGE REFUSES TO DIE DOWN.

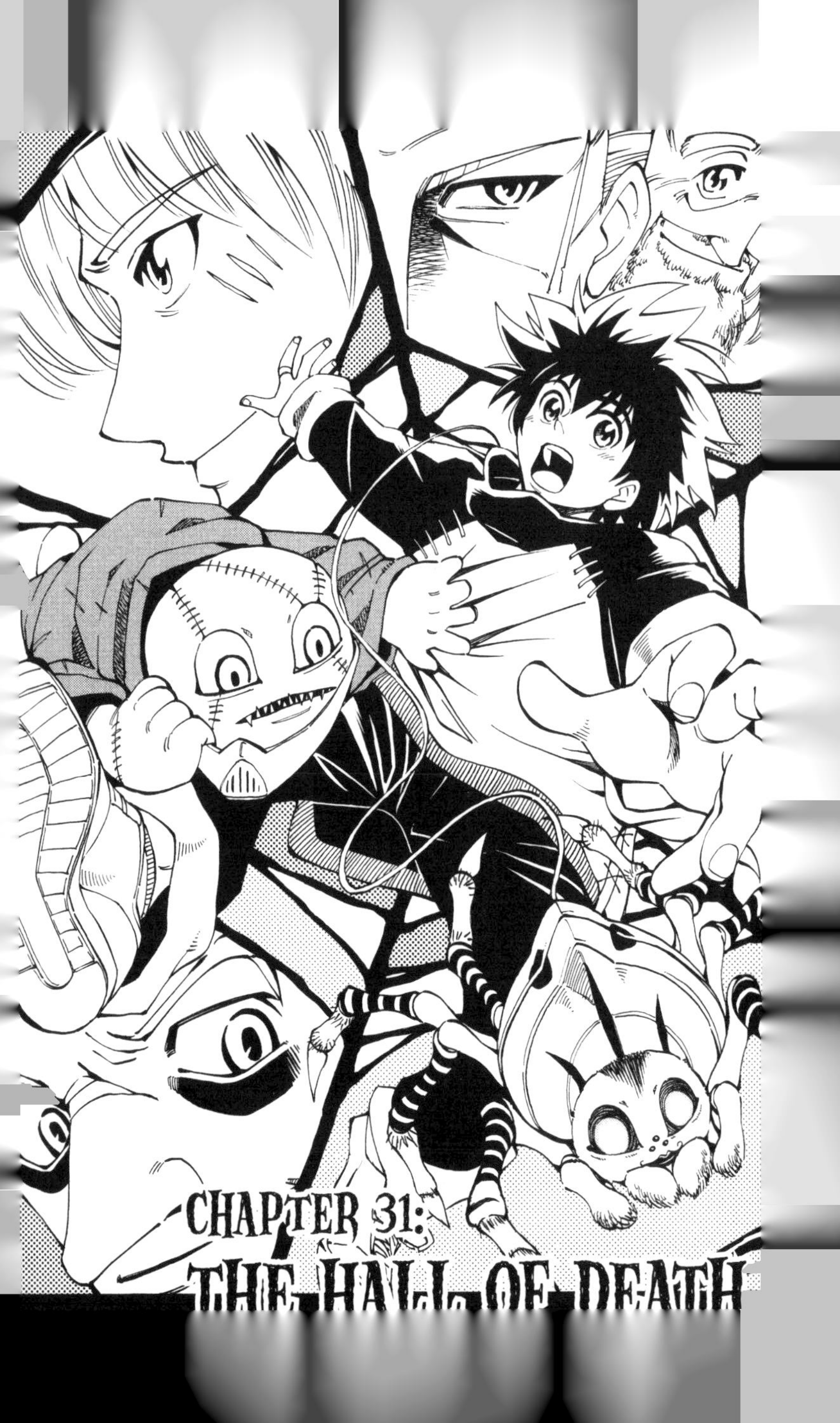

CHAPTER 31: THE HALL OF DEATH

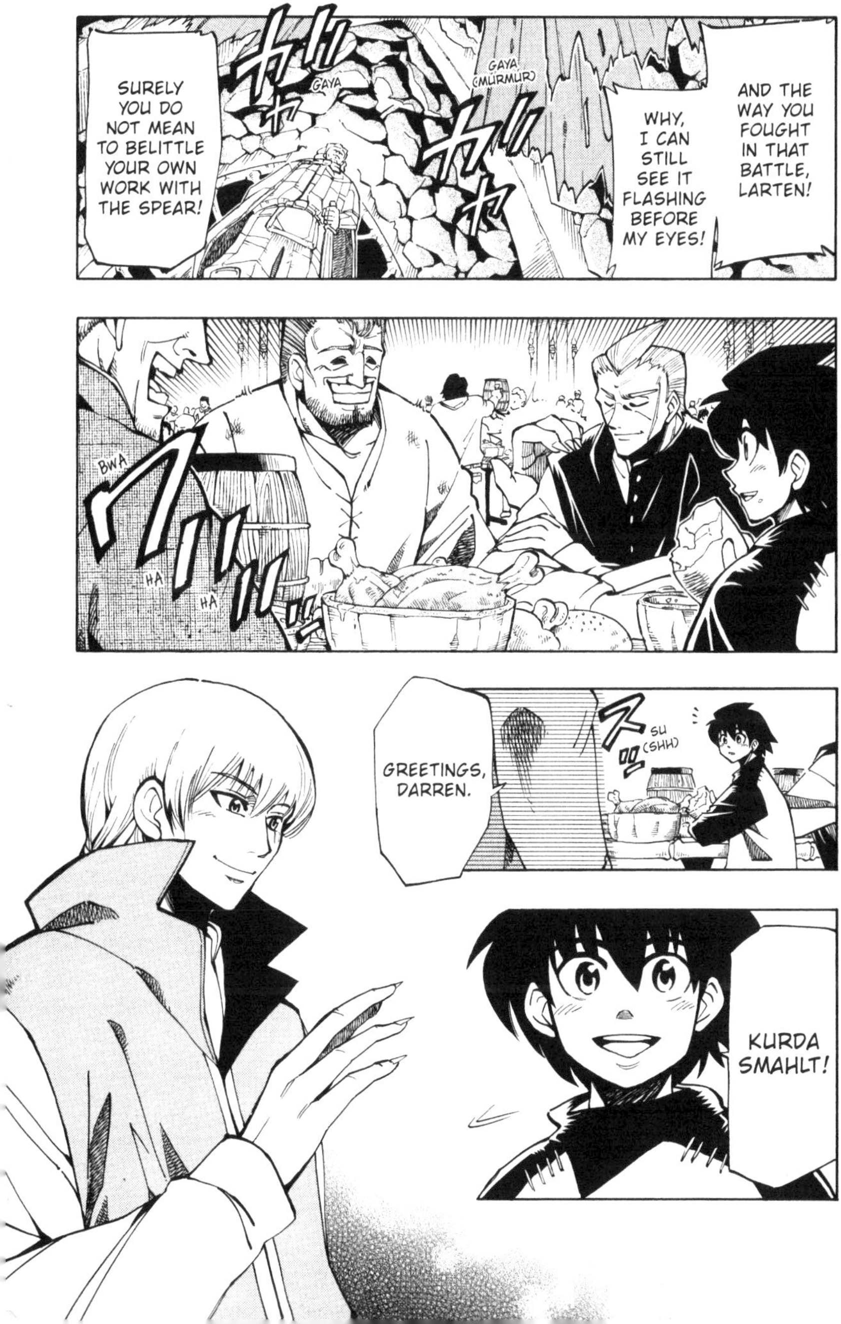
AND THE WAY YOU FOUGHT IN THAT BATTLE, LARTEN!
WHY, I CAN STILL SEE IT FLASHING BEFORE MY EYES!
GAYA (MURMUR)
GAYA
SURELY YOU DO NOT MEAN TO BELITTLE YOUR OWN WORK WITH THE SPEAR!
BWA
HA
HA
SU (SHH)
GREETINGS, DARREN.
KURDA SMAHLT!

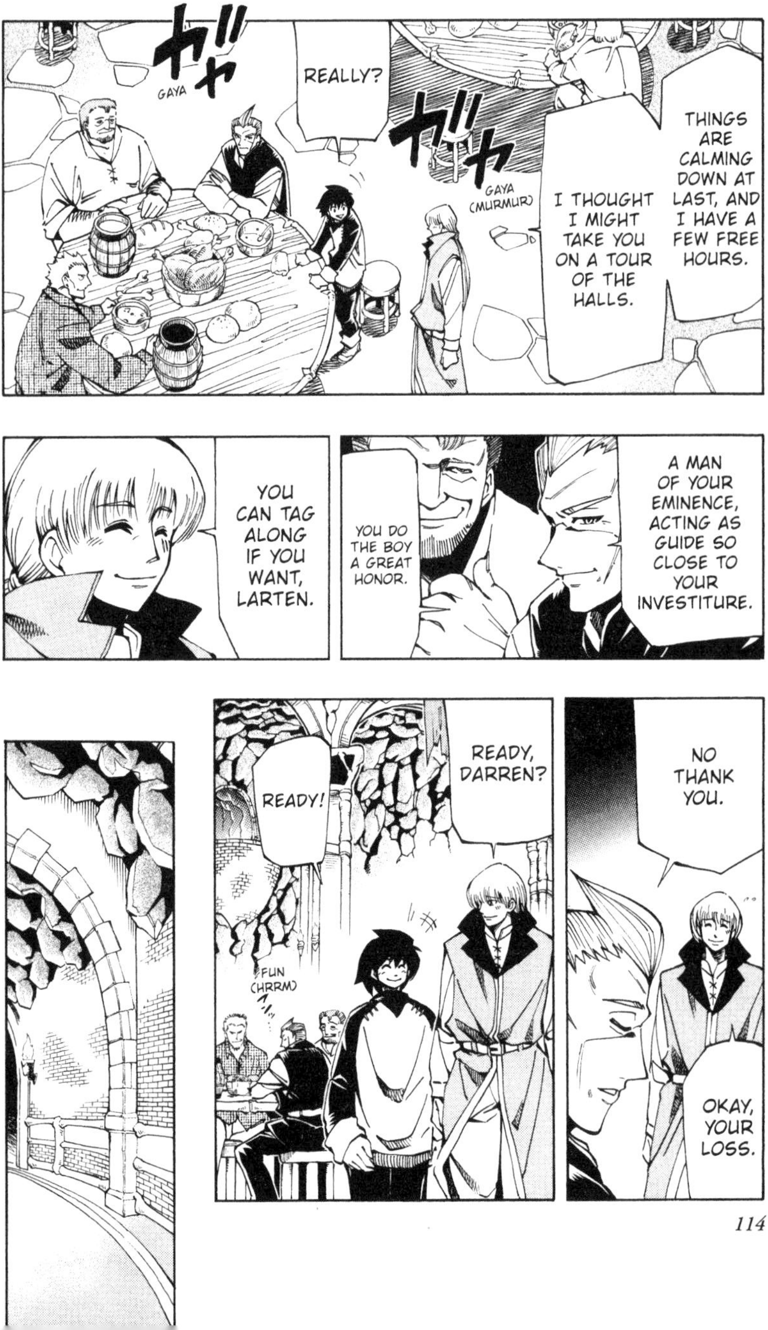
THINGS ARE CALMING DOWN AT LAST, AND I HAVE A FEW FREE HOURS.
I THOUGHT I MIGHT TAKE YOU ON A TOUR OF THE HALLS.
GAYA (MURMUR)
REALLY?
GAYA
A MAN OF YOUR EMINENCE, ACTING AS GUIDE SO CLOSE TO YOUR INVESTITURE.
YOU DO THE BOY A GREAT HONOR.
YOU CAN TAG ALONG IF YOU WANT, LARTEN.
NO THANK YOU.
OKAY, YOUR LOSS.
READY, DARREN?
READY!
FUN (HRRM)

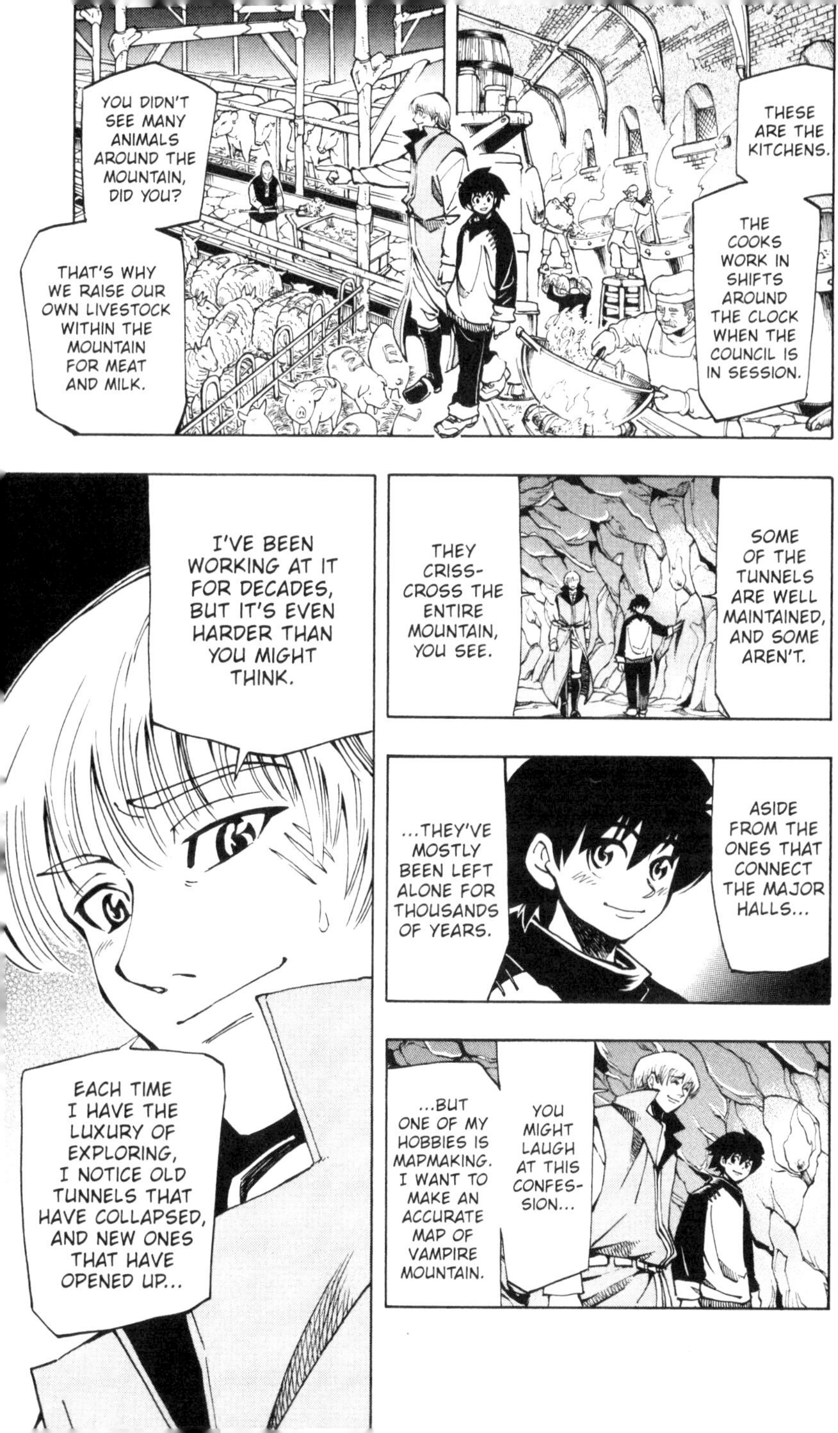
THESE ARE THE KITCHENS.
THE COOKS WORK IN SHIFTS AROUND THE CLOCK WHEN THE COUNCIL IS IN SESSION.
YOU DIDN'T SEE MANY ANIMALS AROUND THE MOUNTAIN, DID YOU?
THAT'S WHY WE RAISE OUR OWN LIVESTOCK WITHIN THE MOUNTAIN FOR MEAT AND MILK.
SOME OF THE TUNNELS ARE WELL MAINTAINED, AND SOME AREN'T.
THEY CRISS-CROSS THE ENTIRE MOUNTAIN, YOU SEE.
ASIDE FROM THE ONES THAT CONNECT THE MAJOR HALLS...
...THEY'VE MOSTLY BEEN LEFT ALONE FOR THOUSANDS OF YEARS.
YOU MIGHT LAUGH AT THIS CONFESSION...
...BUT ONE OF MY HOBBIES IS MAPMAKING. I WANT TO MAKE AN ACCURATE MAP OF VAMPIRE MOUNTAIN.
I'VE BEEN WORKING AT IT FOR DECADES, BUT IT'S EVEN HARDER THAN YOU MIGHT THINK.
EACH TIME I HAVE THE LUXURY OF EXPLORING, I NOTICE OLD TUNNELS THAT HAVE COLLAPSED, AND NEW ONES THAT HAVE OPENED UP...

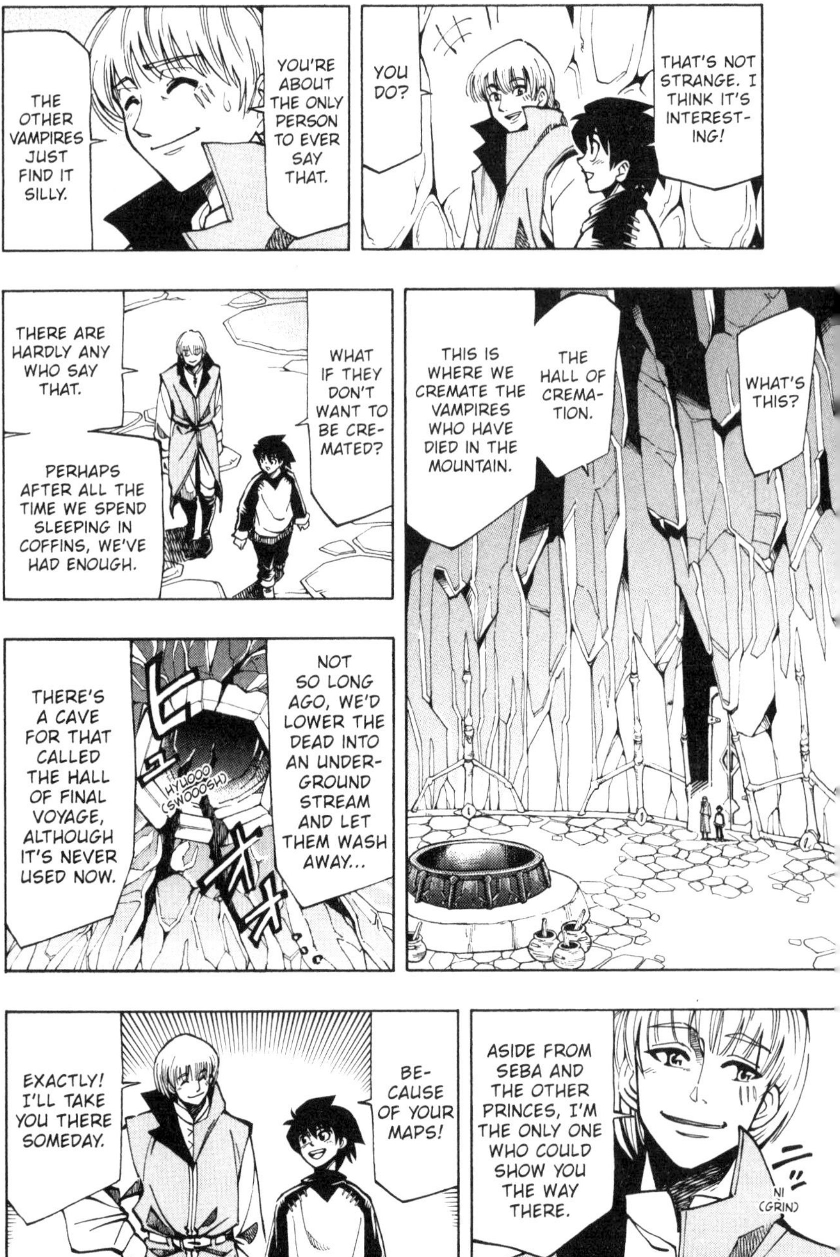
THAT'S NOT STRANGE. I THINK IT'S INTEREST-ING!
YOU DO?
YOU'RE ABOUT THE ONLY PERSON TO EVER SAY THAT.
THE OTHER VAMPIRES JUST FIND IT SILLY.
WHAT'S THIS?
THE HALL OF CREMA-TION.
THIS IS WHERE WE CREMATE THE VAMPIRES WHO HAVE DIED IN THE MOUNTAIN.
WHAT IF THEY DON'T WANT TO BE CRE-MATED?
THERE ARE HARDLY ANY WHO SAY THAT.
PERHAPS AFTER ALL THE TIME WE SPEND SLEEPING IN COFFINS, WE'VE HAD ENOUGH.
NOT SO LONG AGO, WE'D LOWER THE DEAD INTO AN UNDER-GROUND STREAM AND LET THEM WASH AWAY...
HYUOOO (SWOOOSH)
THERE'S A CAVE FOR THAT CALLED THE HALL OF FINAL VOYAGE, ALTHOUGH IT'S NEVER USED NOW.
ASIDE FROM SEBA AND THE OTHER PRINCES, I'M THE ONLY ONE WHO COULD SHOW YOU THE WAY THERE.
NI (GRIN)
BE-CAUSE OF YOUR MAPS!
EXACTLY! I'LL TAKE YOU THERE SOMEDAY.

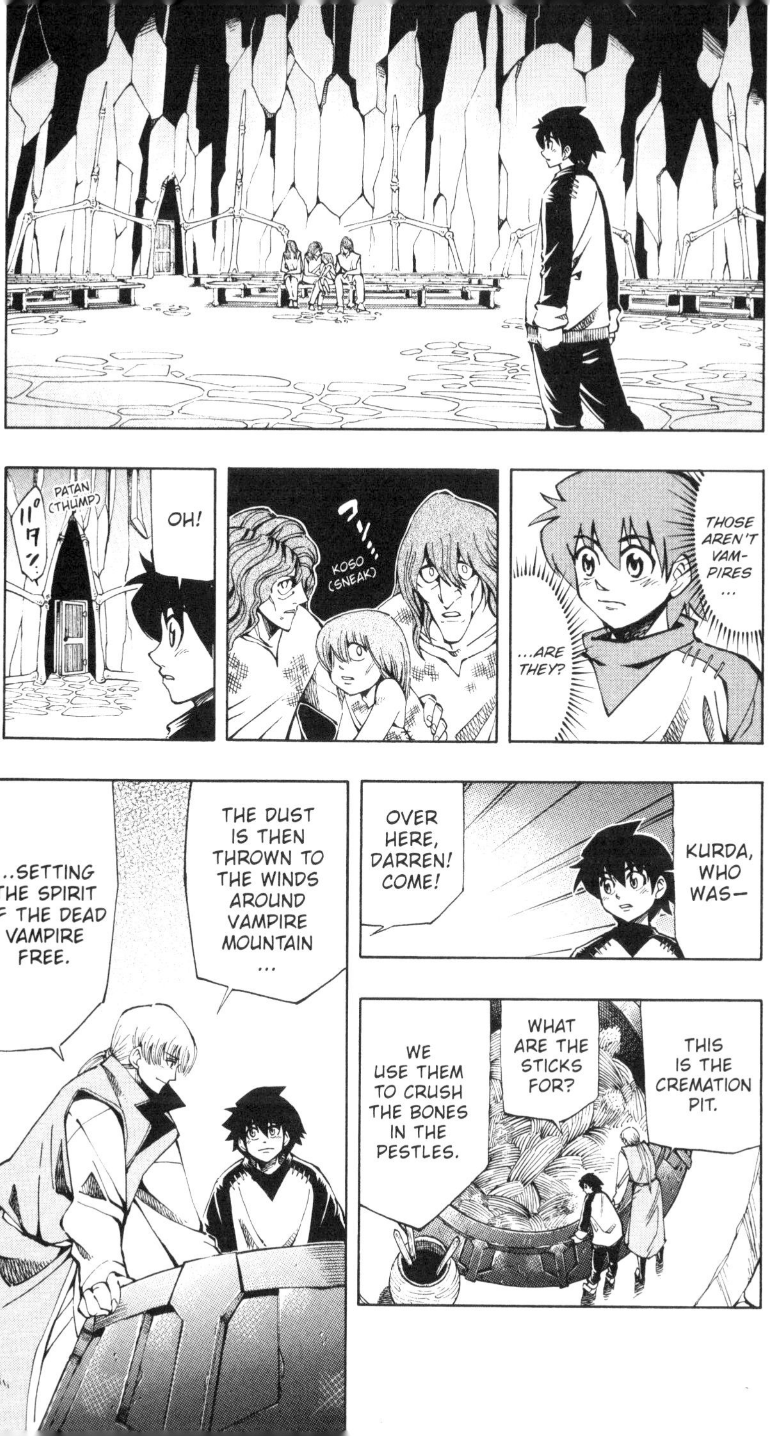
THOSE AREN'T VAMPIRES ...
...ARE THEY?
KOSO (SNEAK)
OH!
PATAN (THUMP)
KURDA, WHO WAS—
OVER HERE, DARREN! COME!
THIS IS THE CREMATION PIT.
WHAT ARE THE STICKS FOR?
WE USE THEM TO CRUSH THE BONES IN THE PESTLES.
THE DUST IS THEN THROWN TO THE WINDS AROUND VAMPIRE MOUNTAIN ...
...SETTING THE SPIRIT OF THE DEAD VAMPIRE FREE.

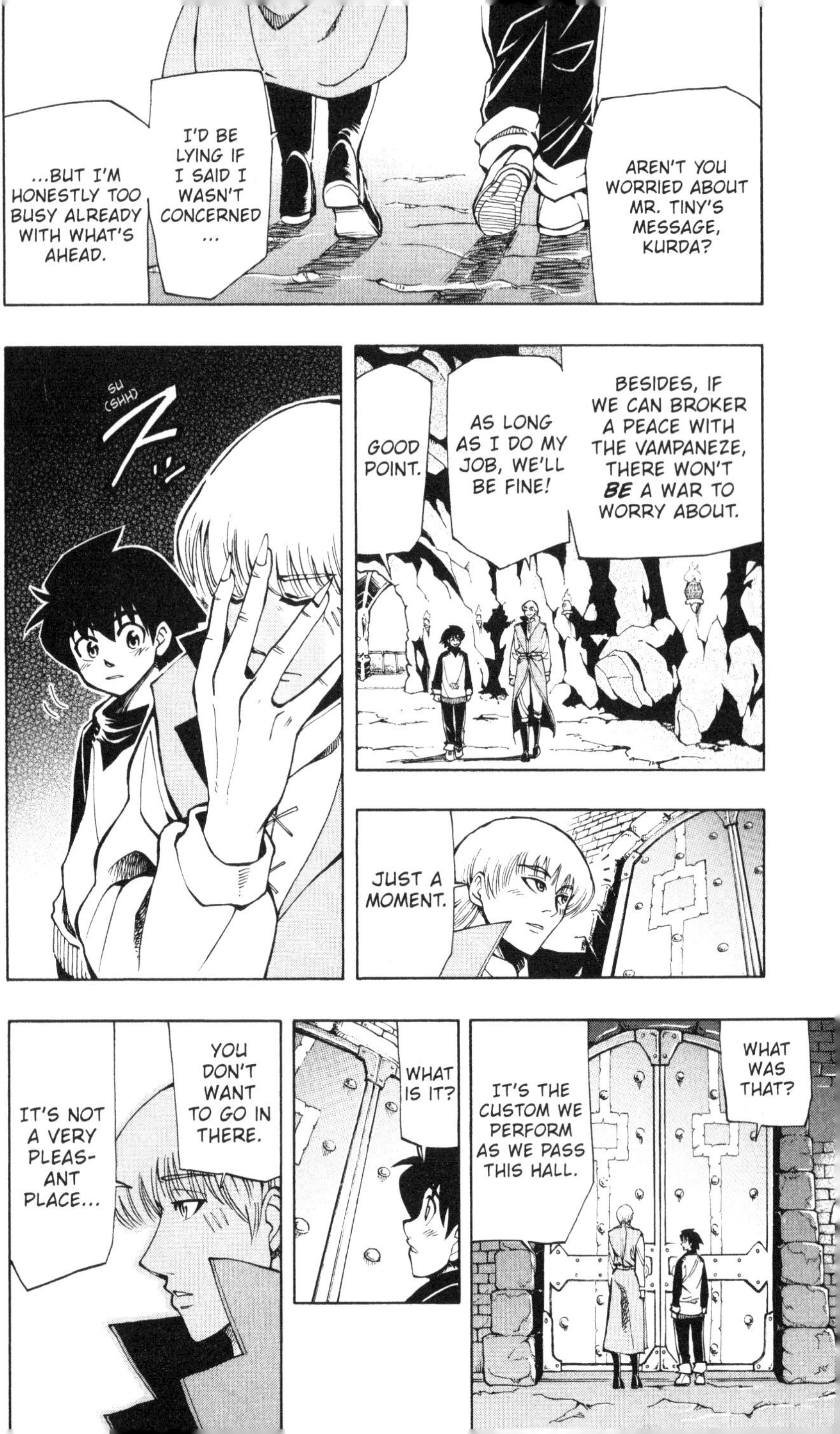
AREN'T YOU WORRIED ABOUT MR. TINY'S MESSAGE, KURDA?
I'D BE LYING IF I SAID I WASN'T CONCERNED ...
...BUT I'M HONESTLY TOO BUSY ALREADY WITH WHAT'S AHEAD.
BESIDES, IF WE CAN BROKER A PEACE WITH THE VAMPANEZE, THERE WON'T *BE* A WAR TO WORRY ABOUT.
AS LONG AS I DO MY JOB, WE'LL BE FINE!
GOOD POINT.
JUST A MOMENT.
SU (SHH)
WHAT WAS THAT?
IT'S THE CUSTOM WE PERFORM AS WE PASS THIS HALL.
WHAT IS IT?
YOU DON'T WANT TO GO IN THERE.
IT'S NOT A VERY PLEAS-ANT PLACE...

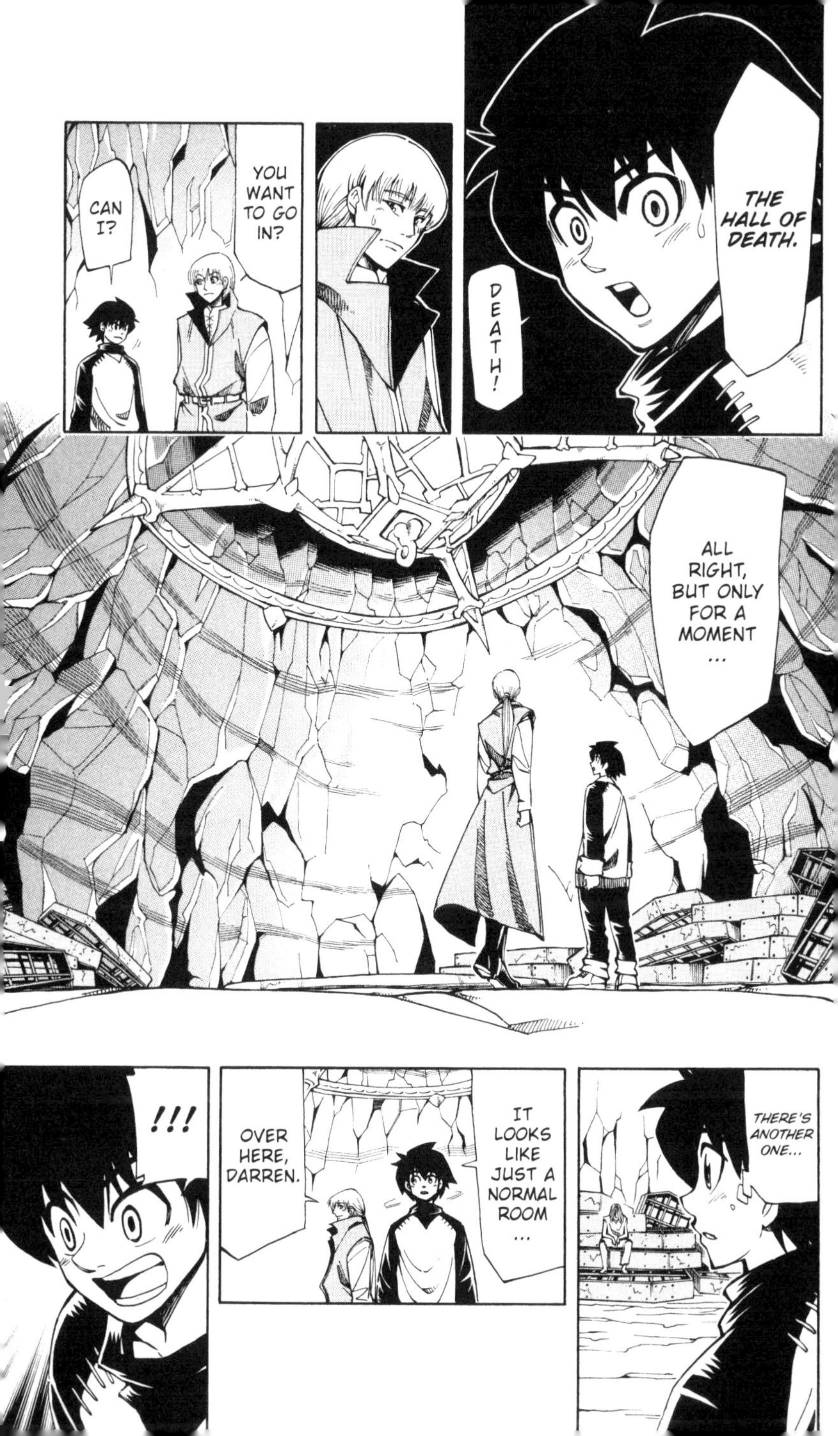
THE HALL OF DEATH.
DEATH!
YOU WANT TO GO IN?
CAN I?
ALL RIGHT, BUT ONLY FOR A MOMENT ...
THERE'S ANOTHER ONE...
IT LOOKS LIKE JUST A NORMAL ROOM ...
OVER HERE, DARREN.
!!!

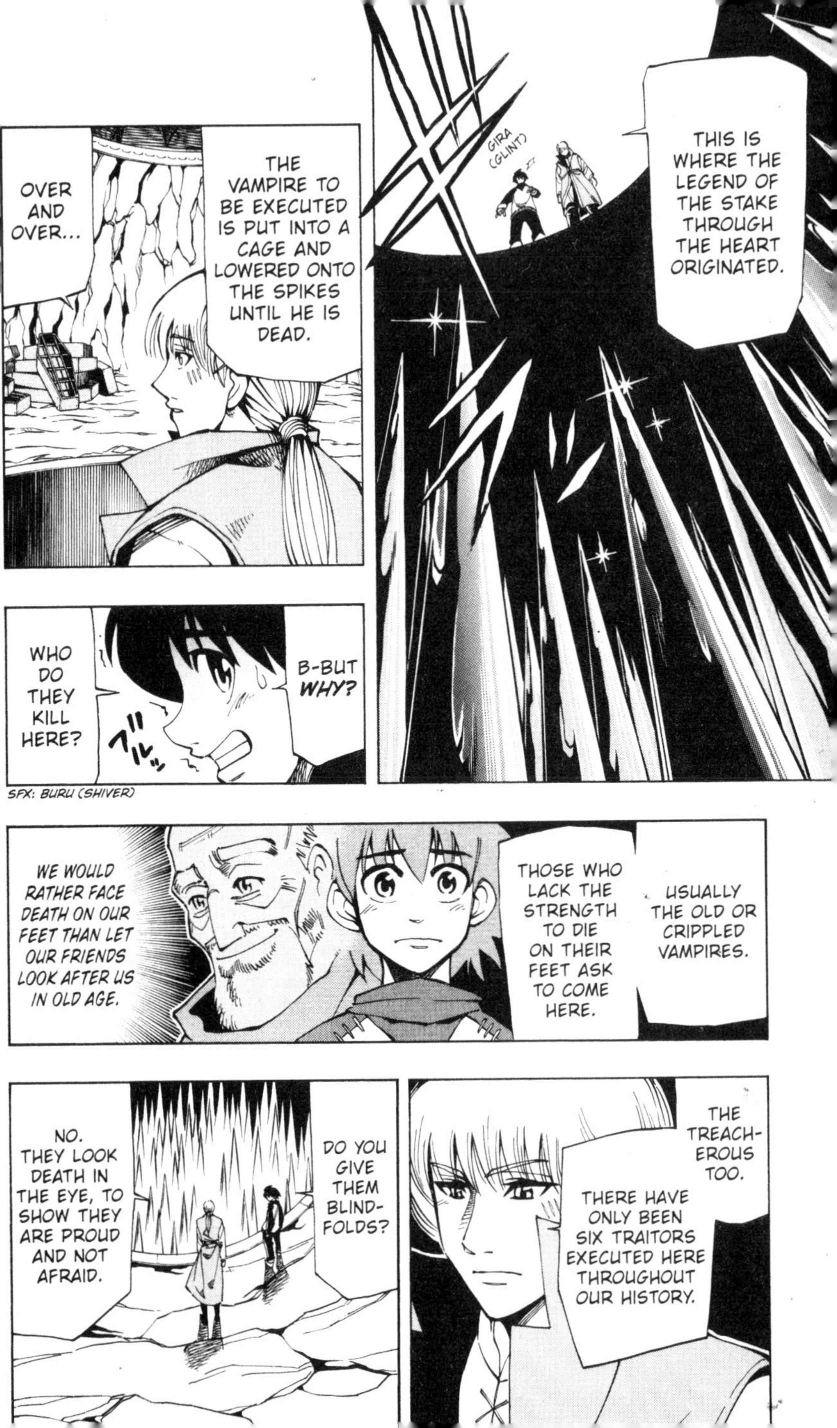
GIRA (GLINT)
THIS IS WHERE THE LEGEND OF THE STAKE THROUGH THE HEART ORIGINATED.
THE VAMPIRE TO BE EXECUTED IS PUT INTO A CAGE AND LOWERED ONTO THE SPIKES UNTIL HE IS DEAD.
OVER AND OVER...
B-BUT *WHY?*
WHO DO THEY KILL HERE?
ブルッ
SFX: BURU (SHIVER)
USUALLY THE OLD OR CRIPPLED VAMPIRES.
THOSE WHO LACK THE STRENGTH TO DIE ON THEIR FEET ASK TO COME HERE.
WE WOULD RATHER FACE DEATH ON OUR FEET THAN LET OUR FRIENDS LOOK AFTER US IN OLD AGE.
THE TREACH-EROUS TOO.
THERE HAVE ONLY BEEN SIX TRAITORS EXECUTED HERE THROUGHOUT OUR HISTORY.
DO YOU GIVE THEM BLIND-FOLDS?
NO. THEY LOOK DEATH IN THE EYE, TO SHOW THEY ARE PROUD AND NOT AFRAID.

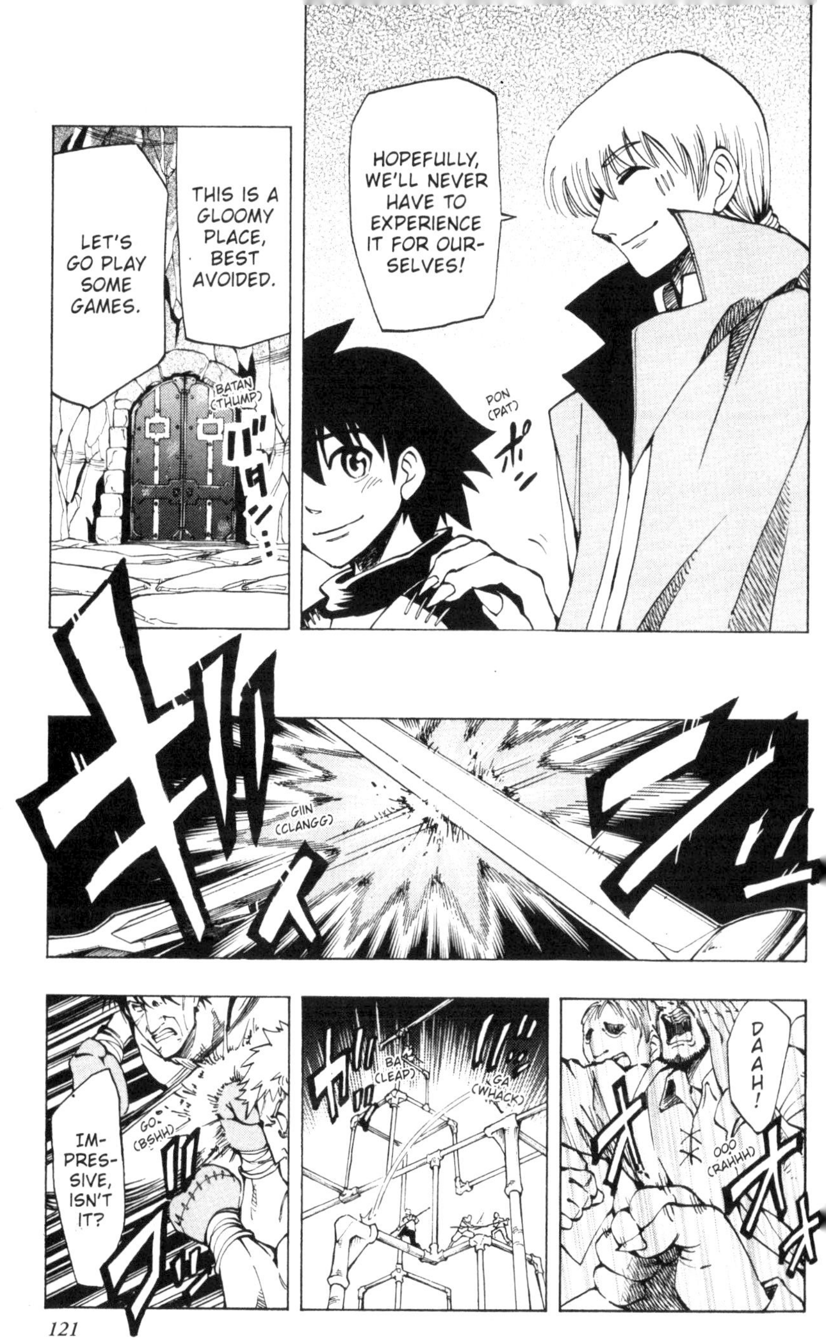
HOPEFULLY, WE'LL NEVER HAVE TO EXPERIENCE IT FOR OUR-SELVES!
PON (PAT)
THIS IS A GLOOMY PLACE, BEST AVOIDED.
LET'S GO PLAY SOME GAMES.
BATAN (THUMP)
GIIN (CLANGG)
DAAH!
OOO (RAHHH)
GA (WHACK)
BA (LEAP)
IM-PRES-SIVE, ISN'T IT?
GO (BSHH)

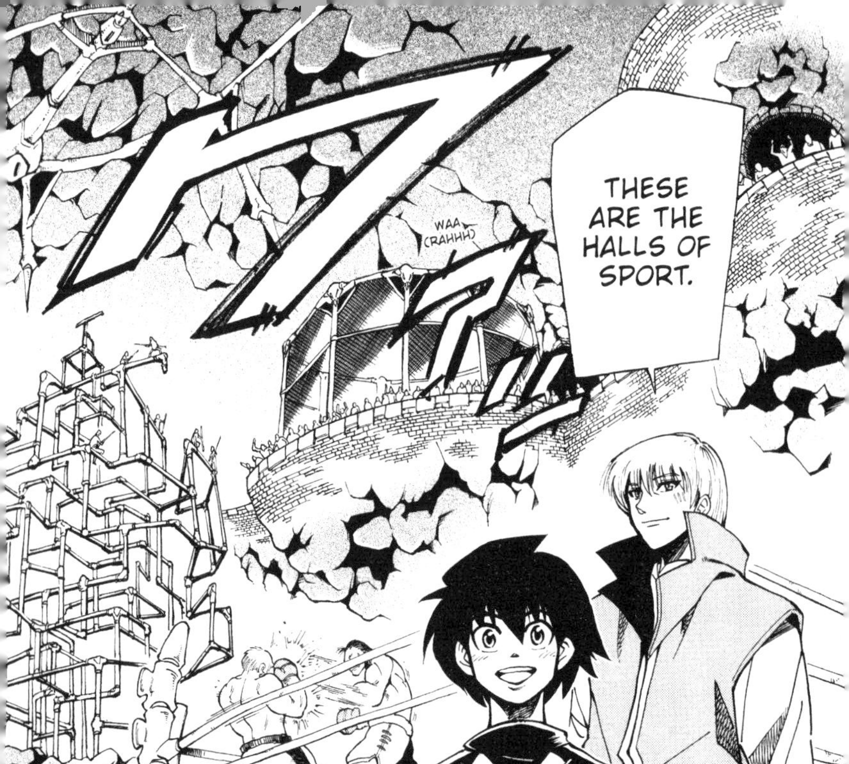
THESE ARE THE HALLS OF SPORT.
WAA (RAHHH)

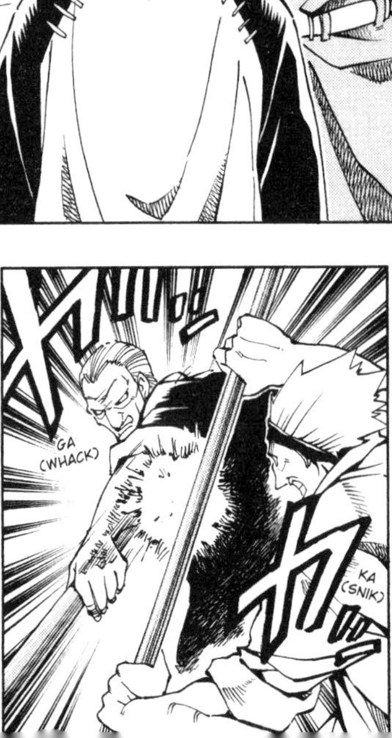
GA (WHACK)
KA (SNIK)

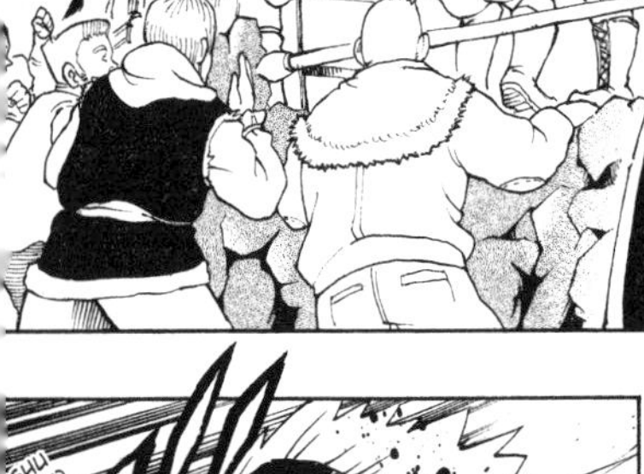
SHU

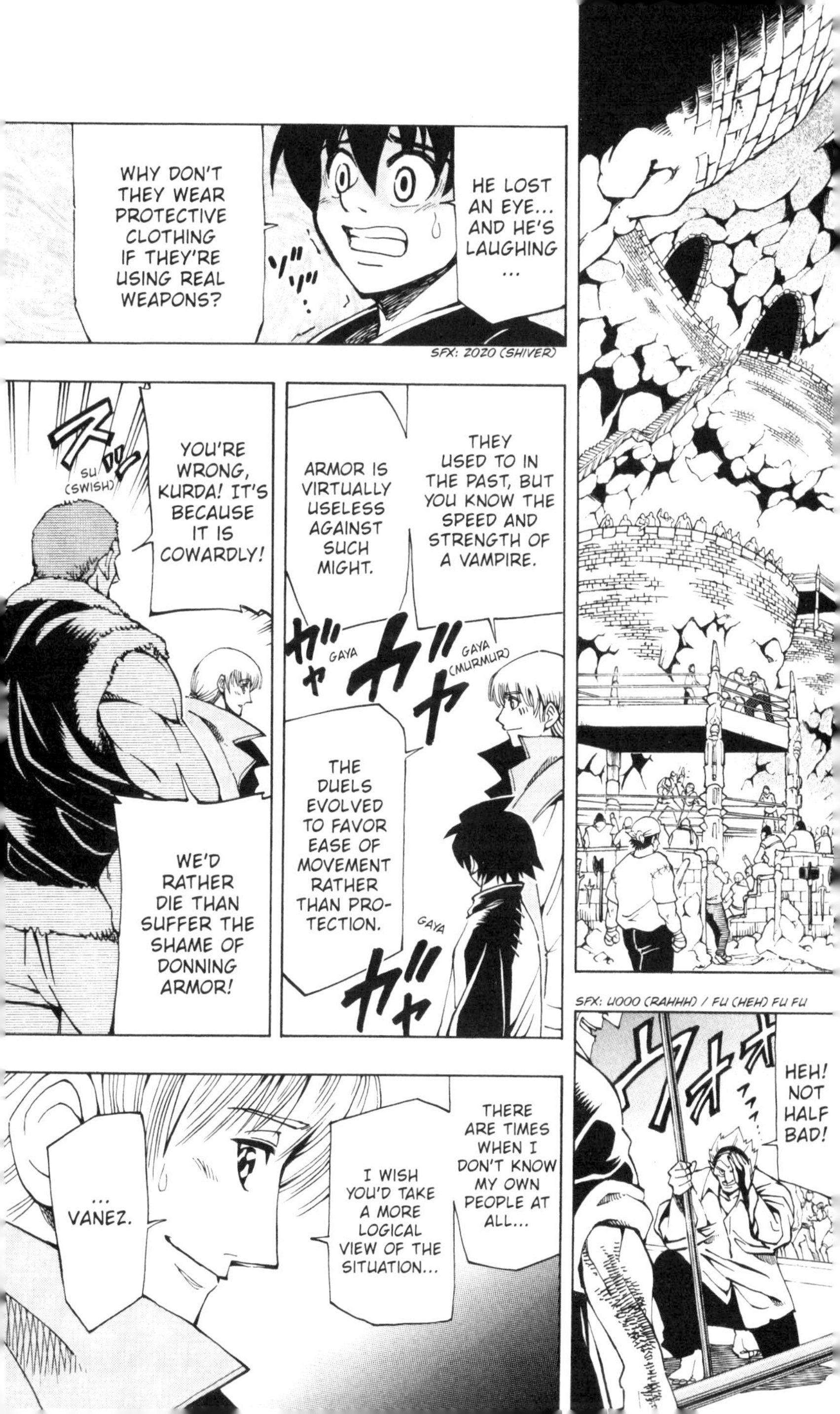
SFX: UOOO (RAHHH) / FU (HEH) FU FU
HE LOST AN EYE... AND HE'S LAUGHING...
WHY DON'T THEY WEAR PROTECTIVE CLOTHING IF THEY'RE USING REAL WEAPONS?
SFX: ZOZO (SHIVER)
THEY USED TO IN THE PAST, BUT YOU KNOW THE SPEED AND STRENGTH OF A VAMPIRE.
ARMOR IS VIRTUALLY USELESS AGAINST SUCH MIGHT.
GAYA (MURMUR)
GAYA
THE DUELS EVOLVED TO FAVOR EASE OF MOVEMENT RATHER THAN PROTECTION.
GAYA
SU (SWISH)
YOU'RE WRONG, KURDA! IT'S BECAUSE IT IS COWARDLY!
WE'D RATHER DIE THAN SUFFER THE SHAME OF DONNING ARMOR!
HEH! NOT HALF BAD!
THERE ARE TIMES WHEN I DON'T KNOW MY OWN PEOPLE AT ALL...
I WISH YOU'D TAKE A MORE LOGICAL VIEW OF THE SITUATION...
... VANEZ.

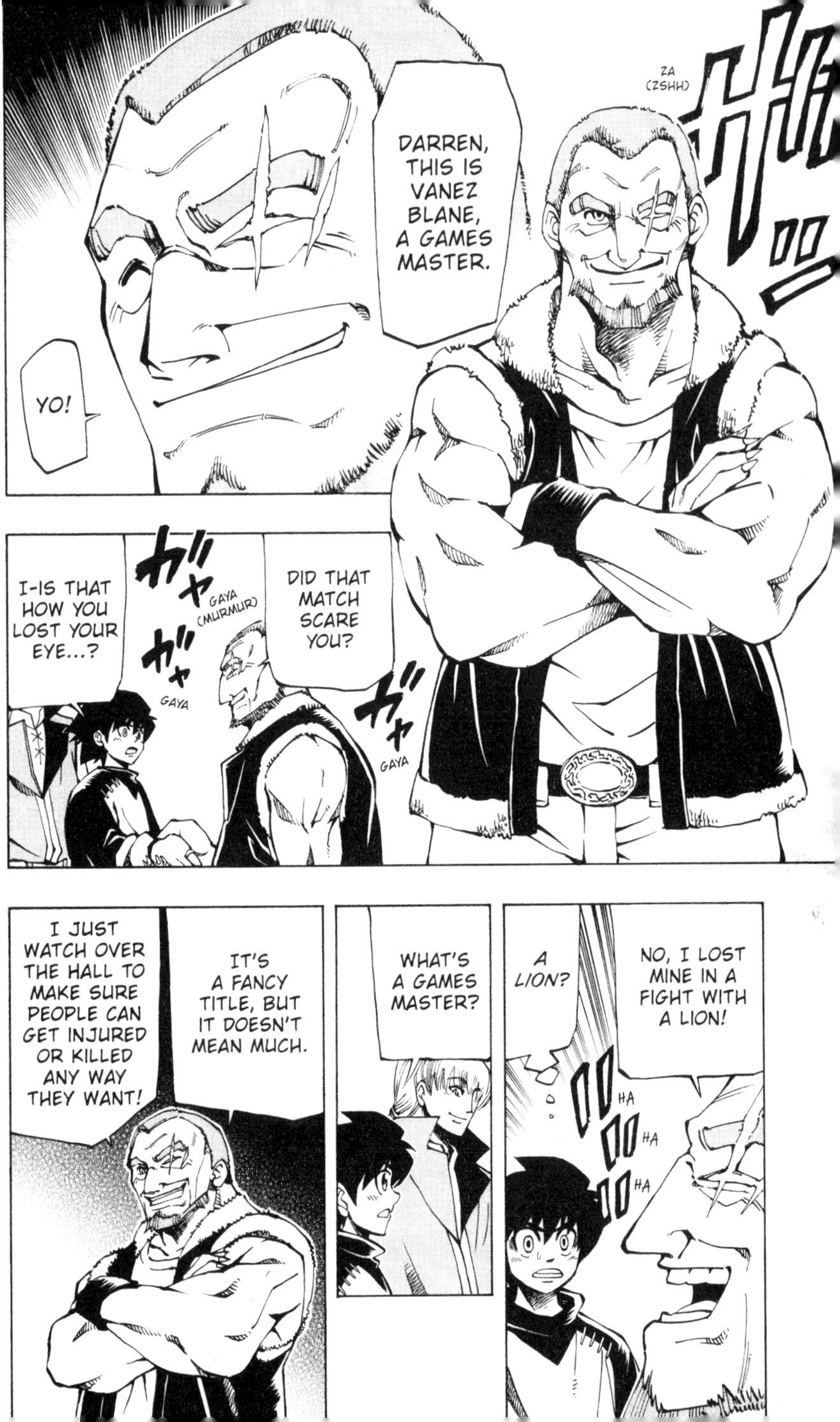
ZA (ZSHH)
DARREN, THIS IS VANEZ BLANE, A GAMES MASTER.
YO!
DID THAT MATCH SCARE YOU?
GAYA
GAYA (MURMUR)
GAYA
I-IS THAT HOW YOU LOST YOUR EYE...?
NO, I LOST MINE IN A FIGHT WITH A LION!
HA HA HA
A LION?
WHAT'S A GAMES MASTER?
IT'S A FANCY TITLE, BUT IT DOESN'T MEAN MUCH.
I JUST WATCH OVER THE HALL TO MAKE SURE PEOPLE CAN GET INJURED OR KILLED ANY WAY THEY WANT!

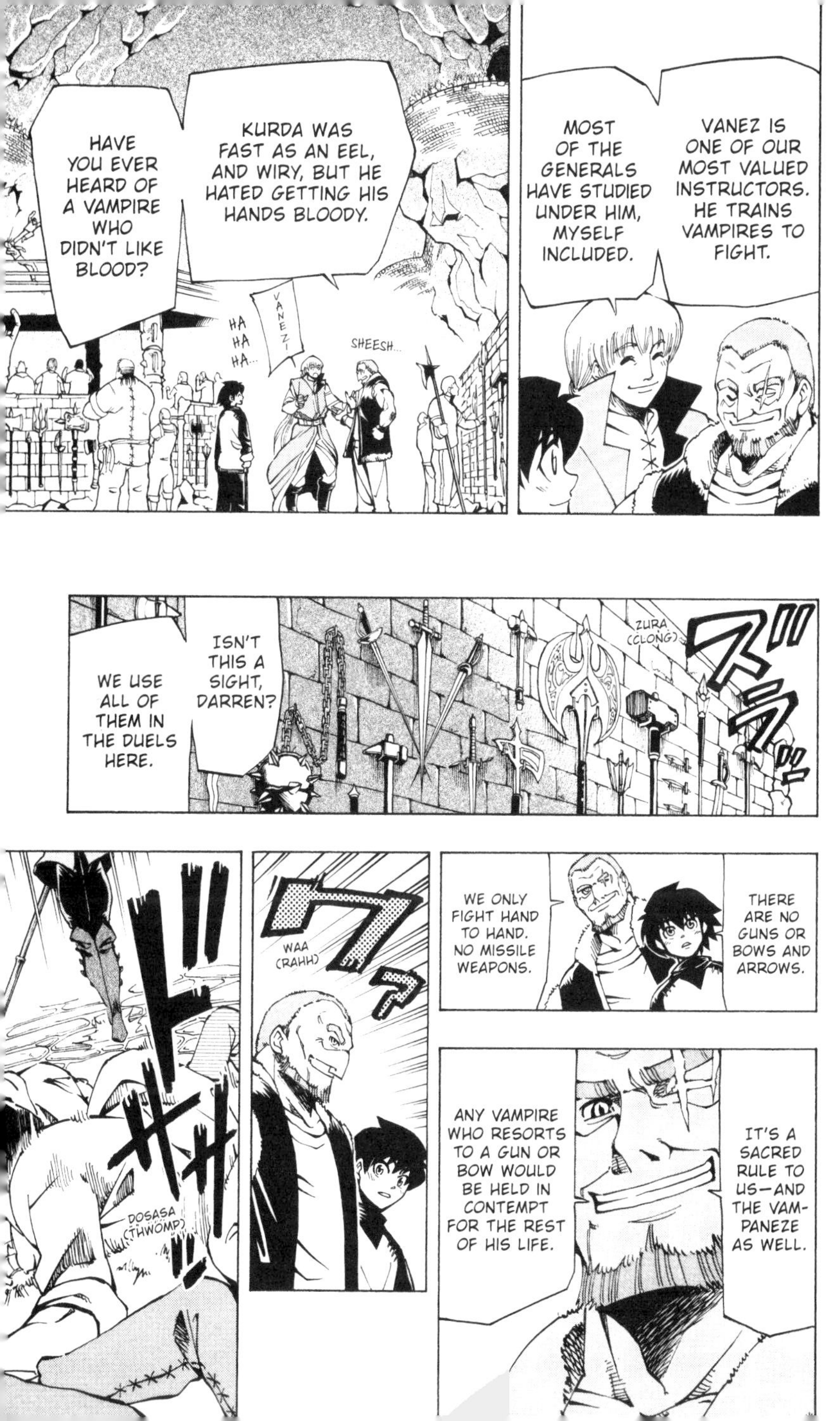
VANEZ IS ONE OF OUR MOST VALUED INSTRUCTORS. HE TRAINS VAMPIRES TO FIGHT.
MOST OF THE GENERALS HAVE STUDIED UNDER HIM, MYSELF INCLUDED.
KURDA WAS FAST AS AN EEL, AND WIRY, BUT HE HATED GETTING HIS HANDS BLOODY.
HAVE YOU EVER HEARD OF A VAMPIRE WHO DIDN'T LIKE BLOOD?
SHEESH...
VANEZ!
HA HA HA...
ZURA (CLONG)
ISN'T THIS A SIGHT, DARREN?
WE USE ALL OF THEM IN THE DUELS HERE.
THERE ARE NO GUNS OR BOWS AND ARROWS.
WE ONLY FIGHT HAND TO HAND. NO MISSILE WEAPONS.
IT'S A SACRED RULE TO US—AND THE VAMPANEZE AS WELL.
ANY VAMPIRE WHO RESORTS TO A GUN OR BOW WOULD BE HELD IN CONTEMPT FOR THE REST OF HIS LIFE.
WAA (RAHH)
DOSASA (THWOMP)

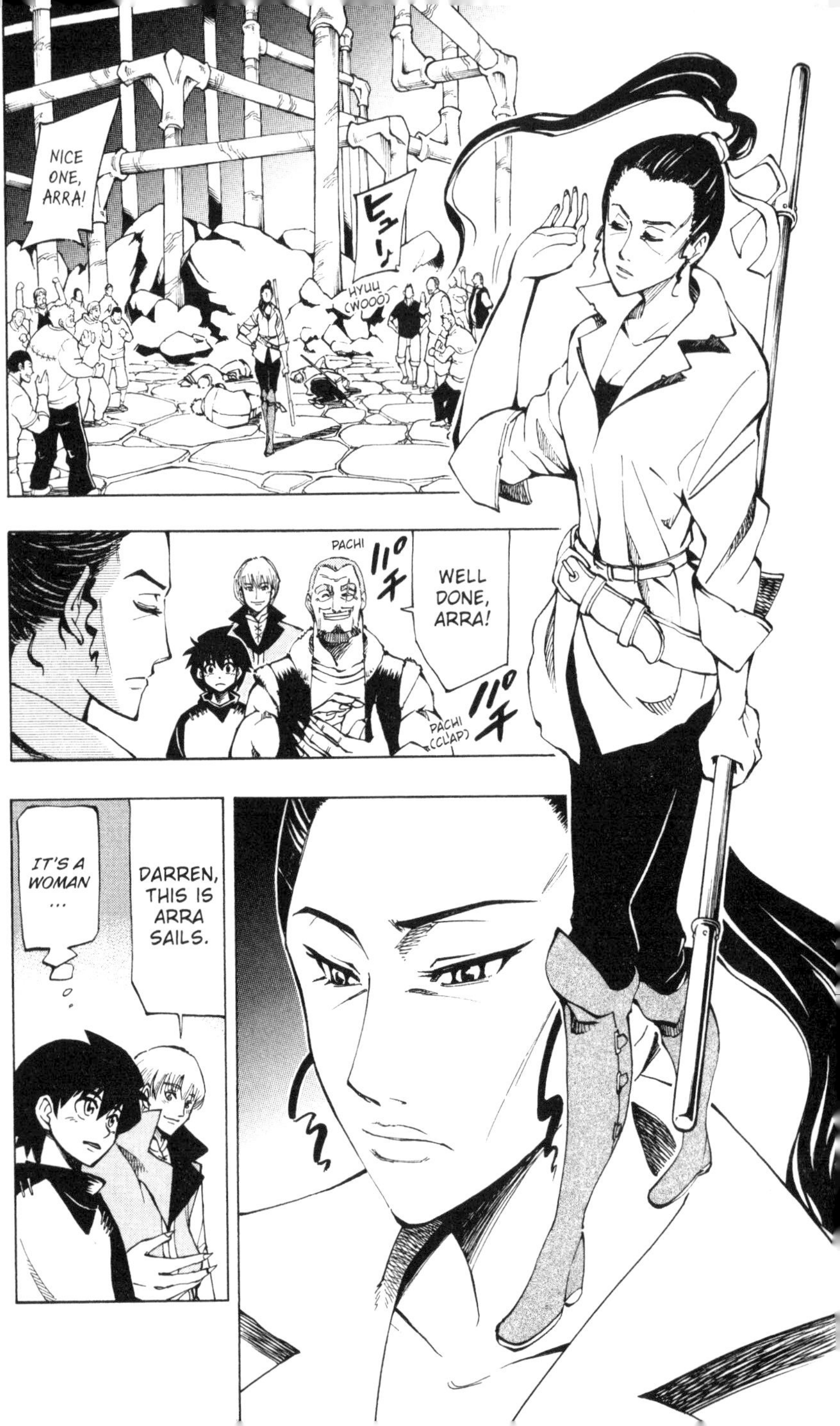
ヒュ～♪
HYUU (WOOO)
NICE ONE, ARRA!
パチ
PACHI
WELL DONE, ARRA!
パチ
PACHI (CLAP)
DARREN, THIS IS ARRA SAILS.
IT'S A WOMAN ...

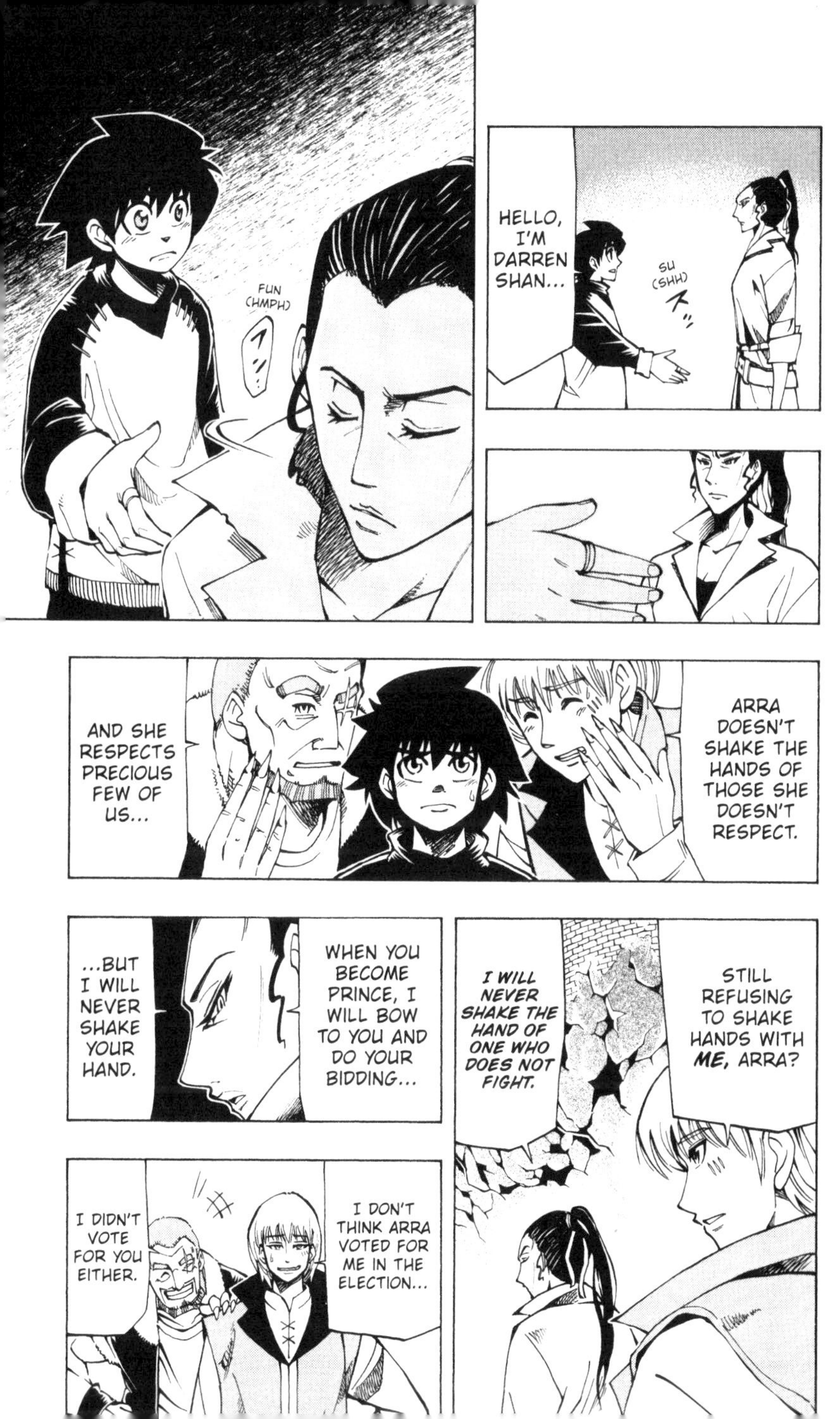
HELLO, I'M DARREN SHAN...
SU (SHH)
FUN (HMPH)
ARRA DOESN'T SHAKE THE HANDS OF THOSE SHE DOESN'T RESPECT.
AND SHE RESPECTS PRECIOUS FEW OF US...
STILL REFUSING TO SHAKE HANDS WITH *ME,* ARRA?
I WILL NEVER SHAKE THE HAND OF ONE WHO DOES NOT FIGHT.
WHEN YOU BECOME PRINCE, I WILL BOW TO YOU AND DO YOUR BIDDING...
...BUT I WILL NEVER SHAKE YOUR HAND.
I DON'T THINK ARRA VOTED FOR ME IN THE ELECTION...
I DIDN'T VOTE FOR YOU EITHER.

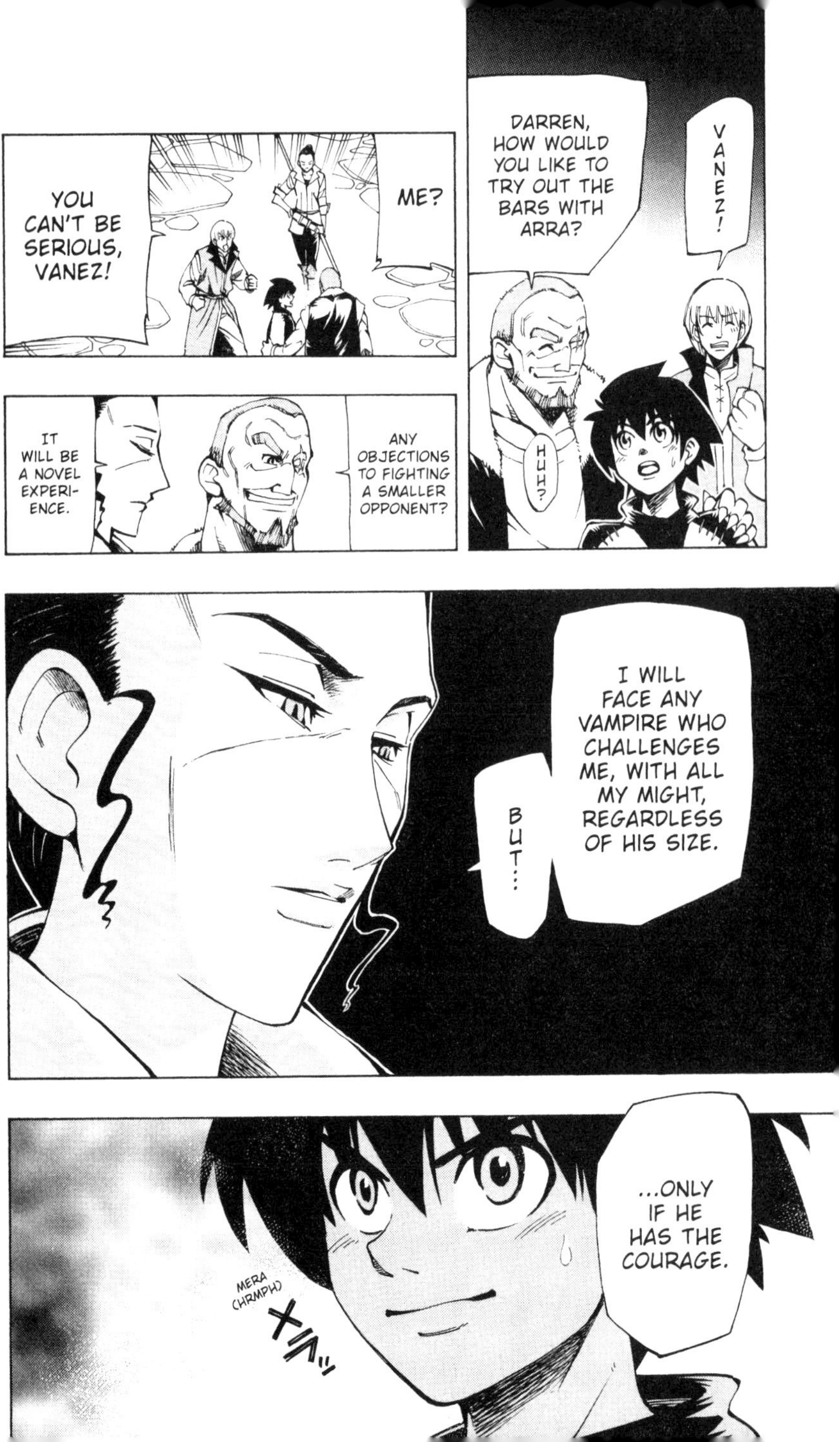
DARREN, HOW WOULD YOU LIKE TO TRY OUT THE BARS WITH ARRA?
VANEZ!
HUH?
ME?
YOU CAN'T BE SERIOUS, VANEZ!
ANY OBJECTIONS TO FIGHTING A SMALLER OPPONENT?
IT WILL BE A NOVEL EXPERIENCE.
I WILL FACE ANY VAMPIRE WHO CHALLENGES ME, WITH ALL MY MIGHT, REGARDLESS OF HIS SIZE.
BUT...
...ONLY IF HE HAS THE COURAGE.
MERA (HRMPH)

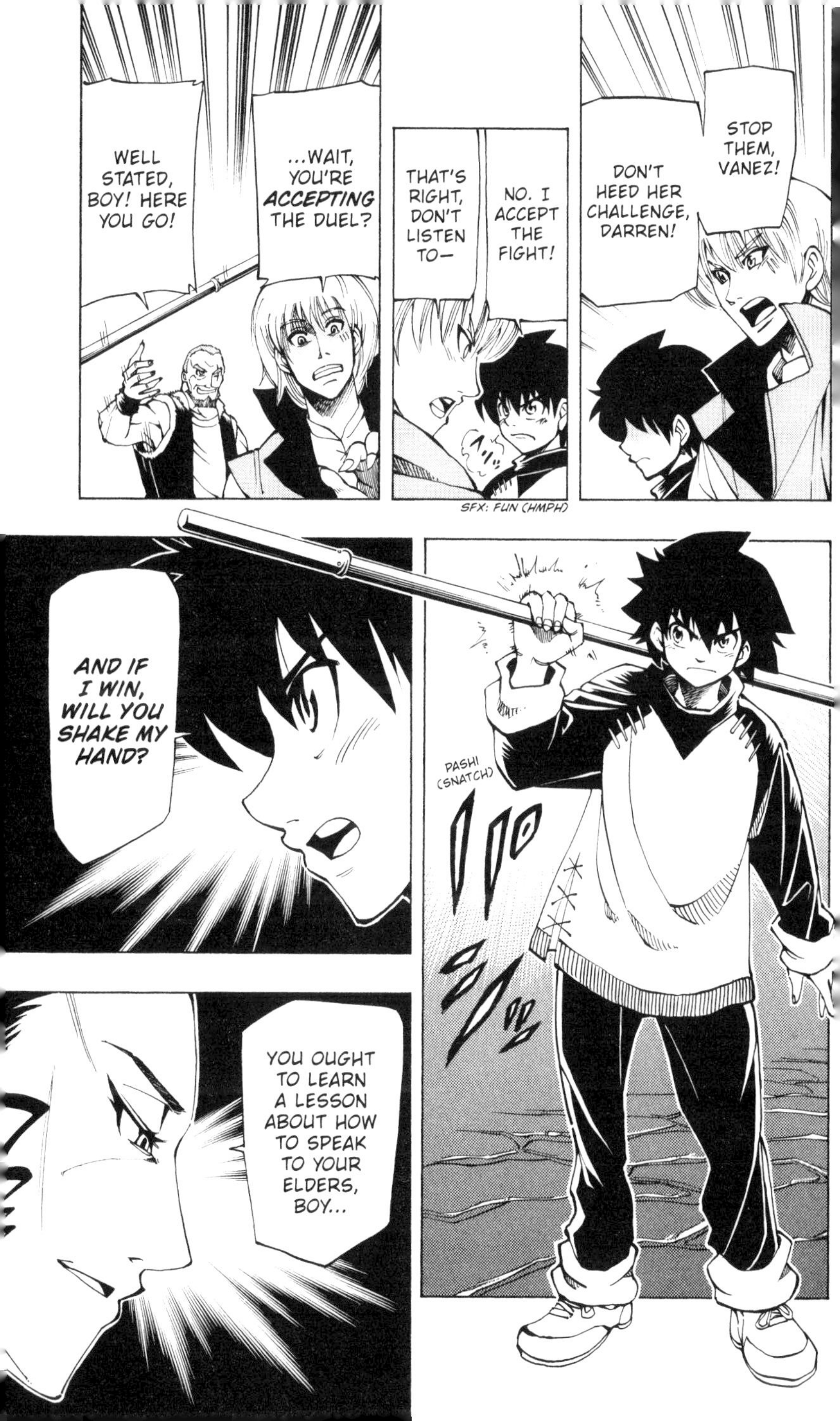
STOP THEM, VANEZ!
DON'T HEED HER CHALLENGE, DARREN!
THAT'S RIGHT, DON'T LISTEN TO—
NO. I ACCEPT THE FIGHT!
SFX: FUN (HMPH)
...WAIT, YOU'RE *ACCEPTING* THE DUEL?
WELL STATED, BOY! HERE YOU GO!
PASHI (SNATCH)
AND IF I WIN, WILL YOU SHAKE MY HAND?
YOU OUGHT TO LEARN A LESSON ABOUT HOW TO SPEAK TO YOUR ELDERS, BOY...

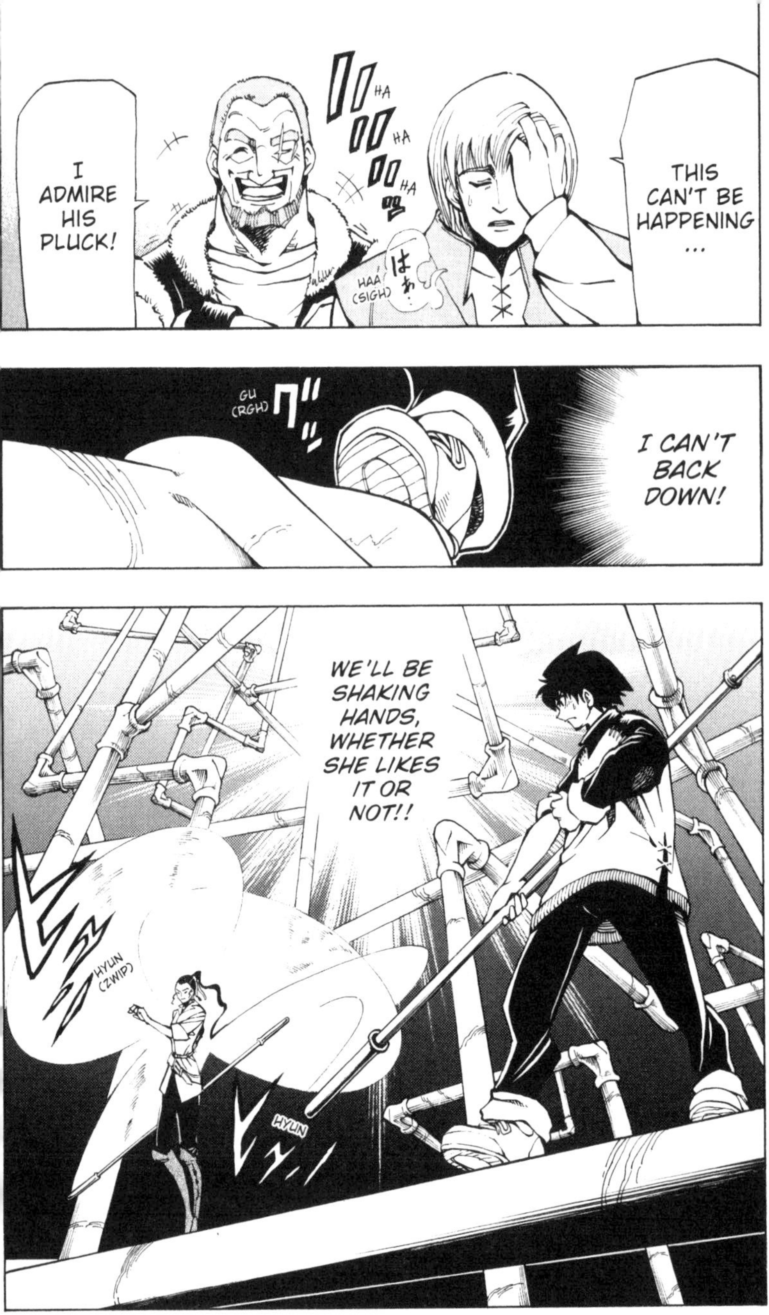
THIS CAN'T BE HAPPENING...
HAA (SIGH) はぁ
HA HA HA
I ADMIRE HIS PLUCK!
I CAN'T BACK DOWN!
GU (RGH) グッ
WE'LL BE SHAKING HANDS, WHETHER SHE LIKES IT OR NOT!!
HYUN
HYUN (ZWIP)

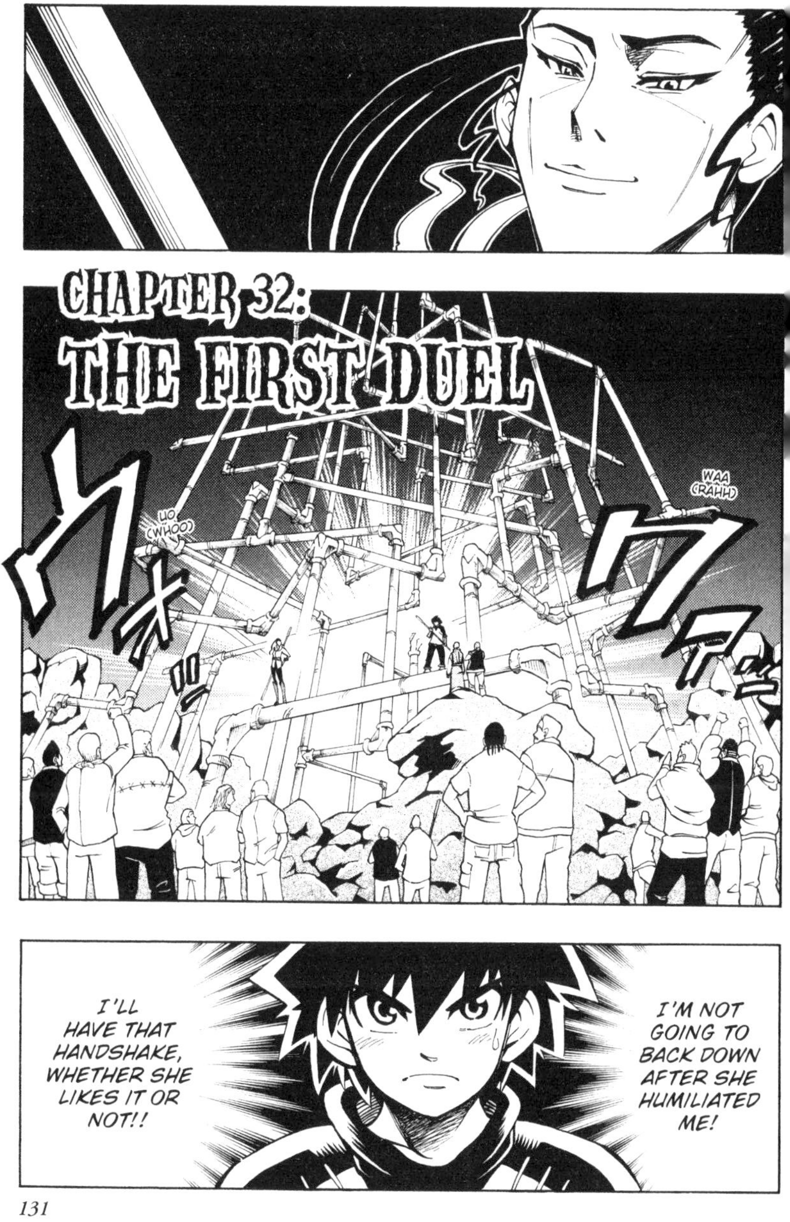
CHAPTER 32:
THE FIRST DUEL
WAA (RAHH)
UO (WHOO)
I'M NOT GOING TO BACK DOWN AFTER SHE HUMILIATED ME!
I'LL HAVE THAT HANDSHAKE, WHETHER SHE LIKES IT OR NOT!!

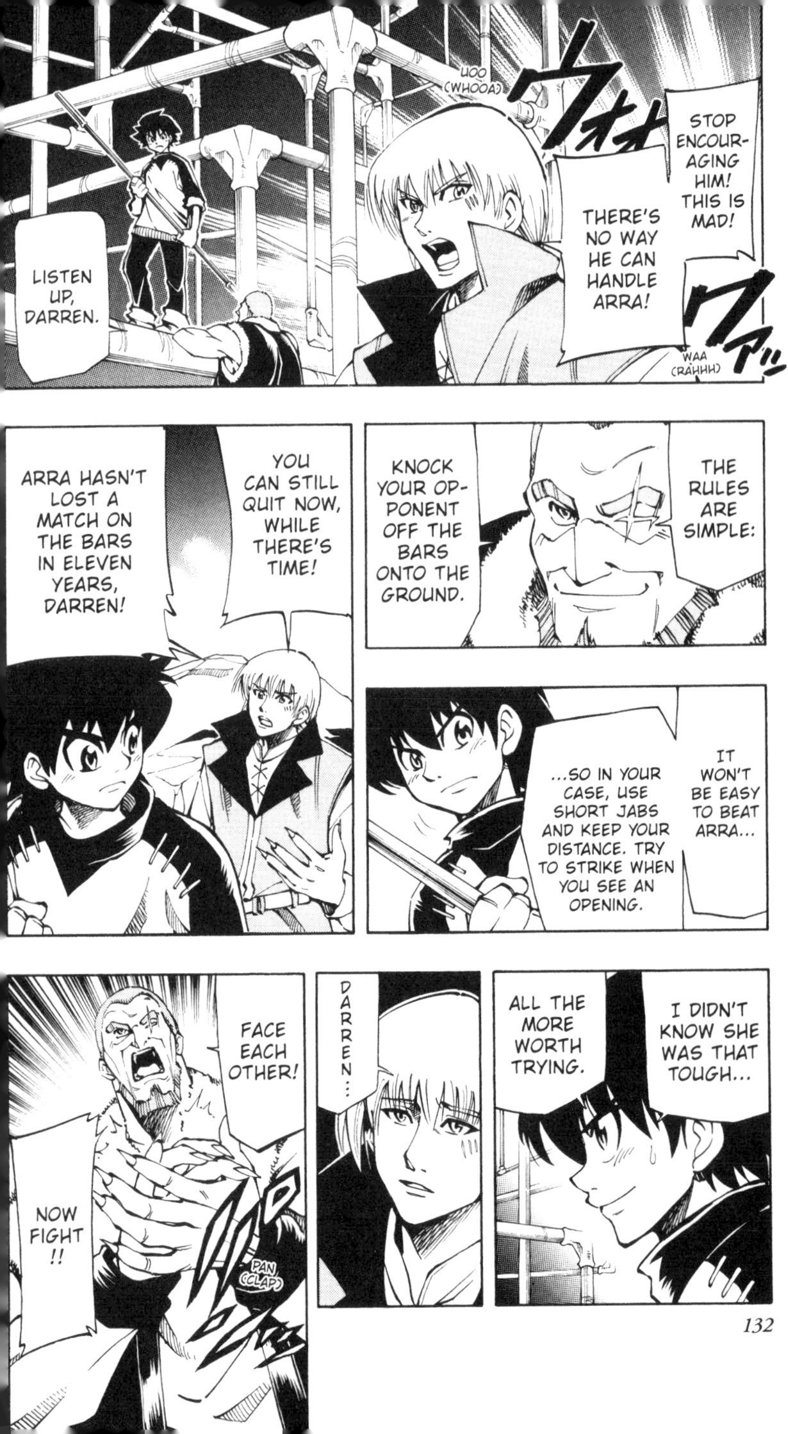
UOO (WHOOA)
STOP ENCOUR-AGING HIM! THIS IS MAD!
THERE'S NO WAY HE CAN HANDLE ARRA!
WAA (RAHHH)
LISTEN UP, DARREN.
THE RULES ARE SIMPLE:
KNOCK YOUR OP-PONENT OFF THE BARS ONTO THE GROUND.
IT WON'T BE EASY TO BEAT ARRA...
...SO IN YOUR CASE, USE SHORT JABS AND KEEP YOUR DISTANCE. TRY TO STRIKE WHEN YOU SEE AN OPENING.
YOU CAN STILL QUIT NOW, WHILE THERE'S TIME!
ARRA HASN'T LOST A MATCH ON THE BARS IN ELEVEN YEARS, DARREN!
I DIDN'T KNOW SHE WAS THAT TOUGH...
ALL THE MORE WORTH TRYING.
DARREN...
FACE EACH OTHER!
NOW FIGHT !!
PAN (CLAP)

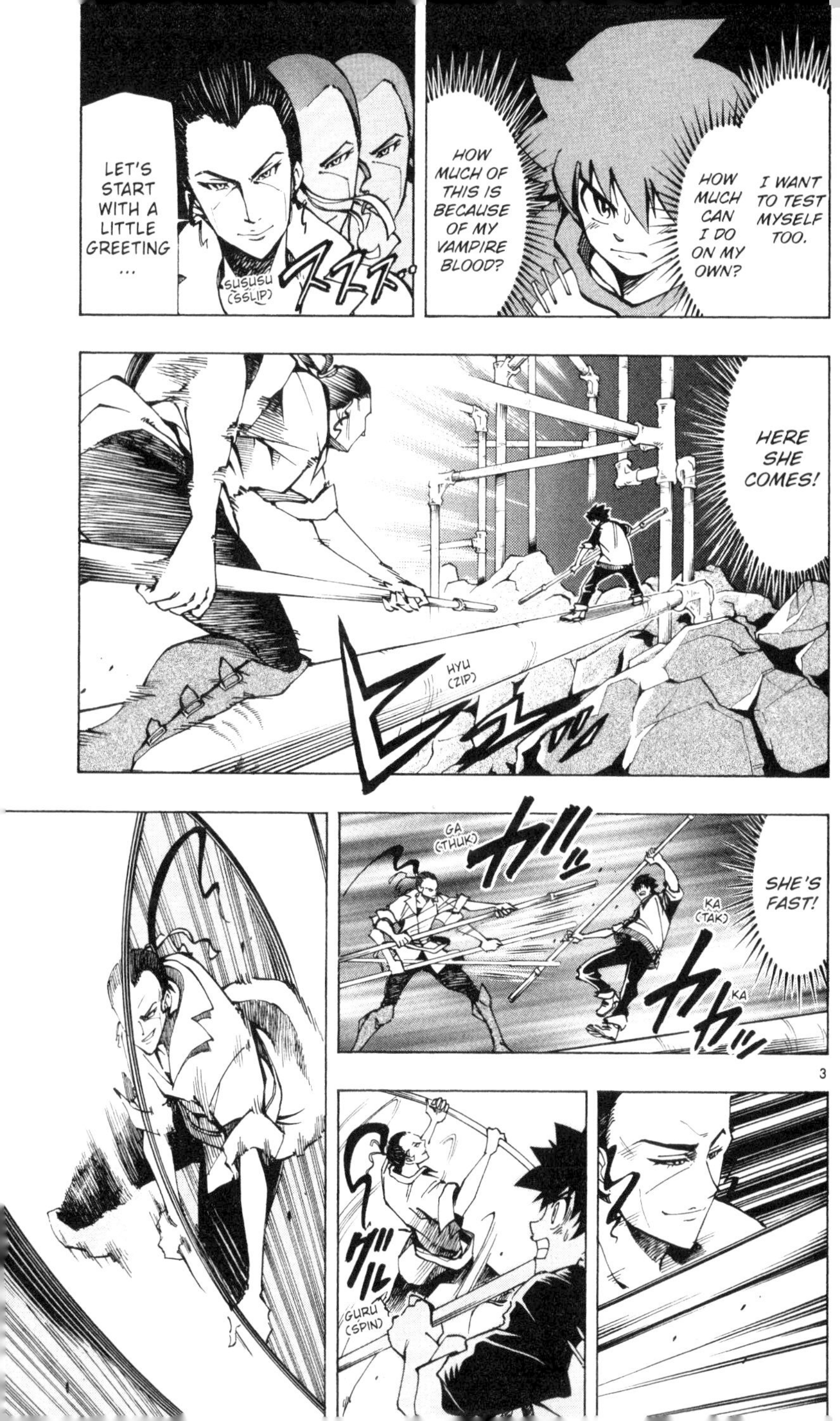

I WANT TO TEST MYSELF TOO.
HOW MUCH CAN I DO ON MY OWN?
HOW MUCH OF THIS IS BECAUSE OF MY VAMPIRE BLOOD?
LET'S START WITH A LITTLE GREETING ...
SUSUSU (SSLIP)
HERE SHE COMES!
HYU (ZIP)
SHE'S FAST!
KA (TAK)
KA
GA (THUK)
GURU (SPIN)

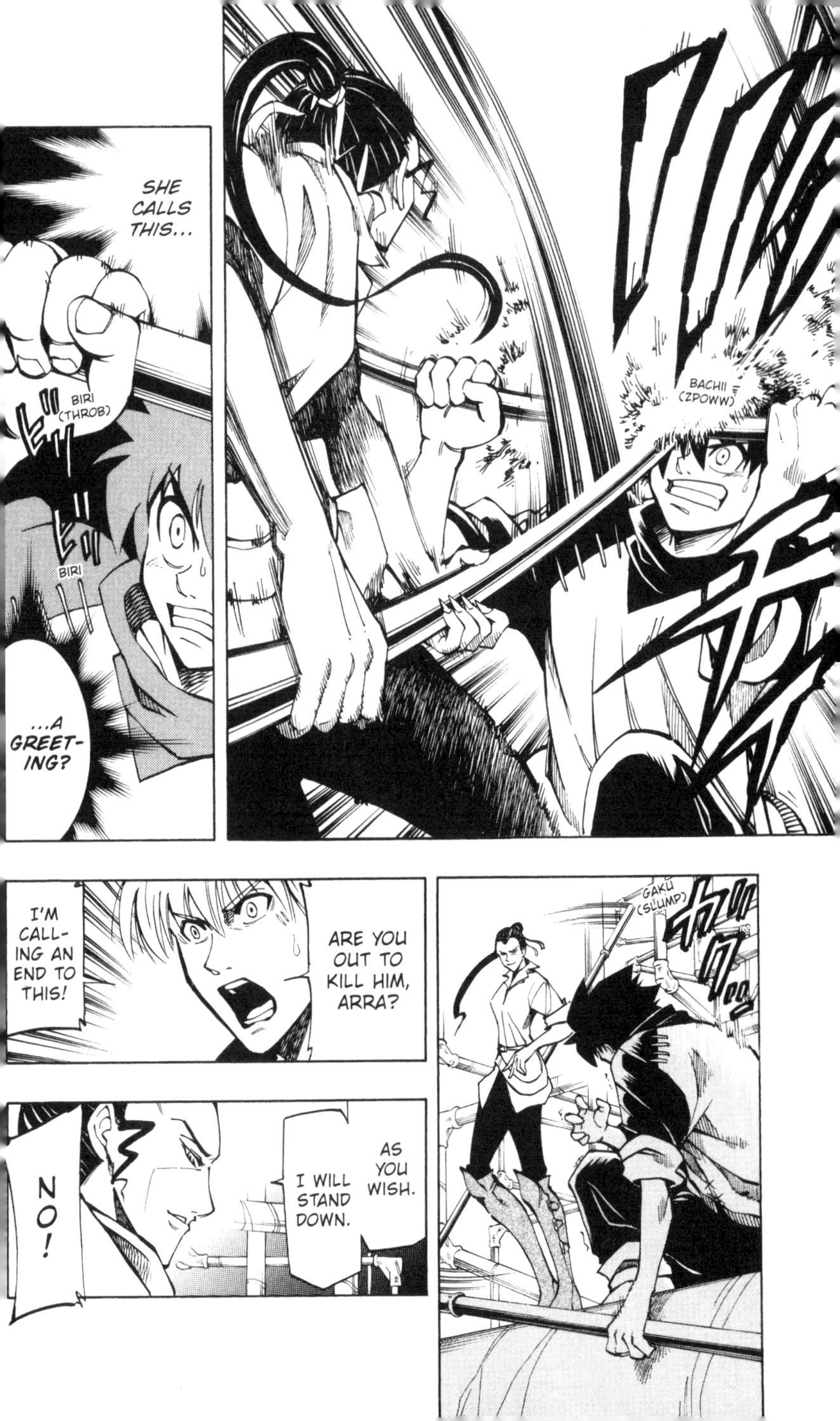
BACHII (ZPOWW)
SHE CALLS THIS...
BIRI (THROB)
BIRI
...A GREETING?
GAKU (SLUMP)
ARE YOU OUT TO KILL HIM, ARRA?
I'M CALLING AN END TO THIS!
AS YOU WISH.
I WILL STAND DOWN.
NO!

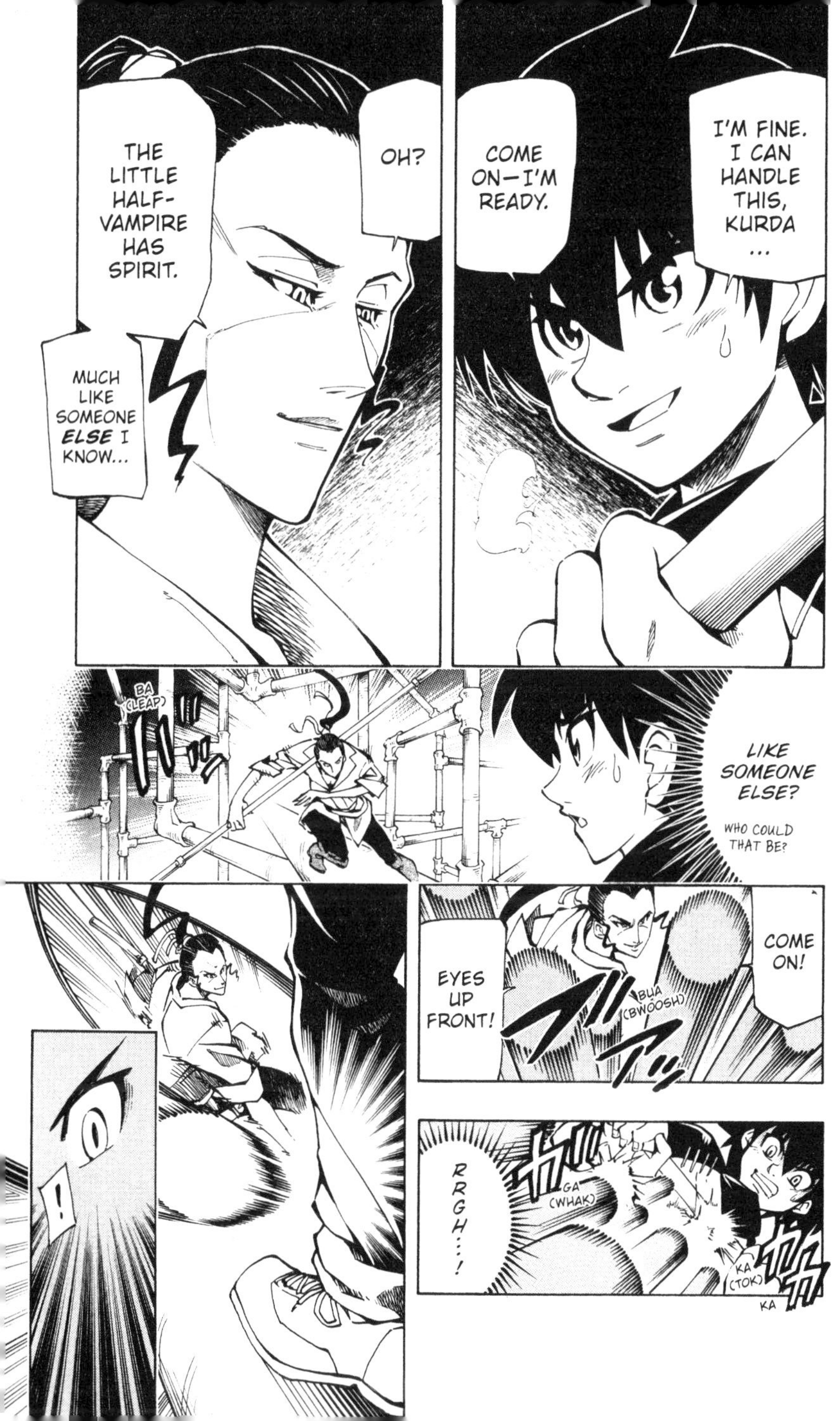
I'M FINE. I CAN HANDLE THIS, KURDA ...
COME ON—I'M READY.
OH?
THE LITTLE HALF-VAMPIRE HAS SPIRIT.
MUCH LIKE SOMEONE ELSE I KNOW...
LIKE SOMEONE ELSE?
WHO COULD THAT BE?
BA (LEAP)
COME ON!
EYES UP FRONT!
BUA (BWOOSH)
GA (WHAK)
KA (TOK)
KA
RRGH...!
!

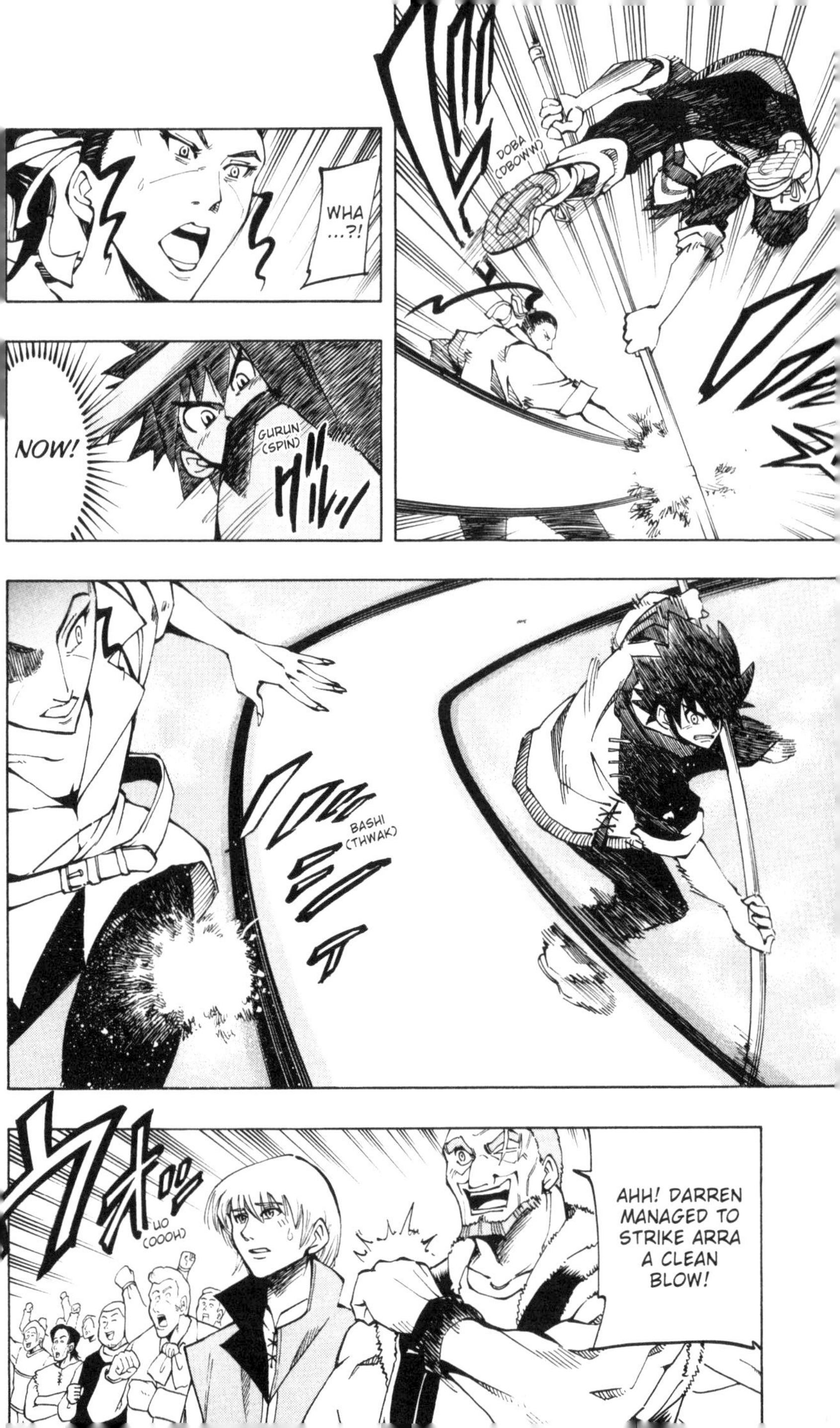
DOBA (DBOWW)
WHA ...?!
NOW!
GURUN (SPIN)
BASHI (THWAK)
AHH! DARREN MANAGED TO STRIKE ARRA A CLEAN BLOW!
UO (OOOH)

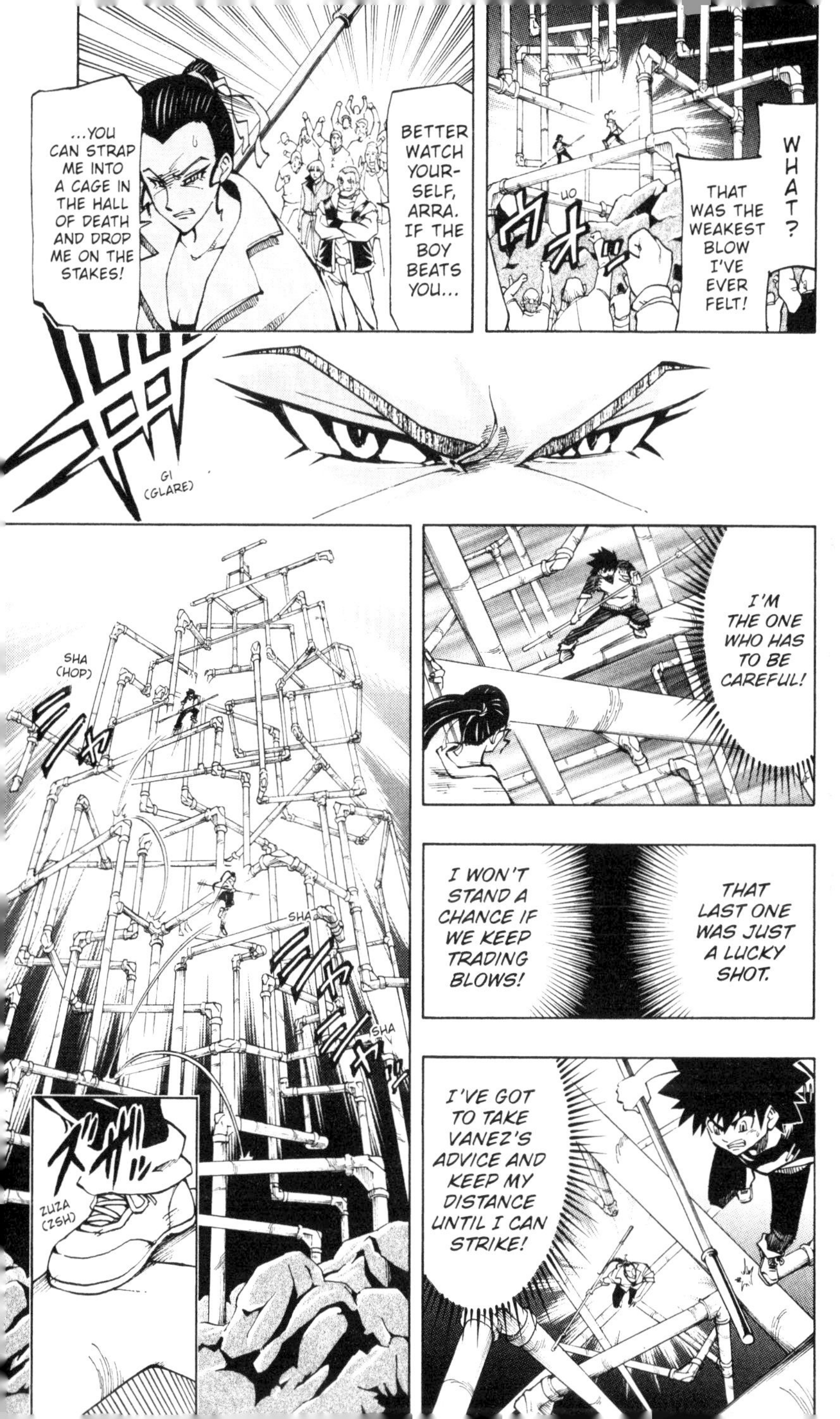
WHAT?
THAT WAS THE WEAKEST BLOW I'VE EVER FELT!
UO
BETTER WATCH YOURSELF, ARRA. IF THE BOY BEATS YOU...
...YOU CAN STRAP ME INTO A CAGE IN THE HALL OF DEATH AND DROP ME ON THE STAKES!
GI (GLARE)
I'M THE ONE WHO HAS TO BE CAREFUL!
THAT LAST ONE WAS JUST A LUCKY SHOT.
I WON'T STAND A CHANCE IF WE KEEP TRADING BLOWS!
I'VE GOT TO TAKE VANEZ'S ADVICE AND KEEP MY DISTANCE UNTIL I CAN STRIKE!
SHA (HOP)
SHA
SHA
ZUZA (ZSH)

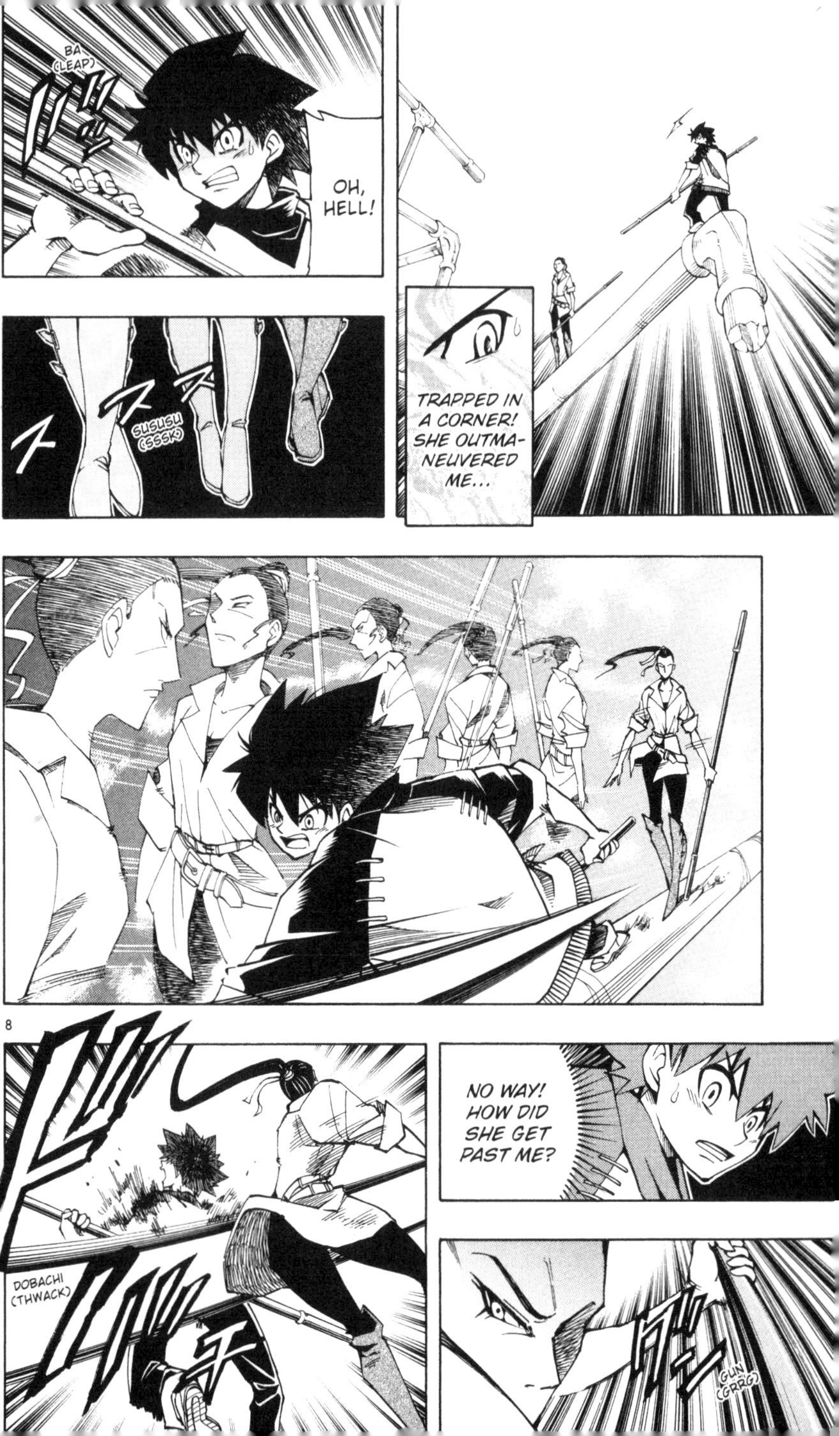
TRAPPED IN A CORNER! SHE OUTMANEUVERED ME...
BA (LEAP)
OH, HELL!
SUSUSU (SSSK)
NO WAY! HOW DID SHE GET PAST ME?
GUN (GRRG)
DOBACHI (THWACK)

8

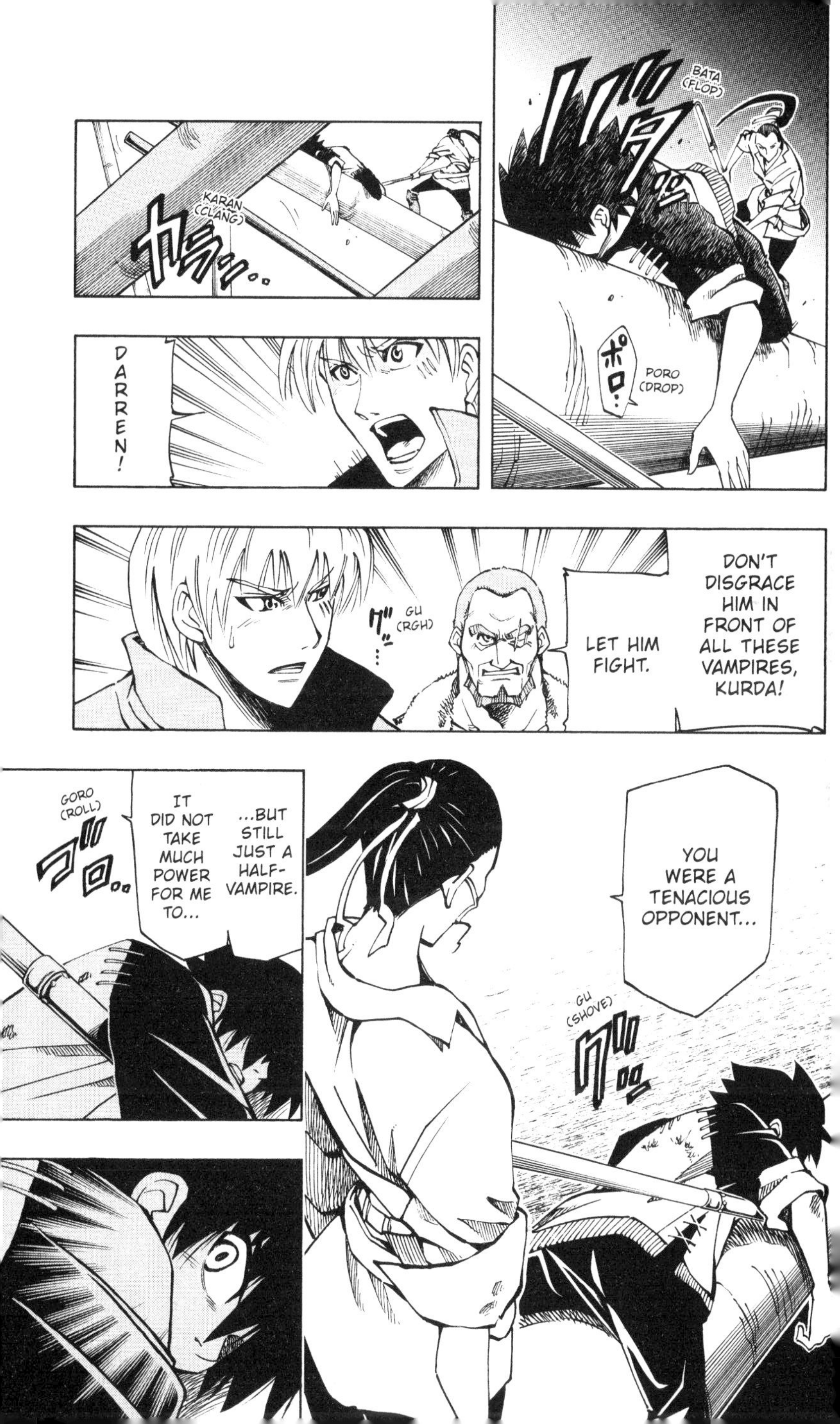
BATA
(FLOP)
PORO
(DROP)
KARAN
(CLANG)
DARREN!
DON'T DISGRACE HIM IN FRONT OF ALL THESE VAMPIRES, KURDA!
LET HIM FIGHT.
GU
(RGH)
YOU WERE A TENACIOUS OPPONENT...
GU
(SHOVE)
...BUT STILL JUST A HALF-VAMPIRE.
IT DID NOT TAKE MUCH POWER FOR ME TO...
GORO
(ROLL)

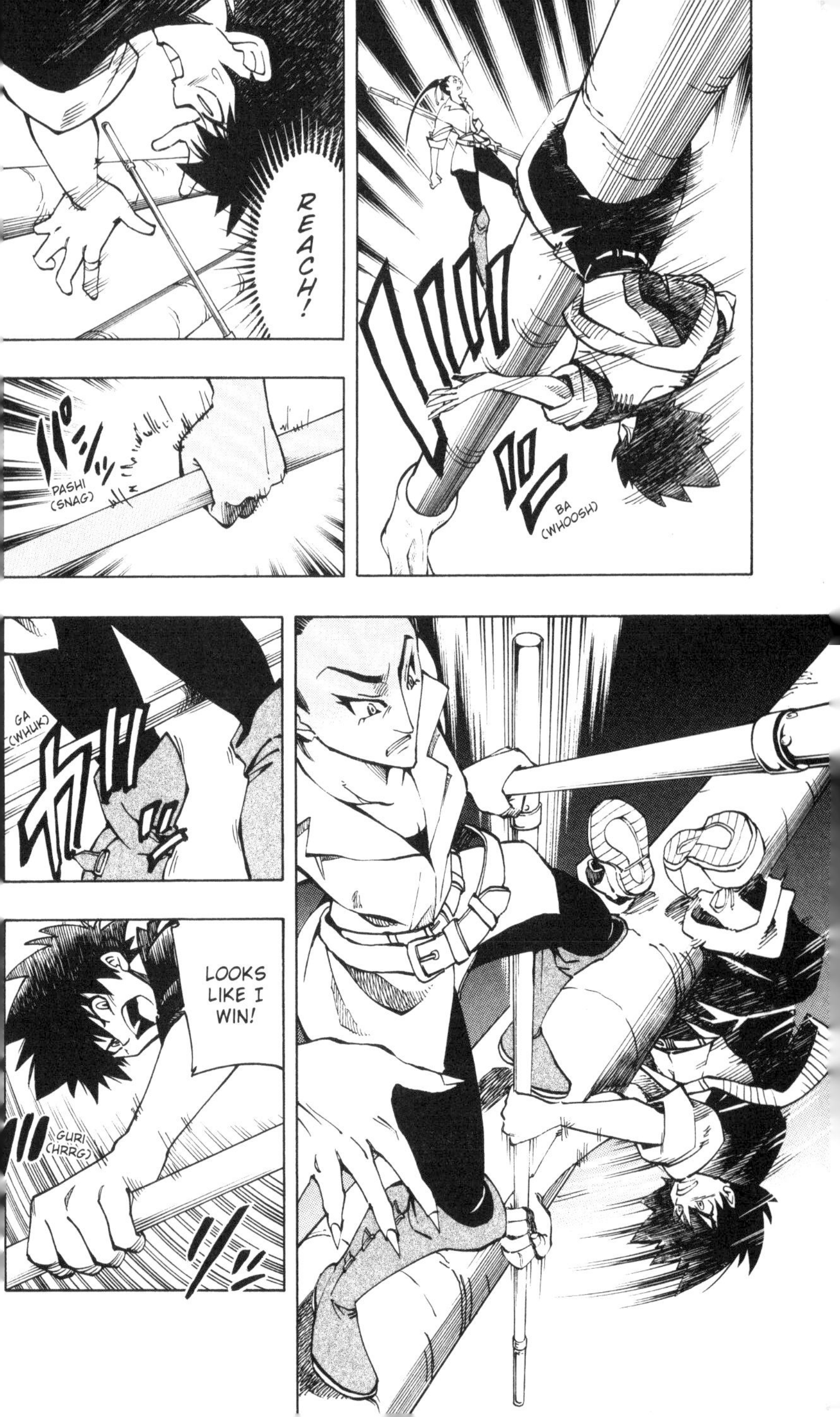
BA (WHOOSH)
REACH!
PASHI (SNAG)
GA (WHUK)
LOOKS LIKE I WIN!
GURI (HRRG)

BA
(SWOOSH)

GASHU
(SNAG)

AH!

PACHI
(CLAP)

PACHI

UOOOO
(WHOAAA)

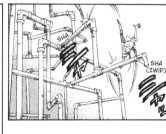

SHA

SHA
(ZWIP)

TA
(TEK)

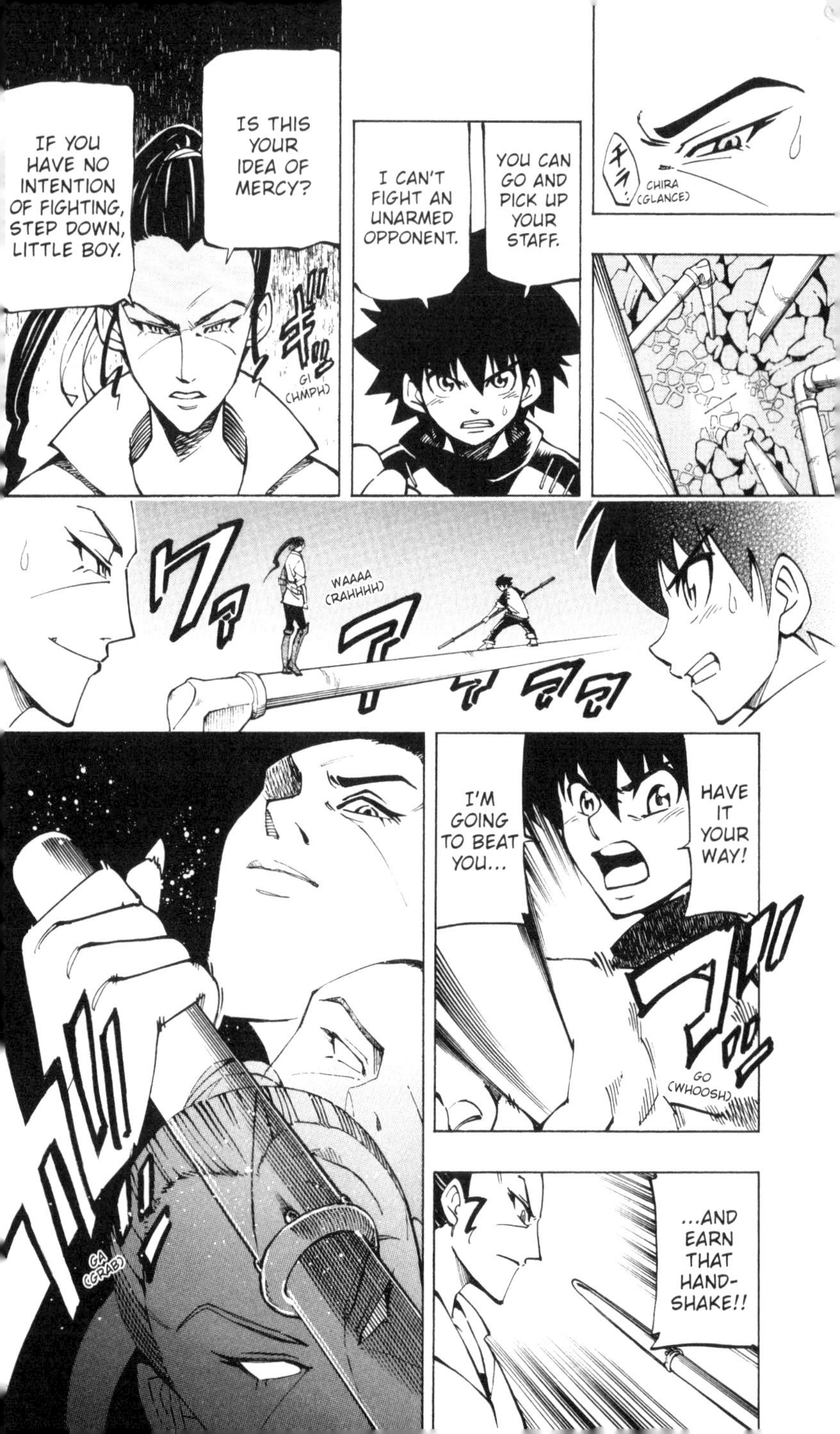
チラ
CHIRA (GLANCE)
YOU CAN GO AND PICK UP YOUR STAFF.
I CAN'T FIGHT AN UNARMED OPPONENT.
IS THIS YOUR IDEA OF MERCY?
IF YOU HAVE NO INTENTION OF FIGHTING, STEP DOWN, LITTLE BOY.
GI (HMPH)
WAAAA (RAHHHH)
HAVE IT YOUR WAY!
I'M GOING TO BEAT YOU...
GO (WHOOSH)
...AND EARN THAT HAND-SHAKE!!
GA (GRAB)

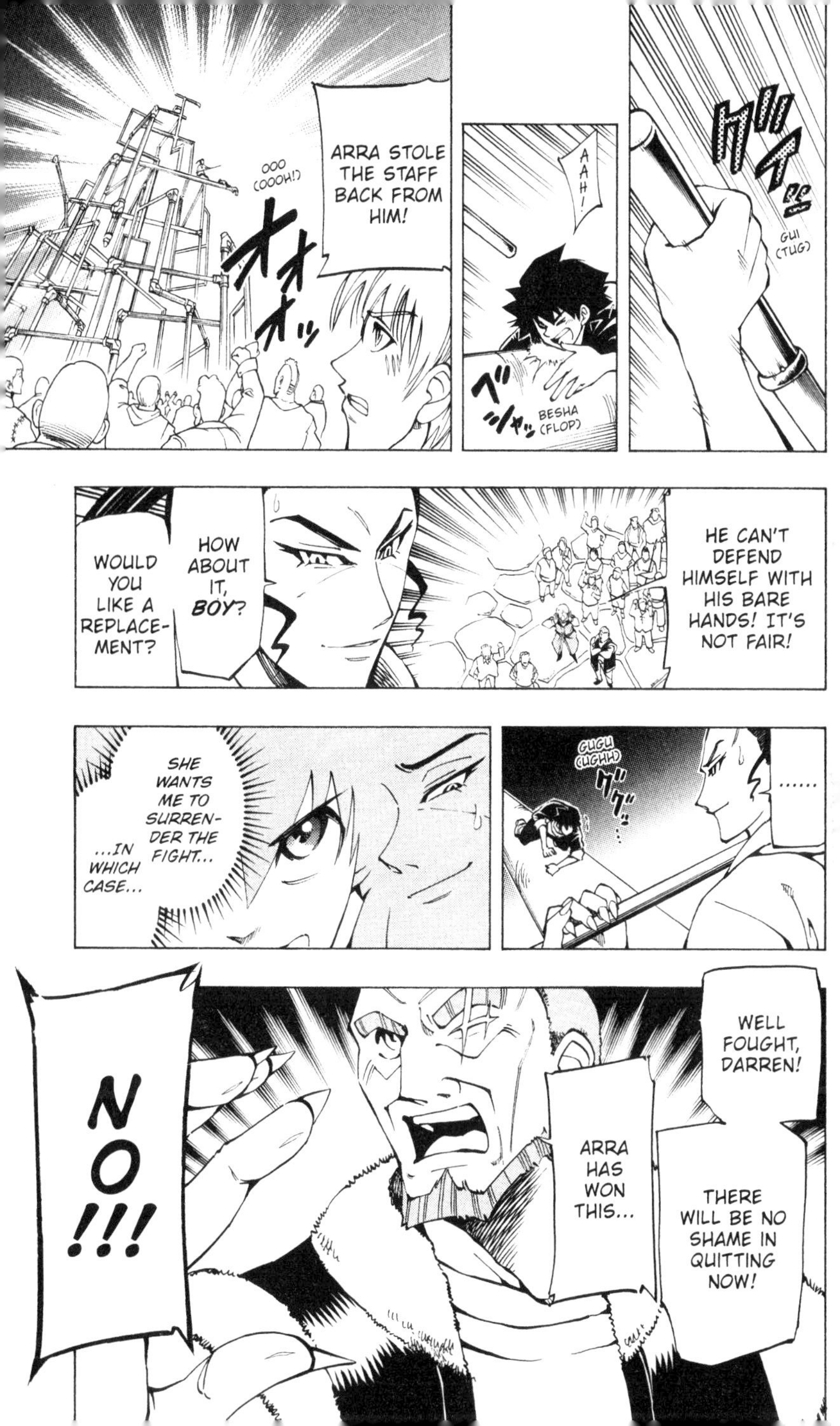
GUI (TUG)
AAH!
BESHA (FLOP)
ARRA STOLE THE STAFF BACK FROM HIM!
OOO (OOOH!)
HE CAN'T DEFEND HIMSELF WITH HIS BARE HANDS! IT'S NOT FAIR!
HOW ABOUT IT, *BOY*?
WOULD YOU LIKE A REPLACE-MENT?
......
GUGU (UGHH)
SHE WANTS ME TO SURREN-DER THE FIGHT...
...IN WHICH CASE...
WELL FOUGHT, DARREN!
ARRA HAS WON THIS...
THERE WILL BE NO SHAME IN QUITTING NOW!
NO!!!

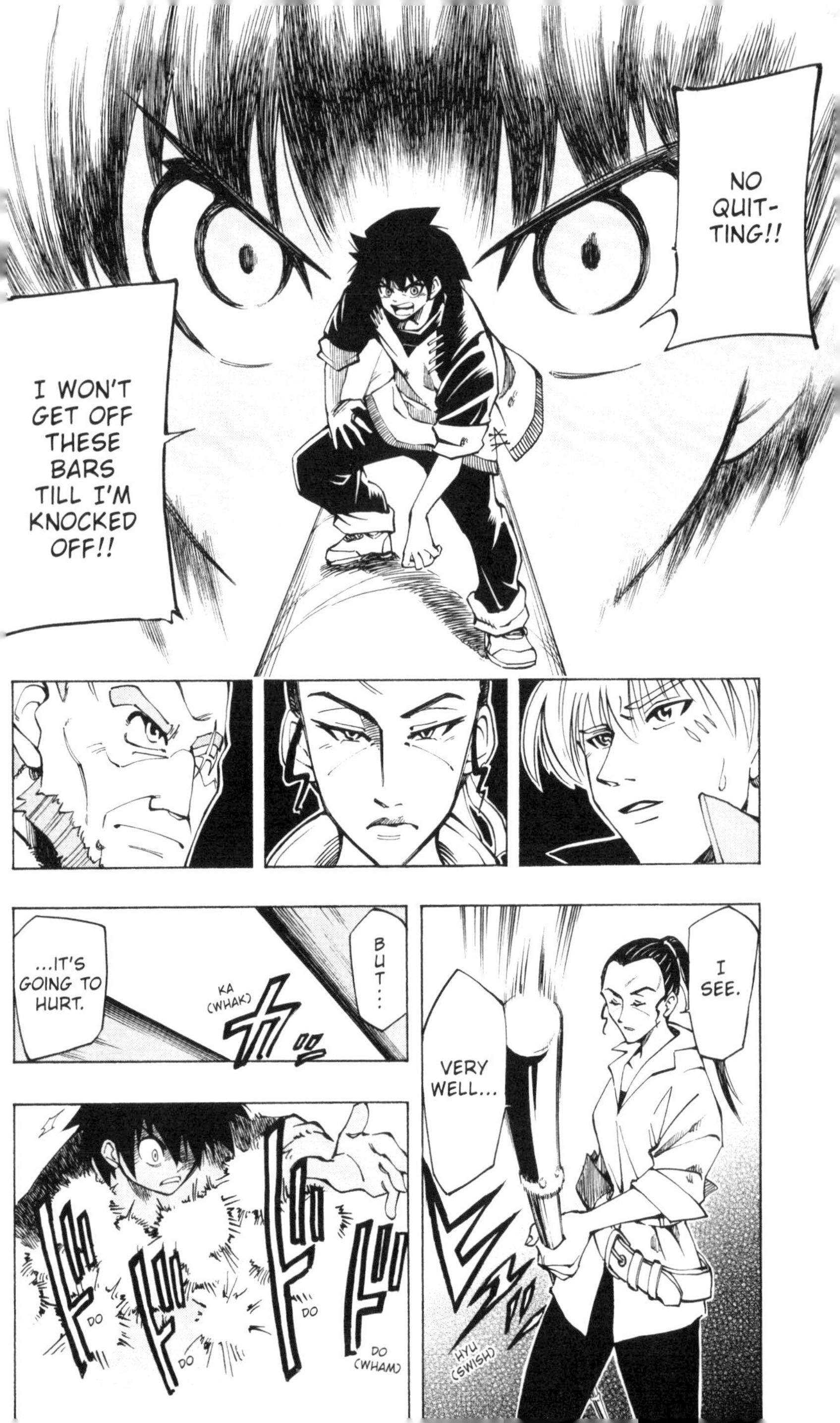
NO QUITTING!!
I WON'T GET OFF THESE BARS TILL I'M KNOCKED OFF!!
I SEE.
VERY WELL...
HYU (SWISH)
BUT...
...IT'S GOING TO HURT.
KA (WHAK)
DO
DO
DO
DO (WHAM)

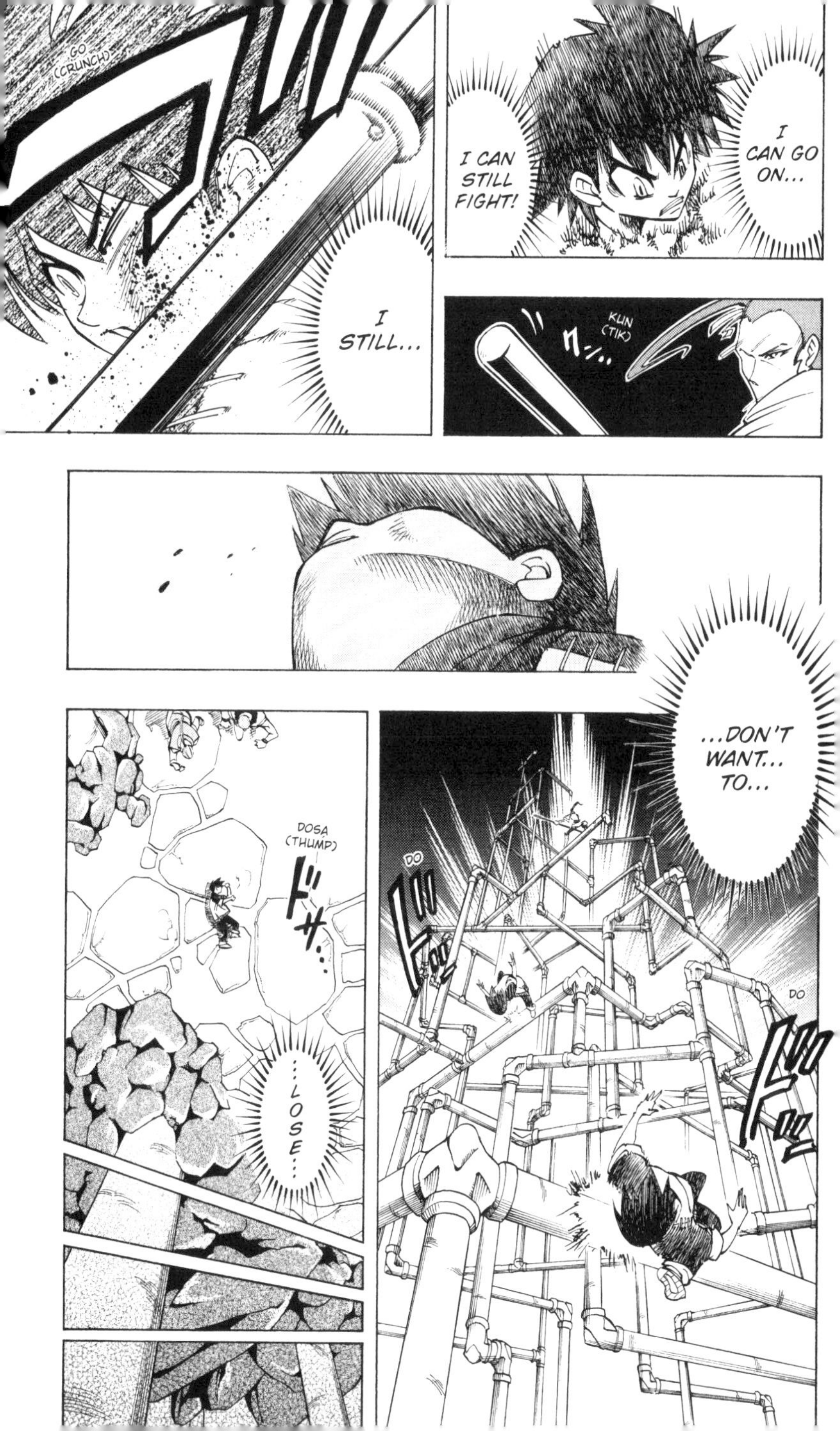
I CAN GO ON...
I CAN STILL FIGHT!
KUN (TIK)
GO (CRUNCH)
I STILL...
...DON'T WANT... TO...
DO
DO
DOSA (THUMP)
...LOSE...

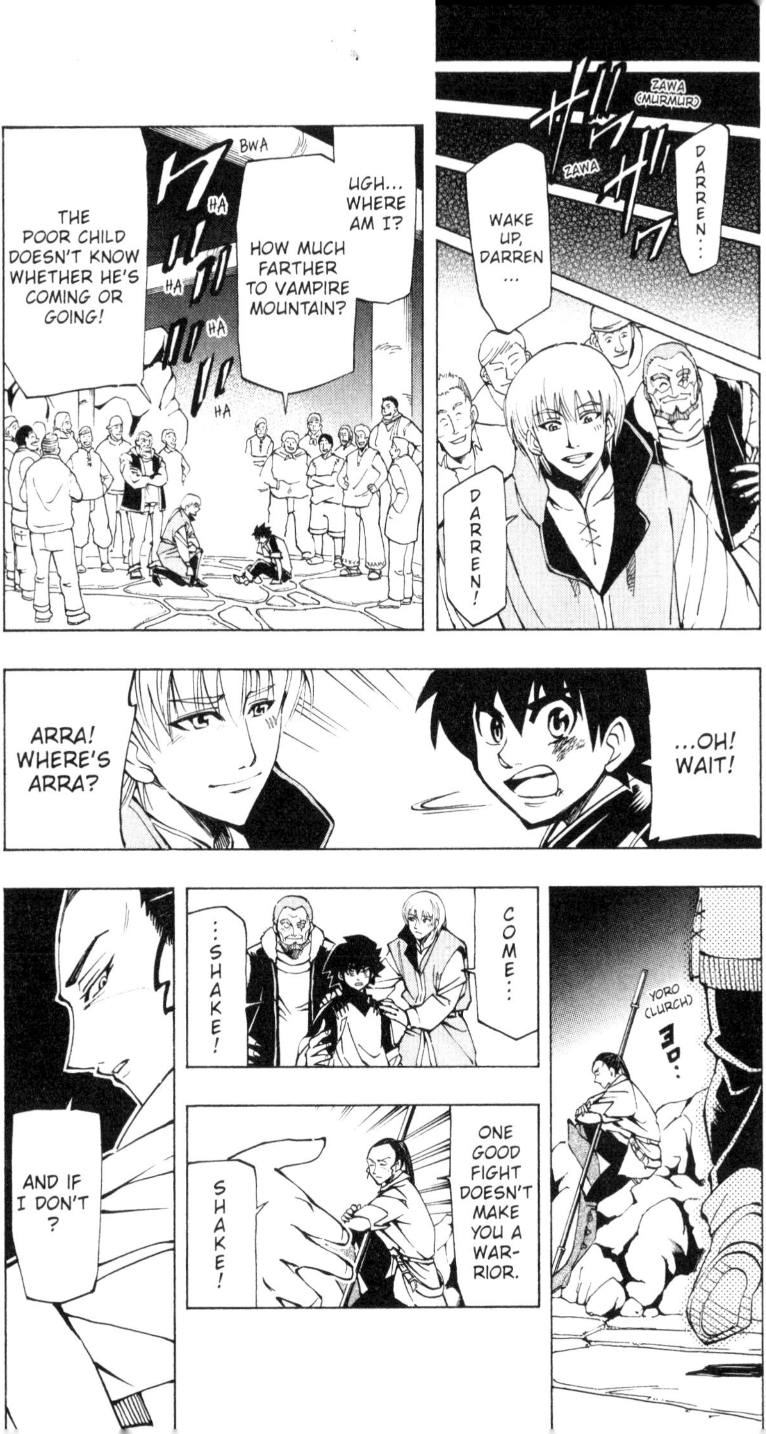
ZAWA (MURMUR)
ZAWA
DARREN...
WAKE UP, DARREN...
DARREN!
UGH... WHERE AM I?
HOW MUCH FARTHER TO VAMPIRE MOUNTAIN?
BWA
HA
HA
HA
HA
THE POOR CHILD DOESN'T KNOW WHETHER HE'S COMING OR GOING!
...OH! WAIT!
ARRA! WHERE'S ARRA?
YORO (LURCH)
COME...
...SHAKE!
ONE GOOD FIGHT DOESN'T MAKE YOU A WARRIOR.
SHAKE!
AND IF I DON'T?

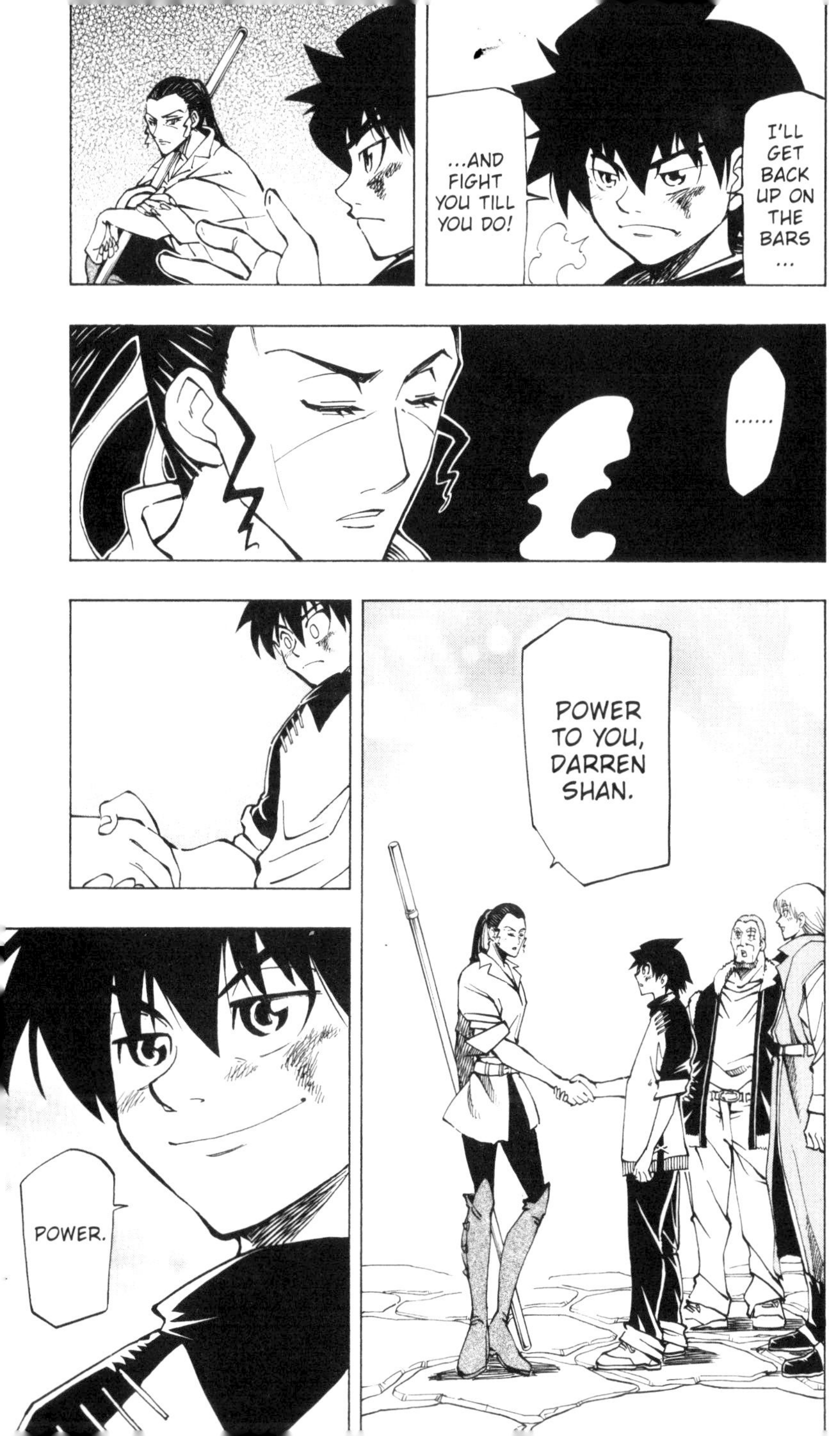
I'LL GET BACK UP ON THE BARS ...
...AND FIGHT YOU TILL YOU DO!
......
POWER TO YOU, DARREN SHAN.
POWER.

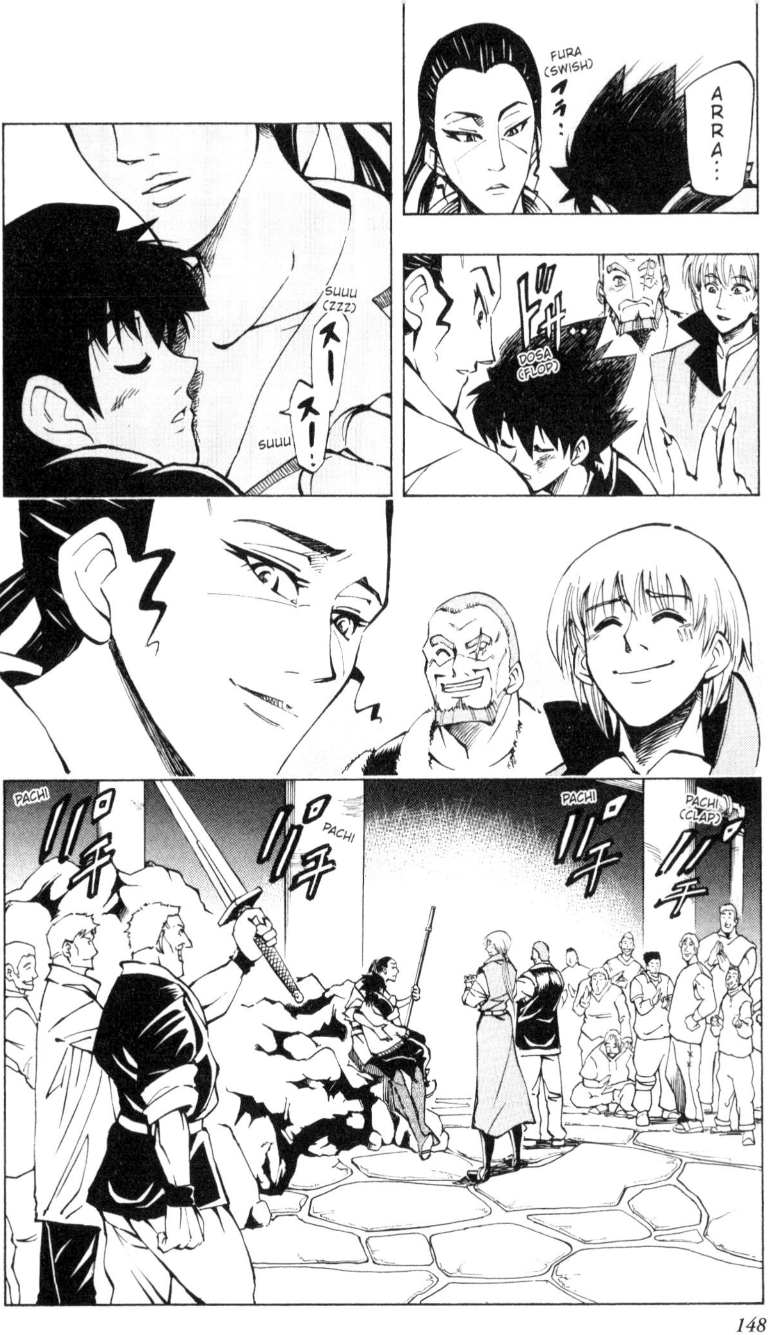
FURA (SWISH)
フラ‥
ARRA...
ドサ‥
DOSA (FLOP)
SUUU (ZZZ)
スー
スー
SUUU
PACHI (CLAP)
パチ
PACHI
パチ
PACHI
パチ
PACHI
パチ

CHAPTER 33: THE HALL OF PRINCES

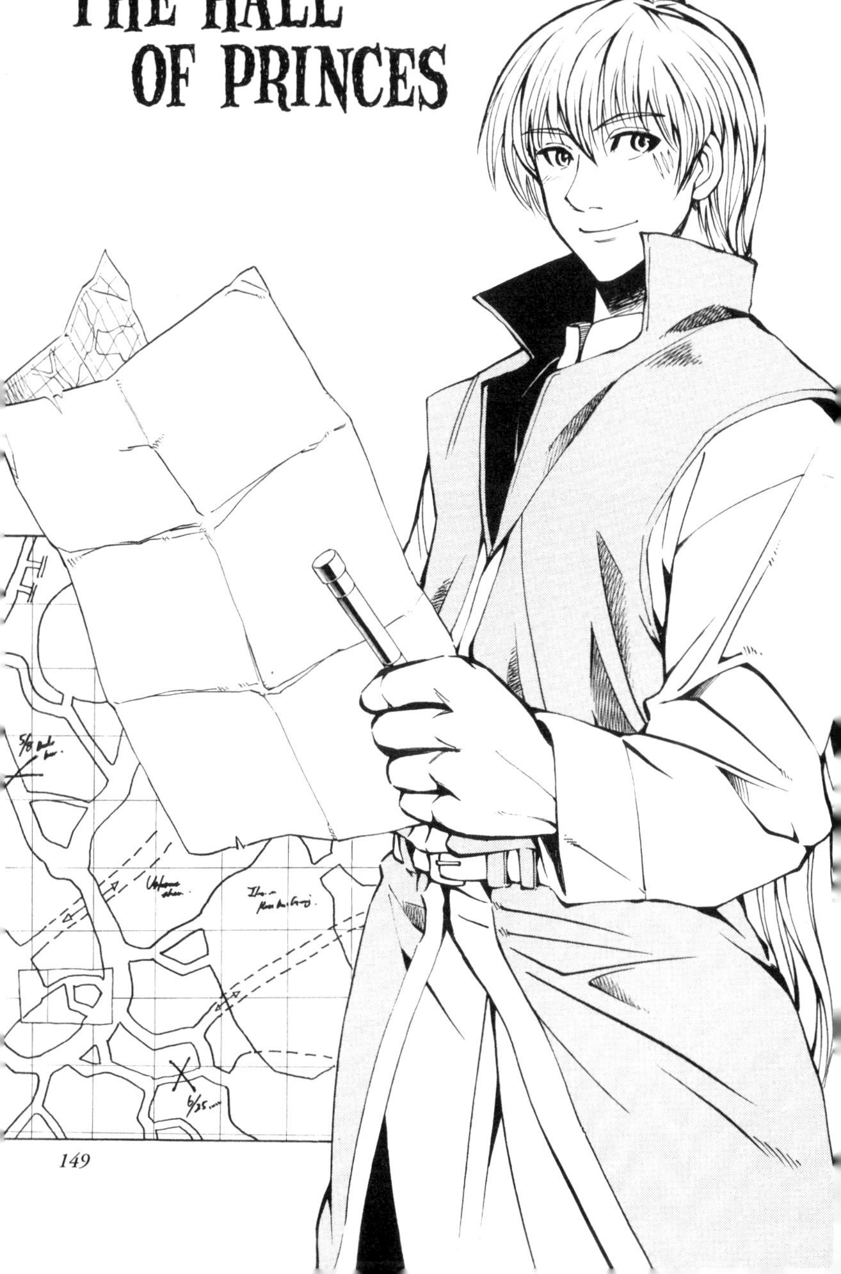

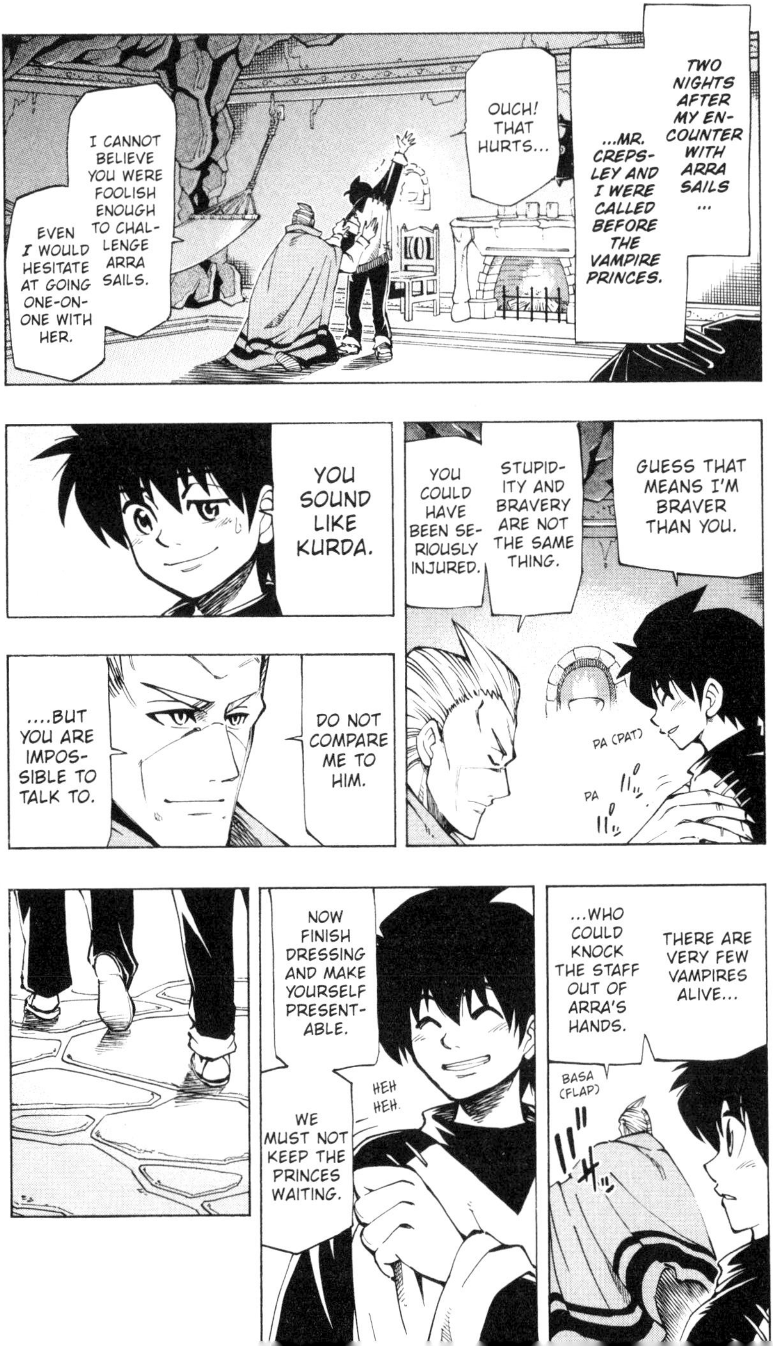
TWO NIGHTS AFTER MY ENCOUNTER WITH ARRA SAILS ...
...MR. CREPSLEY AND I WERE CALLED BEFORE THE VAMPIRE PRINCES.
OUCH! THAT HURTS...
I CANNOT BELIEVE YOU WERE FOOLISH ENOUGH TO CHALLENGE ARRA SAILS.
EVEN *I* WOULD HESITATE AT GOING ONE-ON-ONE WITH HER.
GUESS THAT MEANS I'M BRAVER THAN YOU.
STUPIDITY AND BRAVERY ARE NOT THE SAME THING.
YOU COULD HAVE BEEN SERIOUSLY INJURED.
PA (PAT)
PA
YOU SOUND LIKE KURDA.
DO NOT COMPARE ME TO HIM.
....BUT YOU ARE IMPOSSIBLE TO TALK TO.
THERE ARE VERY FEW VAMPIRES ALIVE...
...WHO COULD KNOCK THE STAFF OUT OF ARRA'S HANDS.
BASA (FLAP)
NOW FINISH DRESSING AND MAKE YOURSELF PRESENTABLE.
HEH HEH.
WE MUST NOT KEEP THE PRINCES WAITING.

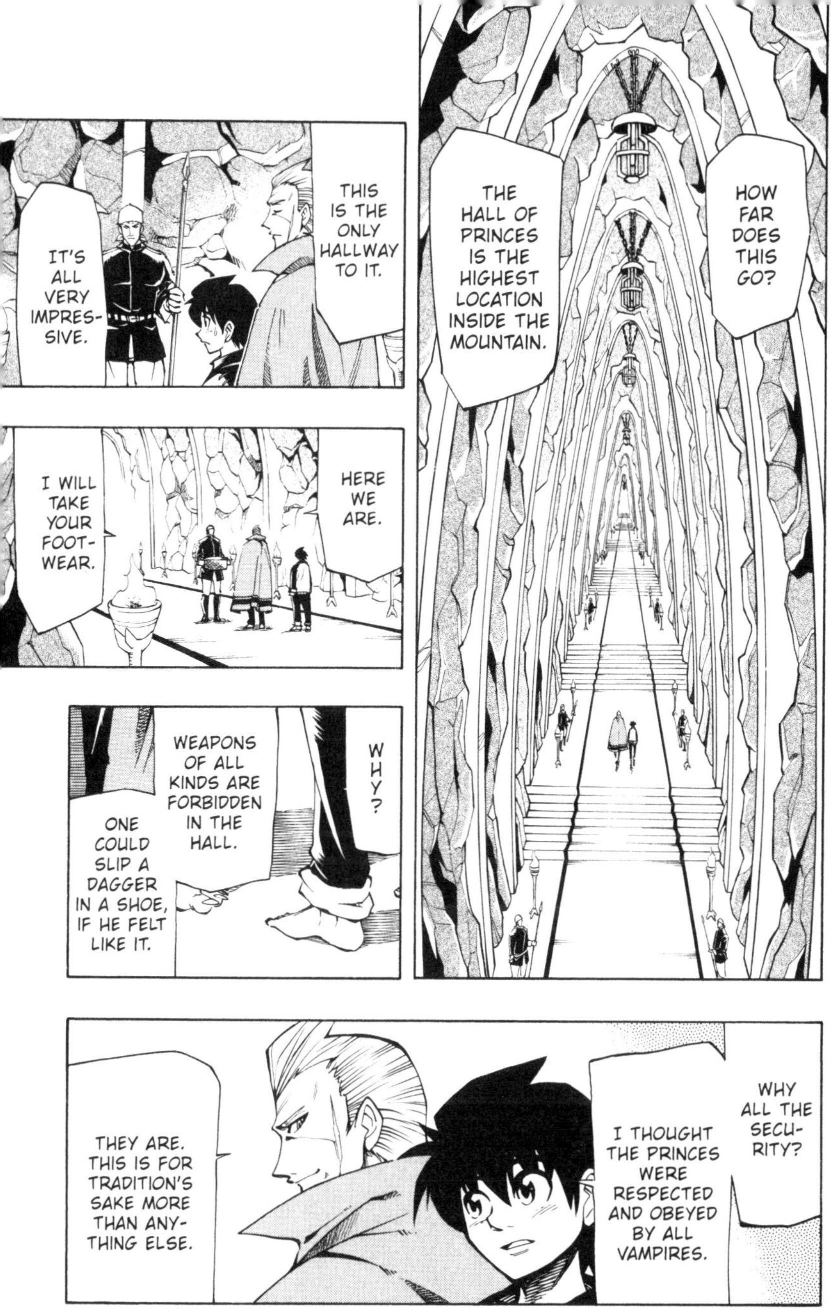
HOW FAR DOES THIS GO?
THE HALL OF PRINCES IS THE HIGHEST LOCATION INSIDE THE MOUNTAIN.
THIS IS THE ONLY HALLWAY TO IT.
IT'S ALL VERY IMPRESSIVE.
HERE WE ARE.
I WILL TAKE YOUR FOOTWEAR.
WHY?
WEAPONS OF ALL KINDS ARE FORBIDDEN IN THE HALL.
ONE COULD SLIP A DAGGER IN A SHOE, IF HE FELT LIKE IT.
WHY ALL THE SECURITY?
I THOUGHT THE PRINCES WERE RESPECTED AND OBEYED BY ALL VAMPIRES.
THEY ARE. THIS IS FOR TRADITION'S SAKE MORE THAN ANYTHING ELSE.

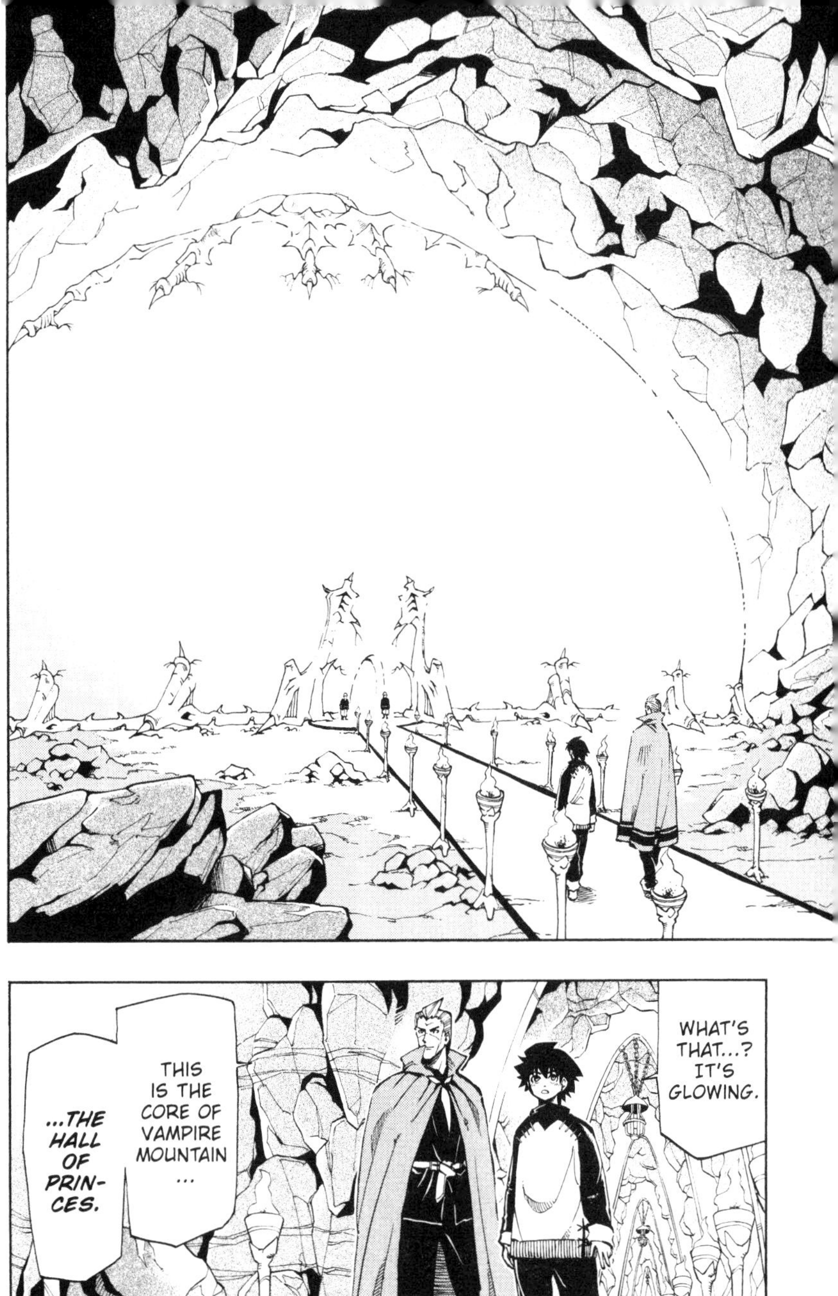
WHAT'S THAT...? IT'S GLOWING.
THIS IS THE CORE OF VAMPIRE MOUNTAIN...
...THE HALL OF PRIN-CES.

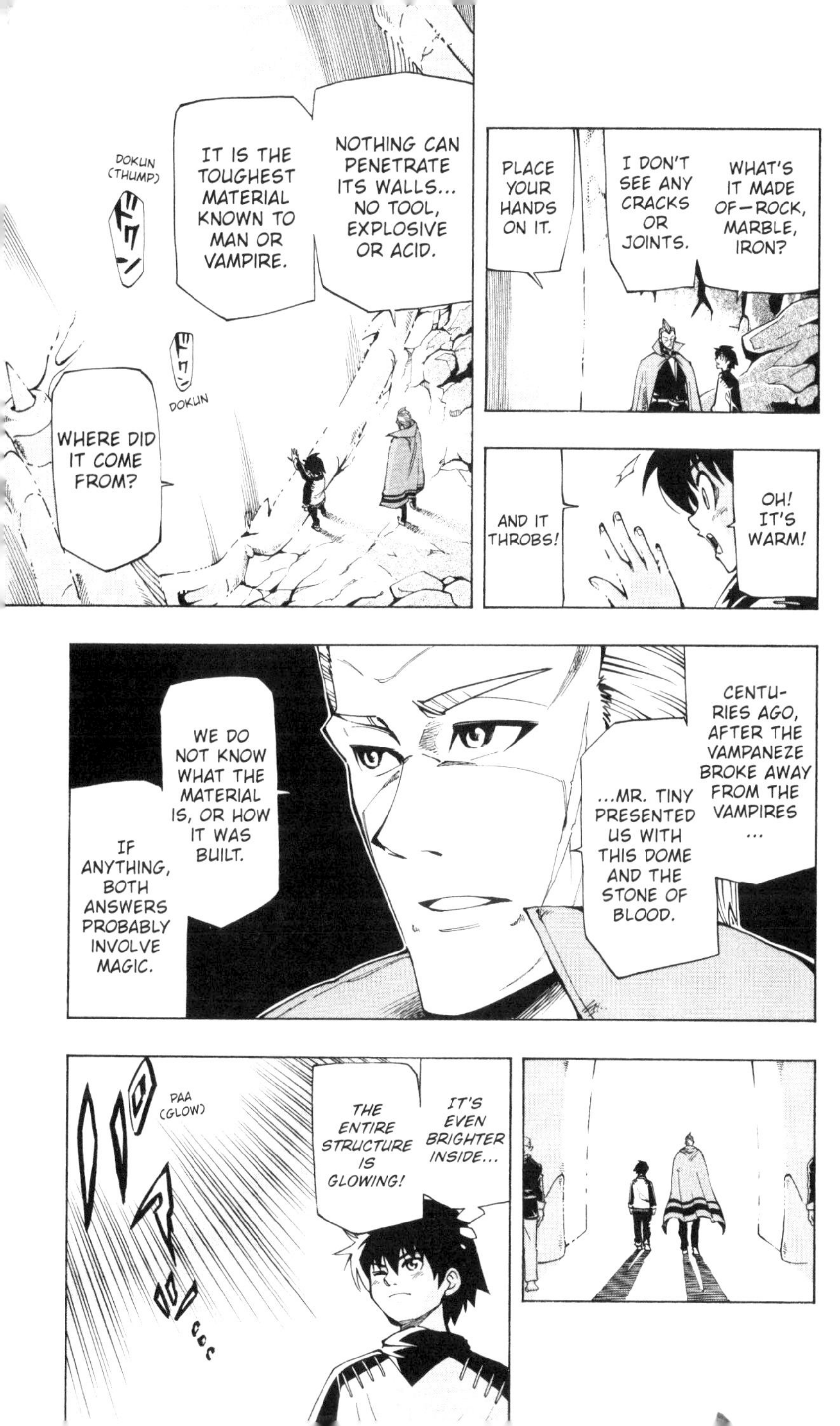
WHAT'S IT MADE OF—ROCK, MARBLE, IRON?
I DON'T SEE ANY CRACKS OR JOINTS.
PLACE YOUR HANDS ON IT.
OH! IT'S WARM!
AND IT THROBS!
NOTHING CAN PENETRATE ITS WALLS... NO TOOL, EXPLOSIVE OR ACID.
IT IS THE TOUGHEST MATERIAL KNOWN TO MAN OR VAMPIRE.
DOKUN (THUMP)
DOKUN
WHERE DID IT COME FROM?
CENTURIES AGO, AFTER THE VAMPANEZE BROKE AWAY FROM THE VAMPIRES ...
...MR. TINY PRESENTED US WITH THIS DOME AND THE STONE OF BLOOD.
WE DO NOT KNOW WHAT THE MATERIAL IS, OR HOW IT WAS BUILT.
IF ANYTHING, BOTH ANSWERS PROBABLY INVOLVE MAGIC.
IT'S EVEN BRIGHTER INSIDE...
THE ENTIRE STRUCTURE IS GLOWING!
PAA (GLOW)

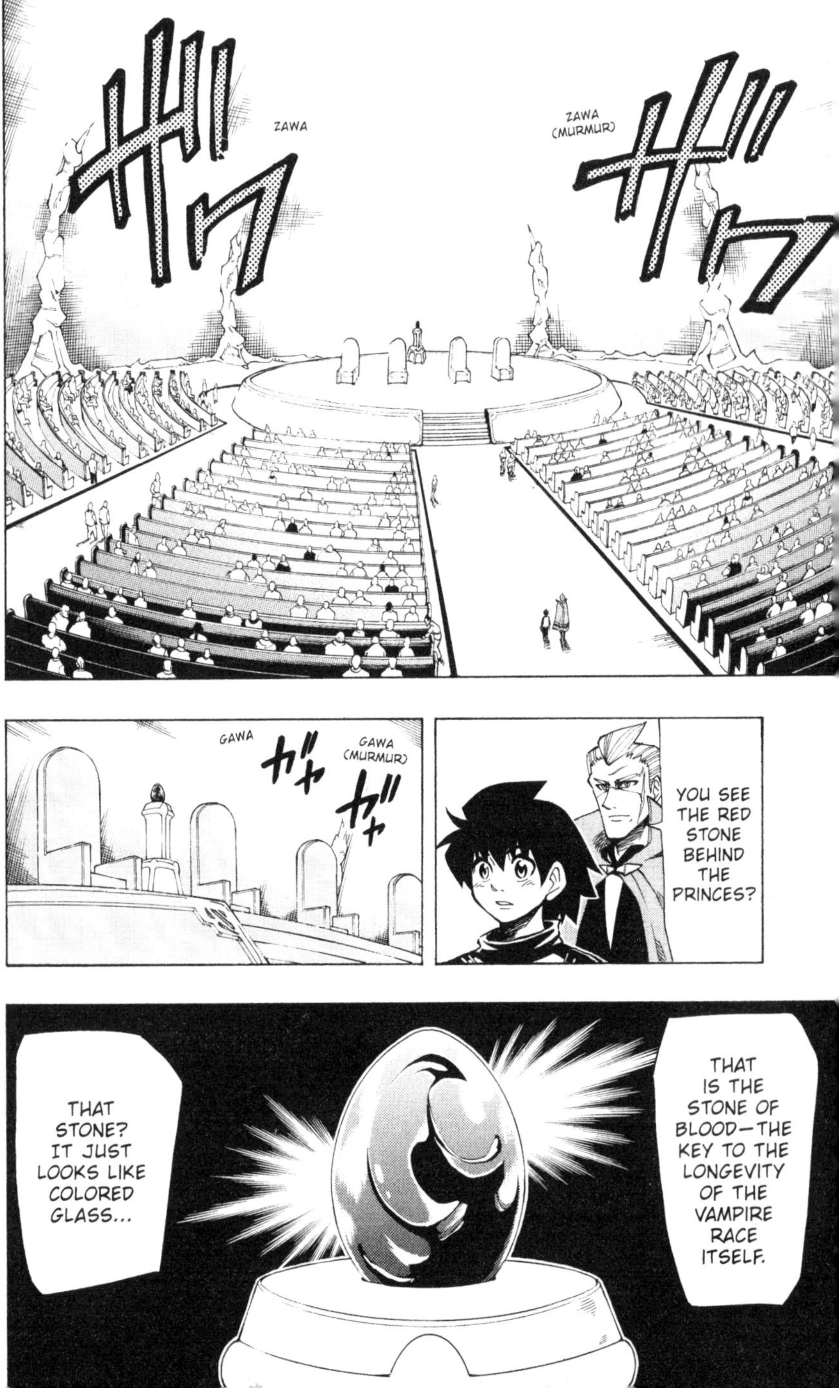
ZAWA (MURMUR)
ZAWA
YOU SEE THE RED STONE BEHIND THE PRINCES?
GAWA (MURMUR)
GAWA
THAT IS THE STONE OF BLOOD—THE KEY TO THE LONGEVITY OF THE VAMPIRE RACE ITSELF.
THAT STONE? IT JUST LOOKS LIKE COLORED GLASS...

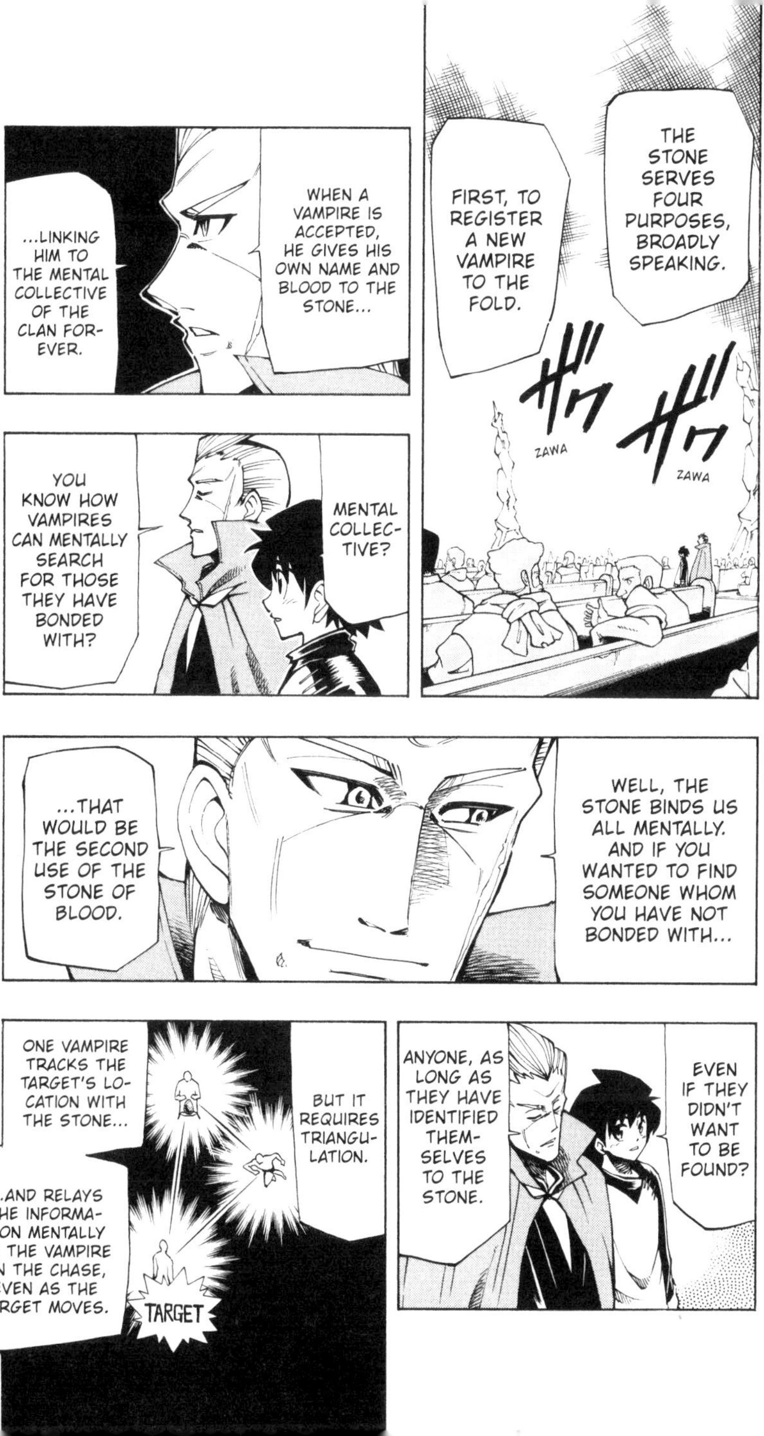
THE STONE SERVES FOUR PURPOSES, BROADLY SPEAKING.
FIRST, TO REGISTER A NEW VAMPIRE TO THE FOLD.
ザワ
ZAWA
ザワ
ZAWA
WHEN A VAMPIRE IS ACCEPTED, HE GIVES HIS OWN NAME AND BLOOD TO THE STONE...
...LINKING HIM TO THE MENTAL COLLECTIVE OF THE CLAN FOR-EVER.
MENTAL COLLEC-TIVE?
YOU KNOW HOW VAMPIRES CAN MENTALLY SEARCH FOR THOSE THEY HAVE BONDED WITH?
WELL, THE STONE BINDS US ALL MENTALLY. AND IF YOU WANTED TO FIND SOMEONE WHOM YOU HAVE NOT BONDED WITH...
...THAT WOULD BE THE SECOND USE OF THE STONE OF BLOOD.
EVEN IF THEY DIDN'T WANT TO BE FOUND?
ANYONE, AS LONG AS THEY HAVE IDENTIFIED THEM-SELVES TO THE STONE.
BUT IT REQUIRES TRIANGU-LATION.
ONE VAMPIRE TRACKS THE TARGET'S LO-CATION WITH THE STONE...
...AND RELAYS THE INFORMA-TION MENTALLY TO THE VAMPIRE ON THE CHASE, EVEN AS THE TARGET MOVES.
TARGET

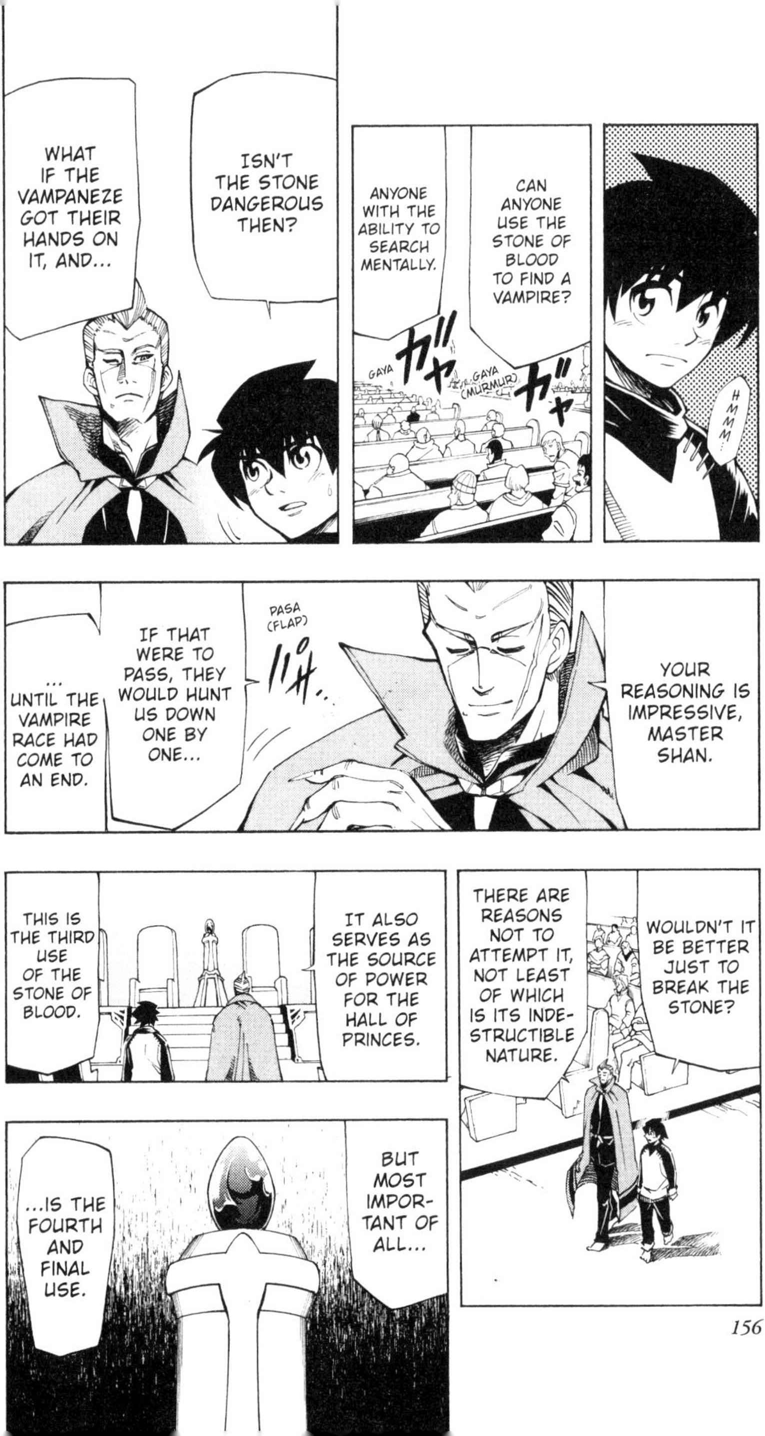
HMMM...
CAN ANYONE USE THE STONE OF BLOOD TO FIND A VAMPIRE?
ANYONE WITH THE ABILITY TO SEARCH MENTALLY.
GAYA (MURMUR)
GAYA
ISN'T THE STONE DANGEROUS THEN?
WHAT IF THE VAMPANEZE GOT THEIR HANDS ON IT, AND...
YOUR REASONING IS IMPRESSIVE, MASTER SHAN.
PASA (FLAP)
IF THAT WERE TO PASS, THEY WOULD HUNT US DOWN ONE BY ONE...
... UNTIL THE VAMPIRE RACE HAD COME TO AN END.
WOULDN'T IT BE BETTER JUST TO BREAK THE STONE?
THERE ARE REASONS NOT TO ATTEMPT IT, NOT LEAST OF WHICH IS ITS INDE-STRUCTIBLE NATURE.
IT ALSO SERVES AS THE SOURCE OF POWER FOR THE HALL OF PRINCES.
THIS IS THE THIRD USE OF THE STONE OF BLOOD.
BUT MOST IMPORTANT OF ALL...
...IS THE FOURTH AND FINAL USE.

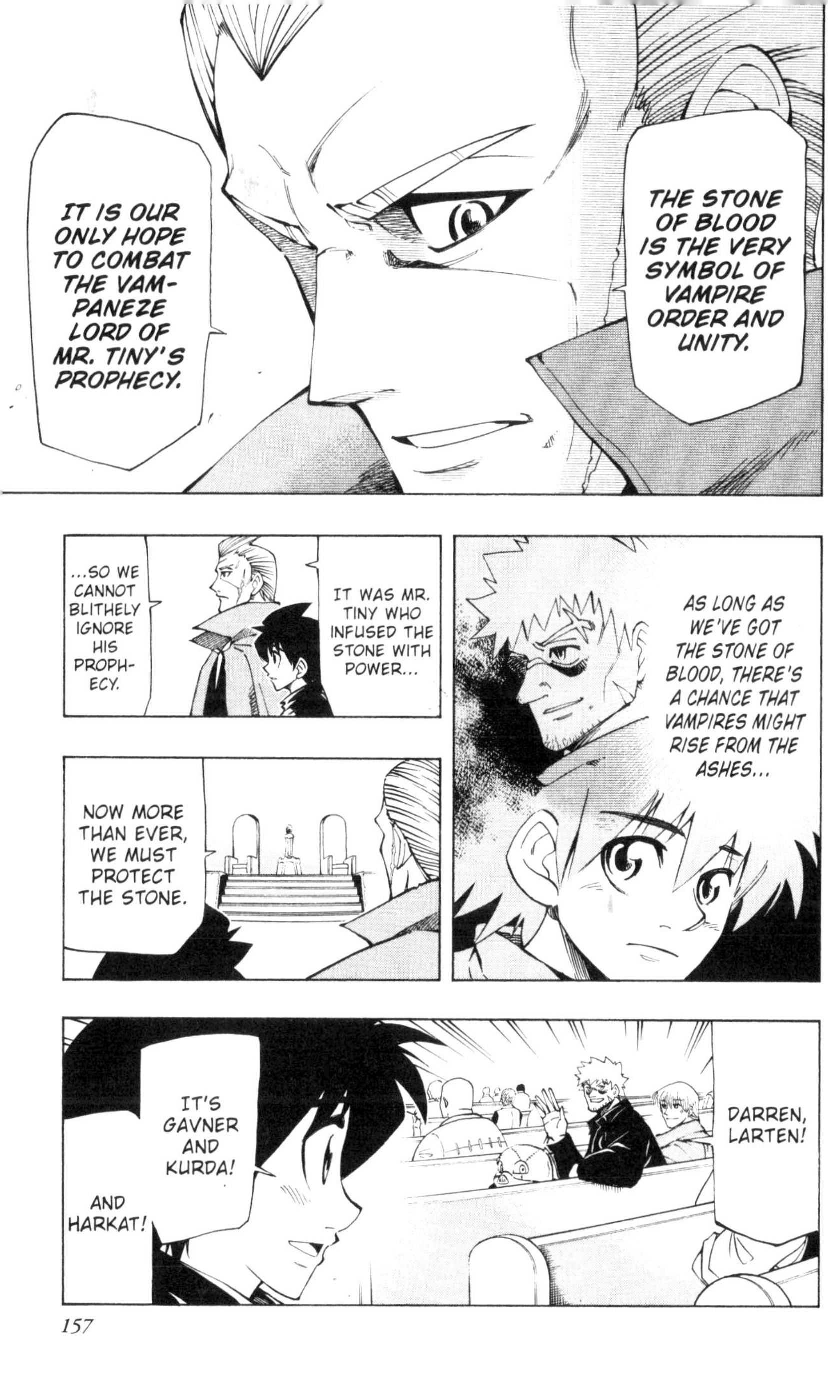
THE STONE OF BLOOD IS THE VERY SYMBOL OF VAMPIRE ORDER AND UNITY.
IT IS OUR ONLY HOPE TO COMBAT THE VAM-PANEZE LORD OF MR. TINY'S PROPHECY.
AS LONG AS WE'VE GOT THE STONE OF BLOOD, THERE'S A CHANCE THAT VAMPIRES MIGHT RISE FROM THE ASHES...
IT WAS MR. TINY WHO INFUSED THE STONE WITH POWER...
...SO WE CANNOT BLITHELY IGNORE HIS PROPH-ECY.
NOW MORE THAN EVER, WE MUST PROTECT THE STONE.
DARREN, LARTEN!
IT'S GAVNER AND KURDA!
AND HARKAT!

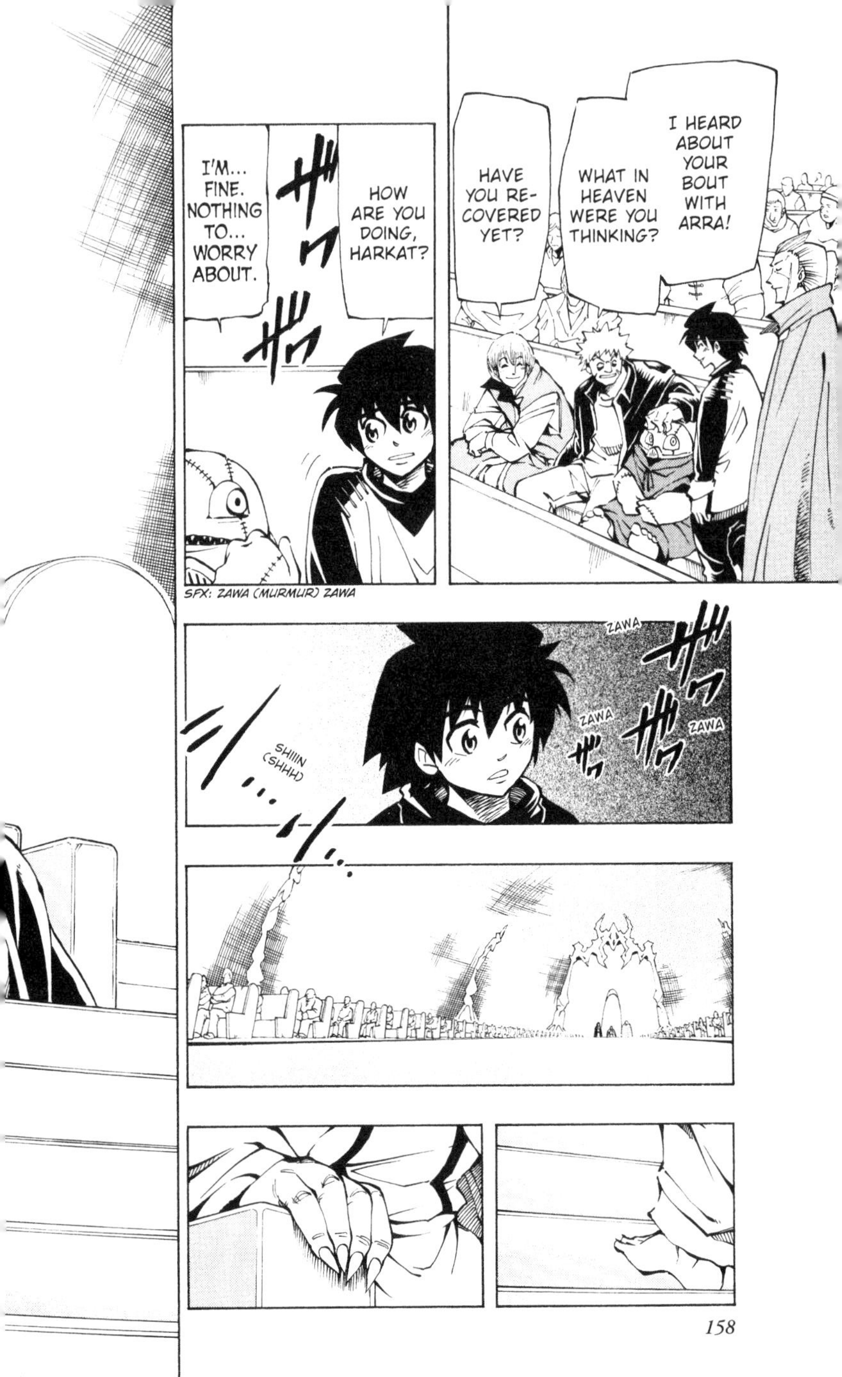
I HEARD ABOUT YOUR BOUT WITH ARRA!
WHAT IN HEAVEN WERE YOU THINKING?
HAVE YOU RE-COVERED YET?
HOW ARE YOU DOING, HARKAT?
I'M... FINE. NOTHING TO... WORRY ABOUT.
SFX: ZAWA (MURMUR) ZAWA
ZAWA
ZAWA
ZAWA
SHIIN (SHHH)

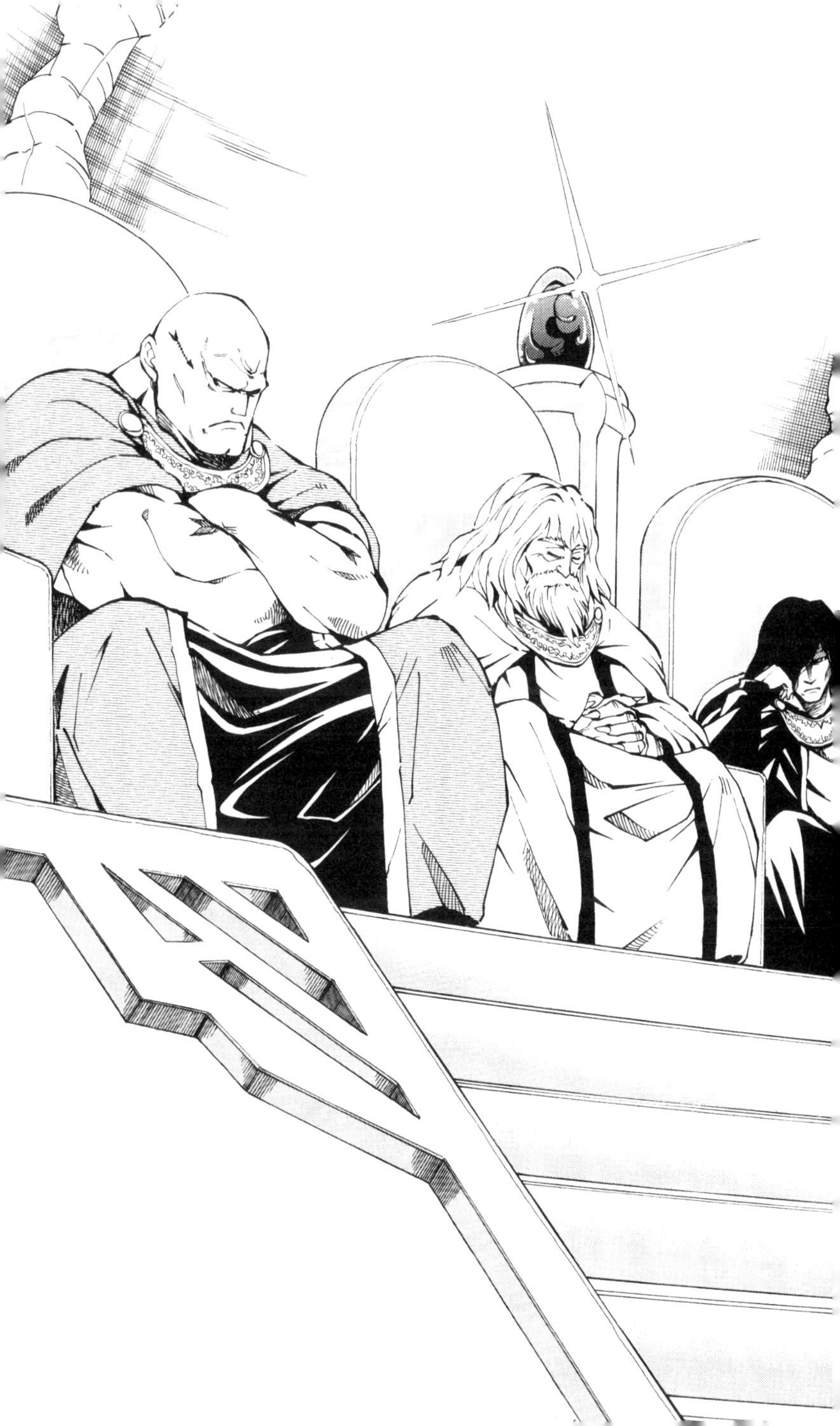

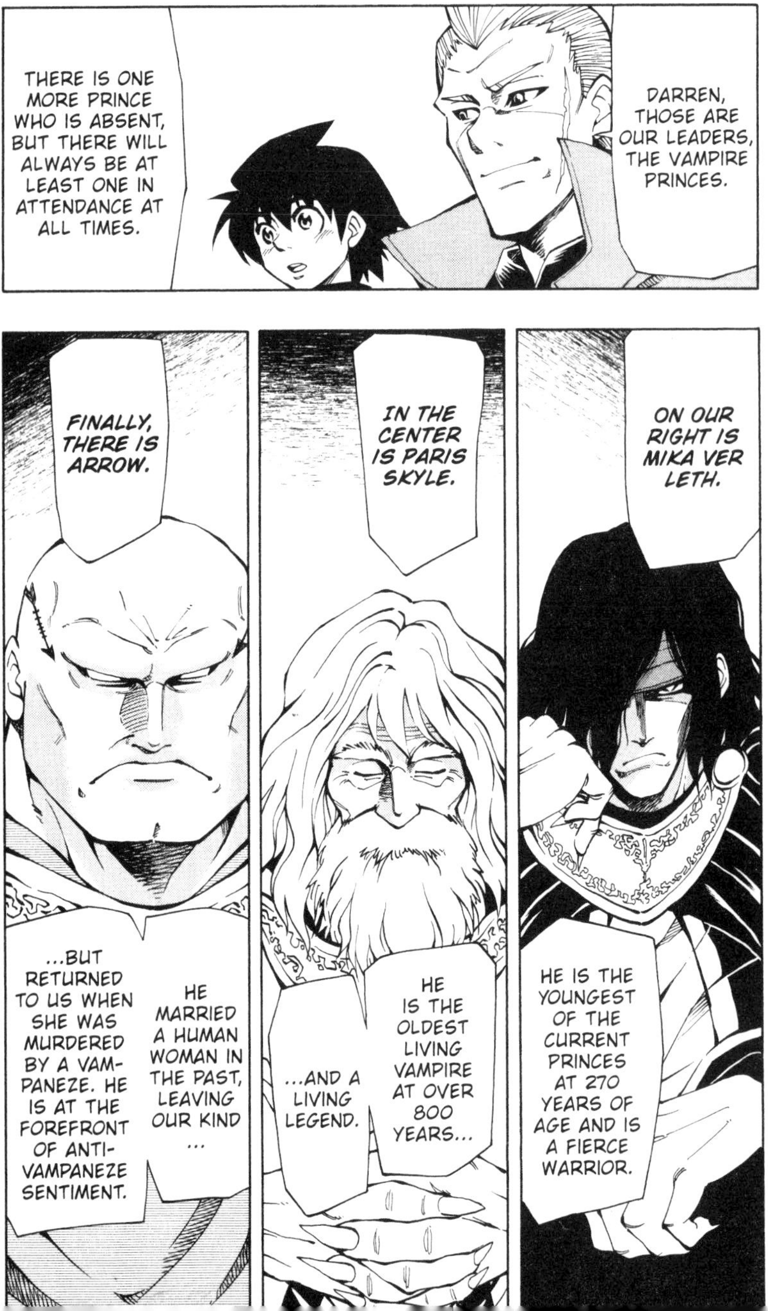
DARREN, THOSE ARE OUR LEADERS, THE VAMPIRE PRINCES.
THERE IS ONE MORE PRINCE WHO IS ABSENT, BUT THERE WILL ALWAYS BE AT LEAST ONE IN ATTENDANCE AT ALL TIMES.
ON OUR RIGHT IS MIKA VER LETH.
HE IS THE YOUNGEST OF THE CURRENT PRINCES AT 270 YEARS OF AGE AND IS A FIERCE WARRIOR.
IN THE CENTER IS PARIS SKYLE.
HE IS THE OLDEST LIVING VAMPIRE AT OVER 800 YEARS...
...AND A LIVING LEGEND.
FINALLY, THERE IS ARROW.
HE MARRIED A HUMAN WOMAN IN THE PAST, LEAVING OUR KIND ...
...BUT RETURNED TO US WHEN SHE WAS MURDERED BY A VAM-PANEZE. HE IS AT THE FOREFRONT OF ANTI-VAMPANEZE SENTIMENT.

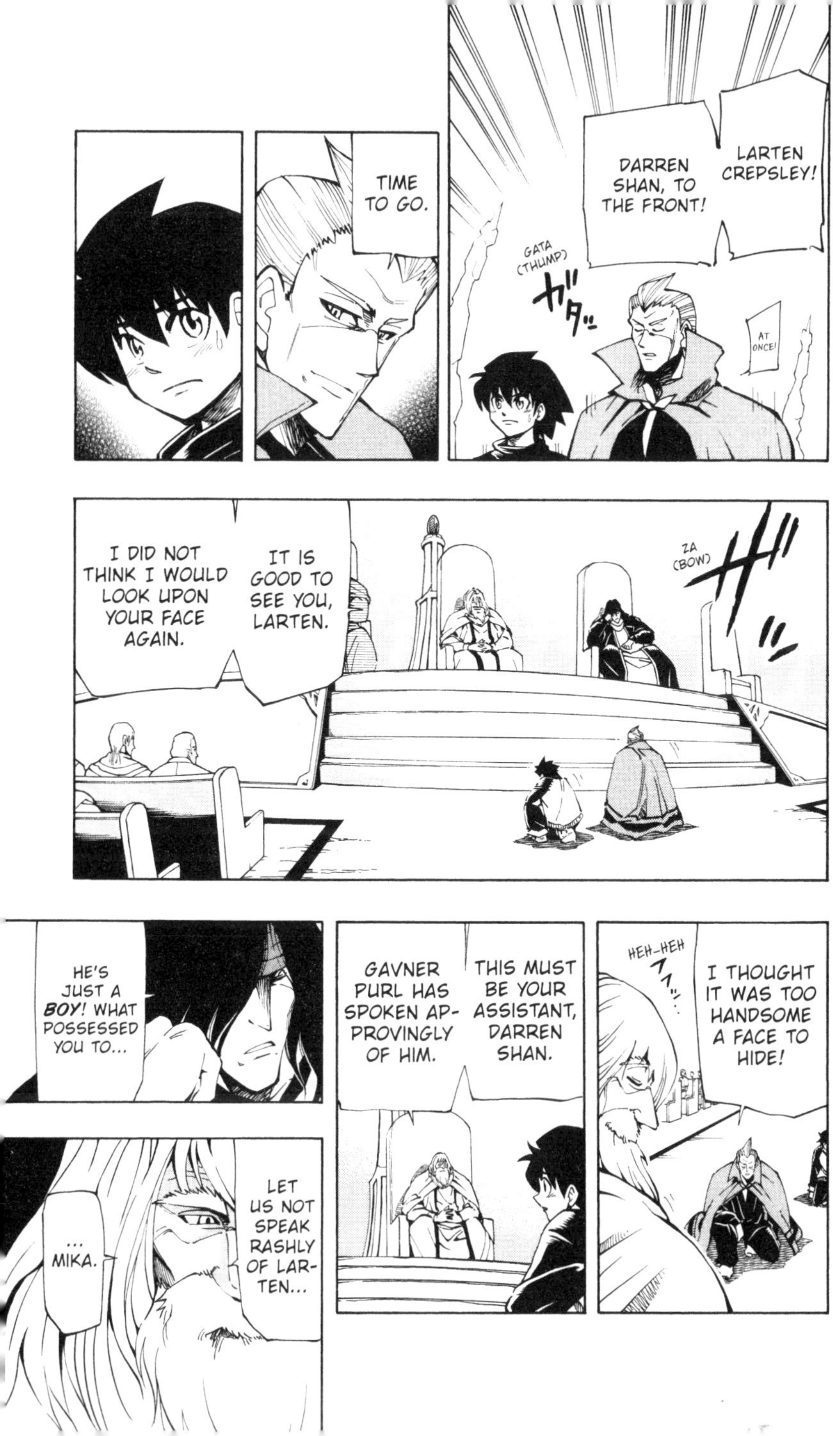
LARTEN CREPSLEY!
DARREN SHAN, TO THE FRONT!
GATA (THUMP)
AT ONCE!
TIME TO GO.
ZA (BOW)
IT IS GOOD TO SEE YOU, LARTEN.
I DID NOT THINK I WOULD LOOK UPON YOUR FACE AGAIN.
HEH-HEH
I THOUGHT IT WAS TOO HANDSOME A FACE TO HIDE!
THIS MUST BE YOUR ASSISTANT, DARREN SHAN.
GAVNER PURL HAS SPOKEN AP-PROVINGLY OF HIM.
HE'S JUST A *BOY*! WHAT POSSESSED YOU TO...
LET US NOT SPEAK RASHLY OF LAR-TEN...
...MIKA.

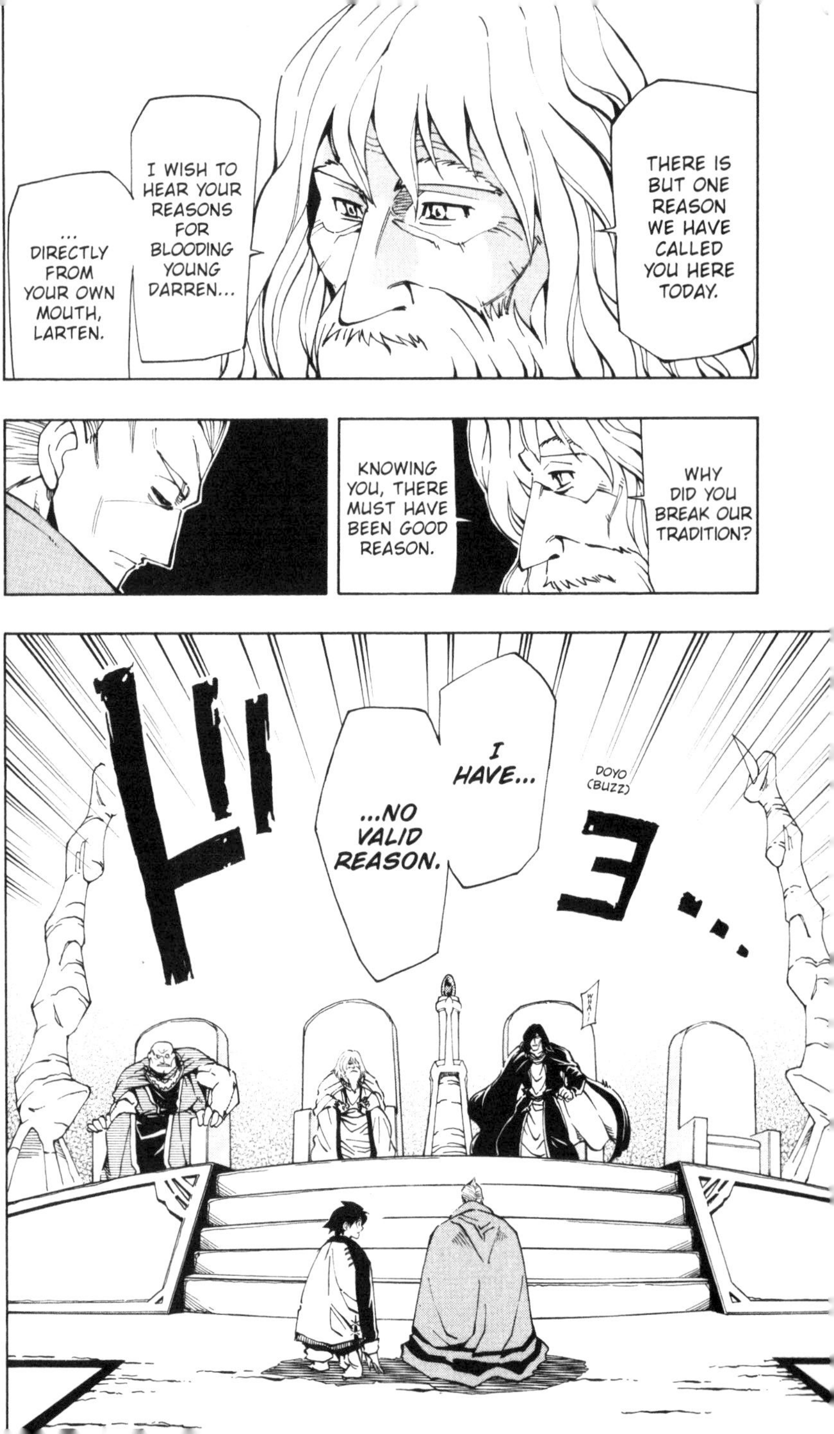
THERE IS BUT ONE REASON WE HAVE CALLED YOU HERE TODAY.
I WISH TO HEAR YOUR REASONS FOR BLOODING YOUNG DARREN...
...DIRECTLY FROM YOUR OWN MOUTH, LARTEN.
WHY DID YOU BREAK OUR TRADITION?
KNOWING YOU, THERE MUST HAVE BEEN GOOD REASON.
DOYO (BUZZ)
I HAVE...
...NO VALID REASON.
WHA!!

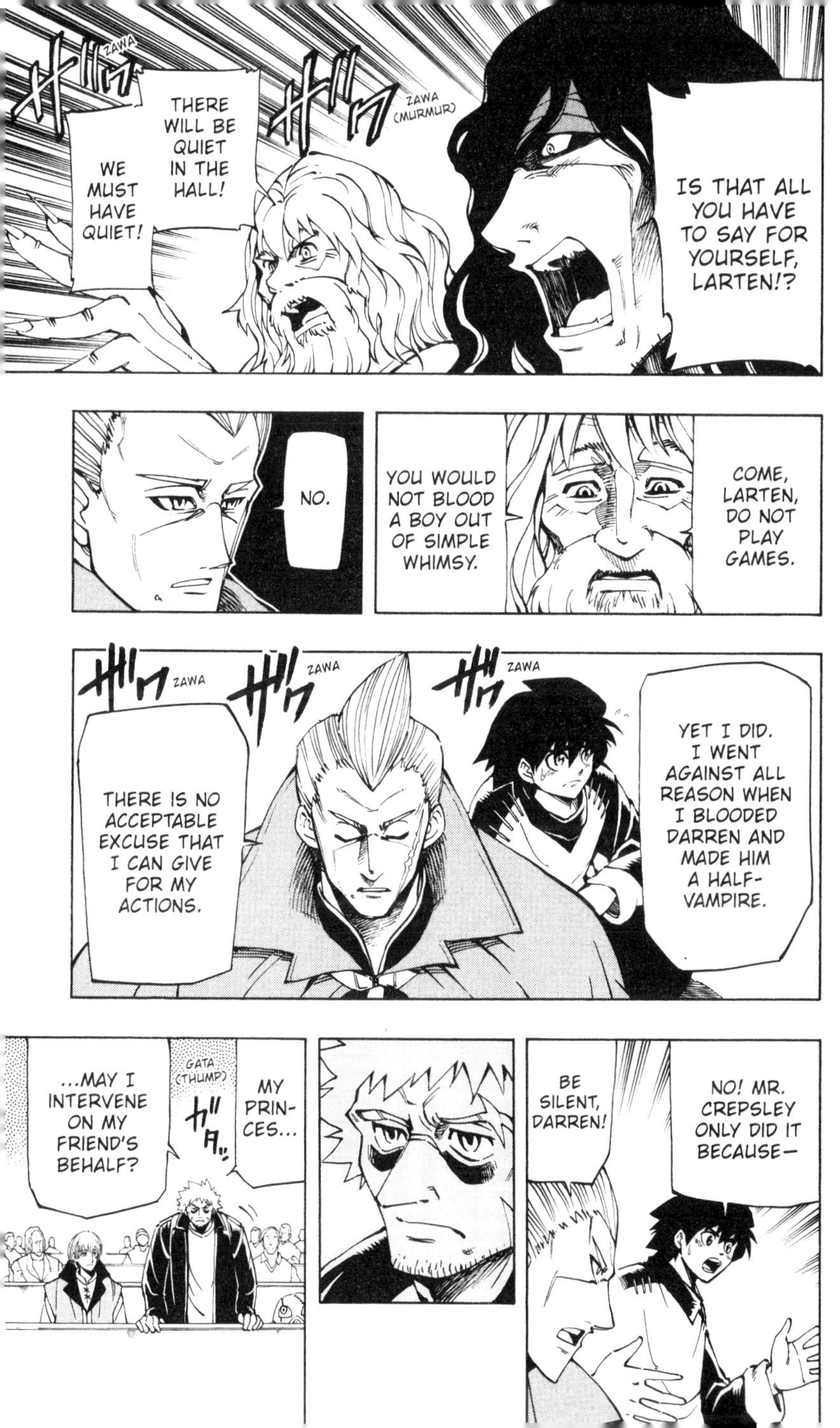
IS THAT ALL YOU HAVE TO SAY FOR YOURSELF, LARTEN!?
ZAWA (MURMUR)
THERE WILL BE QUIET IN THE HALL!
WE MUST HAVE QUIET!
ZAWA
COME, LARTEN, DO NOT PLAY GAMES.
YOU WOULD NOT BLOOD A BOY OUT OF SIMPLE WHIMSY.
NO.
YET I DID. I WENT AGAINST ALL REASON WHEN I BLOODED DARREN AND MADE HIM A HALF-VAMPIRE.
ZAWA
ZAWA
THERE IS NO ACCEPTABLE EXCUSE THAT I CAN GIVE FOR MY ACTIONS.
ZAWA
NO! MR. CREPSLEY ONLY DID IT BECAUSE—
BE SILENT, DARREN!
MY PRIN-CES...
GATA (THUMP)
...MAY I INTERVENE ON MY FRIEND'S BEHALF?

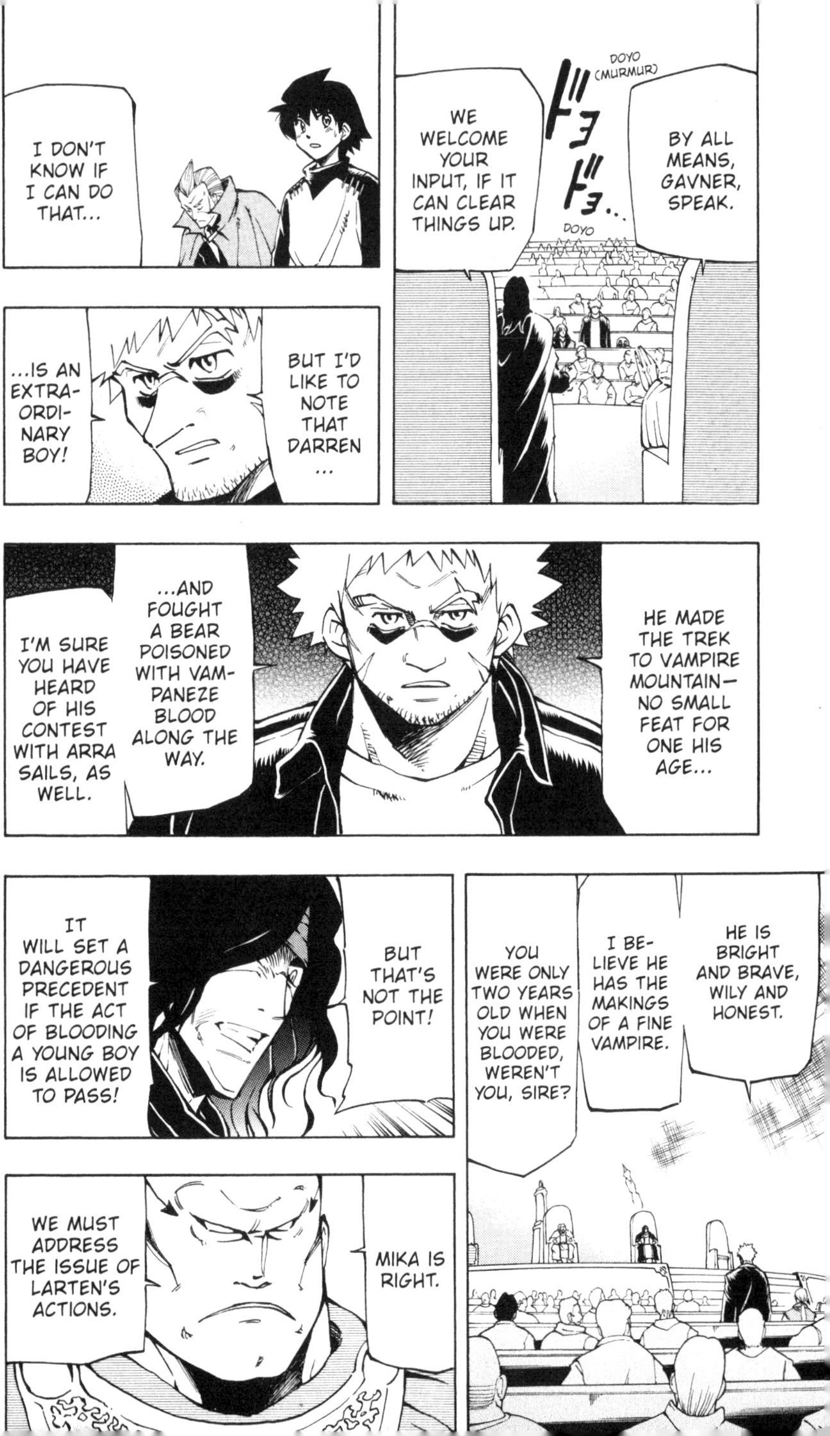
BY ALL MEANS, GAVNER, SPEAK.
DOYO (MURMUR)
DOYO
WE WELCOME YOUR INPUT, IF IT CAN CLEAR THINGS UP.
I DON'T KNOW IF I CAN DO THAT...
BUT I'D LIKE TO NOTE THAT DARREN ...
...IS AN EXTRA-ORDINARY BOY!
HE MADE THE TREK TO VAMPIRE MOUNTAIN—NO SMALL FEAT FOR ONE HIS AGE...
...AND FOUGHT A BEAR POISONED WITH VAMPANEZE BLOOD ALONG THE WAY.
I'M SURE YOU HAVE HEARD OF HIS CONTEST WITH ARRA SAILS, AS WELL.
HE IS BRIGHT AND BRAVE, WILY AND HONEST.
I BELIEVE HE HAS THE MAKINGS OF A FINE VAMPIRE.
YOU WERE ONLY TWO YEARS OLD WHEN YOU WERE BLOODED, WEREN'T YOU, SIRE?
BUT THAT'S NOT THE POINT!
IT WILL SET A DANGEROUS PRECEDENT IF THE ACT OF BLOODING A YOUNG BOY IS ALLOWED TO PASS!
MIKA IS RIGHT.
WE MUST ADDRESS THE ISSUE OF LARTEN'S ACTIONS.

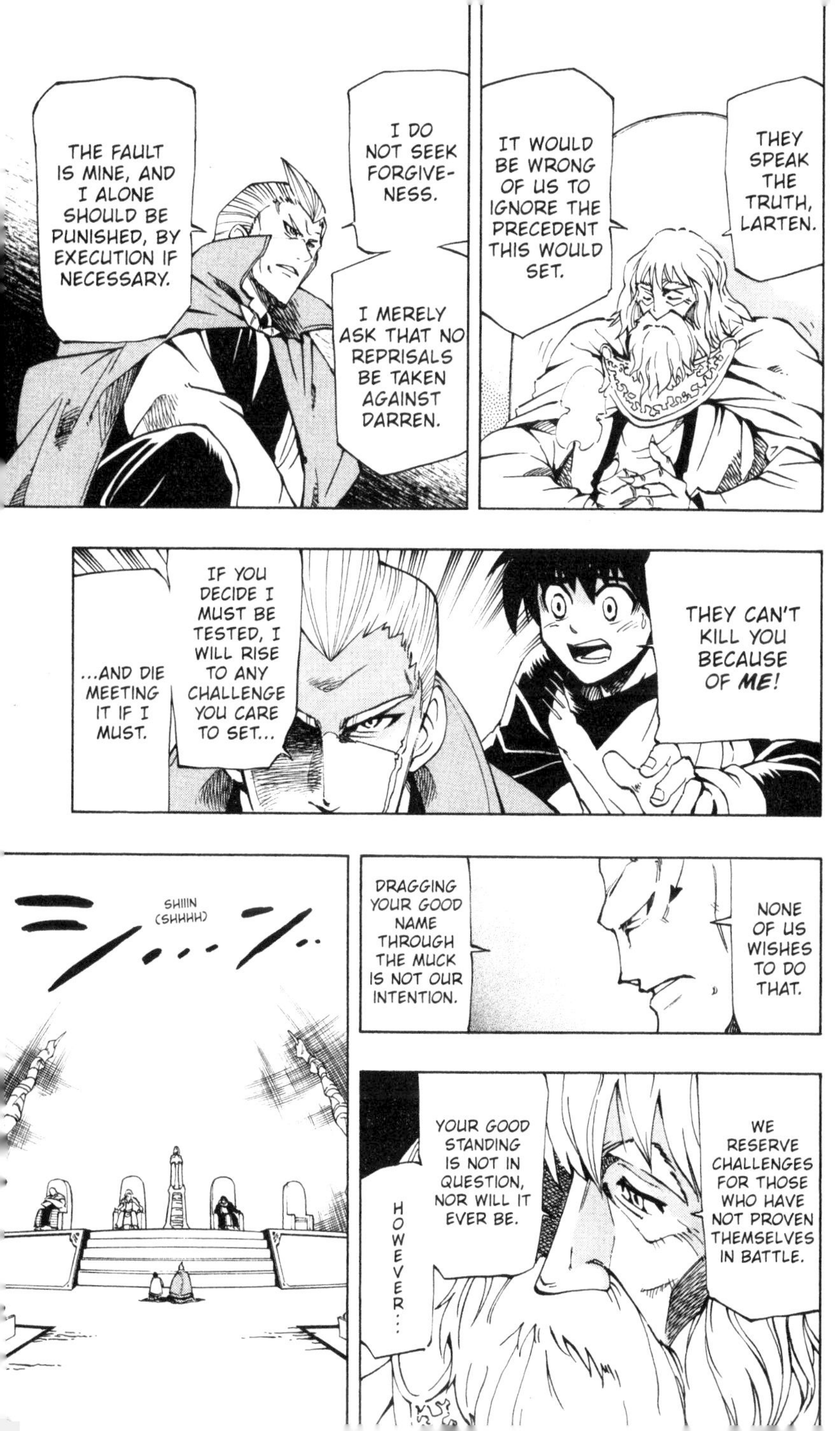
THEY SPEAK THE TRUTH, LARTEN.
IT WOULD BE WRONG OF US TO IGNORE THE PRECEDENT THIS WOULD SET.
I DO NOT SEEK FORGIVE-NESS.
THE FAULT IS MINE, AND I ALONE SHOULD BE PUNISHED, BY EXECUTION IF NECESSARY.
I MERELY ASK THAT NO REPRISALS BE TAKEN AGAINST DARREN.
THEY CAN'T KILL YOU BECAUSE OF *ME*!
IF YOU DECIDE I MUST BE TESTED, I WILL RISE TO ANY CHALLENGE YOU CARE TO SET...
...AND DIE MEETING IT IF I MUST.
NONE OF US WISHES TO DO THAT.
DRAGGING YOUR GOOD NAME THROUGH THE MUCK IS NOT OUR INTENTION.
WE RESERVE CHALLENGES FOR THOSE WHO HAVE NOT PROVEN THEMSELVES IN BATTLE.
YOUR GOOD STANDING IS NOT IN QUESTION, NOR WILL IT EVER BE.
HOWEVER...
SHIIIN (SHHHH)

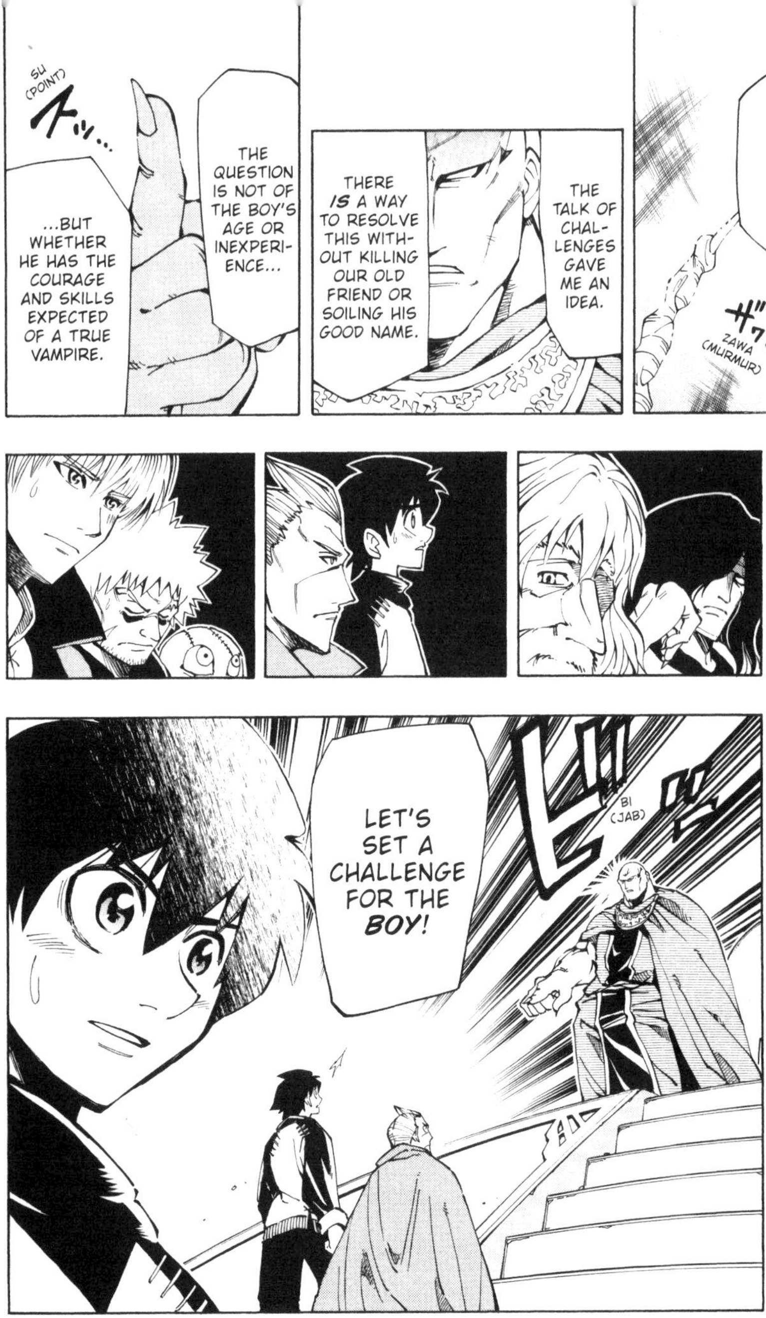
PERHAPS...
ザワ..
ZAWA (MURMUR)
THE TALK OF CHALLENGES GAVE ME AN IDEA.
THERE *IS* A WAY TO RESOLVE THIS WITHOUT KILLING OUR OLD FRIEND OR SOILING HIS GOOD NAME.
THE QUESTION IS NOT OF THE BOY'S AGE OR INEXPERIENCE...
SU (POINT)
スッ...
...BUT WHETHER HE HAS THE COURAGE AND SKILLS EXPECTED OF A TRUE VAMPIRE.
ビッ
BI (JAB)
LET'S SET A CHALLENGE FOR THE *BOY*!

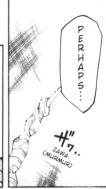

CHAPTER 34:
THE TRIALS OF INITIATION

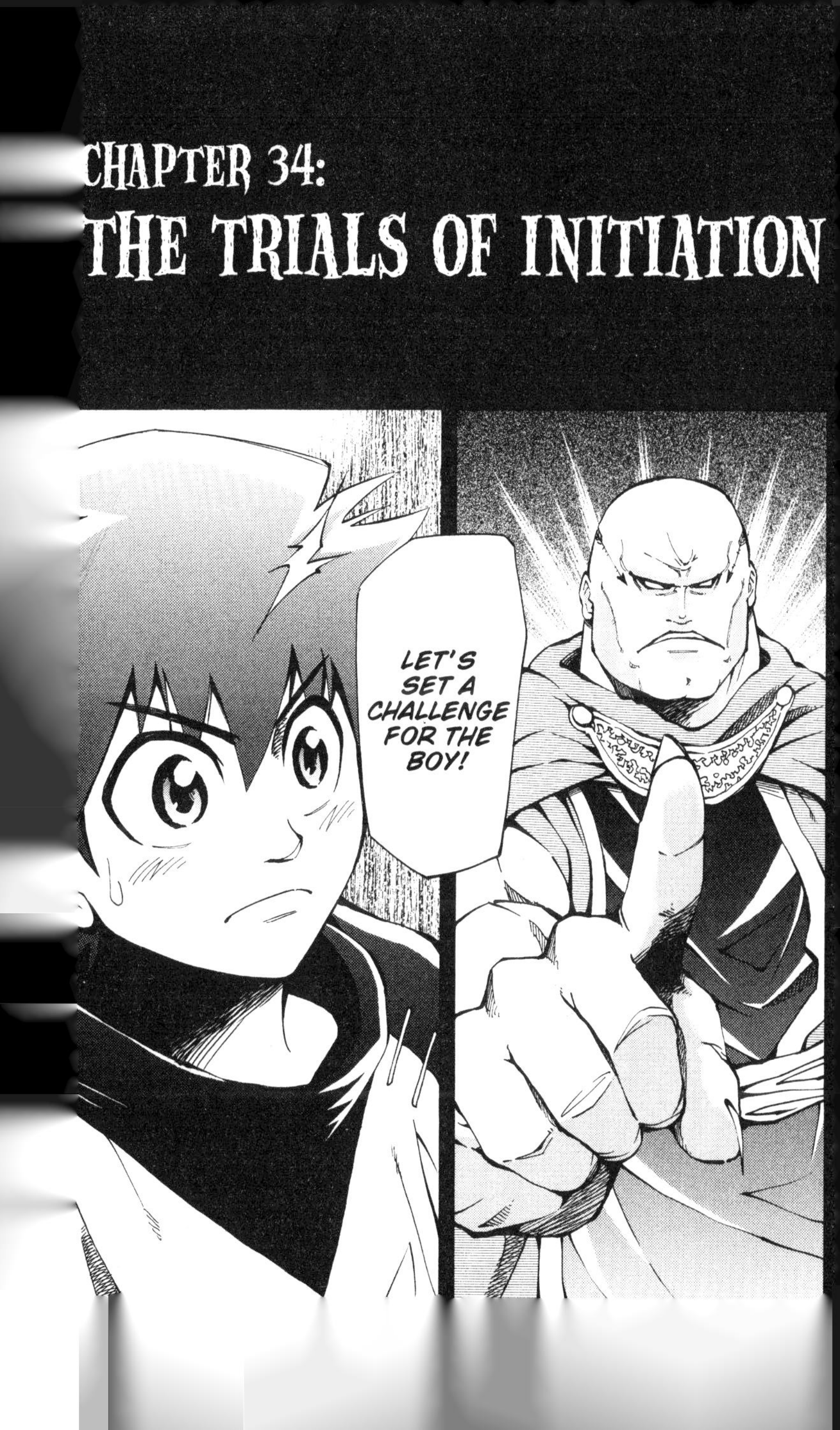
LET'S SET A CHALLENGE FOR THE BOY!

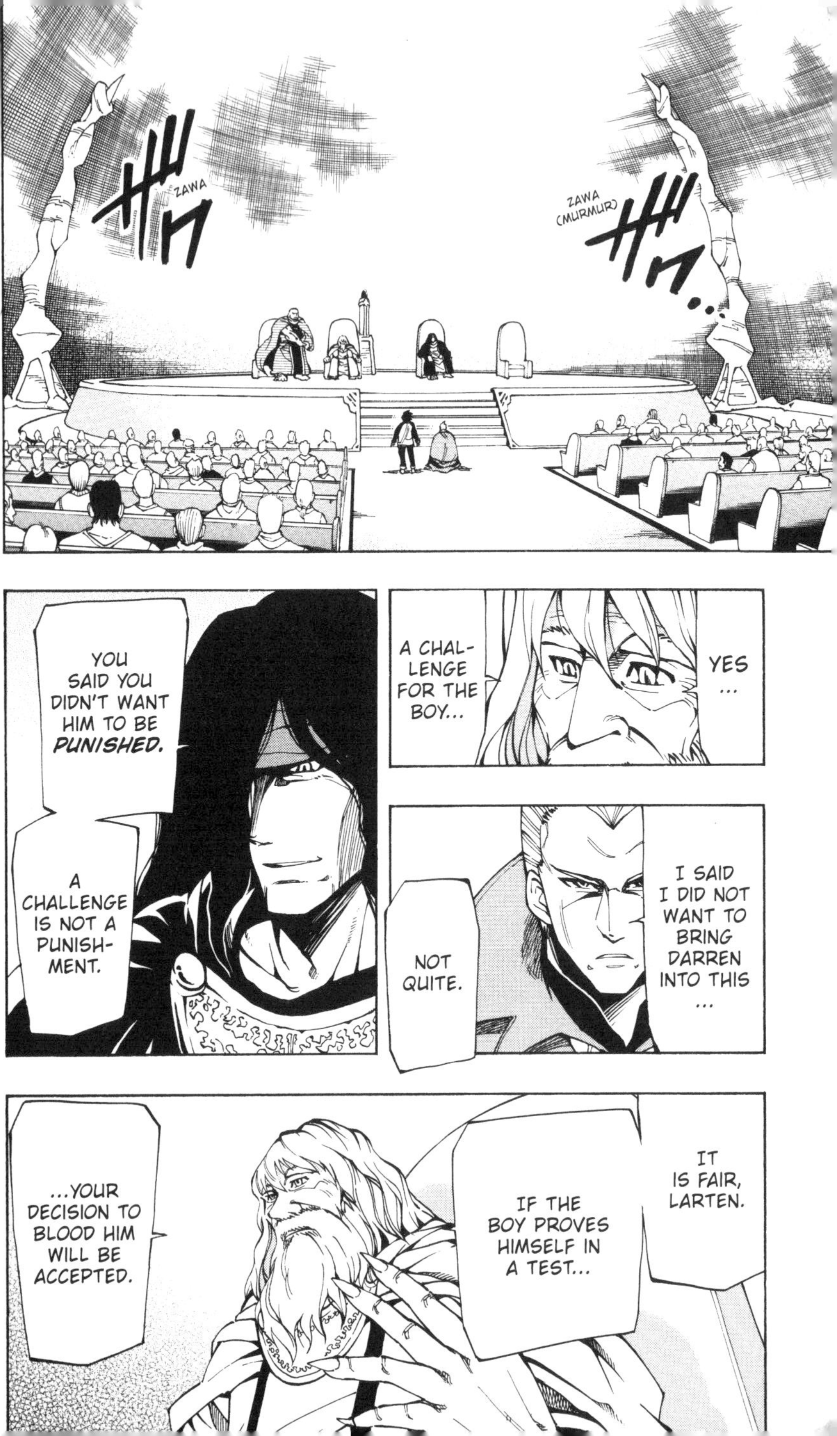
ZAWA (MURMUR)
ZAWA
YES...
A CHAL-LENGE FOR THE BOY...
I SAID I DID NOT WANT TO BRING DARREN INTO THIS...
NOT QUITE.
YOU SAID YOU DIDN'T WANT HIM TO BE ***PUNISHED.***
A CHALLENGE IS NOT A PUNISH-MENT.
IT IS FAIR, LARTEN.
IF THE BOY PROVES HIMSELF IN A TEST...
...YOUR DECISION TO BLOOD HIM WILL BE ACCEPTED.

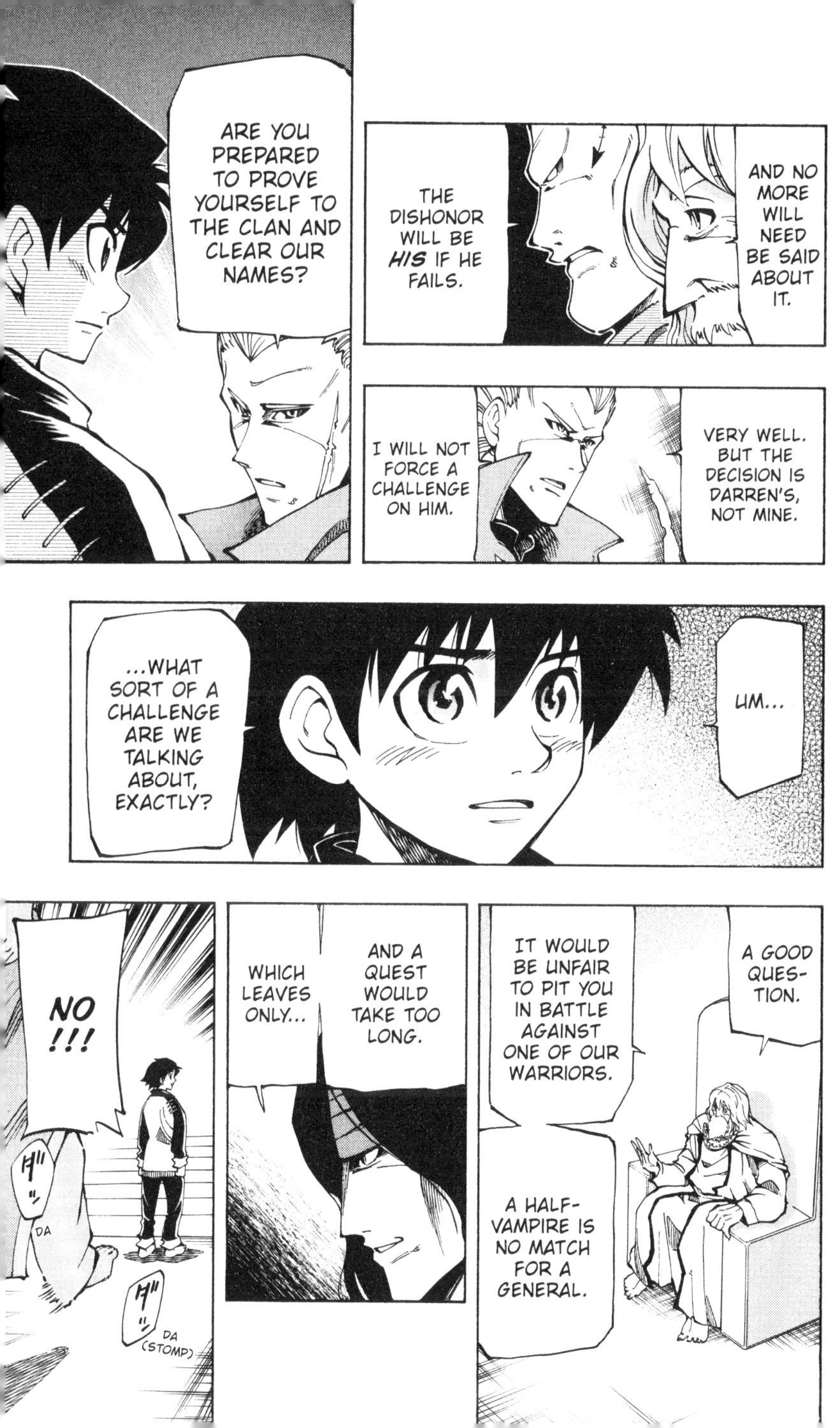
AND NO MORE WILL NEED BE SAID ABOUT IT.
THE DISHONOR WILL BE *HIS* IF HE FAILS.
VERY WELL. BUT THE DECISION IS DARREN'S, NOT MINE.
I WILL NOT FORCE A CHALLENGE ON HIM.
ARE YOU PREPARED TO PROVE YOURSELF TO THE CLAN AND CLEAR OUR NAMES?
UM...
...WHAT SORT OF A CHALLENGE ARE WE TALKING ABOUT, EXACTLY?
A GOOD QUES-TION.
IT WOULD BE UNFAIR TO PIT YOU IN BATTLE AGAINST ONE OF OUR WARRIORS.
A HALF-VAMPIRE IS NO MATCH FOR A GENERAL.
AND A QUEST WOULD TAKE TOO LONG.
WHICH LEAVES ONLY...
NO !!!
DA
DA (STOMP)

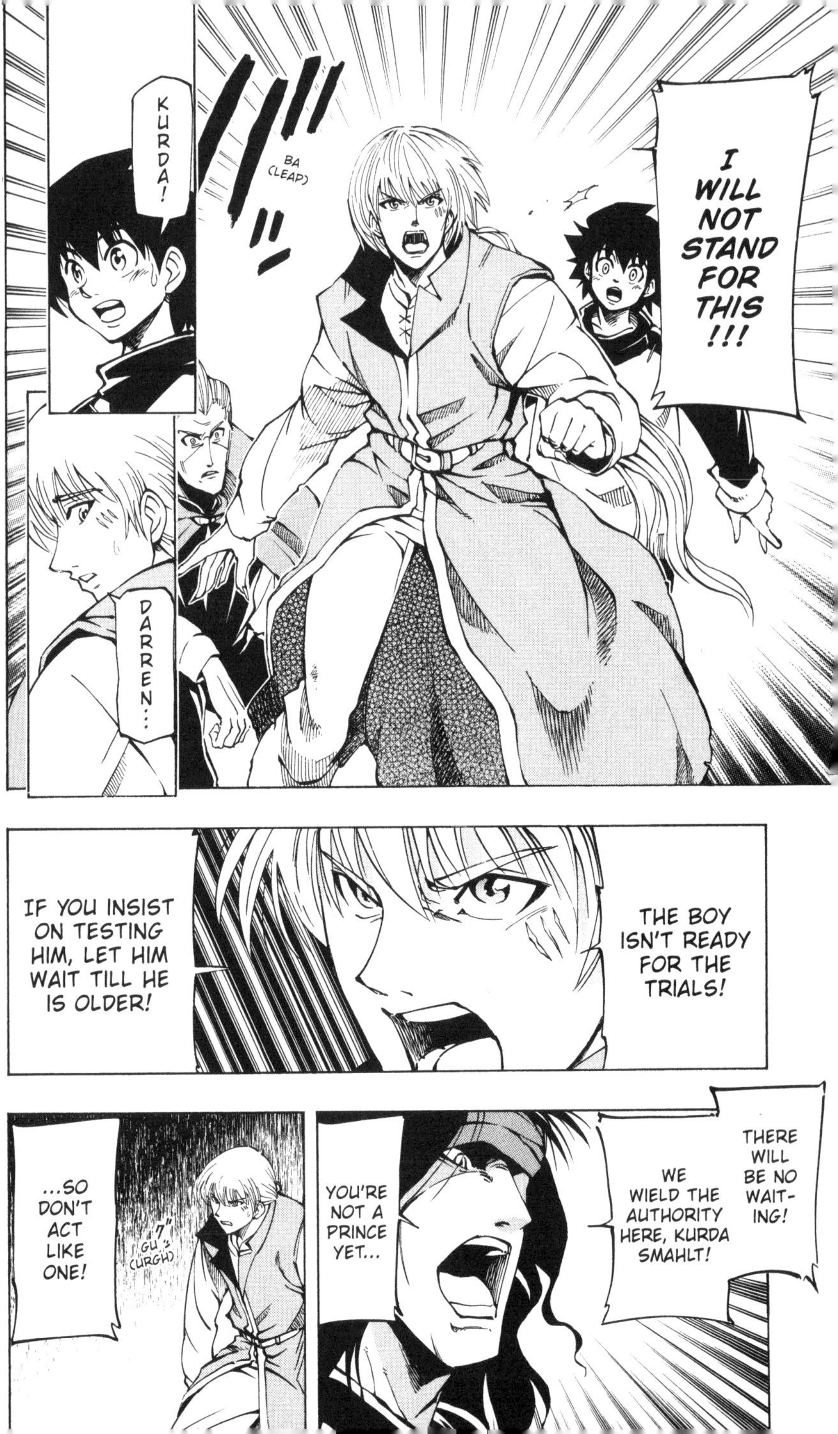
I WILL NOT STAND FOR THIS!!!
BA (LEAP)
KURDA!
DARREN...
THE BOY ISN'T READY FOR THE TRIALS!
IF YOU INSIST ON TESTING HIM, LET HIM WAIT TILL HE IS OLDER!
THERE WILL BE NO WAIT-ING!
WE WIELD THE AUTHORITY HERE, KURDA SMAHLT!
YOU'RE NOT A PRINCE YET...
...SO DON'T ACT LIKE ONE!
GU (URGH)

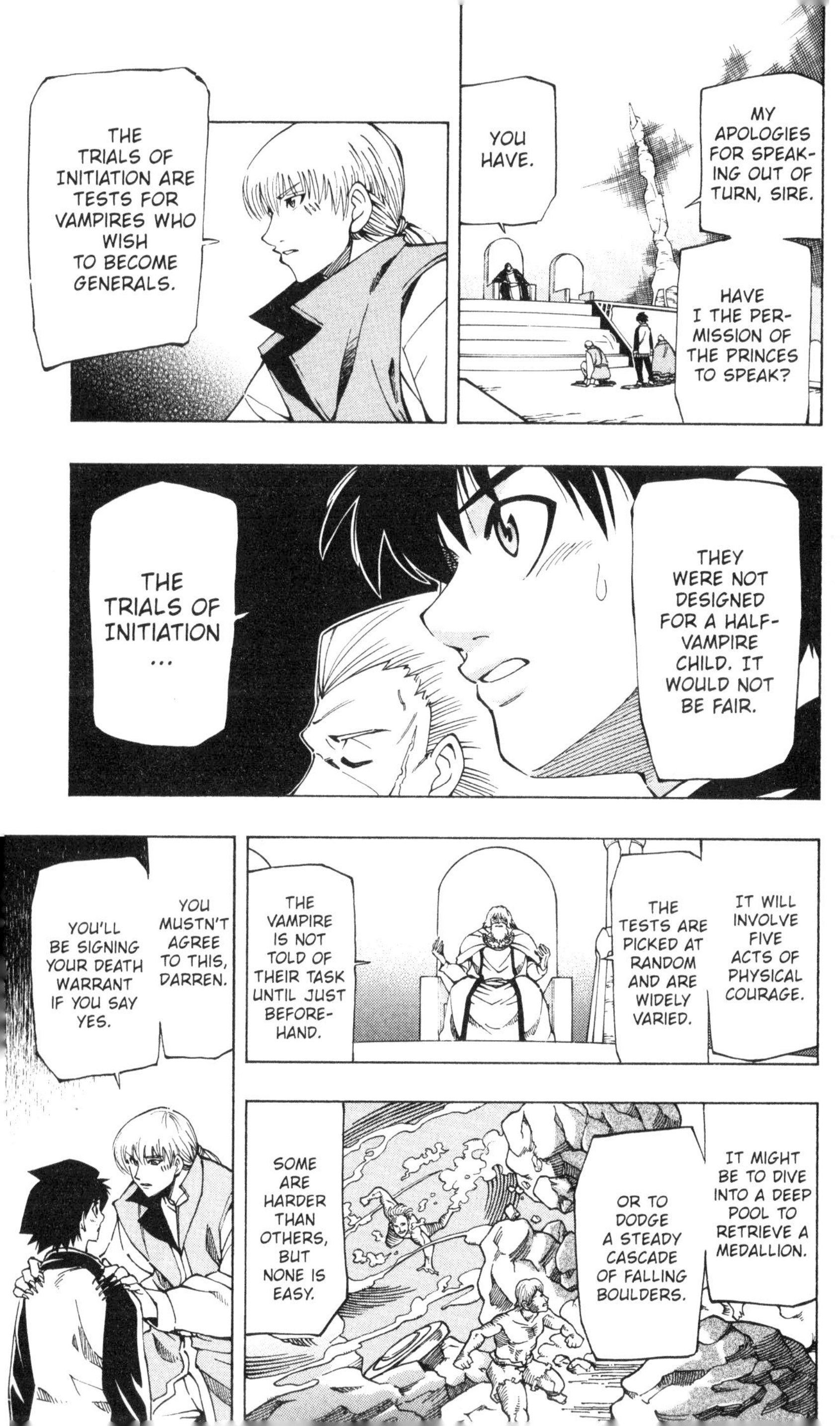
MY APOLOGIES FOR SPEAKING OUT OF TURN, SIRE.
HAVE I THE PERMISSION OF THE PRINCES TO SPEAK?
YOU HAVE.
THE TRIALS OF INITIATION ARE TESTS FOR VAMPIRES WHO WISH TO BECOME GENERALS.
THEY WERE NOT DESIGNED FOR A HALF-VAMPIRE CHILD. IT WOULD NOT BE FAIR.
THE TRIALS OF INITIATION ...
IT WILL INVOLVE FIVE ACTS OF PHYSICAL COURAGE.
THE TESTS ARE PICKED AT RANDOM AND ARE WIDELY VARIED.
THE VAMPIRE IS NOT TOLD OF THEIR TASK UNTIL JUST BEFORE-HAND.
IT MIGHT BE TO DIVE INTO A DEEP POOL TO RETRIEVE A MEDALLION.
OR TO DODGE A STEADY CASCADE OF FALLING BOULDERS.
SOME ARE HARDER THAN OTHERS, BUT NONE IS EASY.
YOU MUSTN'T AGREE TO THIS, DARREN.
YOU'LL BE SIGNING YOUR DEATH WARRANT IF YOU SAY YES.

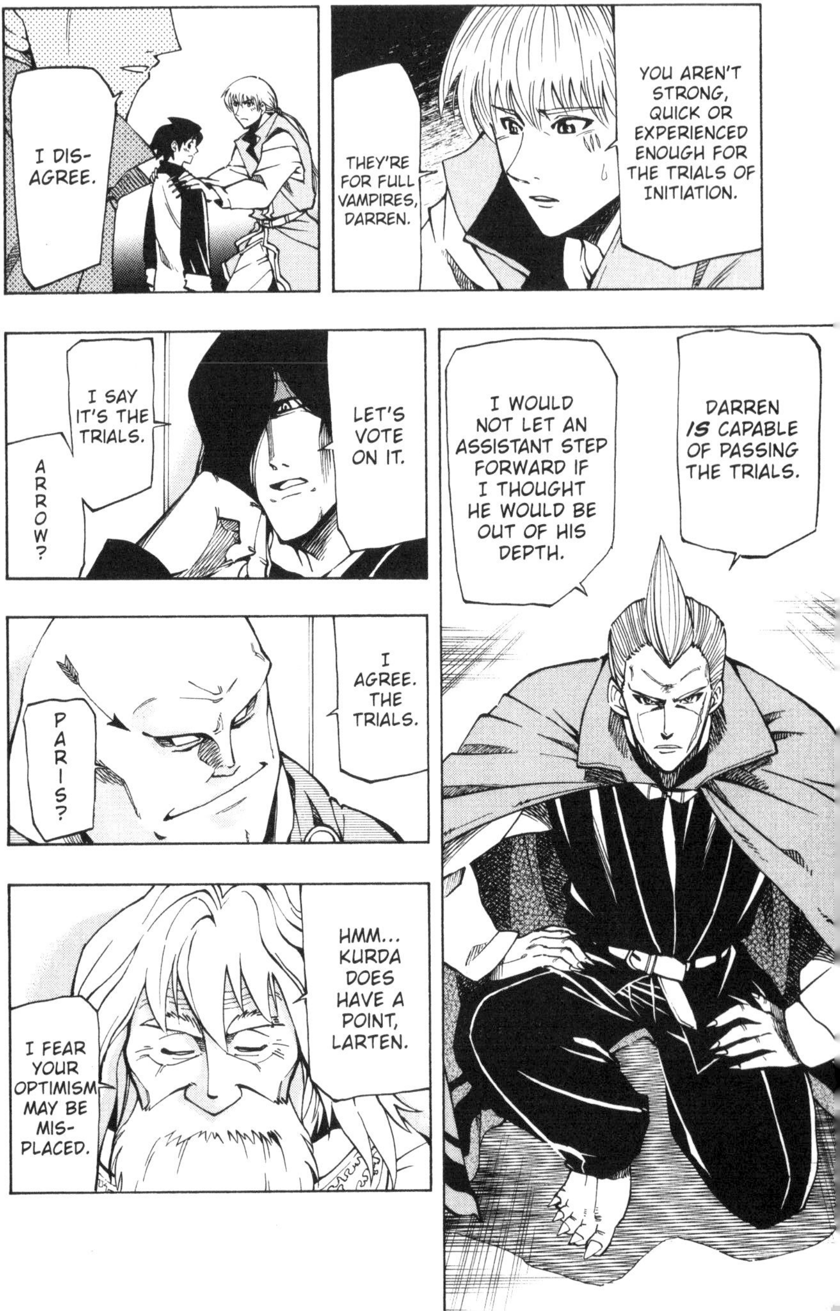
YOU AREN'T STRONG, QUICK OR EXPERIENCED ENOUGH FOR THE TRIALS OF INITIATION.
THEY'RE FOR FULL VAMPIRES, DARREN.
I DIS-AGREE.
DARREN *IS* CAPABLE OF PASSING THE TRIALS.
I WOULD NOT LET AN ASSISTANT STEP FORWARD IF I THOUGHT HE WOULD BE OUT OF HIS DEPTH.
LET'S VOTE ON IT.
ARROW?
I SAY IT'S THE TRIALS.
PARIS?
I AGREE. THE TRIALS.
HMM... KURDA DOES HAVE A POINT, LARTEN.
I FEAR YOUR OPTIMISM MAY BE MIS-PLACED.

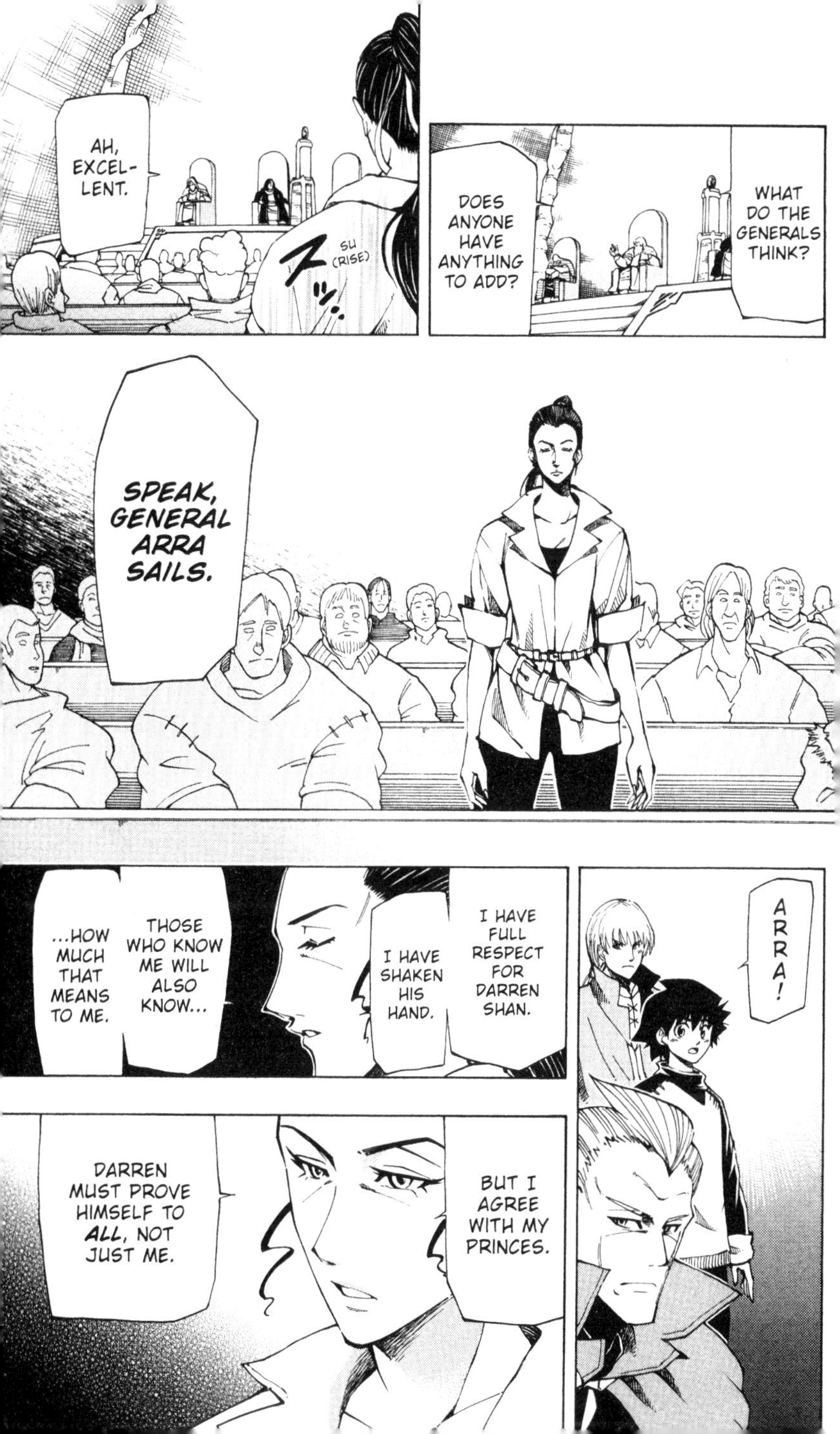

WHAT DO THE GENERALS THINK?
DOES ANYONE HAVE ANYTHING TO ADD?
AH, EXCEL-LENT.
SU (RISE)
SPEAK, GENERAL ARRA SAILS.
ARRA!
I HAVE FULL RESPECT FOR DARREN SHAN.
I HAVE SHAKEN HIS HAND.
THOSE WHO KNOW ME WILL ALSO KNOW...
...HOW MUCH THAT MEANS TO ME.
BUT I AGREE WITH MY PRINCES.
DARREN MUST PROVE HIMSELF TO ALL, NOT JUST ME.

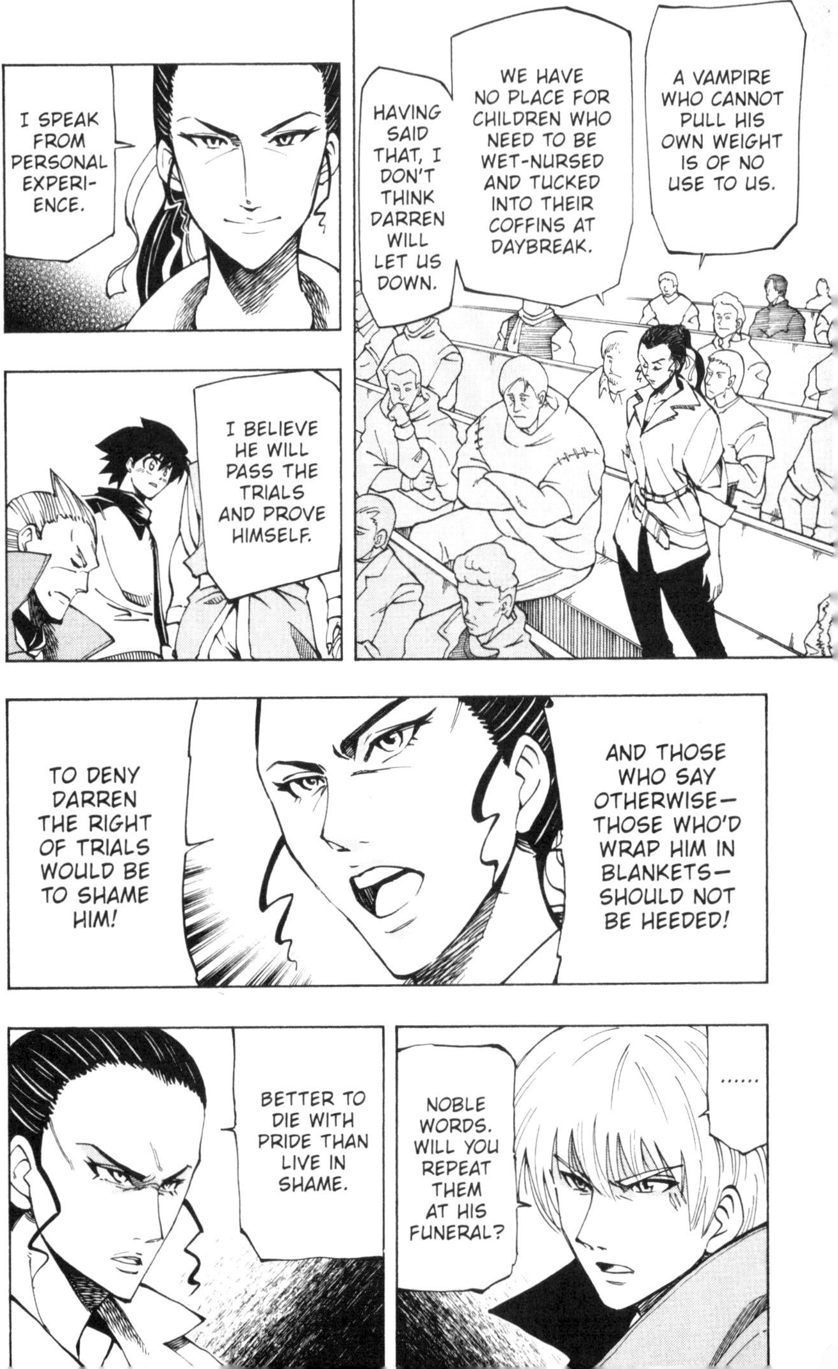
A VAMPIRE WHO CANNOT PULL HIS OWN WEIGHT IS OF NO USE TO US.
WE HAVE NO PLACE FOR CHILDREN WHO NEED TO BE WET-NURSED AND TUCKED INTO THEIR COFFINS AT DAYBREAK.
HAVING SAID THAT, I DON'T THINK DARREN WILL LET US DOWN.
I SPEAK FROM PERSONAL EXPERI-ENCE.
I BELIEVE HE WILL PASS THE TRIALS AND PROVE HIMSELF.
AND THOSE WHO SAY OTHERWISE— THOSE WHO'D WRAP HIM IN BLANKETS— SHOULD NOT BE HEEDED!
TO DENY DARREN THE RIGHT OF TRIALS WOULD BE TO SHAME HIM!
......
NOBLE WORDS. WILL YOU REPEAT THEM AT HIS FUNERAL?
BETTER TO DIE WITH PRIDE THAN LIVE IN SHAME.

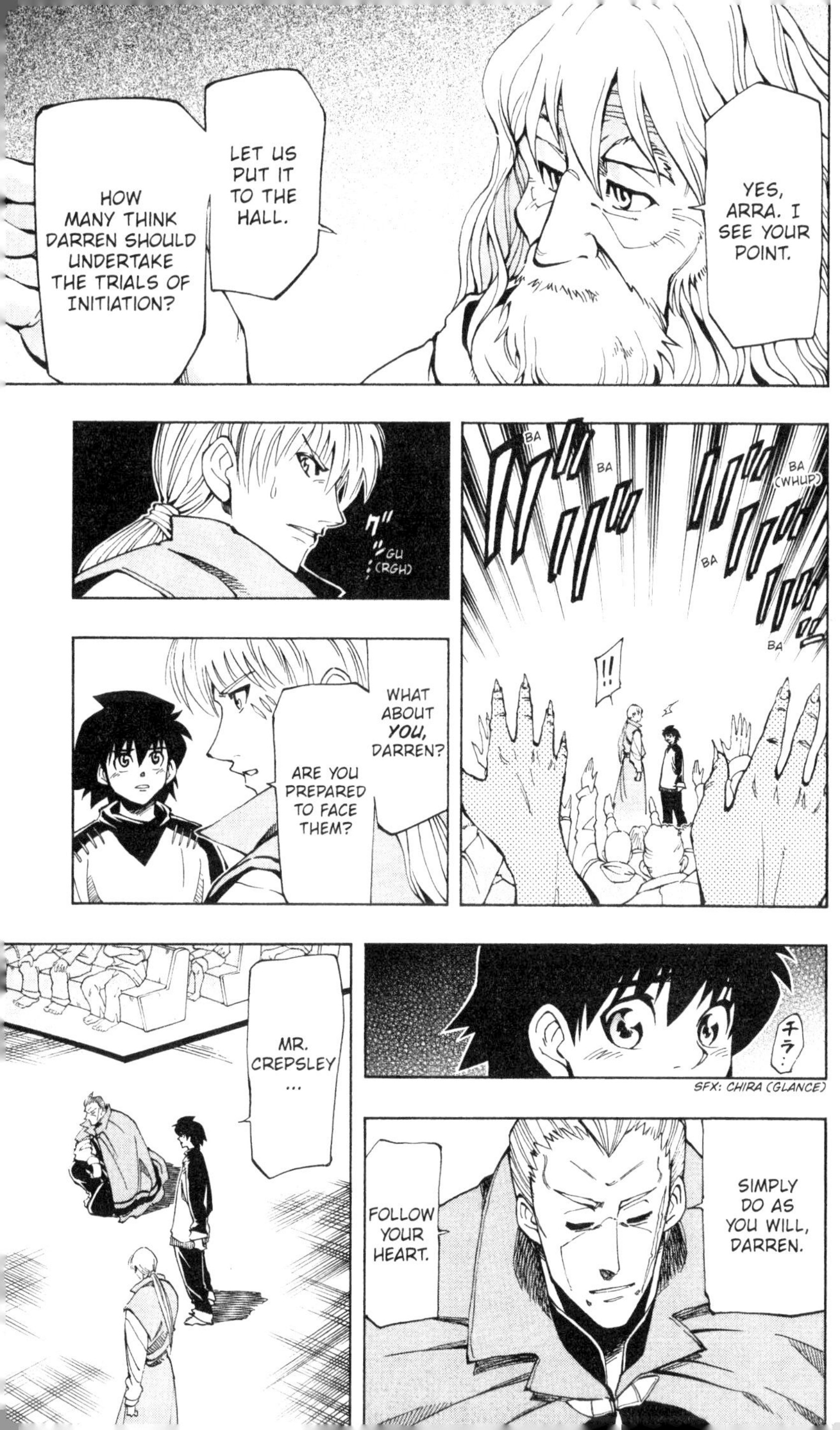
YES, ARRA. I SEE YOUR POINT.
LET US PUT IT TO THE HALL.
HOW MANY THINK DARREN SHOULD UNDERTAKE THE TRIALS OF INITIATION?
BA
BA
BA (WHUP)
BA
BA
!!
グッ
GU (RGH)
WHAT ABOUT *YOU,* DARREN?
ARE YOU PREPARED TO FACE THEM?
チラ…
SFX: CHIRA (GLANCE)
SIMPLY DO AS YOU WILL, DARREN.
FOLLOW YOUR HEART.
MR. CREPSLEY …

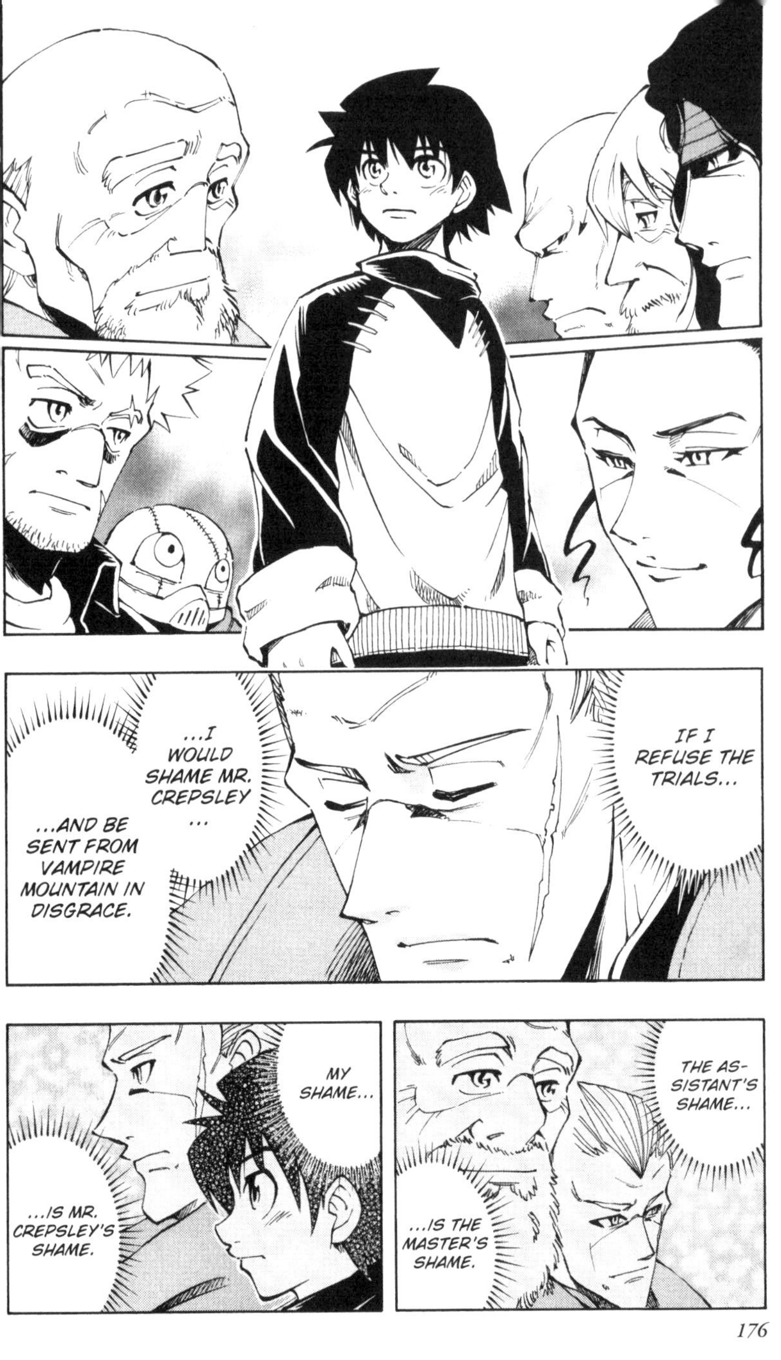
IF I REFUSE THE TRIALS...
...I WOULD SHAME MR. CREPSLEY ...
...AND BE SENT FROM VAMPIRE MOUNTAIN IN DISGRACE.
THE AS-SISTANT'S SHAME...
...IS THE MASTER'S SHAME.
MY SHAME...
...IS MR. CREPSLEY'S SHAME.

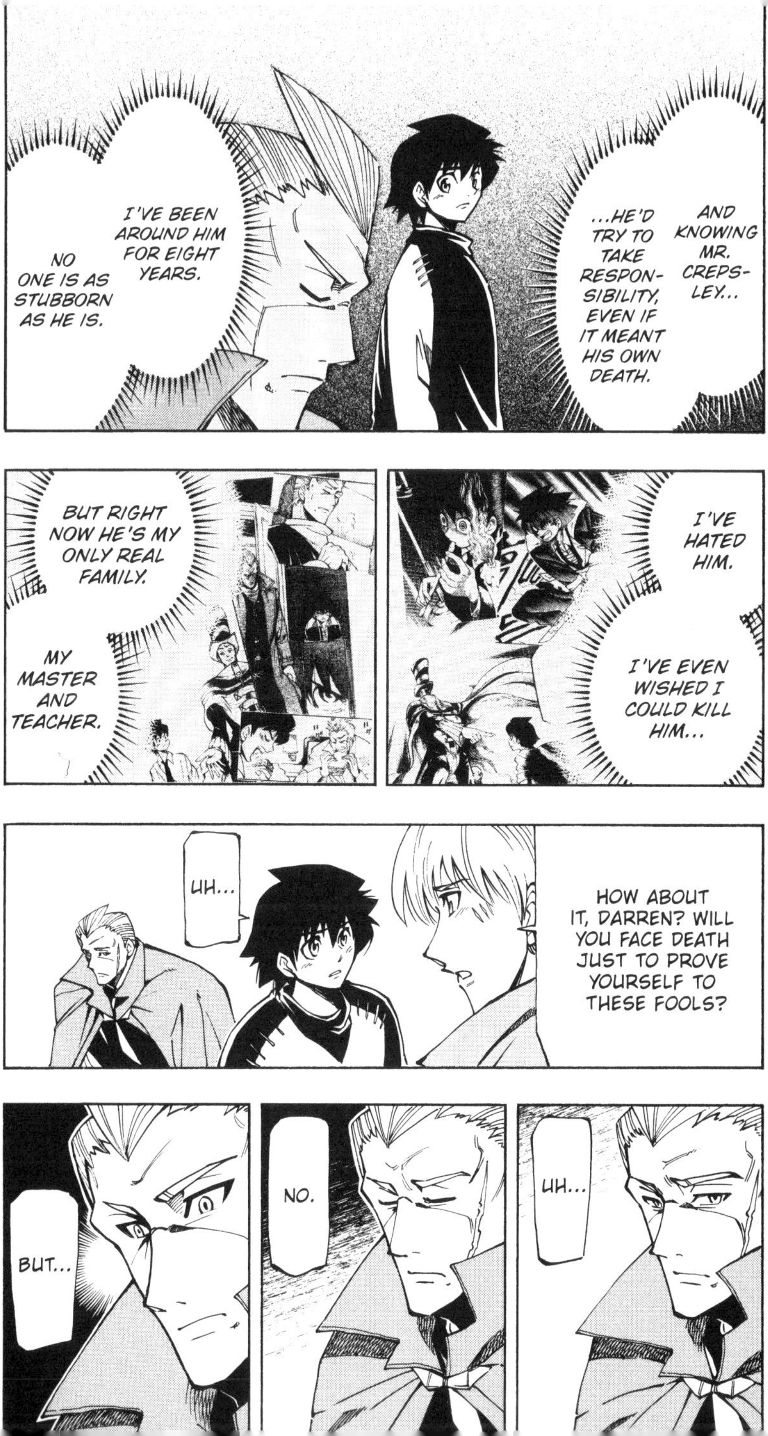
AND KNOWING MR. CREPS-LEY...
...HE'D TRY TO TAKE RESPON-SIBILITY, EVEN IF IT MEANT HIS OWN DEATH.
I'VE BEEN AROUND HIM FOR EIGHT YEARS.
NO ONE IS AS STUBBORN AS HE IS.
I'VE HATED HIM.
I'VE EVEN WISHED I COULD KILL HIM...
BUT RIGHT NOW HE'S MY ONLY REAL FAMILY.
MY MASTER AND TEACHER.
HOW ABOUT IT, DARREN? WILL YOU FACE DEATH JUST TO PROVE YOURSELF TO THESE FOOLS?
UH...
UH...
NO.
BUT...

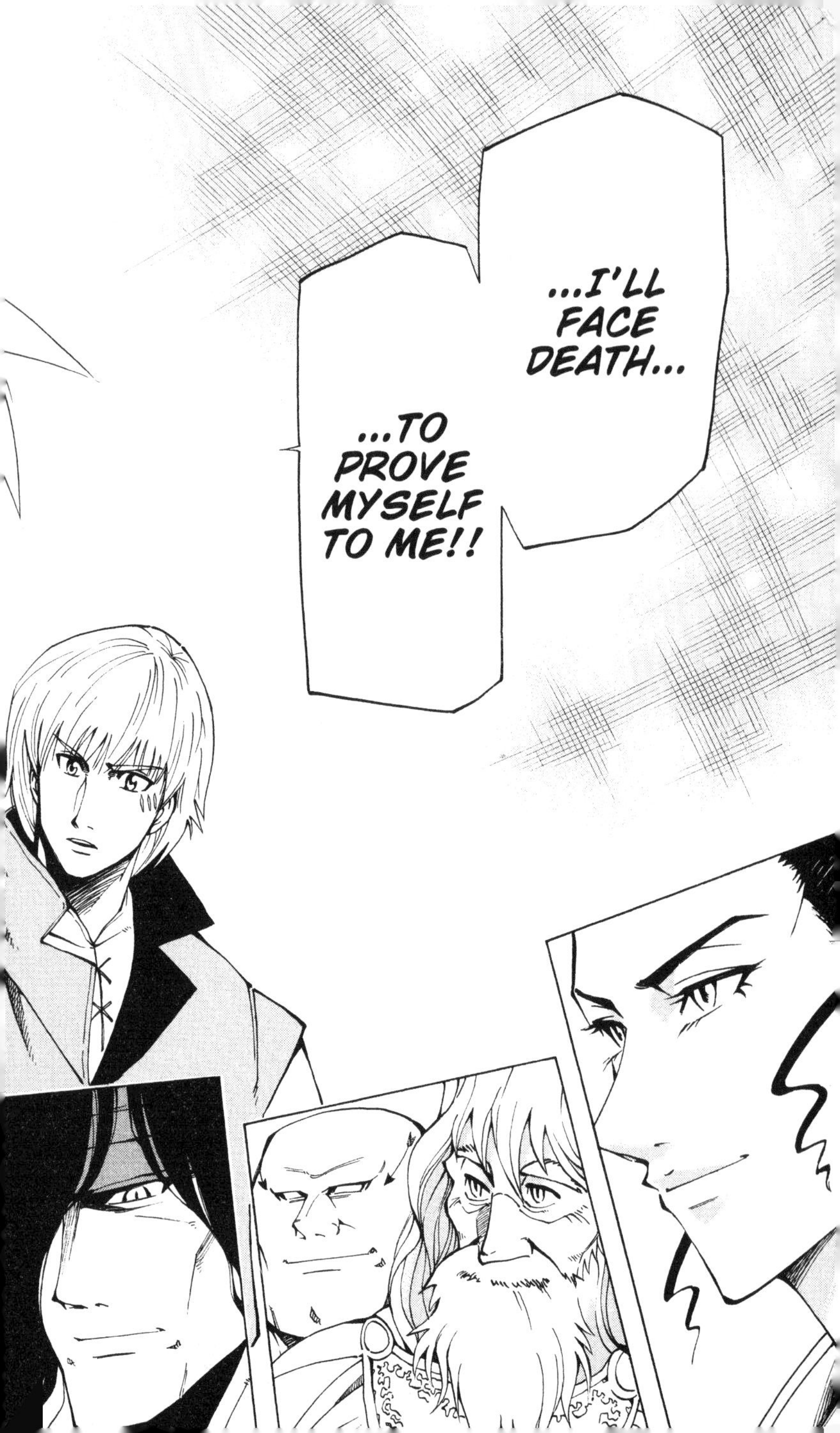
...I'LL FACE DEATH...
...TO PROVE MYSELF TO ME!!

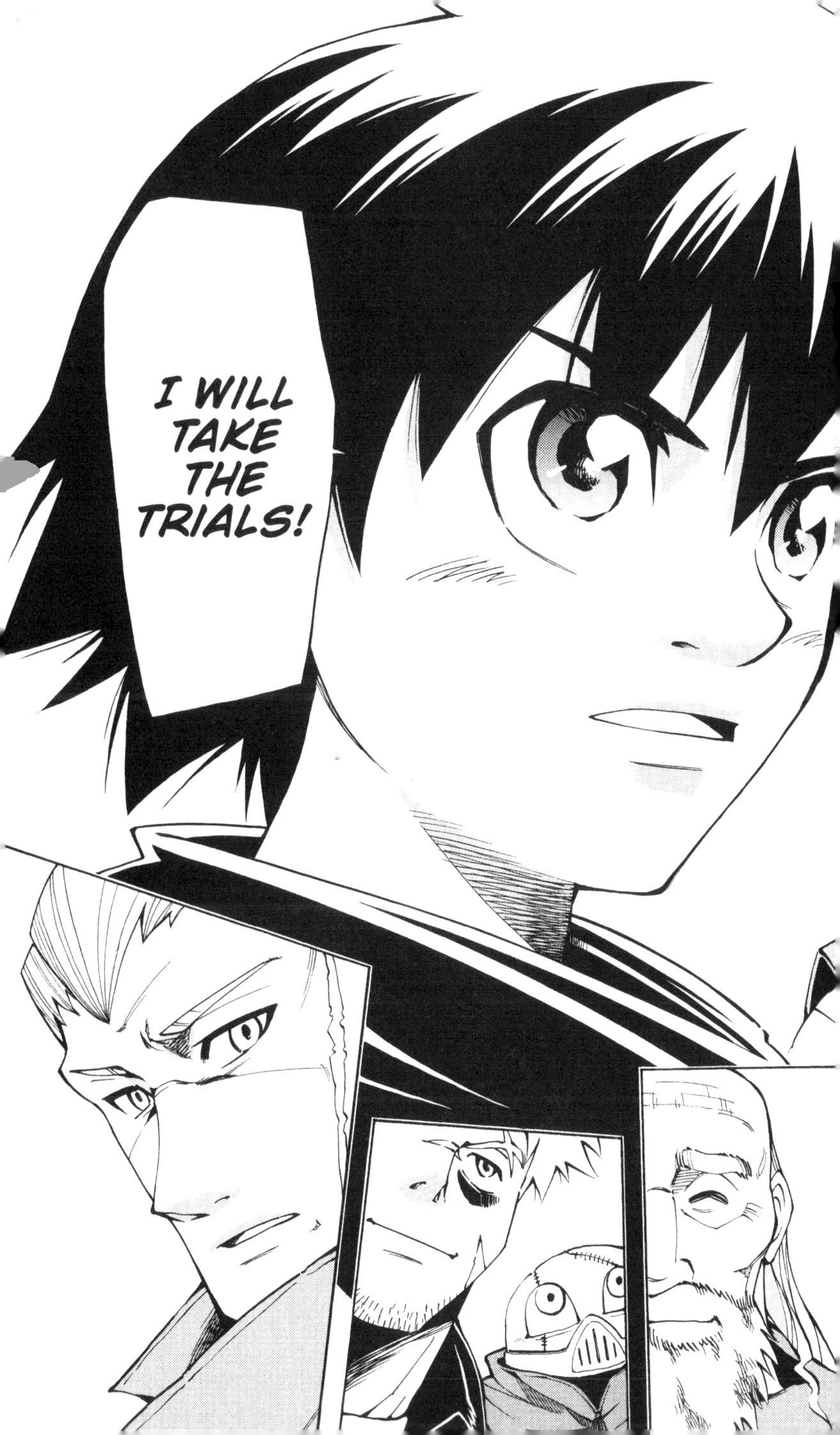
I WILL TAKE THE TRIALS!

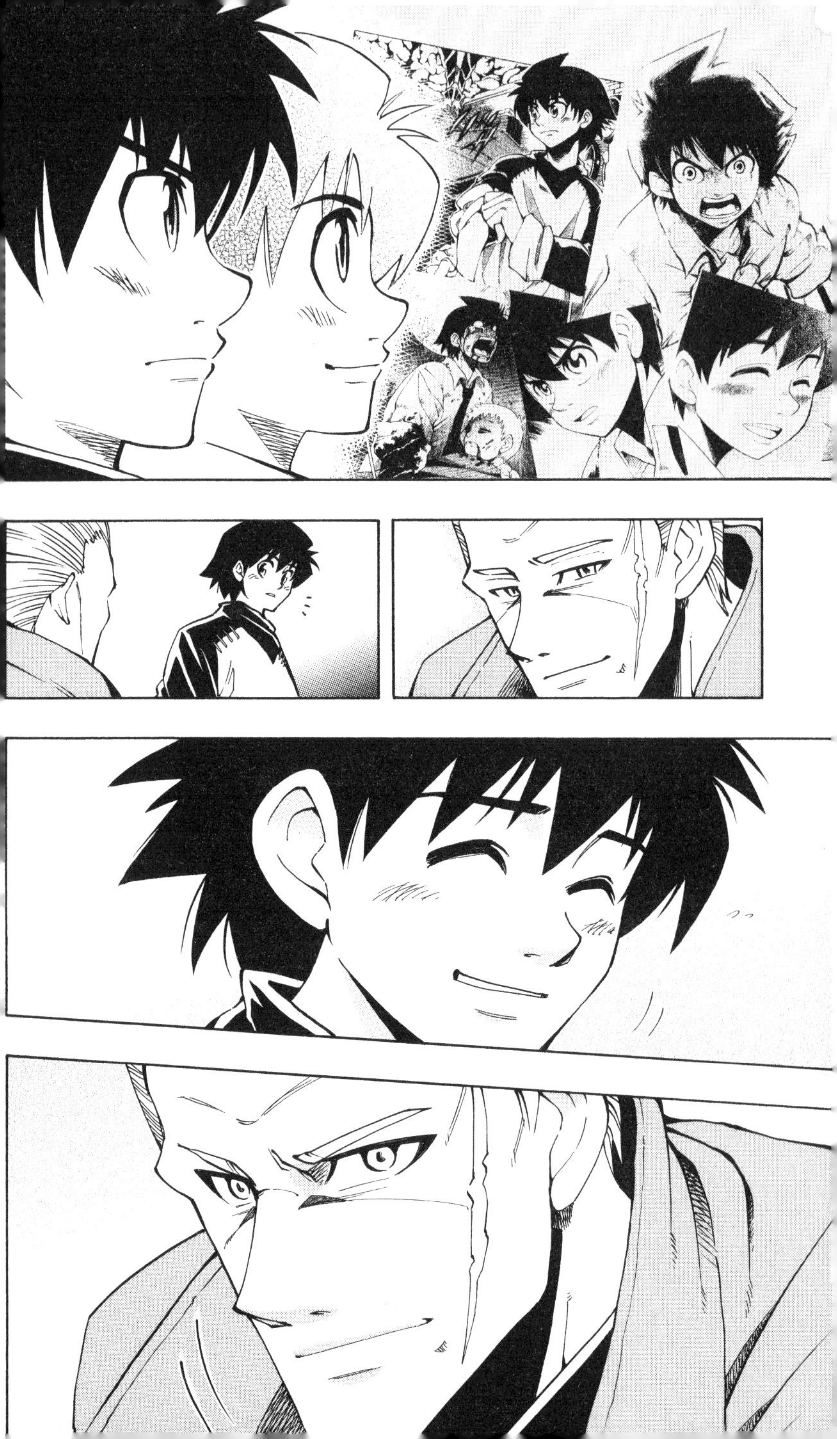

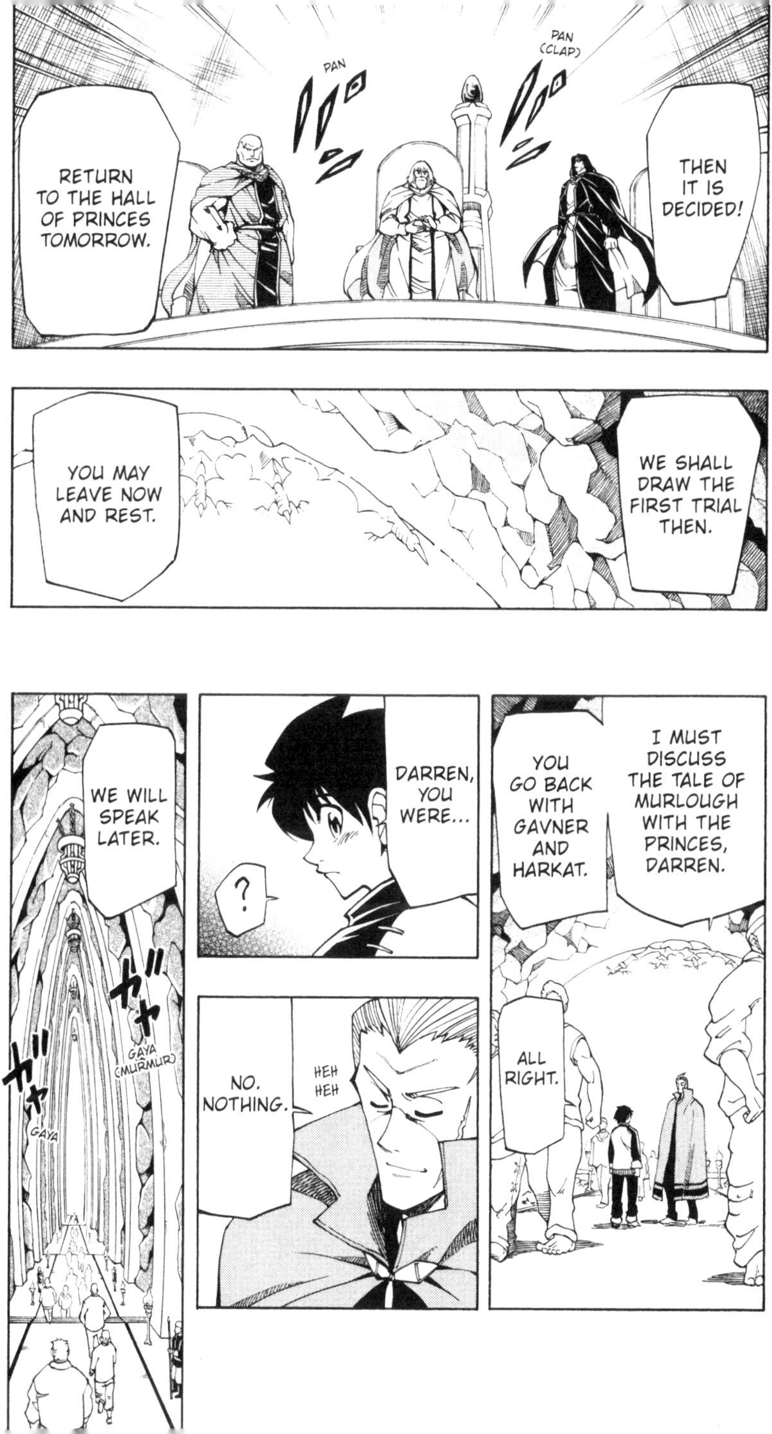

THEN IT IS DECIDED!
PAN (CLAP)
PAN
RETURN TO THE HALL OF PRINCES TOMORROW.
WE SHALL DRAW THE FIRST TRIAL THEN.
YOU MAY LEAVE NOW AND REST.
I MUST DISCUSS THE TALE OF MURLOUGH WITH THE PRINCES, DARREN.
YOU GO BACK WITH GAVNER AND HARKAT.
ALL RIGHT.
DARREN, YOU WERE...
?
HEH HEH
NO. NOTHING.
WE WILL SPEAK LATER.
ガヤ
GAYA (MURMUR)
ガヤ
GAYA

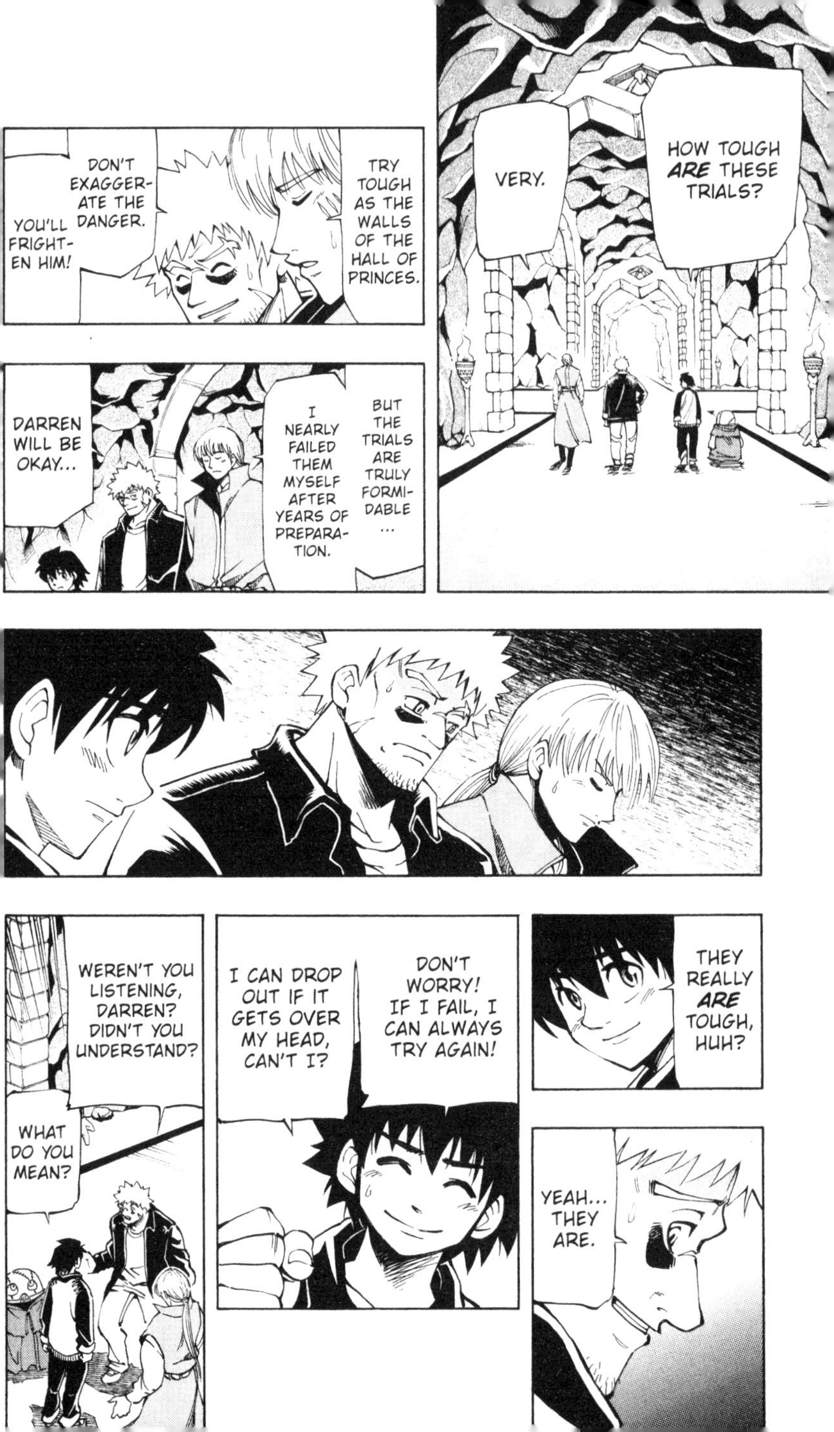
HOW TOUGH ARE THESE TRIALS?
VERY.
TRY TOUGH AS THE WALLS OF THE HALL OF PRINCES.
DON'T EXAGGERATE THE DANGER.
YOU'LL FRIGHTEN HIM!
BUT THE TRIALS ARE TRULY FORMIDABLE...
I NEARLY FAILED THEM MYSELF AFTER YEARS OF PREPARATION.
DARREN WILL BE OKAY...
THEY REALLY ARE TOUGH, HUH?
YEAH... THEY ARE.
DON'T WORRY! IF I FAIL, I CAN ALWAYS TRY AGAIN!
I CAN DROP OUT IF IT GETS OVER MY HEAD, CAN'T I?
WEREN'T YOU LISTENING, DARREN? DIDN'T YOU UNDERSTAND?
WHAT DO YOU MEAN?

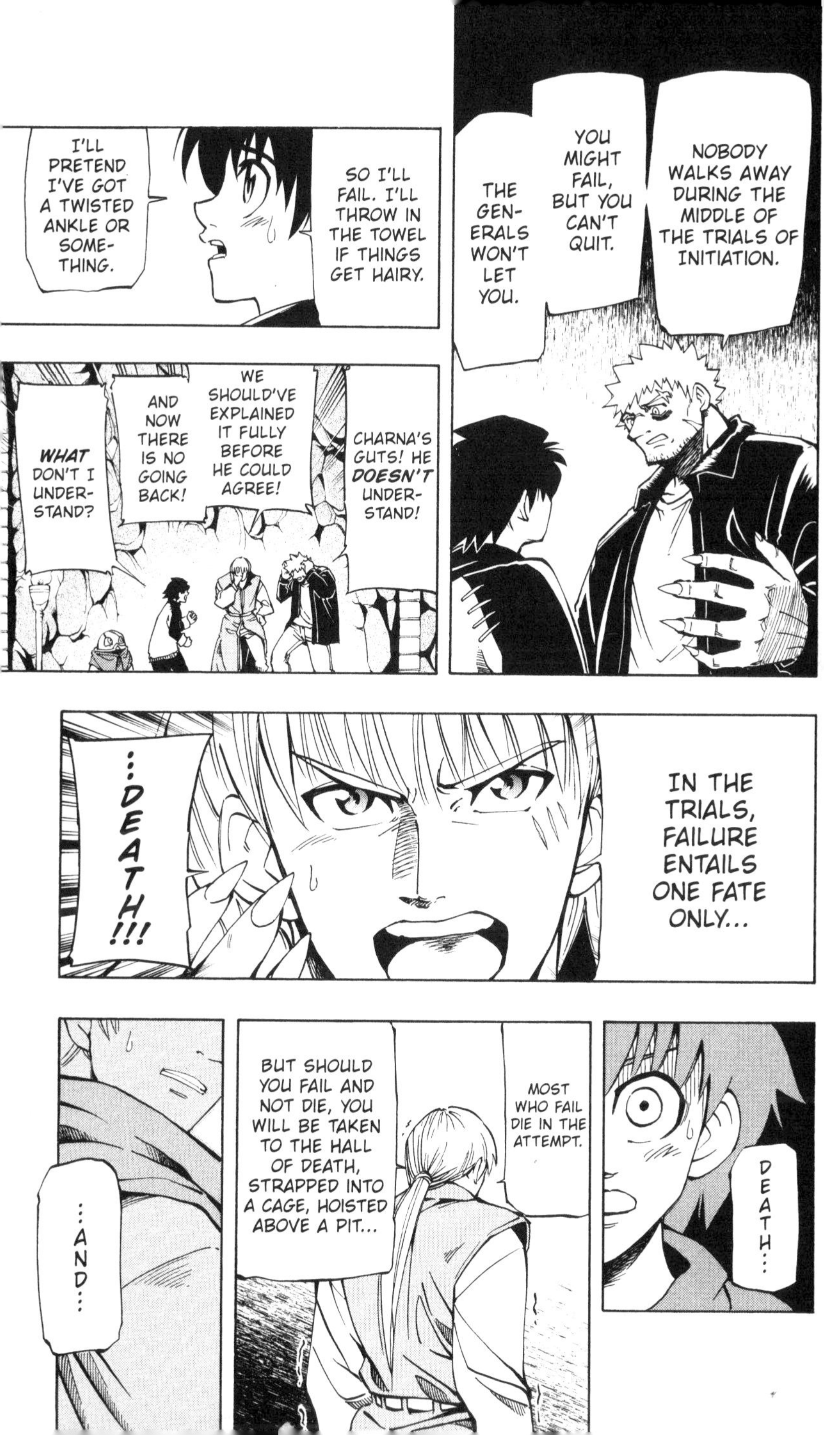
NOBODY WALKS AWAY DURING THE MIDDLE OF THE TRIALS OF INITIATION.
YOU MIGHT FAIL, BUT YOU CAN'T QUIT.
THE GENERALS WON'T LET YOU.
SO I'LL FAIL. I'LL THROW IN THE TOWEL IF THINGS GET HAIRY.
I'LL PRETEND I'VE GOT A TWISTED ANKLE OR SOMETHING.
CHARNA'S GUTS! HE *DOESN'T* UNDERSTAND!
WE SHOULD'VE EXPLAINED IT FULLY BEFORE HE COULD AGREE!
AND NOW THERE IS NO GOING BACK!
WHAT DON'T I UNDERSTAND?
IN THE TRIALS, FAILURE ENTAILS ONE FATE ONLY...
...DEATH!!!
DEATH...
MOST WHO FAIL DIE IN THE ATTEMPT.
BUT SHOULD YOU FAIL AND NOT DIE, YOU WILL BE TAKEN TO THE HALL OF DEATH, STRAPPED INTO A CAGE, HOISTED ABOVE A PIT...
...AND...

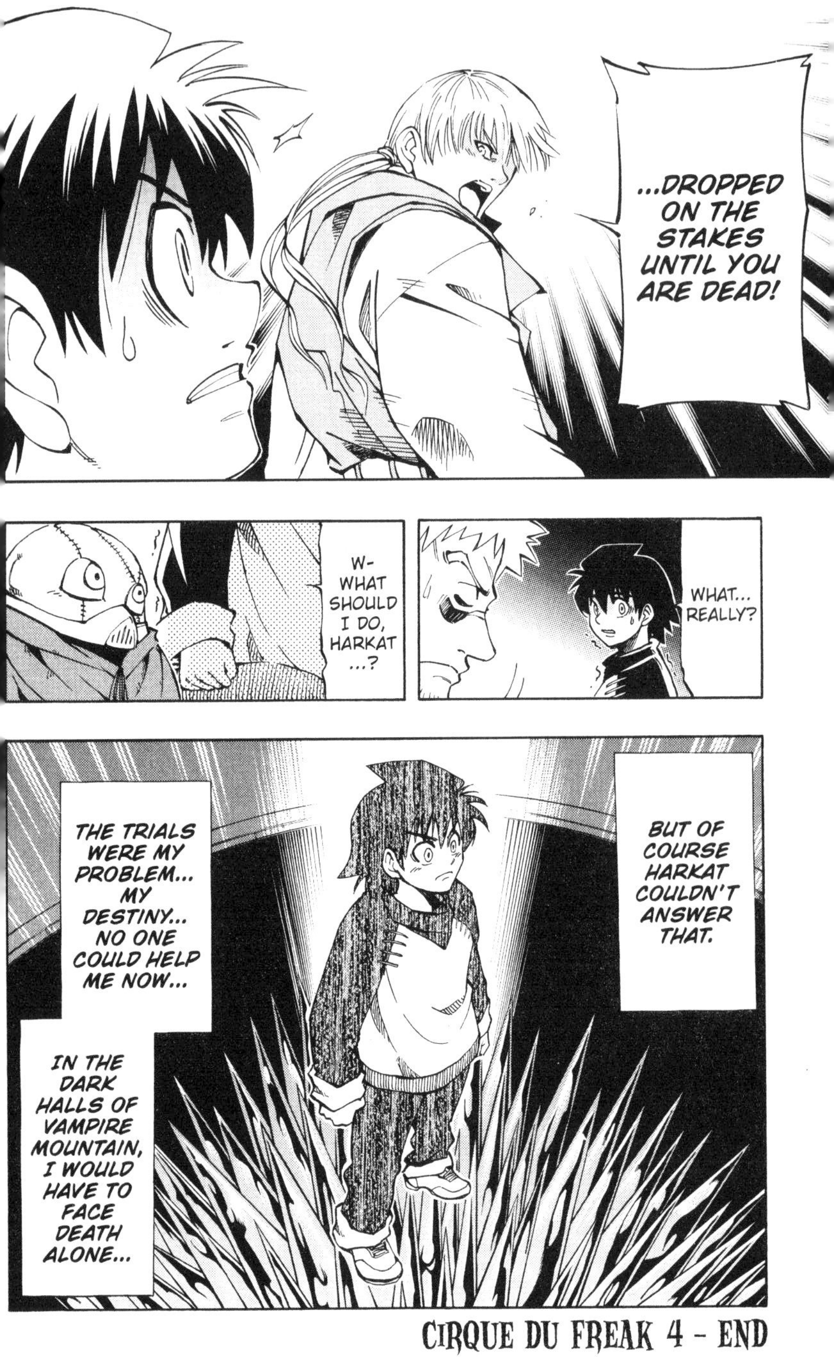
...DROPPED ON THE STAKES UNTIL YOU ARE DEAD!
WHAT... REALLY?
W- WHAT SHOULD I DO, HARKAT ...?
BUT OF COURSE HARKAT COULDN'T ANSWER THAT.
THE TRIALS WERE MY PROBLEM... MY DESTINY... NO ONE COULD HELP ME NOW...
IN THE DARK HALLS OF VAMPIRE MOUNTAIN, I WOULD HAVE TO FACE DEATH ALONE...

CIRQUE DU FREAK 4 - END

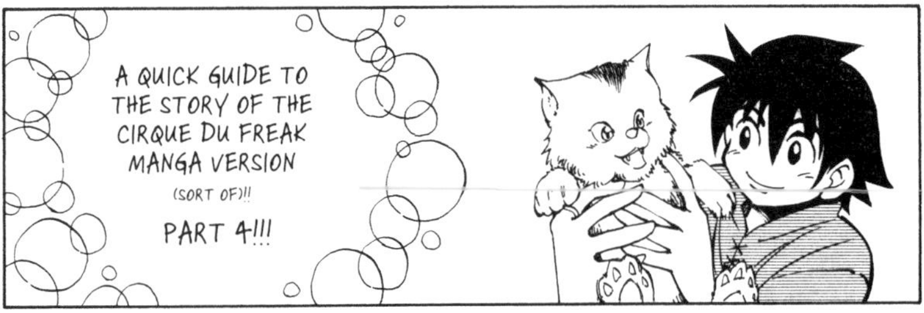
A QUICK GUIDE TO THE STORY OF THE CIRQUE DU FREAK MANGA VERSION
(SORT OF)!!
PART 4!!!

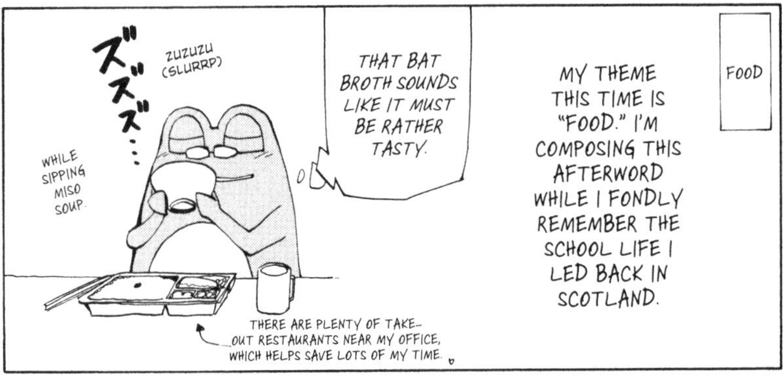
FOOD
MY THEME THIS TIME IS "FOOD." I'M COMPOSING THIS AFTERWORD WHILE I FONDLY REMEMBER THE SCHOOL LIFE I LED BACK IN SCOTLAND.
THAT BAT BROTH SOUNDS LIKE IT MUST BE RATHER TASTY.
ズズズ…
ZUZUZU (SLURRP)
WHILE SIPPING MISO SOUP.
THERE ARE PLENTY OF TAKE-OUT RESTAURANTS NEAR MY OFFICE, WHICH HELPS SAVE LOTS OF MY TIME.

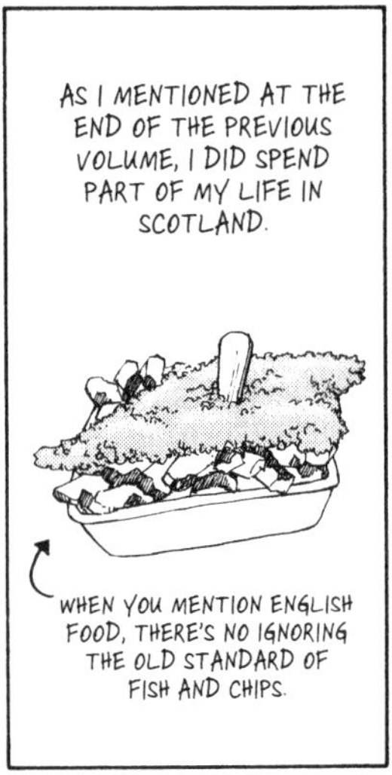
AS I MENTIONED AT THE END OF THE PREVIOUS VOLUME, I DID SPEND PART OF MY LIFE IN SCOTLAND.
WHEN YOU MENTION ENGLISH FOOD, THERE'S NO IGNORING THE OLD STANDARD OF FISH AND CHIPS.

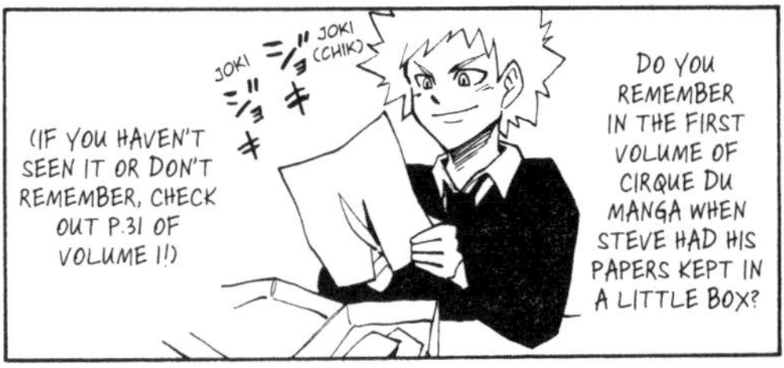
DO YOU REMEMBER IN THE FIRST VOLUME OF CIRQUE DU MANGA WHEN STEVE HAD HIS PAPERS KEPT IN A LITTLE BOX?
ジョ キ
JOKI (CHIK)
ジョ キ
JOKI
(IF YOU HAVEN'T SEEN IT OR DON'T REMEMBER, CHECK OUT P.31 OF VOLUME 1!)

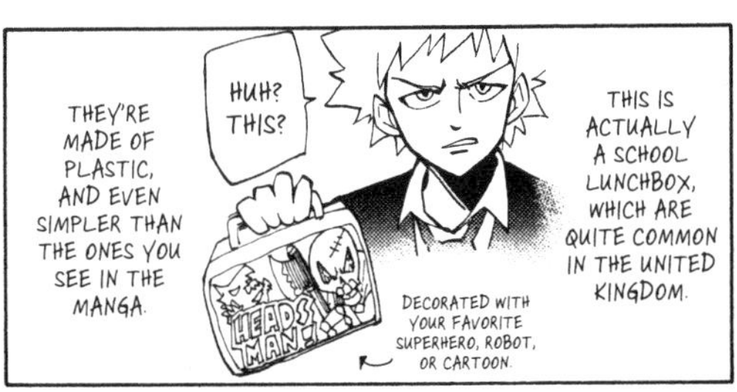
THIS IS ACTUALLY A SCHOOL LUNCHBOX, WHICH ARE QUITE COMMON IN THE UNITED KINGDOM.
HUH? THIS?
THEY'RE MADE OF PLASTIC, AND EVEN SIMPLER THAN THE ONES YOU SEE IN THE MANGA.
HEADSMAN!
DECORATED WITH YOUR FAVORITE SUPERHERO, ROBOT, OR CARTOON.

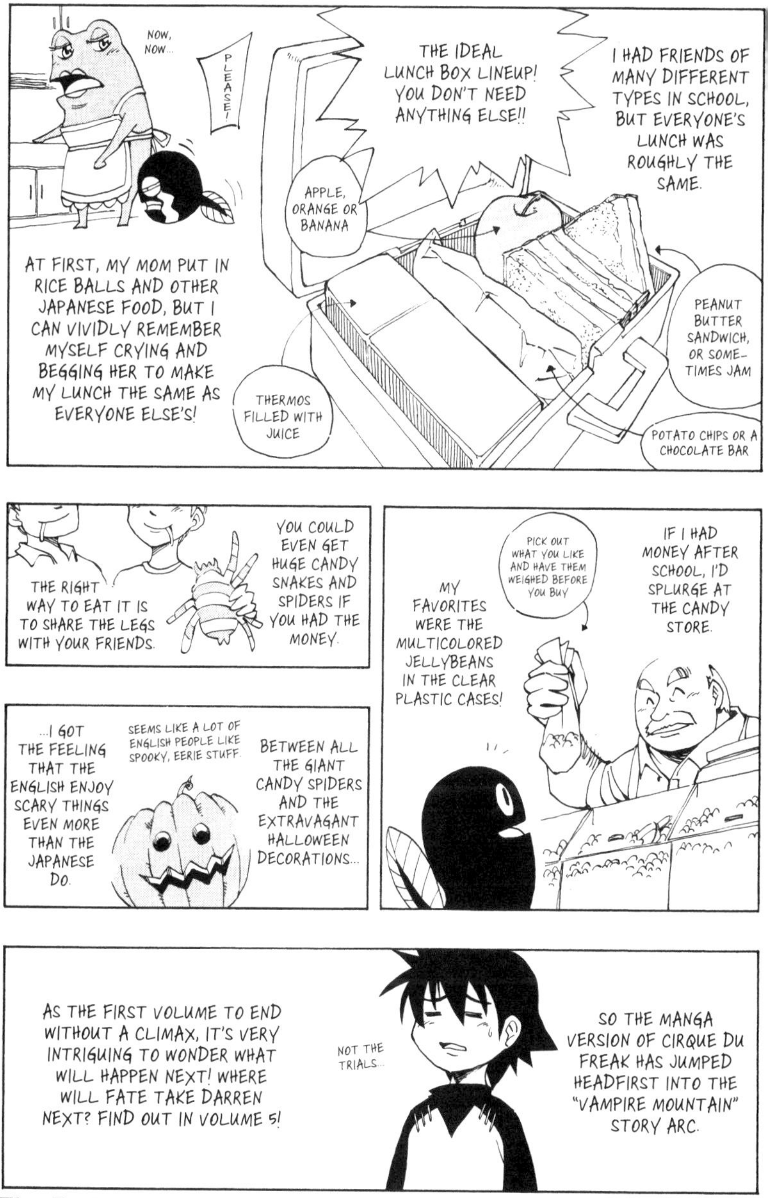
I HAD FRIENDS OF MANY DIFFERENT TYPES IN SCHOOL, BUT EVERYONE'S LUNCH WAS ROUGHLY THE SAME.
THE IDEAL LUNCH BOX LINEUP! YOU DON'T NEED ANYTHING ELSE!!
PLEASE!
NOW, NOW...
APPLE, ORANGE OR BANANA
PEANUT BUTTER SANDWICH, OR SOMETIMES JAM
AT FIRST, MY MOM PUT IN RICE BALLS AND OTHER JAPANESE FOOD, BUT I CAN VIVIDLY REMEMBER MYSELF CRYING AND BEGGING HER TO MAKE MY LUNCH THE SAME AS EVERYONE ELSE'S!
THERMOS FILLED WITH JUICE
POTATO CHIPS OR A CHOCOLATE BAR
IF I HAD MONEY AFTER SCHOOL, I'D SPLURGE AT THE CANDY STORE.
PICK OUT WHAT YOU LIKE AND HAVE THEM WEIGHED BEFORE YOU BUY
MY FAVORITES WERE THE MULTICOLORED JELLYBEANS IN THE CLEAR PLASTIC CASES!
YOU COULD EVEN GET HUGE CANDY SNAKES AND SPIDERS IF YOU HAD THE MONEY.
THE RIGHT WAY TO EAT IT IS TO SHARE THE LEGS WITH YOUR FRIENDS.
BETWEEN ALL THE GIANT CANDY SPIDERS AND THE EXTRAVAGANT HALLOWEEN DECORATIONS...
SEEMS LIKE A LOT OF ENGLISH PEOPLE LIKE SPOOKY, EERIE STUFF.
...I GOT THE FEELING THAT THE ENGLISH ENJOY SCARY THINGS EVEN MORE THAN THE JAPANESE DO.
SO THE MANGA VERSION OF CIRQUE DU FREAK HAS JUMPED HEADFIRST INTO THE "VAMPIRE MOUNTAIN" STORY ARC.
NOT THE TRIALS...
AS THE FIRST VOLUME TO END WITHOUT A CLIMAX, IT'S VERY INTRIGUING TO WONDER WHAT WILL HAPPEN NEXT! WHERE WILL FATE TAKE DARREN NEXT? FIND OUT IN VOLUME 5!

The End

CIRQUE DU FREAK④

DARREN SHAN
TAKAHIRO ARAI

Translation: Stephen Paul   •   Lettering: AndWorld Design
Original Cover Design: Hitoshi SHIRAYAMA + Bay Bridge Studio

DARREN SHAN Vol. 4 © 2007 by Darren Shan, Takahiro ARAI. All rights reserved. Original Japanese edition published in Japan in 2007 by Shogakukan Inc., Tokyo. Artworks reproduction rights in U.S.A. and Canada arranged with Shogakukan Inc. through Tuttle-Mori Agency, Inc., Tokyo.

English translation © 2010 Darren Shan

Yen Press
Hachette Book Group
237 Park Avenue, New York, NY 10017

www.HachetteBookGroup.com
www.YenPress.com

Yen Press is an imprint of Hachette Book Group, Inc. The Yen Press name and logo are trademarks of Hachette Book Group, Inc.

First Yen Press Edition: January 2010

ISBN: 978-0-7595-3039-3

10 9 8 7 6 5 4 3 2 1

BVG

Printed in the United States of America